A SHORT HISTORY of

SHAKESPEAREAN CRITICISM

Arthur M. Eastman is chairman of the department of English at Carnegie-Mellon University in Pittsburgh. He is general editor of *The Norton Reader* and coordinating editor of *The Norton Anthology of Poetry*.

A SHORT
HISTORY *of*
SHAKESPEAREAN
CRITICISM

Arthur M. Eastman

The Norton Library
W · W · NORTON & COMPANY · INC ·
NEW YORK

Acknowledgments

The publisher and author wish to give credit for quotations from the following works:

From *Coleridge's Writings on Shakespeare* edited by Terence Hawkes, originally collected by T. M. Raysor. Copyright © 1959 by G. P. Putnam's Sons. Published by Putnam's & Coward-McCann.

From *Goethe's Literary Essays* edited by J. E. Spingarn, translated by Randolph S. Bourne. Published by Harcourt, Brace & World, Inc.

From *Shaw on Shakespeare* by George Bernard Shaw, edited by Edwin Wilson.

From *Shakespearean Tragedy* by A. C. Bradley. Published by Macmillan & Co. Ltd., London, and St. Martin's Press.

From "On the Influence of the Audience" by Robert Bridges. Published by the Clarendon Press, Oxford.

From *Character and Society in Shakespeare* by Arthur Sewell. Published by the Clarendon Press, Oxford.

From *Hamlet and Oedipus* by Ernest Jones. Published by W. W. Norton & Company, Inc.

From *The Lion and the Fox* by Wyndham Lewis. Published by Methuen & Co. Ltd.

From *The Wheel of Fire* by Wilson Knight. Published by Methuen & Co. Ltd.

From *Shakespeare's Imagination* by Edward A. Armstrong.

From *Shakespeare* by John Middleton Murry. Published by Jonathan Cape Ltd.

From *Shakespeare's Imagery and What It Tells Us* by Caroline Spurgeon. Published by Cambridge University Press.

From *The Development of Shakespeare's Imagery* by Wolfgang Clemen. Published by Harvard University Press and Methuen & Co. Ltd., London.

From *The Sense of Shakespeare's Sonnets* by Edward Hubler. Published by Princeton University Press.

From *Prefaces to Shakespeare* by Harley Granville-Barker. Published by Princeton University Press.

From *Shakespeare's Festive Comedy* by C. L. Barber. Published by Princeton University Press.

From *Shakespeare and the Nature of Man* by Theodore Spencer. Published by The Macmillan Company.

From *Shakespeare and the Rival Traditions* by Alfred Harbage. Published by The Macmillan Company.

From *The Elizabethan World Picture* by E. M. W. Tillyard. Published by The Macmillan Company and Chatto and Windus Ltd.

From *As They Liked It* by Alfred Harbage. Published by Harper & Row, Inc.

From *Shakespeare and the Allegory of Evil* by Bernard Spivack. Published by Columbia University Press.

From *A Natural Perspective* by Northrop Frye. Published by Columbia University Press.

From *The Story of the Night* by John Holloway. Published by Routledge & Kegan Paul Ltd.

From "The Naked Babe and the Cloak of Manliness," *The Well Wrought Urn* by Cleanth Brooks. Published by Harcourt, Brace & World, Inc.

To G. B. H. and W. G. R.—
Wise Counselors,
Warm Friends,
Exemplars

Contents

INTRODUCTION   xix

I.   The First One Hundred Fifty Years   3

*Praise and blame. Shakespeare the poet of Nature: his
creative, imitative, and affective powers. His deficiency
in Art: lack of restraint, generic irregularity—poetic injustice, violation of the unities, tragicomedy—indecorousness.*

II.   Johnson   20

*Shakespeare the poet of general nature, his drama the
mirror of life, his comic dialogue appropriate to the
genius of the language. His multitudinous failings in
art. His essential amorality. Vindication of his violations
of character types, generic purity, and the unities of
time and place. Analysis of his characters. His engaging
the mind.*

III.   Lessing and Schlegel   35

*Lessing's repudiation of French neo-classical perspec-
tives, his conception of genius as fusing imagination and
judgment.* ❧ *Schlegel's grand division of classic and
romantic—Shakespeare the romantic champion. Shake-*

*speare's tragicomedy and violations of the unities vin-
dicated. His unity of interest or impression; his organic
form. Vindication of his anachronisms. Schlegel's structural awarenesses, moral sensitivity, moralistic excess,
wide-ranging perceptiveness.*

IV.   Morgann and Coleridge   52

*Revised view of Shakespeare in late eighteenth-century
England. Morgann's distinction between sensibility and
understanding; his explanation of naturalness and wholeness in Shakespeare's characterization. Character as
historical, as dramatic.* ❦ *Coleridge's defects. His
organicism. His psychological and moral sensitivity:
character analyses, running commentary; defense of
Shakespeare's punning. Ideal theory of poetic creativity:
Coleridge compared to Morgann. "Willing suspension
of disbelief."*

V.   Goethe, Lamb, and Hazlitt   80

*Goethe's Shakespeare: inspired and disciplined, neglect-
ing traditional means but achieving ultimate ends.
Shakespeare's works as falling between Ancient and
Modern; his poetry as deriving from contemplation and
addressing imagination. Apologies for his deficiencies
as dramatist: Hamlet improved.* ❦ *Lamb's attack
against staging Shakespeare except in the theater of his
own mind. Limitations of his theory, subtlety of his
appreciation.* ❦ *Hazlitt's exuberance; his sharp formulations, traditional positions; his feeling for Shakespeare's plasticity. The Characters of Shakespear's Plays
as handbook: general essays, analyses of individual plays
—Richard II. Shakespearean unity as deriving from
analogy. Shakespeare's characters as uniquely individual.*

Hazlitt's political bias. His feeling for the plays as theater.

VI.   Gervinus and Lowell   116

Contemporary influence of the Commentaries. *Gervinus's psychological penetration; his want of measure. Shakespeare's system of morality. Unifying ethical ideas of individual plays.* ❧ *Lowell's appraisal of Elizabethan English as vital, rich, democratic. Development of older topics: Shakespeare's imagination and judgment, punning, action as evolving from character. Allegorical reading of* The Tempest. *Vindication of Hamlet's anachronisms and graveyard comedy; Hamlet's character.*

VII.   Dowden, Swinburne, and Pater   139

The labeled periods of Dowden's Primer *as deriving from his* Shakspere: A Critical Study of His Mind and Art, *their ultimate source in reactions to such critics as Smiles and Taine. Comments trenchant and sentimental. Shakespeare's unity. Shakespeare's objectivity and Dowden's didacticism. Dowden's excessive simplicity.* ❧ *Critical mots from Swinburne. His inquiry into Shakespeare's artistic development: the conflict between rhyme and blank verse.* ❧ *Pater as revealing what and how to appreciate. His elegiac tone, "esthetic" perspective, feeling for unity. Pater compared to Gervinus.*

VIII.   Shaw and Tolstoy   164

Shaw's pejorative wit, reaction against contemporary staging of Shakespeare, critical perceptions. Denigrating portrait of Shakespeare; biographical criticism. Praise of Shakespeare's "problem" plays, attack against his individualism and despair: Shakespeare compared to Bunyan. Shakespeare's word music and imagery. ❦ *Tolstoy as seconding and enlarging Shaw's puritan attack. His studied obtuseness. Insistence on* Lear's *hyperbolic remoteness and artificiality. Shakespeare's unnaturalness in character, thought, and speech. His deficiency in esthetic and ethical authority. Tolstoy's history of Shakespearean criticism.*

IX. Bradley 186

Bradley's aggregational style and rational rhetoric; his "we" and his impressionism. "The Substance of Shakespearean Tragedy": the tragic trait, tragic impression, tragic triumph. "Construction in Shakespeare's Tragedies": exposition, conflict, "fourth-act problem"; Shakespeare's artistic sins; the chief problem in interpreting Shakespeare. The world of Lear, *atmosphere of* Macbeth. *Character interpreted and quickened.*

X. Bridges, Stoll, and Schücking 205

Bridges' indictment of Shakespeare: consistency of character vs. *surprise, new characters for old stories.* ❦ *Stoll as historian and theater-goer. The topicality and unreality of Shakespeare's characters. Gains and losses from the Stollian perspective: restoration and reduction.* ❦ *Schücking's historical objectivity. Primitive conditions of Shakespeare's theater: Shakespeare's art as literal and fragmented. Schücking's obscurations of his own theory.*

XI.   Harris, Jones, and Lewis   219

Harris as redeemer: his Shakespeare. The dark lady.
Limitations and merits of Harris's esthetic. ❧ *Jones*
compared to Harris. Hamlet psychoanalyzed. "Tragedy
and the Mind of the Infant." "The Theme of Matri-
cide." The Oedipal in Shakespeare. Merits and limita-
tions of Jones's approach. ❧ *Lewis's Shakespeare as*
public executioner, as "shamanized" man, contemptu-
ous of king and multitude. His master-subject: past vs.
present, The Lion and the Fox. *Styles appropriate to*
each world. Shakespeare's ambivalent implication in
both worlds. Coriolanus. *Shakespeare's nihilism. Lewis's*
Shakespeare an anti-Shakespeare.

XII.   Knight   238

Taints. Boldness and freshness. "Interpretation." Brad-
ley and Knight on Macbeth. *Visionary unity of individ-*
ual plays, of entire Shakespearean corpus. Seminal com-
parison. The axis of Shakespeare's great plays.

XIII.   Spurgeon, Murry, and Armstrong   252

Whiter's Specimen. *Spurgeon's thesis: Shakespeare's*
imagery as self-revealing. "The Subject-Matter of Shake-
speare's Images." "Shakespeare's Senses." Outdoor in-
terests. Thought. "Shakespeare the Man." Spurgeon's
focus on figure at the expense of thought. Other limita-
tions. Contributions. ❧ *Murry's Shakespeare as Na-*
ture's spokesman. Personal experience in the imagery.
The Bastard as Shakespeare's Adam; Henry V as the
Bastard legitimized, the problem of kingship solved. The

Shakespearean Man and the Shakespearean Woman. Hamlet the final embodiment and catharsis of the Shakespearean Man. Lear the work of a divided Shakespeare. Bridgean perspectives. Rhapsody on Antony and Cleopatra. ❧ *Armstrong on "Linked Images": the dynamics of Shakespeare's imagination. Shakespeare's dualistic awareness: related imagery, unity, puns, ambivalence. Freedom of his associative powers: meanings below consciousness. Inspiration. Attacks against biographical and psychoanalytic criticism. "The Structure of the Imagination."*

XIV.   Spurgeon and Clemen   281

Spurgeon's limitations. Her pioneering exploration of "iterative imagery." Dominating images of individual tragedies. Reinforcement and contradiction of traditional views. Impetus to modern study of imagery: Brooks's criticism of Macbeth. ❧ *Clemen's analysis of Shakespeare's mechanical style in* Titus. Love's Labour's Lost *as showing gain.* Henry VI *as revealing Shakespeare's early uses of imagery.* Richard III: *imagery formal but integrated.* Richard II *a step forward. Shakespeare's middle period as revealing new techniques of associative and fully harmonized imagery.*

XV.   Spencer and Tillyard, Harbage, and Hubler   296

Spencer and Tillyard as illuminators of the "Elizabethan World Picture." The optimistic view: man's end, God's law, geocentric universe, hierarchy of souls, powers of man's mind, kinds of law; correspondences. The pessimistic view. Spencer's thesis; Tillyard's. ❧ *Harbage as historian. His felicitous style. "The Dignity of Man": affirmed in public theaters, undercut in coterie theaters;*

*Shakespeare's aversion to humiliation, his affirmative
characterization. "Sexual Behavior": the popular drama
chaste, the coterie not; Shakespearean broadness analyzed. Limitations and merits of Harbage's approach.
❧ Hubler's analysis of sonnets and plays in the light
of each other. His rhetoric, sympathy. Shakespeare's
wholeness. His healthy, unromantic view of sex. Belief
that the heart must give itself away. Secular frame of
reference of his tragedies: importance of reputation.*

XVI.   Granville-Barker, Harbage, and Spivack   323

*Granville-Barker's stances, his Pirandelloism. Shake-
speare as "genius of the workshop." Granville-Barker as
returning Shakespeare to the platform stage. Preface to
Antony and Cleopatra: the central focus—character in
action in the theater; running commentary; "The Verse
and Its Speaking." Final estimate. ❧ Harbage's
freshness. His thesis: Shakespeare's exciting then reassuring his audience through moral notions. Moral paradoxes, enigmas, unreliable spokesmen to excite. Gratification of our sense of justice to reassure—in the fables,
in the histories. Reservations. Accomplishments. ❧
Spivack's thesis: Iago both Iago and evolving Vice.
Spivack's scholastic style. "Iago": the contradictions in
his motives, emotions, goals. "Iago Revisited": Shakespeare's dramaturgy in the service of moral sentiment;
the natural Iago and Iago-as-Vice. Synthesis of Stoll and
Bradley.*

XVII.   Barber, Holloway, and Frye   354

*Barber's analogy of Shakespeare's plays to holiday enter-
tainments: "through release to clarification." Love's
Labour's Lost. Barber compared to Gervinus and Pater.*

❧ *Holloway's view of Shakespeare's plays as literature of power, not knowledge. King Lear as relating to the legend of world's end, its imagery, society, and characters descending toward the brute; comparison to Job—the common moral vision; personal bonds. Holloway's larger view: tragic pattern as ritual sacrifice of scapegoat hero. Reservations. Appeal of scapegoat role.* ❧ *Frye's view: Shakespeare's comedies as self-contained conventions, deriving from or working toward myth. The New Comedy formula of Renaissance and Shakespearean comedy: an old society giving way to a new, with detached spectators at the end. Shakespearean romance to the contrary. Larger meanings of the endings of Shakespearean romance. Frye's criticism assessed.*

XVIII.   Sewell   383

Relations to other critics, to Knight. Instances of wisdom. The play as a working out of vision. Character as product and agent of vision. Vision in comedy and history static, in tragedy dynamic. The tragic hero's uncovenanted experience. "Tragedy and the 'Kingdom of Ends.'" Reservations and final assessment.

NOTES   395

INDEX   411

Introduction

In military history, said A. W. Schlegel, we do not give the name of every soldier who fought in the files of the hostile armies: "we speak only of generals, and those who performed actions of distinction." The same truth applies to the history of Shakespearean criticism. We do not, perhaps cannot, give the names of all who have fought in the critical battles, denying or asserting Shakespeare's authorship, condemning or celebrating his art, quarreling over the definition of his characters and vision. The "Annotated World Bibliography for 1965" of the *Shakespeare Quarterly* lists no less than 1356 items, ranging from "Shakespeares *Kaufmann von Venedig* in unserer Zeit," to "The Impact of Shakespeare on Urdu Literature," to an article in Japanese on "Ritual Elements in Shakespeare's History Plays," to the query "Was the Bard an Obstetrician?" Exclusive of films, radio broadcasts, television shows, and recordings, there were 3193 items in the "Bibliography" for 1964, the quartercentenary of Shakespeare's birth, 1123 items for 1963, 1159 for 1962. "The bibliography of dissertations and studies devoted to *Hamlet*," says Kott, is already "twice the size of Warsaw's telephone directory."* The sun does not set on Shakespeare; the criticism mounts. In sketching the history of the criticism, therefore, we deal of necessity only with the principal figures—Jonson and Johnson, Dryden and Morgann, Goethe, A. W. Schlegel, Coleridge, Hazlitt, Pater, Bradley, G. Wilson Knight, and a few others.

To study these men is exhilarating. They share a boldness of vision, a courage in following the truth wherever it leads them, a

* Jan Kott, *Shakespeare Our Contemporary*, trans. Boleslaw Taborski (1964), 51.

richness of experience and a depth of sensitivity that make the hours spent in their presence doubly golden—once for the light they reflect from Shakespeare; once for the light they yield from themselves. What I mean should become abundantly clear in the chapters ahead, but I have in mind such triumphs of intellectual honesty as when Ben Jonson couples to his praise of Shakespeare's exuberant natural genius a tribute to Shakespeare's self-disciplining art:

> Yet must I not give Nature all: thy Art,
> My gentle Shakespeare, must enjoy a part.
>
> . . .
>
> For a good poet's made, as well as born.
> And such wert thou!

I think of Samuel Johnson demolishing the indictments that Shakespeare's Romans are insufficiently Roman and his kings insufficiently royal: "these are the petty cavils of petty minds"; or Johnson acknowledging that Shakespearean tragicomedy is "contrary to the rules of criticism" and proceeding, "but there is always an appeal open from criticism to nature." I think of Coleridge who joins some pride, perhaps, with his honesty when he observes of Hamlet's mental inefficiency, "I have a smack of Hamlet myself, if I may say so." And I think, too, of the quixoticism, which is one face of Wilson Knight's genius, that leads him to such conclusions as that, in the "healthy and robust" state of Denmark, where "good-nature, humor, romantic strength, and welfare" abound, the one thing rotten is Hamlet, "the ambassador of death walking amid life."

The great critics share boldness, integrity, and power of mind. They speak with a legitimate authority even when they err, for they see what they see and declare it, while the most of mankind, like Dick Minim, see only what others see and less declare their vision than echo it. This is not to say that what each of the great critics says is entirely new. Fresh eyes, looking on the same objects, will see many of the same things. But each critic gives his own stamp to the common experience as well as to what he alone has witnessed. Each molds the tradition by saying what oft was thought but ne'er so well expressed; each reinvigorates the tradition by asserting what has not before been seen but which, now seen, commends itself to the common understanding as just and valid. When Johnson declares, "This therefore is the praise of Shakespeare, that his drama is the mirror of life," or when Coleridge, speaking to the question of Shakespeare's putative indecencies, asserts that Shakespeare keeps *"at all times the high road of life,"* each is saying what others had said, but saying it with such novel rightness that his formulation echoes down the centuries. When Johnson declares that

> *Polonius is a man bred in courts, exercised in business, stored with observation, confident of his knowledge, proud of his eloquence, and declining into dotage . . . Such a man is positive and confident, because he knows that his mind was once strong, and knows not that it is become weak. Such a man excels in general principles, but fails in the particular application. He is knowing in retrospect, and ignorant in foresight. While he depends upon his memory, and can draw from his repositories of knowledge, he utters weighty sentences, and gives useful counsel; but as the mind in its enfeebled state cannot be kept long busy and intent, the old man is subject to sudden dereliction of his faculties, he loses the order of his ideas, and entangles himself in his own thoughts, till he recovers the leading principle, and falls again into his former train. This idea of dotage encroaching upon wisdom, will solve all the phenomena of the character of Polonius.*

—when Johnson says this of Polonius, or when Coleridge says of Shakespeare that "his judgment is the most wonderful" of his qualities, "more admirable than the rest," each discovers and declares what had not been recognized but which, henceforth, becomes traditional.

The great critics say things each in his own way. Each has his habitual mental stance, his mannerisms, his special stock of critical terms and concepts which a good history should recognize. Schlegel likened literary history to warfare; let me change the figure to that of a gallery. We stroll down the corridors of the centuries. The subjects of the paintings are the same—Shakespeare and his multitudinous progeny—but the pictures differ as, in an actual art gallery, do the varying renditions of the holy family. And as in an art gallery, in the corridor of the Italian Renaissance, say, where the many paintings of Raphael hang one beside another, one would become increasingly conscious of the special style and quality of the individual artist and come to see that this too was part of the content, inseparable from it, so that a Raphael Madonna was not the same Madonna as another's, but unique, the value inhering in both matter and manner, so in our Shakespearean gallery, there are styles to know. When Coleridge enlarges on love in *Romeo and Juliet,* he exhibits that unctuous gallantry which college professors succumb to in lectures before Ladies' Clubs. When he comes to distinguish between the geniuses of Milton and Shakespeare, compeers, not rivals, and ends his panegyric with the apostrophe, "O what great men hast thou not produced, England, my country!" we hear again the note of self-consciousness, as when the speaker exhibits his sensibility by way of asserting his authority. Always we hear this note— among others—in Coleridge. It is part of him and what he says. We must learn to recognize the characteristic rhetoric of Bradley and how he speaks, frequently, not of the plays but of our *impressions* of them, thus removing the matter of debate from the outward theater to the inner. We must catch Granville-Barker's subtle changes of voice and how, at times, he seems to be mere lecturer on the platform, now stage-manager assigning us our parts, now actor, playing a few lines to catch their under-harmonies.

The image of a gallery has other uses than suggesting that

criticism, like painting, uniquely joins manner with matter, the interpreter with the thing interpreted. An important gallery always has more halls than you can get through in the allotted time of the tour, and the same is true of the gallery of Shakespearean criticism. Moreover, though they may be interpreting Shakespeare in Urdu or debating him in Swahili, to those corridors, as long as I in my ignorance am guide, we shall not come. Nor can we do more than glance down most of the corridors of continental criticism, though something of what the French and Germans have said we must scan. And until this century, though Americans have read Shakespeare they have said little significantly new about him—an important essay by Lowell, another by Lanier, a scattered note or two by Poe, Hawthorne, Melville, a panegyric by Emerson, but as McManaway observes, "Not much Shakespeare criticism was published in this country before the first World War."* Our critics will be mainly English, then, until the twentieth century, when Americans join them in importance. Our corridors will be those of the eighteenth century, the nineteenth century, and modern times, the corridors gaining in length as they approach the here and now. Indeed, so numerous are the modern critics and so voluminous their output that they occupy more than half this book, and it has seemed tidy to group them according to their foci or perspectives—the dramatic formalists (Chapters X and XVI), the biographers (XI and XIII), the imagists and symbolists (XIV), the socio-historians (XV), and the anthropologists or archetypists (XVII). First and last our concern will be with the principal critics, their statements and their styles. It should be a pleasant tour.

A NOTE ON SPELLING AND ANNOTATION

Except for the name Shakespeare as it appears in titles (Shakspere, Shakespeare, Schäkespear, etc.), spelling and punc-

* James G. McManaway, "Shakespeare in the United States," *P.M.L.A.*, *LXXIX* (1964), 518.

tuation have been Americanized and modernized. Terminal k's have dropped from old-fashioned "dramatick" and "poetick." British spellings in -our have become the American -or. Eighteenth century italics and intralinear capitalization have disappeared. Capitalization at the beginning of quotations and punctuation at the end have been adjusted to the requirements of my own syntax. Although quotations are frequent, no citations appear if the holder of the work discussed could easily find his way by context, index, or table of contents. As a consequence notes are few and, I hope, unobtrusive—the notes and references may be found at the end of the book, p. 395.

A SHORT HISTORY of
SHAKESPEAREAN CRITICISM

The First One Hundred Fifty Years

Praise and blame. Shakespeare the poet of Nature: his creative, imitative, and affective powers. His deficiency in Art: lack of restraint, generic irregularity—poetic injustice, violation of the unities, tragicomedy—indecorousness.

In 1765, when Samuel Johnson came to write the Preface to his edition of Shakespeare's plays, he set himself to sum up and adjudicate not only his own impressions but those of his predecessors. He was to be judge—dispassionate, calm: "No question," he said, "can be more innocently discussed than a dead poet's pretensions to renown."[1] Johnson's calmness was a rhetorical fiction, his bland reduction of Shakespeare to "a dead poet" with "pretensions to renown" a militant prologue to his cataloguing of Shakespeare's faults, the thoroughness of which distressed bardolaters for a century to come. But judicial Johnson was, and since the evidence he sifted and weighed was all the criticism that preceded him, we can come to understand the criticism of the seventeenth and eighteenth centuries by starting from and returning to him, the last and perhaps the greatest of the spokesmen of neo-classical values.

The critical portion of Johnson's Preface is in two parts, ahistorical and historical. In the first Johnson considers Shakespeare without reference to his temporal or geographical placement, in short, as a classic. In the second he considers him as an English author of the late sixteenth and early seventeenth centuries, writing when "the English nation . . . was yet struggling to emerge from barbarity." In both parts Johnson's method is the same: he begins with praise, he ends with blame. The great paragraph beginning, "This therefore is the praise of Shakespeare, that his drama is the mirror of life," is followed in a few pages with a paragraph beginning, "Shakespeare with his excellencies has likewise faults, and faults sufficient to obscure and overwhelm any other merit." The extraordinary tribute, that "the form, the characters, the language, and the shows of the English drama" are Shakespeare's, heralds the lamentation "that as we owe everything to him, he owes something to us . . . We fix our eyes upon his graces, and turn them from his deformities, and endure in him what we should in another loath or despise."

Praise and blame are poles between which all people and poets live, but not often are they so widely apart as they were in the seventeenth and eighteenth centuries for Shakespeare. However critics spoke of him, hyperbole was their language. "As Plautus and Seneca are accounted the best for comedy and tragedy among the Latins," said Francis Meres (1598), "so Shakespeare among the English is the most excellent in both kinds for the stage." "He was not of an age, but for all time!" said Ben Jonson (1623). "Thou in our wonder and astonishment hast built thyself a live-long monument"—so Milton (1630). "He was the man who of all modern, and perhaps ancient poets, had the largest and most comprehensive soul," said Dryden (1668). For Addison (1714), he was "our inimitable Shakespeare," "born with all the seeds of poetry." "Homer himself," declared Pope (1725), "drew not his art so immediately from the fountains of Nature." And Johnson, in his *Prologue Spoken by Mr. Garrick at the Opening of the Theatre in Drury-Lane* (1747), exuberantly contributed his encomium:

> When Learning's triumph o'er her barb'rous foes
> First rear'd the stage, immortal Shakespeare rose;
> Each change of many-color'd life he drew,

Exhausted worlds, and then imagin'd new:
Existence saw him spurn her bounded reign,
And panting Time toil'd after him in vain:
His pow'rful strokes presiding Truth impress'd,
And unresisted Passion storm'd the Breast."

Not all the hyperbole was praise, however. Thomas Rymer
had this to say about *Othello* (1693):

the moral, sure, of this fable is very instructive.
I. First, this may be a caution to all maidens of quality
how, without their parents' consent, they run away with
blackamoors . . .
   Secondly, this may be a warning to all good wives, that
they look well to their linen.
   Thirdly, this may be a lesson to husbands, that before
their jealousy be tragical, the proofs may be mathematical.

Voltaire speaks with the same atrabilious vigor. Though in
1731 he writes of "the barbarous irregularities" with which *Julius
Caesar* was filled, he professes a gratified astonishment that the
play, written in an age of ignorance, was no worse. By 1748,
however, his astonishment admits more of outrage than gratification. He is speaking of *Hamlet*:

a piece gross and barbarous, that would not be approved by
the lowest populace of France or Italy. Hamlet goes mad in
the second act, his beloved in the third; the prince kills the
father of his beloved, feigning to kill a rat, and the heroine
throws herself into the river. They dig her grave on the stage;
the grave-diggers utter quibbles worthy of them, holding in
their hands the skulls of the dead; prince Hamlet replies to
their grossnesses with nonsense no less disgusting. During this
time one of the players makes the conquest of Poland.
Hamlet, his mother, and his stepfather, drink together on the
stage; they sing at table, they quarrel there, they fight, they

kill. One would think that this work was the fruit of the imagination of a drunken savage.

Most of the time the praise and the blame issue from the same critic. If Jonson sees Shakespeare as one whose writings "neither man, nor muse, can praise too much," he also replies to the players' brag that Shakespeare never blotted a line, "Would he had blotted a thousand." And in his Prologue to *Everyman in His Humour* (1601), Jonson roundly, if indirectly, tasks Shakespeare for violating the unities of the drama and the decorums of the stage. His own play, he says, will not show a child growing to manhood or old age; it will not rehearse the Wars of the Roses *à la Henry VI* with "rusty swords" and "some few foot-and-half-foot words"; it will not "waft you o'er the seas" with a Chorus, as Shakespeare does in *Henry V*; it will not use firecrackers or stage thunder to work up ridiculous excitement. The same balancing of extremely opposed judgments appears repeatedly in the criticism of Dryden, whose revision of *Troilus and Cressida* shows that his love of Shakespeare, like Jonson's, was "this side idolatry." Of *Troilus* he says (1679):

> the author seems to have begun it with some fire; the characters of Pandarus and Thersites are promising enough; but as if he grew weary of his task, after an entrance or two, he lets them fall: and the latter part of the tragedy is nothing but a confusion of drums and trumpets, excursions and alarms. The chief persons . . . are left alive; Cressida is false, and is not punished.

Dryden's more frequent concern is with Shakespeare's style. If Shakespeare describes a thing so that "you more than see it, you feel it too," he is also "many times flat, insipid; his comic wit degenerating into clenches, his serious swelling into bombast" (1668); "the fury of his fancy often transported him beyond the bounds of judgment, either in coining of new words and phrases, or racking words which were in use, into the violence of a catachresis" (1679). Pope is similarly even-handed (1725): "of all English poets Shakespeare must be confessed to be the fairest and fullest subject for criticism, and to afford the most numerous, as well as most conspicuous instances, both of beauties and faults of all sorts." Pope indicates what he means by faults in fair detail:

> The audience was generally composed of the meaner sort of people; and therefore the images of life were to be drawn from those of their own rank: accordingly we find, that not our author's only but almost all the old comedies have their scene among tradesmen and mechanics: and even their historical plays strictly follow the common old stories or vulgar traditions of that kind of people. In tragedy, nothing was so sure to surprise and cause admiration, as the most strange, unexpected, and consequently most unnatural, events and incidents; the most exaggerated thoughts; the most verbose and bombast expression; the most pompous rhymes, and thundering versification. In comedy, nothing was so sure to please, as mean buffoonry, vile ribaldry, and unmannerly jests of fools and clowns . . .

> . . . our authors had no thoughts of writing on the model of the ancients: their tragedies were only histories in dialogue; and their comedies followed the thread of any novel as they found it, no less implicitly than if it had been true history.

For many a modern the seventeenth- and eighteenth-century praise of Shakespeare sounds so right, the blame so outrageously wrong or irrelevant, that the criticism as a whole is hard to take in, much less take seriously. Let us examine it closely, remembering that the consensus of two centuries is not to be lightly neglected, that the critics on whom we are focusing were themselves rare poets, that though they may have tried Shakespeare by laws we deem irrelevant to him, they were chronicling in their criticism their actual experience as they read Shakespeare or saw him.

They praised Shakespeare above all as the poet of Nature. Jonson was learned, but "sweetest Shakespeare, fancy's child,/ Warble[d] his native wood-notes wild" (Milton, 1632?). They thought of him as an irregular genius, an "original," like a forest instead of a garden, like crude instead of refined gold. He was one of the giants before the flood, Othello to their Venice.

They meant by Nature several things. It was, first, the power, in Shakespeare, of creation (Lat. *natura:* birth), whether by inspiration, as from some divine force flowing through him, or by genius, the source of the creative energy god-like within himself. Shakespeare was seminal—in the progeny of his teeming pen:

> Look how the father's face
> Lives in his issue, even so, the race
> Of Shakespeare's mind, and manners brightly shines
> In his well turned, and true-filed lines.
>
> (Jonson, 1623)

The "father of our dramatic poets" (Dryden, 1668), he imparted "to Fletcher wit, to laboring Jonson art" (Dryden, 1667). Like a god, Shakespeare "exhausted worlds, and then imagin'd new" (Johnson, 1747). And always he was seen to possess those special virtues of generating nature, ease and fecundity. "What he thought, he uttered with that easiness, that we have scarce received from him a blot in his papers" (Heminge and Condell, 1623). His "easy numbers flow" (Milton, 1632). He has "the largest and most comprehensive soul" (Dryden, 1668). In him are "*all* the seeds of poetry" (Addison, 1714; my italics).

Nature was the creative power; even more it was the thing imitated—men and manners, talk and thought, sentiment and passion. And it was, finally, the response in us, the sympathetic emotion, whether of joy or terror, the fright at the Ghost in *Hamlet,* the delight with Falstaff. The poet of Nature gave us, in

Dryden's famous phrase, "a just and lively image of human nature" to awaken our recognition, to engage us in his plays.

> So well he hath expressed in his plays all sorts of persons, as one would think he had been transformed into every one of those persons he hath described . . . the clown or jester . . . the king, and privy counsellor . . . the coward . . . the most valiant, and experienced soldier . . . Sir John Falstaff . . . Harry the Fifth . . . Julius Caesar, Augustus Caesar, and Antonius . . . Brutus . . . Cleopatra . . . Nan Page, Mrs. Page, Mrs. Ford . . . Beatrice, Mrs. Quickly, Doll Tearsheet, and others, too many to relate . . . in his tragic vein, he presents passions so naturally, and misfortunes so probably, as he pierces the souls of his readers with such a true sense and feeling thereof, that it forces tears through their eyes, and almost persuades them, they are really actors, or at least present at those tragedies.
>
> (Cavendish, 1664)

"His images are indeed everywhere so lively," said Rowe (1709), "that the thing he would represent stands full before you, and you possess every part of it." "Every single character in Shakespeare," said Pope (1725), "is as much an individual, as those in life itself," and "the heart swells, and the tears burst out, just at the proper places."

So Shakespeare was the poet of Nature, which as Pope said was "at once the source, and end, and test of art." But what of Shakespeare's Art? Jonson had praised Shakespeare's Art as well as his Nature; Dryden said that Shakespeare taught Jonson Art. Yet the style of the praise of Shakespeare, the recurrent image of him as an untutored genius living in a barbarous age, the insistence that he could not be judged "by Aristotle's rules" (Pope, 1725), even Johnson's happy hyperbole of panting Time toiling after Shakespeare, in vain—make clear that it was in his Art Johnson's predecessors found Shakespeare deficient.

Like Nature, Art had several meanings. It was the reason to Nature's passion, the learning to Nature's instinct. It was the education that turned infant savage into adult man, the architecture that reduced the uncouth Gothic to neat modernity, the banks holding in the river, the circumference containing the circle. In a word, Art meant restraint, a virtue insufficiently evident in a poet who scarce blotted a line.

More particularly, Art meant restraint according to the laws of form. In these centuries criticism, both English and continental, concerned itself with the genres and sub-genres of literature, with the principles common to all, and with the special rules peculiar to each. All poetry, as Horace had said and as it was universally agreed, had delight and instruction for its end. And most critics found that fictional poetry, epic or dramatic, accomplished its instruction by conforming the issues of its plot to the requirements of poetic justice. The theory of poetic justice is noble: it is that poetry imitates the ideal justice which history cannot show but which religion promises. In fact, however, the doctrine invited a mechanical distribution of rewards and punishments by the poet, a mechanical standard of judging for the critic. Lesser critics could seize on the doctrine, as did Rymer. Larger men, like Dennis, could become possessed by it, as when he wrote that

> Shakespeare has been wanting in the exact distribution of poetical justice . . . in most of his best tragedies, in which the guilty and the innocent perish promiscuously; as Duncan and Banquo in Macbeth, as likewise Lady Macduff and her children; Desdemona in Othello; Cordelia, Kent, and King Lear . . . Brutus and Portia in Julius Caesar, and young Hamlet in the tragedy of Hamlet . . . The good and the bad then perishing promiscuously in the best of Shakespeare's tragedies, there can be either none or very weak instruction in them.

(1712)

Dryden himself pays lip service to the doctrine when he complains that "Cressida is false, and is not punished" (1679), and when he praises the story of *Antony and Cleopatra* for "the excellency of the moral: . . . the chief persons . . . were famous patterns of unlawful love; and their end accordingly was unfortunate" (1678). Perhaps that is not why we now enjoy the play, but we recognize that popular literature has customarily obeyed poetic justice. Bacon put the reason well when he said that the use of poetry "hath been to give some shadow of satisfaction to the mind of man in those points wherein the nature of things doth deny it, the world being in proportion inferior to the soul" (1605). Poetic justice is the justice not of actuality, but of heart's desire.

All poetry should delight and instruct, but the critics we are considering recognized that the different kinds of poetry achieved their common ends by different means and under differing conditions. They saw that dramatic poetry differed from the epic in that it was to be performed by living actors in a confined space, and therefore they held tragedy and comedy subservient to the unities of time and place, from which the epic was exempt. "The stage should always represent but one place," said Sidney, asserting what is perhaps the strongest single tradition the stage has ever known, "and the uttermost time presupposed in it should be, both by Aristotle's precept and common reason, but one day." Sidney's ridicule of the English dramatic practice, which was to become Shakespeare's, establishes the tone and the logic of Shakespeare's condemners from Jonson to Johnson.

> You shall have Asia of the one side [of the stage], and Afric of the other, and so many other under-kingdoms, that the player, when he cometh in, must ever begin with telling where he is, or else the tale will not be conceived. Now ye shall have three ladies walk to gather flowers, and then we must believe the stage to be a garden. By and by we hear news of shipwreck in the same place, and then we are to blame if

> we accept it not for a rock. Upon the back of that comes out a
> hideous monster with fire and smoke, and then the miserable
> beholders are bound to take it for a cave. While in the mean
> time two armies fly in, represented with four swords and
> bucklers, and then what hard heart will not receive it for a
> pitched field?
>
> Now of time they are much more liberal. For ordinary it
> is that two young princes fall in love; after many traverses she
> is got with child, delivered of a fair boy, he is lost, groweth a
> man, falleth in love, and is ready to get another child, and all
> this in two hours' space; which how absurd it is in sense even
> sense may imagine, and art hath taught, and all ancient
> examples justified.

Except in *Pericles* Shakespeare never makes panting time toil quite
so desperately after him, but his abuses of the unities are so many
that the critics came to value inordinately that one hack play
wherein he obeys them, *The Merry Wives of Windsor*. And if
today the unities seem trivial and the logic by which they were
confirmed silly, perhaps we can momentarily entertain the ancient
feeling about them by thinking of some modern critical doctrine
and the manner of its enforcement. Consider, for example, how
we tend to regard narrative fiction that violates its own point of
view. We do not tolerate it lightly. I recall showing a writer and
critic the passage from Henry Mackenzie's *The Man of Feeling*
where the narrator, having left his friend *alone* with his beloved,
continues to tell us what they said to each other. My critical
friend's remarks had the right Sidneyan ring.

Tragedy and comedy were alike plays, but they were apprehended to be of different kinds. One deals with the lofty and one
with the ordinary. One "openeth the greatest wounds," in Sidney's
formulation, "and showeth forth the ulcers that are covered with
tissue"; the other exposes "the common errors of our life." Accordingly, each characteristically engages a specific segment of the
emotional spectrum: tragedy arouses terror, pity, admiration;

comedy, amusement and scorn. The neo-classicists held that genres thus distinct should be kept apart. And Sidney complains of the plays on the London boards of his day that they are

> neither right tragedies nor right comedies, mingling kings and clowns, not because the matter so carrieth it, but thrust in the clown by head and shoulders to play a part in majestical matters, with neither decency nor discretion; so as neither the admiration and commiseration, nor the right sportfulness, is by their mongrel tragi-comedy obtained.

(1583?)

Till Johnson's day that criticism echoes. The fool in *Lear*, the grave-diggers in *Hamlet*, the drunken porter in *Macbeth*, destroyed with their levities the tragic mood and troubled English critics as well as French, both blaming Shakespeare's practice on the ignorance of his times, the crudity of his audience.

Finally, Art meant restraint according to that all-pervading if elusive concept, decorum. Decorum means fittingness, and as applied to drama it meant not only the maintenance of the genres in their purity but the fittingness of the play to the medium of boards and costumed actors. It meant the fittingness of part to part and part to whole, of speech to character, of cause to consequence. It meant, as well, the fittingness of individual characters to the type they represented, this type conceived ideally— the soldierly soldier, the courtly courtier, the regal king. Decorum meant the propriety of the speech and action of the play according to the standards of taste *reigning in the day of the critic*—hence the recurrent apology for Shakespeare by appealing to the ignorance of his times, the barbarity of his audience. Clearly, though, as Sidney and Jonson testify, there were those alive in Elizabeth's reign to whom Shakespeare's plays were already indecorous in their violation of generic purity, their disunity of time and place, their bustle and commotion, their stage violence and bombast. And in the century and a half thereafter the artistic taste of the English and the French grew in fastidiousness beyond limits we easily imagine today. Voltaire is not being picayune, for a cultivated Enlightenment Frenchman, when he scores Shakespeare for showing people eating on the stage, or fighting. Though his society was as conscious as ours of the ugliness of man's condition, it sought in the elegance of its manners and its art to realize the human potential. The brute actualities of eating and drinking, like those other actualities of bodily evacuation, it could not deny, but it could banish them from the stage and feel legitimately outraged if they appeared there again, bestially obtrusive like a belch from the pulpit.

The fastidiousness of the English about language is harder for us to understand, perhaps impossible for us, in our linguistic permissiveness, to sympathize with, yet it is a solid fact. Young Pope was advised to seek "correctness" in his writing. Swift wrote "A Proposal for Correcting, Improving and Ascertaining the English Tongue." To true and false wit Addison devoted certain of his *Spectator* papers which are, in fact, studies in the proper and improper relations between words and things. The eighteenth century is England's time for arguing over the establishment of an Academy, like the French Academy, to settle the meanings of words and their right relations. It is the century of Johnson's *Dictionary* and the codifying of the "laws" of grammar by Priestley and others. Such facts, however, fail to convey the intense feeling the critics had about language. They paid attention to words with a seriousness most of us have lost. It was like the air they breathed, not to be polluted—or if polluted, then to be lamented. As Johnson put it in his Preface to the *Dictionary*: "Language is only the instrument of science, and words are but the signs of ideas: I wish, however, that the instrument might be less apt to decay, and that signs might be permanent, like the things which they denote."

The definition of this fastidiousness about language remains to arrive at, and here we need illustrations. Addison supplies us with a useful comment on punning: "The seeds of punning are in the minds of all men, and though they may be subdued by reason, reflection, and good sense, they will be very apt to shoot up in the greatest genius, that is not broken and cultivated by the rules of art." The reign of King James, he says, was "the age in which the pun chiefly flourished."

> The greatest authors, in their most serious works, made frequent use of puns. The sermons of Bishop Andrews, and the tragedies of Shakespeare, are full of them. The sinner was punned into repentance by the former, as in the latter nothing is more usual than to see a hero weeping and quibbling for a dozen lines together.

How this could be Addison explains: "the first race of authors, who were the great heroes in writing, were destitute of all rules and arts of criticism; and for that reason, though they excel later writers in greatness of genius, they fall short of them in accuracy and correctness."

Pope supplies us with other examples, of a different sort. When he edited Shakespeare, the variations between the old copies and the presence in the plays of "passages which are excessively bad" convinced him that Shakespeare had been contaminated by the players and the publishers. In his own edition (1725) he "degraded to the bottom of the page" many such "bad" passages, as well as distinguishing by commas in the margin "some of the most shining." Among those he distinguished as shining in *Romeo and Juliet* are the Nurse's tale of Juliet's fall and her husband's jest (I.iii.16–48), Mercutio's celebration of Queen Mab (I.iv.53–95), Mercutio's slander of Benvolio as bellicose ("thou wilt quarrel with a man that hath a hair more, or a hair less, in his beard than thou hast": III.i.16–32), the interchange between Romeo and Juliet on the coming of the dawn (III.v.1–25), and Romeo on the Apothecary's shop (V.i.37–48). Among the passages Pope degraded to the margin are, in Act I alone, the following:

1. A word-playing passage by the Prince. Thrice, he says, the feud has made Verona's citizens cast off the ornaments of peace, "To wield old partisans, in hands as old,/Cankered with peace, to part your cankered hate." (I.i.101–102)

2. Lady Capulet's extended comparison of Paris's face to a volume written on with beauty's pen, his eyes to marginal commentary on the text of his face, his wife to be the binding to this "unbound lover," etc. (I.iii.79–95)

3. Mercutio's punning on "done"—"dun's the mouse"—and more of the same. (I.iv. 39–49)

4. Capulet's tongue-lashing of Tybalt at the ball. (I.v.80–88)

5. The final couplet of the sonnet interchange between Juliet and Romeo, wherein Romeo sues for and receives a kiss, and the witty aftermath. (I.v.107–112)

Johnson supplies our final illustrations. His *Rambler 168* (1751) considers the fluctuations of status which words undergo. What is here regarded as elegant is there seen as mean; what is high today becomes low tomorrow as usage and associations debase it. Johnson takes his illustrations from *Macbeth*:

> Come, thick night!
> And pall thee in the dunnest smoke of hell,
> That my keen knife see not the wound it makes;
> Nor heav'n peep through the blanket of the dark,
> To cry, Hold! hold!

In this passage is exerted all the force of poetry . . . yet, perhaps, scarce any man now peruses it without some disturbance of his attention from the counteraction of the words to the ideas. What can be more dreadful than to implore the presence of night, invested, not in common obscurity, but in the smoke of hell? Yet the efficacy of this invocation is destroyed by the insertion of an epithet now seldom heard but in the stable, and dun night may come or go without any other notice than contempt.

Similarly, "we do not immediately conceive that any crime of importance is to be committed with a *knife*; or who does not, at last, from the long habit of connecting a knife with sordid offices, feel aversion rather than terror?" Again, "I can scarce check my risibility, when the expression forces itself upon my mind; for who, without some relaxation of his gravity, can hear of the avengers of guilt *peeping through a blanket?"*

It is dangerous to generalize about any century's theories of language, difficult to gauge the precise meaning of its own commentators on usage. Clearly Johnson overstates his case to make it; Pope, I believe, took advantage of textual uncertainty to remodel Shakespeare along eighteenth-century lines; Addison obviously enjoyed treating the pun as the lingering taint of original linguistic sin. It seems clear, however, that whether they were retrenching the language from the excesses of the seventeenth-century poets or perfecting the language as the instrument of the new science or simply making the language the reflector of refinements in manners, the critics of this period required that language mirror actuality more narrowly than we now require and they required that it recognize the same distinctions of association they recognized in their daily living.

They found none of the metaphysical or modern delight in ambiguity and open-ended evocation. They demanded of language unambiguous and referential clarity. It should be a map corresponding to actualities of thing or value or feeling. And this is precisely where the pun, the false wit, failed. A pun seemed to point to something out there, something real, but examine it—and nothing. It was a bubble (the century's favorite term for a fraud), bright, shiny, and empty. True wit pointed two ways at once, as does a pun, but each way *it* made sense. In "The Vanity of Human Wishes" Johnson speaks of the guests poisoning the rich old man's mind against his son and daughter: they

> Improve his heady rage with treach'rous skill,
> And mold his passions till they make his will.

Will is true wit. It points to the faculty of the mind which is activated by the passions; it points to the legal instrument. Of such true wit in Shakespeare they recognized the Lord's plenty, but the false wit was there, too, in extraordinary and embarrassing abundance.

The mirroring of actuality meant harmonizing word and feeling. The language of the lover should vibrate to his passion, the mother's affectionate concern should find its appropriate diction, the protest of sincerity should ring true. When it did not, the critical ear heard discord and the feelings were refrigerated. The conceit of young Paris as a volume with text, margin, and binding stops one believing in Lady Capulet's feeling. When Desdemona says she does "abhor" the word "whore" and cannot say it, our faith in her—or in Shakespeare—momentarily withers. And, so often did the "conceited" Shakespeare play with words when he might be working with feeling that the critics cried out in protest.

An old joke about the parlor and the bathroom suggests the final point about the fastidiousness we are exploring. There is a place for this and a place for that, for eating, for sleeping, for living, for playing. Customarily, we keep places apart. We do, as well, for language. We know the registers of formal cordiality, the terms of good-natured equality, the grammars of request, command, plea. But we mix our registers and grammars now more than we used to, and, reading Shakespeare, we blur distinctions because so much time has intervened, because we grow careless, because *he*, after all, is Shakespeare. The critics we are examining tended to feel differently. They did not blur distinctions or grow careless or abdicate responsibility in the face of an idol. They found it hard to respond to the full intensity of Lady Macbeth's invocation when they thought of peeping through holes in a blanket. It was well enough for the Nurse to talk the way garrulous old biddies talk, but the language appropriate to her was not right for the honorable old Capulet. It troubled them when Antony, clasping Cleopatra in his arms, speaks of the "dungy earth." And Shakespeare kept sinning in this way.

In the next chapter we return to Johnson and his Preface. Here we have been examining the Shakespearean criticism that preceded him, the pattern of praising Shakespeare for his nature, of blaming him for the deficiencies of his art. Shakespeare's nature, we have seen, has been his power of creation, though the implications of creativity seem not to have been explored as Coleridge was later to explore them; his power of imitating men, manners, and the phenomenal world; his power of engaging our emotions. His nature, too, has connoted barbarism, which is to say, a lack of art. He has been found deficient in restraint generally, in such laws of form as poetic justice, generic purity, the unities of time and place. More especially, he has been found deficient in the decorums, especially those of language. Johnson fits this tradition, he summarizes it, and, crucially, he modifies it.

ii

Samuel Johnson / 1709–1784

Shakespeare the poet of general nature, his drama the mirror of life, his comic dialogue appropriate to the genius of the language. His multitudinous failings in art. His essential amorality. Vindication of his violations of character types, generic purity, and the unities of time and place. Analysis of his characters. His engaging the mind.

Shakespeare, says Johnson, has "long outlived his century, the term commonly fixed as the test of literary merit." He can no longer benefit from topical allusions, from patronage and puffs, from such propagandistic or factional relevance as his works may once have had. "Unassisted by interest or passion, [his works] have passed through variations of taste and changes of manners, and, as they devolved from one generation to another, have received new honors at every transmission." Why?

> Nothing can please many, and please long, but just representations of general nature. Particular manners can be known to few, and therefore few only can judge how nearly they are copied. The irregular combinations of fanciful invention may delight awhile, by that novelty of which the common satiety of life sends us all in quest; but the pleasures of sudden wonder are soon exhausted, and the mind can only repose on the stability of truth.

> Shakespeare is above all writers, at least above all modern writers, the poet of nature; the poet that holds up to his readers a faithful mirror of manners and of life. His characters . . . are the genuine progeny of common humanity . . . His persons act and speak by the influence of those general passions and principles by which all minds are agitated, and the whole system of life is continued in motion.

Johnson develops this central argument by exuberantly contrasting Shakespeare's "just representations of general nature" with the absurdly unnatural practices of other dramatists.

> The theater, when it is under any other direction, is peopled by such characters as were never seen, conversing in a language which was never heard, upon topics which will never arise in the commerce of mankind . . .
>
> . . . To bring a lover, a lady and a rival into the fable; to entangle them in contradictory obligations, perplex them with oppositions of interest, and harass them with violence of desires inconsistent with each other; to make them meet in rapture and part in agony; to fill their mouths with hyperbolical joy and outrageous sorrow; to distress them as nothing human ever was distressed; to deliver them as nothing human ever was delivered, is the business of a modern dramatist . . .
>
> Other dramatists can only gain attention by hyperbolical or aggravated characters, by fabulous and unexampled excellence or depravity . . . Other writers disguise the most natural passions and most frequent incidents; so that he who contemplates them in the book will not know them in the world.

From this series of hyperbolical contrasts, Johnson comes to the first of his magnificent encomiums:

> This therefore is the praise of Shakespeare, that his
> drama is the mirror of life; that he who has mazed his
> imagination, in following the phantoms which other writers
> raise up before him, may here be cured of his delirious
> ecstasies, by reading human sentiments in human language;
> by scenes from which a hermit may estimate the transactions
> of the world, and a confessor predict the progress of the
> passions.

Just representation of general nature, fidelity to the essence of things—this is what Shakespeare shares with the ancients. He has no "heroes"—Tamburlaines, Almanzors, Supermen—since these are not in nature. If he does depart from this brazen world to give us a Caliban or an Ariel, a Puck, Titania, or Oberon—then he "approximates the remote, and familiarizes the wonderful," endowing with naturalness the beings of fantasy. He is the poet of nature not by inspiration or by virtue of a fecundating imagination, but because he holds up the mirror. "There is a vigilance of observation and accuracy of distinction which books and precepts cannot confer; from this almost all original and native excellence proceeds." Shakespeare possesses this vigilance. He looks at "things as they really exist"; "he gives the image which he receives . . . the ignorant feel his representations to be just, and the learned scc that they are complete."

To this definition of the poet of nature Johnson adds significantly. He says that Shakespeare—starting out "with the world open before him," when the rules were known to few, the public judgment unformed, without any example sufficiently famous to force him to imitation, and without critics of sufficient authority to restrain him—"indulged his natural disposition, and his disposition, as Rymer has remarked, led him to comedy." Typically, Johnson enforces his point by contrasts between Shakespeare's comic gifts and his alleged infelicities at tragedy in a manner sufficiently hyperbolic to outrage later critics. "His tragedy," he avers, "seems to be skill, his comedy to be instinct." Whether

Rymer and Johnson are right, however, need concern us less than Johnson's remark about Shakespeare's comic dialogue:

> *If there be, what I believe there is, in every nation, a style which never becomes obsolete, a certain mode of phraseology so consonant and congenial to the analogy and principles of its respective language as to remain settled and unaltered; this style is probably to be sought in the common intercourse of life, among those who speak only to be understood, without ambition of elegance. The polite are always catching modish innovations, and the learned depart from established forms of speech . . . those who wish for distinction forsake the vulgar, when the vulgar is right; but there is a conversation above grossness and below refinement, where propriety resides, and where this poet seems to have gathered his comic dialogue.*

Johnson here adds to his definition of the poet of nature the attribute of appropriate language—appropriate because natural, because consonant with the genius of the tongue. Shakespeare sees what is there; he gives the image he receives; and he gives it in language pure and stable. So it is, in another of Johnson's splendid encomiums, that "the stream of time, which is continually washing the dissoluble fabrics of other poets, passes without injury by the adamant of Shakespeare."

From praise Johnson turns to blame, to an indictment twelve paragraphs in length which he enjoins with the same vigor he has lavished on commendation. Shakespeare, so runs the charge, (1) "seems to write without any moral purpose." (2) His plots are often "loosely formed" and "carelessly pursued." (3) His last acts are often neglected: the "catastrophe is improbably produced or imperfectly represented." (4) He is guilty of historical, geographical, and chronological improprieties. (5) His comic "reciprocations of smartness and contests of sarcasm" are seldom successful, the jests being gross, the gentlemen and ladies insufficiently distinguished from the clowns. (6) His tragic scenes suffer the more he labors: "whenever he solicits his invention, or strains his faculties, the offspring of his throes is tumor, meanness, tediousness, and obscurity." (7) His narrations are pompous and wearisome. (8) "His declamations or set speeches are commonly cold and weak." (9) He fails to reject unwieldy sentiments that he cannot well express, and (10) he often inflates trivial sentiments and vulgar ideas. (11) "He is not long soft and pathetic without some idle conceit, or contemptible equivocation" that counteracts "terror and pity, as they are rising in the mind." (12) And he is irresistibly fascinated by the quibble, "the fatal Cleopatra for which he lost the world, and was content to lose it."

To be sure we have heard much of this before. This time, however, we have Johnson's notes to the eight volumes of his edition, documenting and, in a sense, legitimizing his complaint. A few notes from the early volumes will illustrate. The second charge spoke of Shakespeare's careless pursuing of his plots. In *Measure for Measure* (IV.v.1), the Duke gives letters to Friar Peter to be delivered "at fit time." Johnson observes: "Peter never delivers the letters, but tells his story without any credentials. The poet forgot the plot which he had formed." In *The Merchant of Venice* (IV.i.105), the Duke tells the court he has sent for Bellario, "a learned Doctor"; Johnson observes: "that the Duke would, on such an occasion, consult a Doctor of great reputation, is not unlikely, but how should this be foreknown by Portia?" He comments similarly on the looseness of *The Two Gentlemen of Verona:* "the author conveys his heroes by sea from one inland town to another in the same country; he places the Emperor at Milan and sends his young men to attend him, but never mentions him more; he makes Proteus, after an interview with Silvia, say he has only seen her picture."

The sixth charge spoke of labored tragic scenes. In *King John* (III.iv.61), where King Philip urges Constance to bind up the tresses she has let down in her grief, Johnson notes: "It was necessary that Constance should be interrupted, because a passion so violent cannot be borne long. I wish the following speeches had been equally happy; but they only serve to show, how difficult it is to maintain the pathetic long." In the first speech in question Constance addresses her thoughts to the joy of meeting Arthur again in heaven; but because canker sorrow will eat her bud (Arthur) "And chase the native beauty from his cheek," and make him "look as hollow as a ghost,/As dim and meager as an ague's fit," his appearance will so have changed at his death that when she meets him in heaven she will know him not: "Therefore never, never/Must I behold my pretty Arthur more." In the second speech, she begins by analogizing her grief to her lost child:

> Grief fills the room up of my absent child,
> Lies in his bed, walks up and down with me,
> Puts on his pretty looks, repeats his words,
> Remembers me of all his gracious parts,
> Stuffs out his vacant garments with his form;
> Then have I reason to be fond of Grief.

There is more, but perhaps this is enough to suggest the basis of Johnson's discontent.

The twelfth charge spoke of the quibble. Johnson draws attention in his notes to such "miserable" equivocations as Launce's arguing (*Two Gentlemen*, II.v.27–34) that his staff *understands* him because it *stands under* him, Portia's hope that she give *light* but not be *light* (*Merchant*, V.i.129), Claudio's play on his beloved's name: "O *Hero*, what a *Hero* hadst thou been" (*Much Ado*, IV.i.101), or Costard's punning on *Ajax* to mean *a jakes*, a privy (*Love's Labour's Lost*, V.ii.581).

The years since Johnson's Preface have ill-fitted us in some ways to read his criticism aright. Babcock[1] speaks of 1766–1791 as the era in which occurred "the genesis of Shakespeare idolatry." Colcridge demanded reverence of Shakespeare's critics, and like Carlyle, regarded Shakespeare more as prophet than poet. Through Shakespeare, in Emerson's view, God spoke. And though detractors as witty and as colossal as Shaw and Tolstoy have had their say, T. J. B. Spencer wittily observes that the detraction of Shakespeare has scarcely survived to the present time. Shakespeare is a dead issue . . . Our most famous living poet, forty years ago, slipped into a paragraph the statement that Shakespeare's most popular tragedy is "most certainly an artistic failure." But the response to this challenge has been disappointing. Even France . . . has capitulated, and the modern French criticism is among the best. No, the spectacle afforded by modern criticism is the shadow-boxing of rival bardolaters. Shakespeare is a dead issue.[2]

Perhaps. At least, it is hard for us to read criticism like Johnson's, summarizing as it does his own experience and that of his critical predecessors and feel it as it should be felt. It is not malevolent or even intentionally severe. It is, as the notes keep demonstrating, the precisely defined if energetically uttered response of disciplined sensitivity to Shakespeare's performance. If we pass from the general indictment of Shakespeare in the Preface to the exact definition of that indictment in the notes, we may surprise ourselves by agreeing with Johnson from time to time. And even if we do not wince at a quibble or possess that sense of fastidious decorum which Johnson shared with his predecessors, we shall find that he accurately points to matters of poetic and dramatic fact in Shakespeare's practice with which our own criticism must come to terms.

Johnson praises Shakespeare for his nature. He blames him for the inadequacies of his art. Like his predecessors, he sees Shakespeare as a noble genius who is also somewhat of a noble savage, deficient in form, excessive in style, guilty now of ignoble sloth and guilty again of misdirected ambition. The cardinal point in Johnson's indictment, however, has little to do with plotting or the rules, nothing to do with decorum. It is less a charge against the plays than against the man who in writing them repeatedly reveals his unconcern for poetry's great end and thus manifests his own amorality.

His first defect is that to which may be imputed most of the evil in books or in men. He sacrifices virtue to convenience, and is so much more careful to please than to instruct, that he seems to write without any moral purpose. From his writing indeed a system of social duty may be selected, for he that thinks reasonably must think morally; but his precepts and axioms drop casually from him; he makes no just distribution of good or evil, nor is always careful to show in the virtuous a disapprobation of the wicked; he carries his persons indifferently through right and wrong, and at the close dismisses them without further care, and leaves their examples to operate by chance. This fault the barbarity of his age cannot extenuate; for it is always a writer's duty to make the world better, and justice is a virtue independent on time or place.

The middle of the paragraph refers to the standard methods of instruction, which Sidney had long ago catalogued: poetic justice, exposure, disapprobation. But Johnson's concern is less with the means of instruction than with the fact, manifest to his eyes, that Shakespeare neglected it. Again, Johnson's notes document and define his distress:

Angelo's crimes [in Measure for Measure] were such, as must sufficiently justify punishment, whether its end be to secure the innocent from wrong, or to deter guilt by example; and I believe every reader feels some indignation when he finds him spared.

I cannot reconcile my heart to Bertram [in All's Well]; a man noble without generosity, and young without truth, who marries Helen as a coward, and leaves her as a profligate: when she is dead by his unkindness, sneaks home to a second marriage, is accused by a woman whom he has wronged, defends himself by a falsehood, and is dismissed to happiness.

> The gratification which would arise from the destruction of
> an usurper and a murderer, is abated by the untimely death of
> Ophelia, the young, the beautiful, the harmless, and the
> pious.

> Shakespeare has suffered the virtue of Cordelia to perish in a
> just cause, contrary to the natural ideas of justice, to the hope
> of the reader, and . . . to the faith of chronicles . . .
> A play in which the wicked prosper, and the virtuous mis-
> carry, may doubtless be good, because it is a just representa-
> tion of the common events of human life: but since all
> reasonable beings naturally love justice, I cannot easily be
> persuaded, that the observation of justice makes a play worse;
> or, that if other excellencies are equal, the audience will not
> always rise better pleased from the final triumph of perse-
> cuted virtue.
> . . . I was many years ago so shocked by Cordelia's
> death, that I know not whether I ever endured to read again
> the last scenes of the play till I undertook to revise them as
> an editor.

Johnson is open-eyed but warm-hearted as a critic. He knows well
enough that in this world justice is not poetic. As his Imlac tells us
in *Rasselas*, "human life is everywhere a state in which much is to
be endured, and little to be enjoyed." But by bringing imagination
to the aid of reason, poetry has the power to create a world both
just and true. Further, it has the power to make us better and so
bring this golden world closer to being. Shakespeare, however,
neither gives us this world nor particularly engages us in its realization. In his amoral impatience to entertain and be done with it, he
fobs us off with the brazen world we already know too well.
Worse, he does this after engaging our feelings. He solicits our
detestation of Angelo and Bertram, our pity for Ophelia, our love of
Cordelia—and then carelessly frustrates our hopes and fears. Johnson's principal charge against Shakespeare is criminal negligence.

The charge arises from a vision of what Shakespeare might have done, from an anguished sense of what he failed to do.

Johnson's catalogue of Shakespeare's faults omits three of which some of his predecessors had made much. One was the failure of his characters to measure up to the ideal types: "Dennis is offended, that Menenius, a senator of Rome, should play the buffoon [in *Coriolanus*]; and Voltaire perhaps thinks decency violated when the Danish Usurper is represented as a drunkard" in *Hamlet*. Second was the practice of tragicomedy. Third was violating the unities of time and place. In a fine enlargement of the critical tradition, Johnson denies that these are faults. He deals with the first summarily, by appealing from accident to essence, from means to end. Shakespeare's "story requires Romans or kings, but he thinks only on men . . . wanting a buffoon, he went into the senate-house for that which the senate-house would certainly have afforded him." Wanting to make Claudius despicable, he "added drunkenness to his other qualities, knowing that kings love wine like other men . . . a poet overlooks the casual distinction of country and condition."

Johnson brings bigger guns to bear on the question of tragicomedy, for the alteration he proposes to effect in the tradition here is larger and the tradition itself more frontally engaged. Shakespeare, he observes, writes neither tragedies nor comedies,

> but compositions of a distinct kind; exhibiting the real state of sublunary nature, which partakes of good and evil, joy and sorrow, . . . in which the loss of one is the gain of another; in which, at the same time, the reveller is hasting to his wine, and the mourner burying his friend; in which the malignity of one is sometimes defeated by the frolic of another; and many mischiefs and many benefits are done and hindered without design.

That this is a practice contrary to the rules Johnson acknowledges, then boldly declares, "but there is always an appeal open from criticism to nature." As before, his appeal is from what he regards as accident to what he regards as essence, from means to end. "The end of writing is to instruct; the end of poetry is to instruct by pleasing." Tragicomedy can convey the instruction of either tragedy or comedy because it contains both in itself, he argues, and it can do yet more in the way of general philosophical education, "by showing how great machinations and slender designs may promote or obviate one another, and the high and the low cooperate in the general system by unavoidable concatenation." (A few years before, in *Rasselas*, Johnson put similar language in the mouth of an optimistic sage whom he was holding up to ridicule, and I cannot escape the sense that he is here playing with an idea, mimicking, as it were, the literal reasoning of the tradition, rather than expressing his own most profound conviction.) Tragicomedy can also please as well as can the separate genres. It is objected that by the changes from serious to light, from high to low, "the passions are interrupted in their progression" and the right emotional effect frustrated. The argument appeals to a psychology more literal than Johnson will accept since it denies his own experience and since it denies Shakespeare's manifest power over our passions: "Fiction cannot move so much, but that the attention may be easily transferred"; Shakespeare "never fails to attain his purpose; as he commands us, we laugh or mourn, or sit silent with quiet expectation, in tranquility without indifference." Since tragicomedy achieves the end of instructing by pleasing, it is, then, legitimate, a valid addition to the dramatic genres of tragedy and comedy. Johnson has again enlarged the tradition.[3]

His great battle, however, is about Shakespeare's neglect of the unities. With the wisdom of hindsight, we may see weaknesses in Johnson's argument. He fails to see in Shakespeare's histories any unity other than that of mere narrative. He fails to see that stage time need not be real time, as the last scenes of *Dr. Faustus* make clear. He is forced to deny dramatic illusion. He has no language of "willing suspension of disbelief," no critical terms so useful as "projection" or "empathy." But this, of course, is precisely why Johnson's argument is so heroic. Against the massed tradition of France and England, with a critical language far more primitive than that which the succeeding two hundred years have made available to us, he must have seemed even to himself, in moments of doubt, to be madly tilting at windmills: "I cannot but recollect how much wit and learning may be produced against me; before such authorities I am afraid to stand . . ." But the windmill went down.

Johnson begins by narrowing the field. Histories he thrusts aside: "being neither tragedies nor comedies, [they] are not subject to any of their laws." He asserts Shakespeare's preservation of the unity of action: "his plan has commonly what Aristotle requires, a beginning, a middle, and an end." And he is left with the unities of time and place. The necessity of observing these, he says, "arises from the supposed necessity of making the drama credible." Johnson develops the traditional argument skillfully, at first attributing it to "the critics," then, deceptively setting it out in its own full force, as the declaration of truth:

> The mind revolts from evident falsehood, and fiction loses its force when it departs from the resemblance of reality . . . The spectator, who knows that he saw the first act at Alexandria, cannot suppose that he sees the next at Rome . . . he knows with certainty that he has not changed his place, and he knows that place cannot change itself.

Then, when the enemy's confidence is aroused, his defenses down, Johnson strikes:

> Such is the triumphant language with which a critic exults over the misery of an irregular poet, and exults commonly without resistance or reply. It is time therefore to tell him by the authority of Shakespeare [!], that he assumes, as an unquestionable principle, a position, which, while his breath is forming it into words, his understanding pronounces

> to be false. It is false, that any representation is mistaken for
> reality; that any dramatic fable in its materiality was ever
> credible, or, for a single moment, was ever credited.

We know that we live today, not in the era of Antony and
Cleopatra; that the trip to the theater was just that, not a voyage
to Egypt; that the actor on the stage is not Antony but our old
friend, David Garrick. There is no delusion. If there were, criticism could no more set limits to it than to the deliriums of fever or
the wanderings of ecstasy.[4]

Johnson's demolition of the esthetic of delusion, and of the
doctrine of the unities of time and place as they derive from it,
satisfies. The esthetic is false, the doctrine baseless.

The esthetic which Johnson substitutes for delusion, however,
does not satisfy. It is both chilly and contrary to our experience.
We come to the theater, he says, not for the rich intellectual and
emotional experience we might have imagined, but "to hear a
certain number of lines recited with just gesture and elegant
modulation." Surely this cure is no better than the disease. Like
Caliban, waking, we cry to sleep again. Whether Johnson was
uncomfortable with his own esthetic it is hard to say, for he was a
contentious man, willing to take a bad position, make it worse,
and then dare his audience to attack it. At any rate, having baldly
set forth this view of the drama as recital, the spectators as self-
possessed judges of gesture and modulation, he returns to more
comfortable language. He speaks of plays as "successive imitations
of successive actions," moving us as do pictures, affecting us as do
good books. Clearly the analogies reinforce his attack on delusion
at the same time they back off from the extremities of his own
position. At the close, he reduces the unities to mere niceties of
art, gratifying perhaps to the curiosity, but showing "rather what
is possible, than what is necessary."

Two other points should be made about Johnson's criticism.
One is the appearance in Johnson's notes of passages that, as D.
Nichol Smith says, "herald the new subject—the study of Shake-

speare's characters, and the study of Shakespeare through his characters."[5] Most often the comments are sharp but summary. The Nurse in *Romeo and Juliet* is "at once loquacious and secret, obsequious and insolent, trusty and dishonest"; Hamlet is "rather an instrument than an agent"; the Bastard in *King John* contains a "mixture of greatness and levity"; Emilia has a virtue "such as we often find, worn loosely, but not cast off, easy to commit small crimes, but quickened and alarmed at atrocious villainies." Occasionally the line lengthens to a paragraph, and then we have such classics of character criticism as the portrait of Polonius or the apostrophe to Falstaff—"unimitated, unimitable *Falstaff*, how shall I describe thee? Thou compound of sense and vice; of sense which may be admired but not esteemed, of vice which may be despised, but hardly detested . . ."

The other point is that Johnson insistently sought in Shakespeare and found there material to engage his mind. Entertainment, we might call it, if the term seems not too trivial, for Johnson sets a very high premium upon it. Shakespeare engages the mind because his works are copious, various, and moving. *Romeo and Juliet*, says Johnson, "is one of the most pleasing of our author's performances. The scenes are busy and various, the incidents numerous and important, the catastrophe irresistibly affecting." The particular excellence of *Hamlet*, says Johnson, is "variety." "The incidents are so numerous, that the argument of the play would make a long tale." And the scenes are "diversified with merriment and solemnity." Does the point seem unimportant? Consider what one might say, if one were called upon to speak in a summary fashion of *King Lear*. And then see what Johnson does say:

> The tragedy of Lear is deservedly celebrated among the dramas of Shakespeare. There is perhaps no play which keeps the attention so strongly fixed; which so much agitates our passions and interests our curiosity. The artful involutions of distinct interests, the striking opposition of contrary charac-

ters, the sudden changes of fortune, and the quick succession
of events, fill the mind with a perpetual tumult of indignation, pity, and hope . . . So powerful is the current of the
poet's imagination, that the mind, which once ventures
within it, is hurried irresistibly along.

From the critic who finds human wishes vain and "the general
condition of life . . . so full of misery, that we are glad to catch
delight without inquiring whence it comes,"[6] who finds the mind
easily slipping into vacuity or its imagination hungrily preying
upon life and demanding employment, who finds that in solitude
we have our dreams to ourselves, and in company we agree to
dream in concert ("the end sought in both is forgetfulness of
ourselves"[7])—from a man who apprehends the common lot so
painfully, the praise of Shakespeare for engaging, occupying, entertaining our minds comes significantly. It makes us feel with
special intensity that Shakespeare, in holding the mirror up to
nature, though he may be thought to fail in one great end of
poetry, instruction, magnificently succeeds in the other, pleasure.

iii

Gotthold Ephraim Lessing / 1729–1781
August Wilhelm von Schlegel / 1767–1845

Lessing's repudiation of French neo-classical perspectives, his conception of genius as fusing imagination and judgment. ❦ *Schlegel's grand division of classic and romantic—Shakespeare the romantic champion. Shakespeare's tragicomedy and violations of the unities vindicated. His unity of interest or impression; his organic form. Vindication of his anachronisms. Schlegel's structural awarenesses, moral sensitivity, moralistic excess, wide-ranging perceptiveness.*

"The English editors and expositors of [Shakespeare's] works were yet under the Gallic yoke," said Gervinus, "when Lessing cast aside the French taste and the opinion of Voltaire, and with one stroke so transformed the age, that *we* now ridiculed the false sublimity of the French drama, as they had formerly laughed at English rudeness."[1] This is right. Lessing did not write much about Shakespeare. His *Hamburg Dramaturgy* (1767–1768) touches on Shakespeare in only a few of its 104 numbers. Yet he says enough to evidence a new perspective. Johnson had dismissed Voltaire's criticism as the petty cavil of a petty mind, but he had taken enormously seriously the great scheme of neo-classical criticism for which Voltaire spoke; and if he permitted himself the bravado of setting the regular critics right by "the authority of

Shakespeare," his diffidence before the unities perhaps more truly expressed his basic attitude. Behind the magnificent rhetoric of his Preface lies the image of Shakespeare as a barbaric genius who, in the last analysis, has to be defended. Lessing's vision differs. For him Shakespeare needs no defense, and the whole tradition of French neo-classicism comes under his attack, or rather, it has already fallen.

His tone is that of amused and ironic superiority, like Mark Twain's when he twits Fenimore Cooper for his literary offenses. He has, for example, a fine passage on Shakespeare's ghost in *Hamlet*, which "appears really to come from another world," and Voltaire's ghost in *Semiramis*:

> Now Voltaire's ghost is not even fit for a bugbear wherewith to frighten children. It is only a disguised actor, who has nothing, says nothing, does nothing that makes it probable that he is that which he pretends to be. All the circumstances moreover, under which he appears, disturb the illusion and betray the creation of a cold poet who would like to deceive and terrify us without knowing how to set about it. Let us only consider this one thing. Voltaire's ghost steps out of his grave in broad daylight, in the midst of an assembly of the royal parliament, preceded by a thunderclap. Now where did M. de Voltaire learn that ghosts are thus bold? What old woman could not have told him that ghosts avoid sunshine and do not willingly visit large assemblies? No doubt Voltaire knew this also; but he was too timid, too delicate to make use of these vulgar conditions, he wanted to show us a ghost but it should be of a higher type, and just this original type marred everything. A ghost that takes liberties which are contrary to all tradition, to all spectral good manners, does not seem to me a right sort of ghost.[2]

Love itself, said a polite art critic, dictated *Zaïre* to Voltaire. "He would have been nearer the truth," says Lessing, "had he said gallantry; I know but one tragedy at which love itself has labored and that is *Romeo and Juliet*."[3] He has a comparable remark to make of Voltaire's jealous Orosman, who "plays a sorry figure beside the jealous Othello of Shakespeare."[4] He speaks of "the great measure of [Shakespeare's] historical plays," which "stand to the tragedies of French taste much as a large fresco stands to a miniature painting intended to adorn a ring."[5]

This new tone, with the critical perspectives which it implies and invites, is perhaps Lessing's principal contribution to the continental judgment of Shakespeare. It expresses his preference for the tradition of Greece to that of France, the authority of Aristotle to that of Corneille, the example of Shakespeare to that of Racine, the tragedy that arouses fear and pity and then purges them to the drama (Lessing did not consider it tragedy) that "excites our pity in order to awaken our fear, in order to purify by this fear the passions which had drawn down misfortunes upon the person we commiserate"[6]—the drama, in other words, of cautionary example, which teaches by poetic justice. Lessing's tone also testifies to a concept of natural genius which fuses rather than separates imagination and judgment, creativity and taste. "Not every critic is a genius," he says, "but every genius is a born critic. He has the proof of all rules within himself."[7]

❦ ❦ ❦

By tumbling French neo-classicism from its long eminence, by appealing to the Greeks, Aristotle, and the idea of tragedy, and by redefining genius to obviate traditional oppositions between nature and art, Lessing heralds the new era of Shakespearean criticism of which Augustus Wilhelm von Schlegel is the extraordinary spokesman. Schlegel's Shakespearean efforts span many years; they include translations that became the German standards and critical articles aplenty; but from our standpoint his great work must be the *Course of Lectures on Dramatic Art and Literature*, delivered in 1808 in Vienna and printed in enlarged form, 1809–11.[8]

Approximately one-fifth of this ambitious survey goes to Shake-speare. Schlegel comes before his audience inviting a wide toler-ance, a sympathy transcending narrow esthetic factionalism. Man is plastic; his art forms evolving, arriving at one perfection in classical antiquity, at another in medieval and Renaissance Europe.

> We will quarrel with no man for his predilection either for the Grecian or the Gothic. The world is wide, and affords room for a great diversity of objects. Narrow and blindly adopted prepossessions will never constitute a genuine critic or connoisseur, who ought, on the contrary, to possess the power of dwelling with liberal impartiality on the most dis-crepant views, renouncing the while all personal inclinations.

So genial and morally appealing is this doctrine that we may fail to see how striking it is. French neo-classical criticism has absolutely disappeared from the equation, and though Shakespeare is again to be seen as Gothic, as the English and French neo-classicists had seen him, the Gothic has now been elevated to a parity with the Grecian! "The Pantheon is not more different from Westminster Abbey . . . than the structure of a tragedy of Sophocles from a drama of Shakespeare . . . But does our admiration of the one compel us to depreciate the other? May we not admit that each is great and admirable in its kind?"

Schlegel's main effort in his opening lecture is to define in a series of antitheses the two equal kinds, into which he grandly divides the history of all art, the ancient or classical or Grecian and what he variously calls the Gothic, the modern, or, most often, the romantic. One kind is pagan, the other Christian; one finite, worldly; the other, infinite and other-worldly. "The poetry of the ancients was the poetry of enjoyment, and ours is that of desire: the former has its foundation in the scene which is present, while the latter hovers betwixt recollection and hope." The ancients sang a poetry of joy, the moderns a poetry predominantly melancholy. For the ancients form and matter naturally unite and harmonize; for the moderns they oppose each other, resisting union. "The Grecian executed what it proposed in the utmost perfection; but the modern can only do justice to its endeavors after what is infinite by approximation; and, from a certain appearance of imperfection, is in greater danger of not being duly appreciated." Given this division, we see where Shakespeare belongs. He is in the forefront of the moderns, as Sophocles is among the ancients; and though Schlegel makes a pretense at equity in his grand division, it is clear that in his eyes Shakespeare champions a greater era, a finer art. Christianity, after all, surpasses paganism; the infinite the finite.

Schlegel's strategies of treating the moderns as at least the equals of the ancients and of measuring them against principles which are inferred from their own practice rather than borrowed from the codifications of Corneille, Horace, or Aristotle, prepare for a new acceptance of Shakespearean tragicomedy. Sidney and most neo-classicists had lamented the mingled mode of Shakespeare's plays. Johnson had vindicated Shakespeare logically and psychologically: tragicomedy imitates aspects of nature which neither tragedy nor comedy alone can imitate, and the mind quickly and easily adjusts to changes of mood—at least, under Shakespeare's manipulation. Lessing, however, had had doubts. Because the mind is finite, it sets up arbitrary limits to save attention from distraction. "If we are witnesses of an important and touching event, and another event of trifling import traverses it, we seek and evade the distractions of our attention thus threatened"—so in actuality, so in art. Only when high and low causally connect can drama justly break down the generic barriers: "if gravity provokes laughter, sadness pleasure or *vice versa*, so directly that an abstraction of the one or the other is impossible to us, then only do we not demand it from art and art knows how to draw a profit from this impossibility."[9] Unfortunately, Lessing neglected to apply his standard to Shakespeare's plays. It is doubtful how many would have passed the test. But for Schlegel there is no test. For him, what Shakespeare does defines the romantic drama and validates it.

> [Romantic drama] delights in indissoluble mixtures; all contrarieties: nature and art, poetry and prose, seriousness and mirth, recollection and anticipation, spirituality and sensuality, terrestrial and celestial, life and death, are by it blended together in the most intimate combination.
>
> It embraces at once the whole of the checkered drama of life with all its circumstances; and while it seems only to represent subjects brought accidentally together, it satisfies the unconscious requisitions of fancy, buries us in reflections on the inexpressible signification of the objects which we view blended by order, nearness and distance, light and color, into one harmonious whole; and thus lends, as it were, a soul to the prospect before us.

These undifferentiated totalities, these indissoluble mixtures, these fusions of opposites in Schlegel's opinion are "not mere licenses, but true beauties in the romantic drama."

Naturally, Schlegel pays no obeisance to the unities—at least in their narrowest definitions. If unity of action be understood to deny multiplicity of plot, Schlegel rejects the limitation out of hand. Plot is not a slender thread, he asserts, but a mighty stream, springing perhaps from different sources, receiving into itself other rivers.

> Why should not the poet be allowed to carry on several, and, for a while, independent streams of human passions and endeavors, down to the moment of their raging junction, if only he can place the spectator on an eminence from whence he may overlook the whole of their course? And if this great and swollen body of waters again divide into several branches,

and pour itself into the sea by several mouths, is it not still
one and the same stream?

To the extent that the unities derive their support from an
esthetic of delusion, Schlegel joins Johnson in denying their
authority. He does not, however, argue that we attend the theater
"to hear a certain number of lines recited with just gesture and
elegant modulation." Instead he speaks of the theatrical illusion as
"a waking dream, to which we voluntarily surrender ourselves."
The astronomical time to which our bodies are subjected is
nothing to the mind, which has its own ideal time. "In this
measure of time the intervals of an indifferent inactivity pass for
nothing, and two important moments, though they lie years apart,
link themselves immediately to each other." In the theater, the
mind "dwells solely on the decisive moments placed before it, by
the compression of which the poet gives wings to the lazy course
of days and hours." Schlegel feels little of Johnson's timidity,
whether real or feigned, about attacking the unities, but, like
Johnson, he adds one argument to another. The ancients, he
argues, themselves violated the unity of astronomical time and
concerned themselves only with "the *seeming* continuity of time"
—more things happen during the choric songs than actually could,
as when Agamemnon returns to Argos from Troy during the
singing of an ode. And the ancients concerned themselves with
this seeming unity because of the "constant presence of the
Chorus." When the Chorus leaves the stage, as between the parts
of a trilogy, the gaps could be as long as anyone could wish. As to
the unity of place, Schlegel explicitly accepts Johnson's argument
against delusion and argues with him that the imagination can fly
easily enough from one place to another.

Schlegel argues, of course, not to abolish the unities but to
deny them solely sovereign sway. They are perfectly valid as one
kind of means to one kind of end (and here again we see Schlegel's grand division): they express the plastic or sculptural sense of

antiquity, which Schlegel opposes to the picturesque sense of modernity.

> Sculpture directs our attention exclusively to the group which it sets before us, it divests it as far as possible from all external accompaniments, and where they cannot be dispensed with, it indicates them as slightly as possible. Painting, on the other hand, delights in exhibiting, along with the principal figures, all the details of the surrounding locality and all secondary circumstances, to open a prospect into a boundless distance in the background; and light and shade with perspective are its peculiar charms. Hence the dramatic, and especially the tragic art, of the ancients, annihilates in some measure the external circumstances of space and time; while, by their changes, the romantic drama adorns its more varied pictures. Or, to express myself in other terms, the principle of the antique poetry is ideal; that of the romantic is mystical: the former subjects space and time to the internal free-agency of the mind; the latter honors these incomprehensible essences as supernatural powers, in which there is somewhat of indwelling divinity.

These things being so, the important unity for picturesque drama is none of the traditional ones but a unity of interest or impression. "The separate parts of a work of art . . . must not be taken in by the eye and ear alone, but also comprehended by the understanding. Collectively, however, they are all subservient to one common aim, namely, to produce a joint impression on the mind." Thus the story of *Romeo and Juliet*, as Shakespeare found it, Schlegel declares,

> will always excite a tender sympathy: but it was reserved for Shakespeare to join in one ideal picture purity of heart with warmth of imagination; sweetness and dignity of manners with passionate intensity of feeling . . . All that is most

intoxicating in the odor of a southern spring,—all that is languishing in the song of the nightingale, or voluptuous in the first opening of the rose, all alike breathe forth from this poem . . . The sweetest and the bitterest love and hatred, festive rejoicings and dark forebodings, tender embraces and sepulchral horrors, the fullness of life and self-annihilation, are here all brought close to each other; and yet these contrasts are so blended into a unity of impression, that the echo which the whole leaves behind in the mind resembles a single but endless sigh.

Schlegel sees Shakespeare as genuine successor and true rival of the ancients. He sees Shakespeare's plays as romantic drama, a genre separate from but equal to the ancient genres of tragedy and comedy, reflective of the picturesque or mystical propensities of the modern mind. Inevitably he regards the traditional assessment of Shakespeare as a wildly luxuriant genius as misguided: "I consider, generally speaking, all that has been said on the subject a mere fable." He rejects the analytical separation of genius and taste on which the traditional view was based. "Genius," he declares, "is the almost unconscious choice of the highest degree of excellence, and, consequently, it is taste in its highest activity." If the activity of genius seems unconscious,

it by no means follows, that the thinking power had not a great share in it. It is from the very rapidity and certainty of the mental process, from the utmost clearness of understanding, that thinking in a poet is not perceived as something abstracted, does not wear the appearance of reflex meditation.

We recall Lessing's observation that "every genius is a born critic." The two men are using the same kind of language to make the same kind of point, which they do handsomely. The language, however, is a touch unsympathetic to their purposes. By naming, it separates the powers and activities of the mind which the criticism is trying to bring together. It sets or seems to set against each other mental imagination and judgment, genius and taste, nature and art. It is disjunctive. But Schlegel also finds a different, a conjunctive language in the enormously influential imagery of organic form.

> Organical form . . . is innate; it unfolds itself from within, and acquires its determination contemporaneously with the perfect development of the germ. We everywhere discover such forms in nature throughout the whole range of living powers, from the crystallization of salts and minerals to plants and flowers, and from these again to the human body. In the fine arts, as well as in the domain of nature—the supreme artist, all genuine forms are organical, that is, determined by the quality of the work. In a word, the form is nothing but a significant exterior, the speaking physiognomy of each thing.

This is the great central and seminal idea in Schlegel's new esthetic. Genius unites creativity and restraint. It issues in organic forms according to laws derivable from its own essence. Its works are connected wholes, complete and satisfactory within themselves. The multiple parts of any one work, however diverse superficially they may be, cooperate "to produce a joint impression on the mind"; and the mind, responsive to the forces stamping upon it this unified impression, submits as in a waking sleep, voluntarily surrendering itself.

This esthetic of unity, creative and responsive, enables Schlegel to refute or dismiss various other traditional complaints against Shakespeare—for example, the anachronisms which Pope had endeavored, "with more zeal than judgment," as Johnson put it, "to transfer to [Shakespeare's] imagined interpolators." Shakespeare knew as well as we, says Schlegel, that Bohemia has no seacoast, but he is only faithful to factual details in his domestic stories—his stories placed in England.

*In the novels on which he worked, he avoided disturbing the
associations of his audience, to whom they were known, by
novelties—the correction of errors in secondary and unimportant particulars. The more wonderful the story, the more it
ranged in a purely poetical region, which he transfers at will
to an indefinite distance. These plays, whatever names they
bear, take place in the true land of romance, and in the very
century of wonderful love stories.*

The argument builds dizzily. Shakespeare, with consummate tact,
avoids disturbing his audience. He transports them to the land of
romance, where anything may happen, where any conjunction of
times and traits may occur. Shakespeare "had not to do with a hair-
splitting, hypercritical age like ours," grumbles Schlegel: "his
audience entered the theater, not to learn true chronology, geog-
raphy, and natural history, but to witness a vivid exhibition."
Then, the enthusiastic fit seizing him, Schlegel boldly undertakes
"to prove that Shakespeare's anachronisms are, for the most part,
committed of set purpose and deliberately." The tone of modish
modernity in *Hamlet* was necessary to make it credible that
Hamlet be "a philosophical inquirer." Richard III's mention of
Machiavelli is only a shorthand reference to principles of government that "have been in existence ever since the existence of
tyrants." Perhaps Johnson would have judged of Schlegel's success
no more favorably than he did of Pope's, but we note the
insistence on the audience's submissiveness and the suggestion of
artistic purpose. The hypothesis of unity receptive and creative
turns the neo-classical sin, at worst, into an irrelevance; at best,
into a prudent stroke of artistry in the interest, paradoxically, of
probability.

More usefully, perhaps, the esthetic of organic unity invites
(or reflects) a series of structural awarenesses. Schlegel sees that
Theseus and Hippolyta provide a frame for A *Midsummer Night's
Dream,* that the choruses of *Henry* V provide a lyric enlargement
of the theme of war that the stage itself could not legitimately

provide, that the "sententious rhymes full of antitheses" help set off the play-within-the-play in *Hamlet*, that the banishment of Alcibiades parallels the rejection by his former friends of Timon: "they are both examples of ingratitude." The second plot in *King Lear*, which Warton had condemned[10] and which Johnson had justified by appeals to variety, to plot, and to the moral "that villainy is never at a stop, that crimes lead to crimes, and at last terminate in ruin," Schlegel apprehends with an enlarging awareness:

> two such un-heard of examples taking place at the same time have the appearance of a great commotion in the moral world: the picture becomes gigantic, and fills us with such alarm as we should entertain at the idea that the heavenly bodies might one day fall from their appointed orbits.

Schlegel recognizes the use of foils: "Shakespeare makes each of his principal characters the glass in which the others are reflected, and by like means enables us to discover what could not be immediately revealed to us." So Hamlet, Laertes, and Fortinbras reflect themselves and each other. So the "ideal follies" of the higher characters in *Twelfth Night* define and are defined by the "naked absurdities" of the low. Schlegel recognizes the parodic value of various comic scenes: we think of Pyramus and Thisbe in *A Midsummer Night's Dream* commenting on the love of the aristocratic young couples; of the Gadshill robbery in *Henry IV, Part I*, with its burlesquing of the rebellion, or of the ring business at the end of *The Merchant of Venice* ironically replaying the pound of flesh plot of contract, forfeit, humiliation, and forgiveness. Schlegel has an especially sharp eye for the way Shakespeare blends contrasting elements, or manipulates contrasting emotional responses in his audience, to achieve his harmonies. Shakespeare softens Hero's distress at the altar "to prepare for a fortunate catastrophe." That is, against our distress at her embarrassment he pits our knowledge that Don John's plot has already been detected, and detected by the happily idiot Dogberry and Verges whose interrogation of the scoundrels delights us. Shakespeare blends with the apparent tragicality of Fidele's funeral in *Cymbeline* a musicality that mitigates the impression without weakening it. He presents in Richard III a repulsive villain yet engages our interest by endowing him with "profound skill in dissimulation . . . wit . . . prudence . . . presence of mind . . . quick activity . . . valor." Though he gives Richard what history gave him, an heroic death, which might have outraged us, he gratifies our moral sense in the tent scene by the curses which the apparitions heap upon Richard. "The repugnance inspired by [Iago's] aims becomes tolerable from the attention of the spectators being directed to his means: these furnish endless employment to the understanding."

Schlegel's Shakespearean criticism, like Johnson's, is first general, then particular. The lectures on the comedies, tragedies, and histories, from which I have just been drawing illustrations, contain short summaries of the plays and may seem all too hurried, in handbook fashion. Yet they reveal Schlegel's traits in a way his more general remarks perhaps do not. If one of these traits is a fine sense of structure, particularly as it uses and unifies contraries, another is a moral sensibility. This prevents Schlegel from shrugging off Bertram's "unfeeling pride and light-hearted perversity," though it lets him recognize in Bertram "the good qualities of a soldier" and, in the world, a phlegmatic acceptance of "man's injustice to woman, if so-called family honor is preserved." Schlegel sees "the true significance" of *Measure for Measure* in "the triumph of mercy over strict justice," but he considers the Duke "too fond of roundabout ways." "His vanity is flattered with acting invisibly like an earthly providence; he takes more pleasure in overhearing his subjects than governing them in the customary way of princes." Furthermore, "as he ultimately extends a free pardon to all the guilty, we do not see how his original purpose, in committing the execution of the laws to other hands, of restoring their strictness, has in any wise been accomplished." Schlegel sees "the heartless littleness of Octavius" in *Antony and Cleopatra*; the "mixture of hardness, moderation, and prudence" in Bolingbroke in *Richard II*; the fusion in Hotspur of "rude manners, arrogance, and boyish obstinacy" with "the majestic image of his noble youth": "we are carried away by his fiery spirit at the very moment we would most censure it." After cataloguing Hamlet's virtues, Schlegel then turns toward his shortcomings, which he sees in a sharp moral light. Hamlet

> has a natural inclination for crooked ways; he is a hypocrite towards himself; his far-fetched scruples are often mere pretexts to cover his want of determination . . . he is too much overwhelmed with his own sorrow to have any compassion to spare for others . . . On the other hand, we evidently perceive in him a malicious joy . . . Hamlet has no firm belief either in himself or in anything else.

Not until Santayana and L. C. Knights is the melancholy Prince to receive such another scourging.[11]

Without his moral sensitivity Schlegel could not begin to be the critic he is. Yet it limits his criticism where the criticism of another moralist, Johnson, is free. Johnson repines that Shakespeare sacrifices virtue to convenience and neglects opportunities to instruct. He regards the plays as things in nature, in a sense, from which moral lessons may be drawn, but he does not treat the lessons as intentional. The "important moral" of the double plot in *Lear*, "that villainy is never at a stop" is only "incidentally enforced." Johnson looks at Falstaff and speaks, not of the moral Shakespeare intended, but simply of "the moral to be drawn." Schlegel, on the other hand, both draws morals and attributes them to Shakespeare's intent. The result is a contraction or narrowing of his criticism that makes it seem, at times, both less than full and faintly corrupted by a doctrinaire Christianity. In *Macbeth*, he says, Shakespeare wishes to show that the conflict of good and evil in this world can only take place by the permission of Providence, which converts the curse that individual mortals draw down on their heads into a blessing to others. An accurate scale is followed in the retaliation.

The punishment, that is to say, fits the crime, the crimes themselves being nicely graded, and the fact of pain or suffering is, *ipso facto*, evidence of guilt. So "Banquo, by an early death, atones for the ambitious curiosity which prompted the wish to know his glorious descendants." When he comes to examine *King Lear* Schlegel seems free from the worst excesses of the doctrine of poetic justice—at least, he finds no fault with "Cordelia's heavenly beauty of soul," and sees her death, not as reflective of her moral nature but as instrumental in bringing Lear fitly to his own death. But then doctrine has its say:

According to Shakespeare's plan the guilty, it is true, are all punished, for wickedness destroys itself; but the virtues that would bring help and succor are everywhere too late, or over-matched by the cunning activity of malice. The persons of this drama have only such a faint belief in Providence as heathens may be supposed to have; and the poet here wishes to show us that this belief requires a wider range than the dark pilgrimage on earth to be established in full extent.

If at times Schlegel's criticism of the individual plays wraps them thus in darkness visible, more often it illuminates the individual character or the nature of his hold upon our minds. Indeed, the moral criticism divorced from the doctrinal schema is immensely valuable. It expresses a perceptiveness broader-ranging than this discussion has yet indicated and of which the following brief samples may serve as final witness. A century and a half before Tillyard and Lily Bess Campbell,[12] Schlegel perceives the histories as "one great whole . . . an historical heroic poem in the dramatic form," and he sees this heroic poem as a mirror for monarchs. Sidney had repudiated the imitation of war by stage tumults, and Johnson had neglected to comment on them (perhaps as reader of the plays rather than spectator he had less cause to be offended). With a smile Schlegel grants the absurdity of a "handful of awkward warriors in mock armor, by means of two or three swords, with which we clearly see they take especial care not to do the slightest injury to one another," deciding "the fate of mighty kingdoms"; but he recognizes that the effort on the stage to make battles seem real—by using cavalry, noise, throngs of actors—renders "the spectator incapable of bestowing that attention which a poetical work of art demands." He sees the need, then, of an artful middle course, a stagecraft that will suggest that the main business of battle is elsewhere, that we are witnessing momentarily "separate groups of an enormous picture." Schlegel recognizes the incredibility of the bond plot in *The Merchant of Venice* and the equal incredibility of the casket plot but observes that "the one . . . is rendered natural and probable by means of the other." Schlegel emancipates *The Winter's Tale* from the claims of realism—"the calculation of probabilities has nothing to do with such wonderful and fleeting adventures"—and pleasantly consigns those who affect to be displeased at neglect of dramatic decorum in *As You Like It* "to the wise fool, to be led gently out of [the forest of Arden] to some prosaical region." In terms not unlike those of Mack and Levin[13] some one hundred fifty years later, Schlegel says of *Hamlet* that it "resembles those irrational equations in which a fraction of unknown magnitude always remains, that will in no way admit of solution." Johnson had dismissed the histories from his considerations on the unities. Schlegel proposed that "under the apparent artlessness of adhering closely to history as he found it," Shakespeare concealed "an uncommon degree of art." Shakespeare "knows how to seize the true poetical point of view, and to give unity and rounding to a series of events detached from the immeasurable extent of history without in any degree changing them." Like Johnson before him and Bradley after, Schlegel tries to catch the special or unique quality of the individual plays, especially the tragedies. For him, as for how many after, *Hamlet* is a tragedy of thought, *Macbeth* of terror, *King Lear* of compassion.

Johnson has a happy comparison between a critic recommending Shakespeare by the citation of individual passages and the pedant "who, when he offered his house to sale, carried a brick in his pocket as a specimen." I confess to feeling like that pedant, trying to convey the range, the genial tolerance, and the sharp perceptiveness of Schlegel's critical mind. Perhaps if we recognize in it the union of many and precise percepts with large, liberating concepts we do him justice. Along with hundreds on hundreds of awarenesses that came to him about speeches, characters, episodes, and the individual plays as he translated and mulled over Shakespeare, Schlegel made his own and made applicable to Shakespeare a new esthetic, inclusive and organic. Hence, with an eye to what two centuries of predecessors had found wrong with the Bard, and with a humor exemplary of his own critical spaciousness, he was able to write this passage as the peroration of his general examination:

> *Each of his compositions is like a world of its own, moving in its own sphere. They are works of art, finished in one pervading style, which revealed the freedom and judicious choice of their author. If the formation of a work throughout, even in its minutest parts, in conformity with a leading idea; if the domination of one animating spirit over all the means of execution, deserves the name of correctness . . . we shall then, after allowing to Shakespeare all the higher qualities which demand our admiration, be also compelled, in most cases, to concede to him the title of a correct poet.*

Maurice Morgann / 1726–1802
Samuel Taylor Coleridge / 1722–1834

Revised view of Shakespeare in late eighteenth-century England. Morgann's distinction between sensibility and understanding; his explanation of naturalness and wholeness in Shakespeare's characterization. Character as historical, as dramatic. 🌿 *Coleridge's defects. His organicism. His psychological and moral sensitivity: character analyses, running commentary; defense of Shakespeare's punning. Ideal theory of poetic creativity: Coleridge compared to Morgann. "Willing suspension of disbelief."*

Shakespeare, once condemned, then defended, is in England, in the years after Johnson's *Shakespeare*, increasingly and unreservedly praised. Voltaire is ridiculed. Violations of the unities and indulgence in tragicomedy now manifest genius: "The early eighteenth-century explanation of Shakespeare's eccentricities as those of a poet of nature became by the end of the century a glorification of Shakespeare *in toto* in terms of the rising deification of original genius as such."[1] "Sweetest Shakespeare, Fancy's child," becomes conscious artist, moral philosopher. Attention focuses on the richness or truth or beauty of individual passages, which are held up for delectation, instruction, and awe. More importantly, attention focuses steadily, analytically, on the characters—Iago and Shylock, King Lear, Macbeth, Falstaff, Hamlet—in the interests of esthetic, psychological, and moral understanding. A smattering of titles suggests the varying emphases and acknowledges, too, the principal critical figures of this period: Thomas Tyrwhitt, *Observations and Conjectures upon Some Passages of Shakespeare* (1766), Mrs. Elizabeth Montagu, *Essay on the Genius and Writings of Shakespear, Compared with the Greek and French Dramatic Poets with Some Remarks upon the Misrepresentations of Mons. de Voltaire* (1769), William Richardson, *A Philosophical Analysis and Illustration of Some of Shakespeare's Remarkable Characters* (1774), Mrs. Elizabeth Griffith, *The Morality of Shakespeare's Drama Illustrated* (1775), Maurice Morgann, *An Essay on the Dramatic Character of Sir John Falstaff* (1777), Thomas Whately, *Remarks on Some of the Characters of Shakespeare* (1785).

Among these critics Maurice Morgann is extraordinary. Like a lesser Philip Sidney, like a more cultivated Harry Bailly, he genially invites his reader on an intellectual ramble. The object? To prove Falstaff no coward. But listen:

> The vindication of Falstaff's courage is truly no otherwise the object than some old fantastic oak, or grotesque rock, may be the object of a morning's ride; yet being proposed as such, may serve to limit the distance, and shape the course. The real object is exercise, and the delight which a rich, beautiful, picturesque, and perhaps unknown country, may excite from every side. Such an exercise may admit of some little excursion, keeping however the road in view, but seems to exclude every appearance of labor and of toil.

It's a lovely invitation, and it images truly the order of Morgann's essay, but it expresses, of course, its author's sophisticated if unobtrusive art. Morgann has meditated his topics long and fruitfully. He has explored the techniques of comedy, the nature of illusion, the operations of the imagination. If he seems to proceed at random, interrupting himself at times to inquire after the reader's comfort, pausing again to breathe before attempting some particularly difficult critical ascent, he is, in truth, artfully winding toward a series of connected awarenesses. When the journey is over, Morgann points back over the course we have come, and we can see that it has been less casual than he made it seem:

> So ended this singular buffoon; and with him ends an essay
> . . . professing to treat of the courage of Falstaff, but extend-
> ing itself to his whole character, to the arts and genius of his
> poetic-maker, Shakespeare, and through him sometimes, with
> ambitious aim, even to the principles of human nature itself.

The main principle of human nature Morgann deals with is the existence in man of "a certain mental sense," "an imperfect sort of instinct" (I propose to call it "sensibility"), which operates by laws different from those of the understanding to arrive, frequently, at opposing conclusions. Sensibility takes "mental impressions" "from the most minute circumstances, and frequently from such as the understanding cannot estimate, or even recognize; whereas the understanding delights in abstraction, and in general propositions." Sensibility determines the virtue of actions by reference to its impressions of character; understanding determines the virtue of character by reference to actions. Sensibility values the deed because it loves the doer whereas understanding determines how to regard the doer by judging the deed in itself. We love or hate at first sight because of mental impressions; the understanding merely rationalizes the verdict of the sensibility. Morgann is at pains to make this distinction since it permits him to frame his proposition about Falstaff thus: "the art of Shakespeare . . . has contrived to make secret impressions upon us of courage, and to preserve those impressions in favor of a character . . . held up for sport and laughter on account of actions of apparent cowardice and dishonor."[2]

Delightful as Morgann's defense of Fat Jack is, I propose to neglect it in the interests of defining his more general critical contributions. He starts from this distinction between sensibility and understanding, often apprehended to be at odds. He proceeds to a notion of that gift by which Shakespeare creates his characters—not by "a minute and laborious attention," but by "a certain comprehensive energy of mind, involving within itself all the effects of system and labor."

> There are certain qualities and capacities which he seems to have considered as first principles; the chief of which are [1] certain energies of courage and activity, according to their degrees; together with [2] different degrees and sorts of sensibilities, and [3] a capacity, varying likewise in degree, of discernment and intelligence. The rest of the composition is drawn in from an atmosphere of surrounding things

—laws, religions, governments, social ranks, professions, etc. According to these principles, then, and to the accidental influence of environment, with an intuitive sense of what traits go together, and in what degrees, Shakespeare formed his characters "with the most perfect truth and coherence." Further, he compressed "his own spirit into these images," an act impossible "*from without;* he must have *felt* every varied situation, and have spoken through the organ he had formed."

> The reader will not now be surprised if I affirm that those characters in Shakespeare, which are seen only in part, are yet capable of being unfolded and understood in the whole; every part being in fact relative, and inferring all the rest. It is true that the point of action or sentiment, which we are most concerned in, is always held out for our special notice. But who does not perceive that there is a peculiarity about it, which conveys a relish of the whole? And very frequently, when no particular point presses, he boldly makes a character act and speak from those parts of the composition which are

inferred only, and not distinctly shown. This produces a wonderful effect; it seems to carry us beyond the poet to nature itself, and gives an integrity and truth to facts and character, which they could not otherwise obtain. And this is in reality that art in Shakespeare which, being withdrawn from our notice, we more emphatically call nature. A felt propriety and truth from causes unseen, I take to be the highest point of poetic composition. If the characters of Shakespeare are thus whole, and as it were original, while those of almost all other writers are mere imitation, it may be fit to consider them rather as historic than dramatic beings; and, when occasion requires, to account for their conduct from the whole of character, from general principles, from latent motives, and from policies not avowed.

Shakespeare blends energy, sensibility, and intelligence in their proper degrees, adjusts to time, place, and environment, informs with his own energy, and feels himself into every situation. By virtue of this method and power, he is able to render his dramatic characters like real people, letting them speak and act out of motives and histories not immediately evident or conveyed in the usual way of exposition. So Shakespeare can operate on his audience as nature does, stealing upon us impressions that run counter to our understandings, and endowing our responses to his characters with that same rich ambivalence we accord our acquaintance and friends. This is the heart of Morgann's criticism. Other dramatists, in his view, proceed by other means. They think out their characters rationally, they handle their exposition efficiently; but the characters are not historical or actual beings, they are manifestly copies. In them the dramatist harmonizes the appeals to our sensibilities and our understandings so that, instead of being in doubt how to feel, or instead of feeling and thinking contradictory things, we respond simply and, though we may not notice it, unnaturally. But Shakespeare—

He differs essentially from all other writers. Him we may profess rather to feel than to understand; and it is safer to say, on many occasions, that we are possessed by him, than that we possess him. And no wonder;—he scatters the seeds of things, the principles of character and action, with so cunning a hand, yet with so careless an air, and, master of our feelings, submits himself so little to our judgment, that everything seems superior. We discern not his course, we see no connection of cause and effect, we are rapt in ignorant admiration, and claim no kindred with his abilities. All the incidents, all the parts, look like chance, whilst we feel and are sensible that the whole is design.

If one is careless, he sees Morgann's account as simply one more eulogy of Shakespeare's protean gift. I have tried to make clear that it explains as well as eulogizes and deserves, therefore, a certain prominence in the history of Shakespearean criticism. Morgann both acknowledges Shakespeare's power over our passions and discovers, at least hypothesizes, the cause. He confronts the nature-art opposition that underlies Shakespearean criticism from Jonson to Johnson and solves it. His language, to be sure, possesses only in passing that wonderful organicism of Schlegel's but he goes further than Schlegel in analyzing Shakespeare's method and in pinpointing its effects.

Morgann's understanding of Shakespeare permits him to dismiss the unities almost in passing. They are not so much contemptible as irrelevant. Derived originally from "the narrow circle of the Chorus," which forced the Greek dramatists to practice precision and copy the details of nature, they constitute an appeal to the understanding. Shakespeare, emancipated from the formal chorus, providing choral commentary from individual characters—Enobarbus in *Antony and Cleopatra,* for example, or Menenius in *Coriolanus*—appeals to the sensibility more than to the understanding, and operating by means of impressions rather than rational demonstrations, achieves "a larger circle . . . a more compendious *nature* . . . a nature of *effects* only, to which neither the relations of place, or continuity of time, are always essential."

To the eye of history it is clear that Morgann opened Pandora's box when he analogized Shakespeare's characters to historical beings. In that moment was born Mary Cowden Clarke's *The Girlhood of Shakespeare's Heroines* and Lord knows how many other critical aberrations. But Morgann had, I believe, half an eye to the dangers. Between life and art, between characters historical and characters dramatic, he always maintained the distinction. His title, be it remembered, is *An Essay on the Dramatic Character of Sir John Falstaff*. The meaning of character as dramatic will be clearer after we examine Morgann's treatment of the characters as actual. The extreme form of this treatment is to give the character a biography by way of accounting for him as he comes before us in the play. So the extraordinary analysis of Falstaff:

> He seems, by nature, to have had a mind free of malice or any evil principle; but he never took the trouble of acquiring any good one. He found himself esteemed and beloved with all his faults; nay for his faults, which were all connected with humor, and for the most part grew out of it. As he had, possibly, no vices but such as he thought might be openly professed, so he appeared more dissolute through ostentation. To the character of wit and humor, to which all his other qualities seem to have conformed themselves, he appears to have added a very necessary support, that of the profession of a soldier. He had from nature, as I presume to say, a spirit of boldness and enterprise; which in a military age, though employment was only occasional, kept him always above contempt, secured him an honorable reception among the great, and suited best both his particular mode of humor and

of vice. Thus living continually in society, nay even in taverns, and indulging himself, and being indulged by others, in every debauchery; drinking, whoring, gluttony, and ease; assuming a liberty of fiction, necessary perhaps to his wit, and often falling into falsity and lies, he seems to have set, by degrees, all sober reputation at defiance; and finding eternal resources in his wit, he borrows, shifts, defrauds, and even robs, without dishonor. Laughter and approbation attend his greatest excesses; and being governed visibly by no settled bad principle or ill design, fun and humor account for and cover all. By degrees, however, and through indulgence, he acquires bad habits, becomes an humorist, grows enormously corpulent, and falls into the infirmities of age; yet never quits, all the time, one single levity or vice of youth, or loses any of that cheerfulness of mind which had enabled him to pass through this course with ease to himself and delight to others; and thus, at last, mixing youth and age, enterprise and corpulency, wit and folly, poverty and expense, title and buffoonery, innocence as to purpose, and wickedness as to practice; neither incurring hatred by bad principle, or contempt by cowardice, yet involved in circumstances productive of imputation in both; a butt and a wit, a humorist and a man of humor, a touchstone and a laughing stock, a jester and a jest, has Sir John Falstaff, taken at that period of his life in which we see him, become the most perfect comic character that perhaps ever was exhibited.

It may be argued that the roadway in the painting of a landscape continues not an inch beyond the picture's frame, or that the people in portraits have no trunks or members beyond what we see, but most of us do not believe it. What lies outside the frame is there but unspecified, not to-be-looked-at but to be not-looked-at. Morgann looks. Yet he looks only quickly, generally, without embarrassing facts or events. And if his biography goes too far in one sense, it has this important merit: by suggesting how such a being as Fat Jack could in actuality be, it demonstrates that the incongruities composing him are, however absurd, natural.

More importantly Morgann's treatment of the characters as actual opens them up to richly subtle analysis both psychological and moral. It discovers the varying depths in the plays that engage the reader or spectator more profoundly than would mere entertainment. John of Lancaster's rebuke of Falstaff near the end of *Henry IV, Part II*, illustrates:

> Now, Falstaff, where have you been all this while?
> When everything is over, then you come:
> These tardy tricks of yours will, on my life,
> One time or other break some gallows' back.

This is, says Morgann, a formidable passage. It is spoken in the hearing of the army, by one entitled to speak on military conduct, and the absence of condign punishment may be imputed to Falstaff's standing in with the Prince of Wales. But Morgann reminds us of the perfidious maneuver by which Lancaster has just mastered the rebels and sees no reason "to be surprised if we find him practicing a more petty fraud with suitable skill and address." The analysis proceeds:

> He appears in truth to have been what Falstaff calls him, a cold, reserved, sober-blooded boy; a politician, as it should seem, by nature; bred up moreover in the school of Bolingbroke his father, and tutored to betray: with sufficient courage and ability perhaps, but with too much of the knave in his composition, and too little of enthusiasm, ever to be a great and superior character. That such a youth as this should, even from the propensities of character alone, take any plausible occasion to injure a frank unguarded man of wit and pleasure, will not appear unnatural. But he had other inducements. Falstaff had given very general scandal by his distinguished wit and noted poverty, insomuch that a little cruelty and

*injustice towards him was likely to pass, in the eye of the
grave and prudent part of mankind, as a very creditable piece
of fraud, and to be accounted to Lancaster for virtue and
good service. But Lancaster had motives more prevailing;
Falstaff was a favorite, without the power which belongs to
that character; and the tone of the court was strongly against
him, as the misleader and corrupter of the Prince, who was
now at too great a distance to afford him immediate counte-
nance and protection. A scratch then, between jest and
earnest as it were, something that would not too much offend
the prince, yet would leave behind a disgraceful scar on
Falstaff, was very suitable to the temper and situation of
parties and affairs.*

The critic assumes a life beyond that of stage and text. Behind the
words lie complex and cooperating motives blending aggression
and restraint, fear and caution. The mere four lines express
Lancaster's circumspect awareness of Falstaff and the attendant
army, of the absent Prince of Wales and the court circle. The lines
witness in their speaker to a rearing in cold calculation, a temperament deficient in warmth, a morality short on goodness.
Moreover, Morgann treats the words as having a particular tone—
girding, jocularly ambiguous—as though they were actually
spoken, by one man to another, in all the specificity of past event.
On the stage, of course, they are. The actor dons the role and gives
it particular shape. In uttering the words, he selects from among
the multiplicity of tones and implications one narrow set thereof.
He takes the script, which is a map of infinity, and reduces it to
uniqueness. To some extent the critic does the same, though his
judgments may be tentative, his readings suspended between
different tones, his assessments of character deliberately open and
flexible. Morgann's, however, are not. Perhaps one thing to see
about his practice, then, is that with the full force of his extraordinary sensitivity and intelligence, he commits himself and invites
the century and a half to come to commit itself to a view of the

characters as so richly, intricately, engagingly alive that they require and reward the most elaborate study. With Morgann the close scrutiny of the Shakespearean text for all its moral and psychological latencies comes of age.

For Morgann the characters are richly alive but the plays *are* plays, not history. This can be so because historical characters and dramatic characters, though related, are not identical. Historical characters are realities. Dramatic characters are less than real—and more. They are appearances. Shakespeare creates an historical Falstaff, then renders him to us in an illusory way. We see this if we subject Falstaff to moral scrutiny. He is, Morgann observes, "a robber, a glutton, a cheat, a drunkard, and a liar; lascivious, vain, insolent, profligate, and profane." In actuality such attributes would render the fat knight obnoxious. The malicious motives and evil principles would evoke our disgust; the evil consequences either threatened to or suffered by the victims would arouse our grief or terror. Yet though the historic Falstaff would thus affect us, the dramatic Falstaff does not. Shakespeare has hidden his motives and denied his effects. In this Falstaff, vice, denied both cause and consequence, operates as mere incongruity, the source of laughter. At the end of a fine development of this argument, Morgann says:

> This completes the dramatic character of Falstaff, and gives him that appearance of perfect good nature, pleasantry, mellowness, and hilarity of mind, for which we admire and almost love him, though we feel certain reserves which forbid our going that length; the true reason of which is, that there will be always found a difference between mere appearances and reality.

On this earth Falstaff might indeed be real and harshly evil, but we see him on the stage—as through a glass—lightly.

❦ ❦ ❦

Coleridge's Shakespearean criticism spreads over a quarter of a century in scattered lectures, for many of which there are no records, for many, mere fragments.[3] Some of it is caught in newspaper accounts, some in the notes of Crabb Robinson and Collier, some in Coleridge's manuscripts and undated marginalia. Only a few essays are fully worked out. Only the material in *Biographia Literaria* ever went through the appropriate polishings before publication. This means that we do not see Coleridge steadily and whole; we see him in critical undress—from the wrong side of the footlights, as it were. Our notes, like the notes taken year after year by undergraduates of varying degree of acumen and commitment, show that the lecturer said the same thing, that he annually dusted off old distinctions, acted out sudden inspirations, disingenuously evaded certain topics for which he had perhaps inadequately prepared himself. If he apologized once for one of his expressions, by way of stressing it, he did it a hundred times.

Our notes show that Coleridge spoke, not as expositor but as advocate or champion, in a style straining with superlatives and vibrant with the speaker's own personal commitment—as in these remarks on Hamlet's "Angels and ministers of grace defend us!" at the first sight of his father's ghost:

> Here Shakespeare adapts himself so admirably to the situation—in other words, so puts himself into it—that, though poetry, his language is the very language of nature. No terms associated with such feelings can occur to us so proper as those which he has employed, especially on the highest, the most august and the most awful subjects that can interest a human being in this sentient world. That this is no mere fancy, I can undertake to establish from hundreds, I might say thousands, of passages. No character he has drawn in the whole list of his plays could so well and fitly express himself as in the language Shakespeare has put into his mouth.

Our notes show finally, as we grow familiar with the literature, that Coleridge, with exceedingly sparse acknowledgment,
borrowed a great deal of material from others, most especially
from Schlegel. "In a rough count of pages," says Raysor, "Schlegel
might be given credit for forty odd pages of Coleridge's Shakespearean criticism, not mentioning criticism merely suggested by
ideas from Schlegel."[4] The precise meaning of this indebtedness is
ethically and intellectually difficult to establish. A single acknowledgment in a lecture may, conceivably, cover a hundred in-
debtednesses, and it may be that, had he brought his own notes to
publication, Coleridge would have paid full tribute to his sources.
The fact is, that he takes from Schlegel the grand division between
classical and romantic drama and the antithesis between sculpture
and painting. He takes the distinction between mechanic and
organic form, the emphasis on unity of impression or interest
instead of unity of action, the passage on the union of opposites in
Romeo and Juliet.

For the fragmentation and repetitiousness of the notes, for the
intrusive stridency of the lecturer's tone, for the borrowings from
Schlegel we may find apologies, extenuations, other faces. We may
say that few lecturers could meet the test of being known by the
kind of notes Coleridge left behind him; that Shakespeare stood in
need of a champion, and the more so that England had not
developed the casy detachment from neo-classical regulations
which the Germans had achieved; and that what Coleridge found
of greatest importance in Schlegel was not particular passages but
the sanction of a congenial perspective. As Anna Augusta Helmholtz observes,

> After Coleridge had read the Vorlesungen [Lectures], a new
> tone is apparent in his criticism. Where before it was in-
> definite, it becomes definite; the principles with which he had
> been darkly working, but which he had not been able to
> express in words, he now enunciates with certainty of their
> truth.[5]

All these apologies are surely valid, but they do not explain how, in the face of such handicaps, Harbage is able to assert that Coleridge is "the greatest of Shakespearean critics"[6] and why he is able to list in support of his judgment historians and critics as eminent and wide-ranging as George Saintsbury, Augustus Ralli, T. M. Raysor, D. N. Smith, George Santayana, and T. S. Eliot. To understand this unanimity of praise, we must look to the criticism more closely.

Coleridge's criticism, like Schlegel's and Johnson's, divides between the general and the particular. In the general his great message has to do with that old distinction between nature and art by means of which two centuries of critics had praised Shakespeare and condemned him too:

> *Are the plays of Shakespeare works of rude uncultivated genius, in which the splendor of the parts compensates, if aught can compensate, for the barbarous shapelessness and irregularity of the whole? To which not only the French critics, but even his own English admirers, say yes. Or is the form equally admirable with the matter, the judgment of the great poet not less deserving of our wonder than his genius? Or to repeat the question in other words, is Shakespeare a great dramatic poet on account only of these beauties and excellencies which he possesses in common with the ancients, but with diminished claims to our love and honor to the full extent of his difference from them? Or are these very differences additional proofs of poetic wisdom, at once results and symbols of living power as contrasted with lifeless mechanism, of free and rival originality as contradistinguished from servile imitation, or more accurately, from a blind copying of effects instead of a true imitation of the essential principles? Imagine not I am about to oppose genius to rules. No! the comparative value of these rules is the very cause to be tried. The spirit of poetry, like all other living powers, must of necessity circumscribe itself by rules, were it only to unite power with beauty.*

> It must embody in order to reveal itself; but a living body is of
> necessity an organized one,—and what is organization, but
> the connection of parts to a whole, so that each part is at once
> end and means! . . .
>
> No work of true genius dare want its appropriate form;
> neither indeed is there any danger of this. As it must not, so
> neither can it, be lawless! For it is even this that constitutes it
> genius—the power of acting creatively under laws of its own
> origination.

In his repudiation of the old distinction, in his substitution therefore of the doctrine of organic unity, Coleridge sounds the knell of
neo-classicism in England as surely as did German voices on the
continent. He sounds the knell often, for systems of thought die
slowly. He heaps happy ridicule on the notion (Pope's) that
Shakespeare grew "immortal in his own despite," that he was "a
delightful monster . . . like the inspired idiots so much venerated
in the East, uttering, amid the strangest follies, the sublimest
truths." He insists on a revolutionary upgrading of Shakespeare's
judgment: "If it were possible to say which of [Shakespeare's]
great powers and qualifications is more admirable than the rest, it
unquestionably appears to me that his judgment is the most
wonderful"!

Like Schlegel, Coleridge often employs an unsympathetic
language to assert his doctrine of organic unity. He speaks still of
"genius" and "judgment," the old terms, and "preparation,"
which suggests mechanical prudence rather than natural growth,
and all this so often that his criticism has a characteristic accent to
it, as of a cultured immigrant who has not quite mastered the
idiom of his new tongue. So he speaks of Shakespeare's "accus-
tomed judgment" in opening *Romeo and Juliet* with "a lively
picture of all the impulses of the play" and of "Shakespeare's skill
in justifying Romeo from inconstancy." He speaks of "the exquisite judgment of Shakespeare" in the first scene of *Hamlet*,
where "the preparation *informative* of the audience is just as much

as was precisely necessary." There is "judgment in having two of the persons present . . . having seen [the ghost] twice before," and, when Hamlet sees it, "the co-presence of Horatio, Marcellus and Bernardo is most judiciously contrived." With "exquisite judgment" *The Tempest* "opens with a busy scene" which "prepares and initiates the excitement required for the entire piece." "In the exercise of his admirable judgment," Shakespeare has kept Ariel engaged in Prospero's success as the avenue to his own freedom, and "another instance of admirable judgment and excellent preparation is to be found in the creature contrasted with Ariel—Caliban."

This faint oddity of the critical accent relates, presumably, to Coleridge's distinctions between the primary and secondary imagination, the first of which is "the living Power," the second that power "coexisting with the conscious will," the first relating to what the eighteenth century had called "Nature," the second to what it called "Art."[7] But whatever the cause, the effect of the accent is to catch our ear and reveal to us how very often Coleridge is promulgating his doctrine of unity. The more we listen, the more we hear it. It informs his concept of poetry as a kind of composition "permitting a pleasure from the whole consistent with a consciousness of pleasure from the component parts—and the perfection of which is, to communicate from each part the greatest immediate pleasure compatible with the largest sum of pleasure on the whole." It informs his varying acceptances of tragicomedy, whether in the Johnsonian terms of truth to life, or the Schlegelian terms of the accommodation of opposites. It enters into Coleridge's exploration of Shakespeare's wit, which is "blended with the other qualities of his works"—not "a combination of words, but . . . a combination of images." It informs his definition of Shakespeare's imagination as

> the power by which one image or feeling is made to modify many others, and by a sort of fusion to force many into one—that which afterwards showed itself in such might and energy

in Lear, where the deep anguish of a father spreads the feeling of ingratitude and cruelty over the very elements of heaven—combining many circumstances into one moment of thought to produce the ultimate end of human thought and human feeling, unity.

Quantity changes quality. The frequency of Coleridge's insistence on unity transforms the idea into an attitude, an expectancy, a faith. He comes, and by his reiterated examples invites others to come to Shakespeare, not to judge but to find.

Shakespeare knew the human mind and its most minute and intimate workings, and he never introduces a word or a thought in vain or out of place: if we do not understand him, it is our own fault or the fault of copyists and typographers; but study, and the possession of some small stock of the knowledge by which he worked, will enable us often to detect and explain his meaning. He never wrote at random, or hit upon points of character and conduct by chance; and the smallest fragment of his mind not unfrequently gives a clue to a most perfect, regular and consistent whole.

In this faith, which is itself the consequence of extended critical experience, Coleridge brings us before the plays to discover their underlying harmonies, their encompassing unities. So brilliantly do his own discoveries witness for his faith, we accept its sacraments. At least, most of the nineteenth century did. The brilliance is measured by the multiplicity and the delicacy of the items shown to be united—as in the following passage on the opening of *King Lear*:

The strange yet by no means unnatural mixture of selfishness, sensibility and habit of feeling derived from and fostered by the particular rank and usages of the individual; the intense desire to be intensely beloved, selfish and yet characteristic of the selfishness of a loving and kindly nature—a feeble selfishness, self-supportless and leaning for all pleasure on another's breast; the selfish craving after a sympathy with a prodigal disinterestedness, contradicted by its own ostentation and the mode and nature of its claims; the anxiety, the distrust, the jealousy, which more or less accompany all selfish affections and are among the surest contradistinctions of mere fondness from love, and which originate Lear's eager wish to enjoy his daughter's violent professions, while the inveterate habits of sovereignty convert the wish into claim and positive right, and the incompliance with it into crime and treason—these facts, these passions, these moral verities, on which the whole tragedy is founded, are all prepared for, and will to the retrospect be found implied in, these first four or five lines of the play.

It is difficult not to quote and quote again to enforce this point about Coleridge since it is his performance that persuades as his mere precept never could. Goethe had spoken of the unity of the plays. Johnson had apprehended their unity of action. Schlegel had demonstrated, and brilliantly, the interlinking of the parts of *Romeo and Juliet*. But Coleridge apprehends unity so subtly and intricately, as entailing such a honeycombed multiplicity of tones, moods, motives, conditions, circumstances, that his testimony is almost to another kind of unity, or if that unity still be called organic, then his testimony communicates the organicism to our feelings as Schlegel communicated it, perhaps, only to our intellects.

"The fundamental principle of Coleridge's Shakespeare criticism," says Middleton Murry, is "that his work is completely coherent and harmonious, and that the material which he borrowed was subdued to his own high artistic purpose. The principle was pregnant."[8] But Murry has an important reservation. "It has come to be realized that the criticism of Coleridge, which justly set Shakespeare on a pinnacle, was ultimately unjust to him by severing the solid connections of that pinnacle with the age from which it was built." Coleridge, so runs the indictment, presented Shakespeare "as a miracle of universality" and forgot his particularity. He made Shakespeare "into the supreme and ideal romantic poet, whereas he was in fact an Elizabethan playwright." Murry is right, of course, and the criticism of the twentieth century has had to recover the Elizabethan particularity Coleridge overlooked or denied. But the felt concept of organic unity remains still the most fruitful of all the critical awarenesses brought to Shakespeare.

The doctrine, the discovery, the experience of organic unity is part of Coleridge's contribution to the history of Shakespearean criticism. Another, as already indicated, is a subtlety of psychological and moral sensitivity that helps us see how very deeply and truly Shakespeare's plays mirror life. Coleridge enlarges the tradition already fed by Johnson and Morgann and Schlegel when he pens psycho-moral portraits of Iago ("the motive-hunting of motiveless malignity"), Thersites ("intellectual power deserted by all grace, all moral principle, all not momentary purpose"), Roderigo ("the want of character and the power of the passions,— like the wind loudest in empty houses, form his character"), York in *Richard II* ("a man giving up all energy under a feeling of despair"). Richard II he characterizes as "a man not deficient in immediate courage . . . or in powers of mind . . . still, he is weak, variable, and womanish, and possesses feelings which, amiable in a female, are misplaced in a man and altogether unfit for a king." Lady Macbeth, "of high rank, left much alone, and feeding herself with day-dreams of ambition, . . . mistakes the courage of fantasy for the power of bearing the consequences of the realities of guilt. Hers is the mock fortitude of a mind deluded by ambition." In Othello, Coleridge finds "no predisposition to suspicion," hence no jealousy in the true sense of the word. "If Desdemona had, in fact, been guilty, no one would have thought of calling Othello's conduct that of a jealous man." "Hamlet's character is the prevalence of the abstracting and generalizing habit over the practical. He does not want courage, skill, will or opportunity, but every incident sets him thinking; and it is curious and at the same time strictly natural that Hamlet, who all the play seems reason itself, should be impelled at last by mere accident to effect his object."

Such portraits appear most often simply as parts of Coleridge's running commentary on the play in question. One excerpts them because they are so neatly quotable—Coleridge's pinpoint phrase-making is famous. But the original audience must have responded quite as much to the nervous copiousness of Coleridge's style, to the special authority he derived from the minute and complex fidelity of his commentary to both the text of Shakespeare and the experience of his audience. The sense of cumulative illumination must have been extraordinary. Imagine how it must have been to attend the lecture on *Hamlet* of which the following are Coleridge's notes for the opening lines:

> *That Shakespeare meant to put an effect in the actor's power in the very first words, "Who's there?" is evident from the impatience expressed in the words that follow. "Nay, answer me: stand and unfold yourself." A brave man is never so peremptory as when he fears that he is afraid.*
>
> *The gradual transition from the silence and the recent habit of listening in Francisco's "I think I hear them," and the more cheerful call out, which a good actor would observe, in the "Stand ho! Who is there?" Bernardo's enquiry after Horatio, and the repetition of his name, and in his own presence, indicate respect or eagerness that implies him as one of the persons who are to appear in the foreground; and the skepticism attributed to him—*
>
>> Horatio says, 'tis but our phantasy;
>> And will not let belief take hold of him—
>
> *preparing us for Hamlet's after eulogy on him as one whose blood and judgement were happily commingled. The indefiniteness of the first opening out of the occasion of this anx-*

iety: "Welcome, Horatio!" (gladness); "welcome, good Marcellus" (courtesy).

MAR.: What has *this thing* appear'd again to-night?

rising with the next speech into

Touching this dreaded sight twice seen of us.

Horatio's confirmation of his disbelief—

Tush, tush, 'twill not appear—

and the silence with which the scene opened again restored by the narration. The solemnity of it and the exquisite proof of the narrator's deep feeling of what he is himself about to relate, shown by his turning off from it as from a something that is forcing him too deep into himself, to the outward objects, the realities of nature that had accompanied it—

BER.: Last night of all,
When yond same star that's westward from the pole
Had made his course to illume that part of heaven
Where now it burns, Marcellus and myself,
The bell then beating one—

seem to contradict the critical law that what is told makes a faint impression compared with what is beheld, and do indeed convey to the mind more than the eye can see; and note the interruption of the narration at the very moment when we are most intensely listening for the sequel, and have our thoughts diverted from the dreaded sight in expectation of the desired yet almost dreaded tale, thus giving all the suddenness and surprise of the original appearance—

Peace, break thee off! look where it comes again!

The judgment in having two of the persons present as having seen it twice before, hence naturally confirming their former opinions, while the skeptic is silent, and after he has twice been addressed by his friends, answers with two hasty syllables, "Most like," and a confession of horror—

It harrows me with fear and wonder.

Coleridge's sensitivity to the psychologically subtle leads him to try to "palliate" Shakespeare's sin of quibbling. Dryden, Addison, and Pope, it will be recalled, found Shakespeare's word playing barbarous, but a fault of the times. Johnson had effervesced at the end of his observations on *Romeo and Juliet* that Shakespeare's "persons, however distressed, *have a conceit left them in their misery, a miserable conceit*"; and so playfully had he expatiated in his Preface on Shakespeare's losing the world for a quibble and being content to lose it, one suspects he did not find punning quite the social nuisance his predecessors had. Morgann offered Shakespeare the traditional left-handed defense in a footnote, intimating that many of the quibbles were interpolated, but he went on to vindicate one kind of pun as both natural and pathetic. When Antonio in the trial scene says that if Shylock cut but deep enough, he will pay the forfeiture with all his heart, Morgann sees him striving with telltale failure for the gaiety of fortitude: "a skillful actor, well managing his tone and action, might with this miserable pun steep a whole audience suddenly in tears." Coleridge's defense is of the same order. Playing with language is not itself a source of power or a sign of the integrative imagination at work, but it is a natural trait, in certain circumstances, which, in certain places, Shakespeare judiciously imitates. Thus, when Hamlet says "A little more than kin, and less than kind," Coleridge writes the following note:

> *Play on words either due to (1) exuberant activity of mind, as in Shakespeare's higher comedy; or (2) imitation of it as a fashion; . . . or (3) contemptuous exultation in minds vulgarized and overset by their success, like Milton's Devils; or (4) as the language of resentment, in order to express con-*

tempt—most common among the lower orders, and the origin of nicknames; or lastly, as the language of suppressed passion, especially of hardly smothered dislike. Three of these combine in the present instance.

Like Schlegel, Coleridge brings to Shakespeare a bent both moral and moralizing—and with similar gains and losses. The sensitivity to nuances of character and to Shakespeare's manipulating of his audience's moral-emotional responses are the gains. The losses are the constriction of the play's meanings, the forcing on them of patterns of thought and feeling which are only fractionally relevant. We may doubt that in *Hamlet* "Shakespeare wished to impress upon us the truth that action is the chief end of existence" or that in *Venus and Adonis* he "represented the animal impulse . . . so as to preclude all sympathy with it." As Schlegel in examining *Macbeth* fell momentary victim to his doctrine of poetic justice, we may descry Coleridge falling momentarily victim to Iago's racist cant:

> No doubt Desdemona saw Othello's visage in his mind; yet, as we are constituted, and most surely as an English audience was disposed in the beginning of the seventeenth century, it would be something monstrous to conceive this beautiful Venetian girl falling in love with a veritable Negro. It would argue a disproportionateness, a want of balance, in Desdemona . . .

Generally, however, though Coleridge impresses on us his own ethical values, he remains true to his conviction that a poem or a play proposes "for its *immediate* object pleasure, not truth." To the question of Shakespeare's morality, especially as this comes under Bowdlerian fire, he has a response not unlike Johnson's. Johnson had seen that Shakespeare's plays, though they might neglect opportunities for instruction, were nevertheless instructive: they justly imitated general nature and general nature is moral.

Morality, that is, is a dimension of actuality. Similarly Coleridge finds Shakespeare never taking pains "to make his characters win your esteem, but leaves it to the general command of the passions, and to poetic justice." Shakespeare may occasionally be gross, yet in such a way as to evoke a salutary gust of laughter "that would . . . blow away all impure ideas." He may risk what is "both morally and poetically unsafe" by presenting "what is admirable . . . in the mind, and what is most detestable in the heart, as coexisting in the same individual without any apparent connection or any modification of the one by the other"—this in Iago, a *tour de force*—but this is not his usual way. In his writing (and Coleridge echoes Schlegel here), Shakespeare kept to

> the high road of life. With him there were no innocent adulteries; he never rendered that amiable which religion and reason taught us to detest; he never clothed vice in the garb of virtue . . . his fathers were roused by ingratitude, his husbands were stung by unfaithfulness; the affections were wounded in those points where all may and all must feel.

From the sensitive psychology which mediates between the plays and the nature they morally image we may return to Coleridge's organicism. His belief in the unity of each of the plays expresses a series of assumptions about poetic creativity different from certain earlier assumptions and destined to influence succeeding criticism profoundly. Johnson had spoken of Shakespeare's "vigilance of observation," his "exact knowledge of many modes of life, and many casts of native dispositions," his exact surveying "of the inanimate world": "Shakespeare . . . shows plainly, that he has seen with his own eyes; he gives the image which he receives." In other words, he holds the mirror up to nature. Addison, earlier, had made much of Shakespeare's witches and elves, his Ariels and Calibans—precisely because in these exemplars of "the fairy way of writing" Shakespeare was *not* holding the mirror to nature. "It shows a greater genius in Shakespeare to have drawn his Caliban, than his Hotspur, or Julius Caesar: the one was to be supplied out of his own imagination, whereas the other might have been formed upon tradition, history and observation."[9] The opposition here is between theories of poetry as mimetic and as imaginative. According to one theory, poetry discovers (invents), arranges, rearranges what is already out there; according to the other, poetry creates from within. Before Coleridge, though Shakespeare was seen to have creative power, which made his Calibans such special achievements, his principal strength had been held to be his mimetic gift, his compellingly just representations of general nature. Coleridge brings all the mimetic *within* the imaginative; he endows all the characters with the attributes hitherto held to belong to the few.

Repeatedly Coleridge tells us that Shakespeare's characters are "ideal, and the result of his own meditation." He appeals confidently to his hearers "whether the closest observation of the manners of one or two old nurses would have enabled Shakespeare to draw this character of admirable generalization"—the Nurse of *Romeo and Juliet*. Where, he demands, "was Shakespeare to observe such language" as Othello's, unless "with the inward eye of meditation?" Meditation means self-examination, self-exploration. Shakespeare

> had only to imitate certain parts of his own character, or to exaggerate such as existed in possibility, and they were at once true to nature, and fragments of the divine mind that drew them.

> In the meanest characters, it was still Shakespeare; it was not the mere Nurse in Romeo and Juliet, or the Dogberry in Much Ado About Nothing, or the blundering Constable in Measure for Measure, but it was this great and mighty being changing himself into the Nurse or the blundering Constable, that gave delight.

> Shakespeare's mode of conceiving characters out of his own intellectual and moral faculties [was] by conceiving any one intellectual or moral faculty in morbid excess and then placing himself, thus mutilated and diseased, under given circumstances.

Here is a theory, less schematic than Morgann's, that attempts to account for the same phenomenon, the inferential and vital wholeness of the characters. Morgann starts from Shakespeare the observer or contemplator; Coleridge from the self-observer, the introspector. Morgann proposes a Shakespeare feeling his way into the roles he has conceived; Coleridge, a Shakespeare feeling his way down the avenues of his own real or potential being. The earlier critic accurately describes the data of the characterization; the later more nearly accounts for its dynamics. Morgann, moreover, in his concern for character, pays scant attention to the play. *Henry IV, Parts I* and *II*, and *Henry V* weave together for him into the single magnificent tapestry of Falstaff, to which he devotes himself at the expense of the unity of action or impression of the parts. Coleridge's theory accords due attention to the unity of the individual character and to the unity of the play in which he lives, sees the one relating to and expressing the other. The mere observer, says Coleridge, can only offer parts and fragments; the meditator, by contrast, peering with the eye of philosophical interest, offers wholes. So Coleridge notes of Capulet's upbraiding of Tybalt at the ball, "the old man's impetuosity at once contrasting, yet harmonized with, the young Tybalt's—but this it would be endless to repeat. Every leaf is different on an oak; but still we can only say, our tongues defrauding our eyes, this is another oak leaf." Morgann sees the leaf: Coleridge the leaf, the leaves, the tree.

If characters derive from within, a study of the characters might reveal the author from whom they derive. Dowden, Frank Harris, Ernest Jones, and Middleton Murry in the years to come explore this hypothesis. Coleridge too offers some interesting observations on Shakespeare. Shakespeare's characters, he says, may be reduced to a few classes, the members of which, though strikingly individual, possess certain central, Shakespearean attributes. He illustrates with the gentlemen: "Biron is seen again in Mercutio, in Benedick and in several others. They are men who combine the politeness of the courtier with the faculties of high intellect—those powers of combination and severance which only belong to an intellectual mind." At another time he says,

> Mercutio is a man possessing all the elements of a poet: the whole world was, as it were, subject to his law of association. Whenever he wishes to impress anything, all things become his servants for the purpose: all things tell the same tale, and sound in unison. This faculty, moreover, is combined with the manners and feelings of a perfect gentleman, himself utterly unconscious of his powers.

We can imagine Coleridge consciously connecting this expression of happy poetic intellect with the expression of unhappy poetic intellect in Richard II and Hamlet, and proceeding to some sort of biographical or characterological analysis. Coleridge, however, seems not to have been tempted. Perhaps it was because Shakespeare, despite the reducibility of his characters to a few classes, remained too oceanic, too "myriad-minded," as Coleridge was fond of calling him. With Shakespeare's "astonishing and intuitive knowledge of what man must be at all times, and under all circumstances, he is rather to be looked upon as a prophet than as a poet"—and so beyond the biographer's analysis. Perhaps, too, like August Wilhelm Schlegel's brother, Friedrich, Coleridge found Shakespeare objective and elusive as well as subjective,[10] and his characters less transparent windows into his nature than beautifying and magnifying mirrors reflecting our own. We can "see ourselves in all he wrote," says the critic, but, he adds in another place, "decorated with such hues of beauty and magnified to such proportions of grandeur that, while we know the figure, we know also how much it has been refined and exalted by the poet."

Coleridge's final contribution to the understanding of Shakespeare lies in his declaration that it is a "willing suspension of disbelief for the moment, which constitutes poetic faith." The formulation is extraordinarily complex. It launches out on the affirmative *willing*, doubles back with its paired negatives of *suspension* and *disbelief*, balances on the precarious qualification *for the moment*, and comes to rest under the faintly oxymoronic *poetic faith*. Complex though the formulation is, we sense it at once as sound, as delineating our own experience precisely. And so it emancipates Shakespeare simultaneously from the esthetics of delusion, which said that poetic faith was the *un*willing suspension of belief, and from the esthetics of recitation, which denied that either belief or disbelief were suspended or that there could be such a thing as poetic faith. Coleridge's formulation, toward which many a critic had been working, is to be seen, ultimately, as the necessary corollary of his theories. It harmonizes with his conviction that the poet creates from within and that the works themselves are organically unified. It defines the posture of response, of commitment, of faith which most spectators and readers have naturally and which the critic must have if he is to enter the Shakespearean heaven.

v

Johann Wolfgang von Goethe / 1749–1832
Charles Lamb / 1775–1834
William Hazlitt / 1778–1830

Goethe's Shakespeare: inspired and disciplined, neglecting traditional means but achieving ultimate ends. Shakespeare's works as falling between Ancient and Modern; his poetry as deriving from contemplation and addressing imagination. Apologies for his deficiencies as dramatist: Hamlet improved. ❧ *Lamb's attack against staging Shakespeare except in the theater of his own mind. Limitations of his theory, subtlety of his appreciation.* ❧ *Hazlitt's exuberance; his sharp formulations, traditional positions; his feeling for Shakespeare's plasticity.* The Characters of Shakespear's Plays *as handbook: general essays, analyses of individual plays—Richard II. Shakespearean unity as deriving from analogy. Shakespeare's characters as uniquely individual. Hazlitt's political bias. His feeling for the plays as theater.*

Schlegel had intended his remarks on Hamlet as a reply to Goethe's running analysis of that character in *Wilhelm Meister's Apprenticeship* (1795), of which the following is the summary, the climax, and probably the most famous of all the remarks ever made about a Shakespearean character:

Shakespeare meant . . . to represent the effects of a great
action laid upon a soul unfit for the performance of it . . .
There is an oak tree planted in a costly jar, which should have
borne only pleasant flowers in its bosom; the roots expand,
the jar is shivered.

    A lovely, pure, noble and most moral nature, without the
strength of nerve which forms a hero, sinks beneath a burden
which it cannot bear and must not cast away. All duties are
holy for him; the present is too hard. Impossibilities have
been required of him; not in themselves impossibilities, but
such for him. He winds, and turns, and torments himself; he
advances and recoils; is ever put in mind, ever puts himself in
mind; at last does all but lose his purpose from his thoughts;
yet still without recovering his peace of mind.[1]

Goethe is the most philosophical of Shakespeare's great continental critics, and the least enchanted. More precisely than his
predecessors and contemporaries he fixes Shakespeare's place in
the continuum of drama and poetry. Less enthusiastically than his
contemporaries, more like his neo-classical predecessors, he sees
the unity of Shakespeare's plays as large and loose. Like almost all
of Shakespeare's critics, he regards him as a genius of many talents.
"Shakespeare," he said, "has already exhausted the whole of
human nature in all its tendencies, in all its heights and depths."[2]

Eckermann once asked Goethe whether there weren't means
of calling forth the productive mood or of increasing it. No,
replied Goethe, production of the highest kind is not at man's
command. The great seminal thoughts are like unexpected gifts,
children of God. But what one does with these entails productive-
ness of another nature, within man's control. Shakespeare received
from on high his inspiration for Hamlet.

But the individual scenes, and the dialogue of the characters,
he had completely in his power, so that he might produce
them daily and hourly, and work at them for weeks if he

liked. And, indeed, we see in all that he has achieved, constantly the same power of production; and in all his plays we never come to a passage of which it could be said "this was not written in the proper humor, or with the most perfect faculty." Whilst we read him, we receive the impression of a man thoroughly strong and healthy, both in mind and body.[3]

This healthy Shakespeare, who works up his inspirations with professional discipline and taste,

associates himself with the World-Spirit; like it he explores the world; from neither is anything hidden. But whereas it is the business of the World-Spirit to keep its secrets both before and after the event, it is the work of the poet to tell them, and take us into his confidence before the event or in the very action itself.

Shakespeare, in other words, gives us nature, but nature self-revealing, as Morgann had observed. Men,

the most mysterious and complex productions of creation, here act before us as if they were watches, whose dial-plates and cases were of crystal; which pointed out, according to their use, the course of the hours and minutes; while, at the same time, you could discern the combination of wheels and springs that turned them.[4]

Goethe joins the critics whose psychological and esthetic sensitivity to Shakespeare's characters pays tribute to the sensitivity of their creator. He vindicates the lasciviousness of Ophelia's songs as expressing the secret desires of one who lived within herself and presumably "attempted, like an unskilful nurse, to lull her senses to repose with songs which only kept them the more awake," one who, "in the innocence of insanity" solaces herself with the echo of those songs.[5] He apprehends Polonius as blending "emptiness and . . . significance," "exterior gracefulness and interior meanness," "frankness and sycophancy," "sincere roguery and deceitful truth"—a "respectable gray-haired, enduring, time-serving, half-knave" who speaks like a book when he is prepared beforehand but like an ass when he utters the overflowings of his heart.[6] His analysis of Hamlet we have already seen, but we may observe his method, for it accords with Morgann's and credits Shakespeare's characters with historical roundness. He speaks through Wilhelm Meister, describing his perplexity until—

> *I set about investigating every trace of Hamlet's character, as it had shown itself before his father's death; I endeavored to distinguish what in it was independent of this mournful event; independent of the terrible events that followed; and what most probably the young man would have been, had no such thing occurred.*[7]

He sees that Rosencrantz and Guildenstern must be two, cannot be one:

> *These soft approaches, this smirking and bowing, this assenting, wheedling, flattering, this whisking agility, this wagging of the tail, this allness and emptiness, this legal knavery, this ineptitude and insipidity—how can they be expressed by a single man? There ought to be at least a dozen of these people, if they could be had: for it is only in society that they are anything; they are society itself . . . Besides, . . . as a couple [they] may be contrasted with the single, noble, excellent Horatio.*[8]

And Goethe offers a fine vindication of the player's speech on Pyrrhus. The player's emotion affects Hamlet and sharpens his conscience; the scene thus becomes a prelude to the play-within-the-play, which operates in the same way upon Claudius.

Shakespeare, thus strong, healthy, sensitive, associating himself with the World-Spirit, neglects traditional means but achieves ultimate esthetic ends. Esthetic ends are effects in the minds of the spectator. One such effect is comprehension, to the achievement of which the three unities are means. "The pieces of Shakespeare deviate, as far as possible, from the unities of time and place; but they are comprehensible—nothing more so—and on this account, the Greeks would have found no fault in them."[9] Another effect is the release or gratification that comes from variety—Goethe speaks of the "law of required change"[10]—and this, too, Shakespeare achieves, with those lively scenes that make his tragedies into tragicomedies. (Goethe's explanation of Shakespeare's mixed mode differs from his predecessors' but relates, clearly, to Johnson's feeling for novelty as escape from the mind's vacancy, for variety as momentary satisfaction of the incessantly hungering imagination.) Yet a third effect is the felt, the natural impact of each detail. What is involved here is, once again, a celebrating of Shakespeare for his neglect of a unity or decorum that neo-classical criticism has espoused.

Goethe's argument emerges from a discussion with Eckermann. He invites Eckermann to examine an evening pastoral by Reubens, to discover that "the figures cast their shadows into the picture; the group of trees, on the contrary, cast theirs towards the spectator. We have, thus, light from two different sides, which is quite contrary to nature." "That is the point," says Goethe. "It is by this that Reubens proves himself great, and shows to the world that he, with a free spirit, stands *above* nature."

> The artist has a twofold relation to nature; he is at once her master and her slave. He is her slave, inasmuch as he must work with earthly things, in order to be understood; but he is her master, inasmuch as he subjects these earthly means to his higher intentions, and renders them subservient.[11]

Shakespeare contradicts himself just as does Reubens. Lady Macbeth says, "I have given suck." Later Macduff says of Macbeth,

"He has no children." "These words of Macduff contradict those of Lady Macbeth; but this does not trouble Shakespeare. The grand point with him is the force of each speech."[12] Similarly, Macbeth's words, "Bring forth men children only," though they might be taken to imply in Lady Macbeth a youthful childlessness, exist not in a legal realm of interlocking evidence, factual and circumstantial, but simply as rhetorical testimony to Lady Macbeth's impact upon him. We may question Goethe's reading of Macduff's "He has no children," but we recognize his defense of Shakespeare as according with Schlegel's vindication of the anachronisms. It testifies to a sense of the drama as a flowing immediacy of gratefully received impressions. It looks forward almost a century to Robert Bridges' elaborate analysis of Shakespearean ambiguity.

Goethe's defense of Shakespeare for his apparent violations of unity finds its counterpart in the special praise he gives to the unity of idea in each individual play.

> *Coriolanus is permeated by the idea of anger at the refusal of the lower classes to recognize the superiority of their betters. In Julius Caesar everything hinges on the idea that the upper classes are not willing to see the highest place in the state occupied, since they wrongly imagine that they are able to act together. Antony and Cleopatra expresses with a thousand tongues the idea that pleasure and action are ever incompatible.*

The language comes a hair's breadth this side of moralizing, considerably further than that from indisputable accuracy, but it points to the critical conviction these pages have been annotating, that the inspired and industrious Shakespeare, healthy and strong, psychologically sensitive and esthetically cunning, neglectful of outer form to the gain of inner vitality, achieves in his separate works a harmony of unities, unity of idea being one.

We turn from Goethe's various tributes to Shakespeare's genius to his efforts to define Shakespeare's place. In a narrow scope, this gives rise to a special definition of the place of *Hamlet* in the continuum of art narrative and dramatic. At one pole is the novel, wherein "it is chiefly *sentiments* and *events* that are exhibited"; at the other, "in the drama, it is *characters* and *deeds*."[13]

> The novel must go slowly forward; and the sentiments of the hero, by some means or another, must restrain the tendency of the whole to unfold itself and to conclude. The drama, on the other hand, must hasten, and the character of the hero must press forward to the end; it does not restrain, but is restrained. The novel-hero must be suffering, at least he must not in a high degree be active; in the dramatic one, we look for activity and deeds.

In the novel there is scope for chance; in the drama, only for fate. But chance must be led by the sentiments of the personages while fate, which can exist only in the drama, carries men forward to unforeseen catastrophes. Chance may produce pathetic situations but never tragic ones; while fate "ought always to be terrible; and is in the highest sense tragic, when it brings into a ruinous concatenation the guilty man, and the guiltless that was unconcerned with him." These considerations lead Wilhelm Meister and Serlo, his manager,

> back to the play of Hamlet, and the peculiarities of its composition. The hero . . . is endowed more properly with sentiments than with a character; it is events alone that push him on; and accordingly the piece has in some measure the expansion of a novel. But as it is Fate that draws the plan; as the story issues from a deed of terror, and the hero is continually driven forward to a deed of terror, the work is tragic in the highest sense, and admits of no other than a tragic end.

To certain of the implications of this analysis we shall return hereafter. We can see now that it attempts to distinguish, by antitheses perhaps too neatly paired, the two literary forms, and that between them it fixes *Hamlet* in a way to make us sense the peculiarity of the play's nature. *Hamlet* is extended; its hero suffers rather than acts; he has sentiments, perhaps, more than character (in the rather limited definition Goethe appears to give his terms), and there is undeniably something of the novel's loose-ranging multiplicity of place, personage, and incident to this bemusing play that makes it different from other plays.

More generally, Goethe attempts to place all of Shakespeare's plays in terms of antitheses between Ancient and Modern of the kind which had provided Schlegel his grand strategy.

Ancient	Modern
Natural	Sentimental
Pagan	Christian
Classic	Romantic
Realistic	Idealistic
Necessity	Freedom
Duty (*sollen*)	Will (*wollen*)

The final pair of antitheses is Goethe's special contribution to the tradition. "Duty," he says, "is imposed upon men; 'must' is a bitter pill. The will man imposes upon himself; man's will is his kingdom of heaven." "Ancient tragedy was based on inescapable necessity, which was only sharpened and accelerated by an opposing will. Here is the seat of all that is fearful in the oracles, the region in which Oedipus lords it over all." "All necessity is despotic, whether it belong to the realm of Reason, like custom and civil law, or to Nature, like the laws of Becoming, and Growing and Passing-away, of Life and of Death. Before all these we tremble, without realizing that it is the good of the *whole* that is aimed at." By contrast, modern drama is based on the will, which overcomes and dissolves necessity, which "is free, appears free, and is advantageous to the *individual*." "Through the motive of Necessity, tragedy became mighty and strong; through the motive of Will, weak and feeble."

At these antitheses, as with those between the drama and the novel, we may fruitfully cavil; my concern, though, is with Goethe's fixing of Shakespeare not in one camp or the other, *à la* Schlegel, but between them—and not midway, either, but nearer to the Ancients: "In his plays Will and Necessity struggle to maintain an equilibrium; both contend powerfully, yet always so that Will remains at a disadvantage." Goethe is saying something about Shakespeare, I apprehend, so different in degree from the assertions of his predecessor that it amounts to a statement different in kind. He is fixing the special blend of attributes that make Shakespeare's plays amenable to Aristotle's most basic laws, significantly analogous to Sophocles' plays, communal in their import, and filled with a sense of Necessity or Law superior to human will, yet simultaneously modern in their tone, individual in their thrust, and filled with the claims of the free will. In Goethe's assertions we seem to see the final swing of an Hegelian pendulum. First there were the Ancients and, barbarously different from and beneath them, the Gothic or Romantic artists of whom Shakespeare was the benighted chief. Then there were the Ancients and, splendidly different from if not superior to them, the Gothic and Romantic artists of whom Shakespeare was the emancipating chief. For Goethe, there are the Ancients, there are the Romantic Moderns; and between them, reconciling their opposition, providing a new direction for dramatic endeavor, Shakespeare, the unique. The full force of Goethe's synthesis appears in this passage:

> No one has shown perhaps better than he the connection between Necessity and Will in the individual character. The person, considered as a character, is under a certain necessity; he is constrained, appointed to a certain particular line of

action; but as a human being he has a will, which is unconfined and universal in its demands. Thus arises an inner conflict, and Shakespeare is superior to all other writers in the significance with which he endows this. But now an outer conflict may arise, and the individual through it may become so aroused that an insufficient will is raised through circumstance to the level of irremissible necessity. These motives I have referred to earlier in the case of Hamlet; but the motive is repeated constantly in Shakespeare—Hamlet through the agency of the ghost; Macbeth through the witches, Hecate, and his wife; Brutus through his friends gets into a dilemma and situation to which they were not equal; even in Coriolanus the same motive is found. This Will, which reaches beyond the power of the individual, is decidedly modern. But since in Shakespeare it does not spring from within, but is developed through external circumstance, it becomes a sort of Necessity, and approaches the classical motive. For all the heroes of ancient poetry willed only what was possible to men, and from this arose that beautiful balance between Necessity, Will, and Accomplishment. Still their Necessity is a little too severe for it really to be able to please us, even though we may wonder at and admire it. A Necessity which more or less, or even completely, excludes human freedom does not chime with our views any longer. It is true that Shakespeare in his own way has approximated this, but in making this Necessity a moral necessity he has, to our pleasure and astonishment, united the spirit of the ancient and the modern worlds. If we are to learn anything from him, here is the point where we must study in his school.

Goethe fixes Shakespeare's place in one other important way, in which Lamb (as we shall see) and Coleridge had in part preceded him. "If we call Shakespeare one of the greatest poets," he says, "we mean that few have perceived the world as accurately as he, that few who have expressed their inner contemplation of it have given the reader deeper insight into its meaning and consciousness." Goethe celebrates the perception in Shakespeare which Johnson praised, but he attributes the poetry, as did Coleridge, to contemplation. The contemplation, moreover, is self-contemplation, for "the full consciousness of his own feelings and thoughts" gives man "the means of knowing intimately the hearts of others"; but Goethe does not explicitly go the Coleridgian length of considering Shakespeare's characters as so many embodiments of Shakespearean selves. In Shakespeare's contemplation, however, he sees the assimilative or ordering process by which the world "becomes for us completely transparent: we find ourselves at once in the most intimate touch with virtue and vice, greatness and meanness, nobility and infamy, and all this through the simplest of means." Contemplation is the process, and the means are words, living words, speaking not to such outer senses as the eye, delicate though that be, but to the inner sense, which is more delicate still—in short, to the imagination.

> Shakespeare speaks always to our inner sense. Through this, the picture world of imagination becomes animated, and a complete effect results, of which we can give no reckoning. Precisely here lies the ground for the illusion that everything is taking place before our eyes. But if we study the works of Shakespeare enough, we find that they contain much more of spiritual truth than of spectacular action. He makes happen what can easily be conceived by the imagination, indeed what can be better imagined than seen. Hamlet's ghost, Macbeth's witches, many fearful incidents, get their value only through the power of the imagination, and many of the minor scenes get their force from the same source. In reading, all these things pass easily through our minds, and seem quite appropriate, whereas in representation on the stage they would strike us unfavorably and appear not only unpleasant but even disgusting.

This is also Lamb's point, but in a different context, defining the workings of the Shakespearean dynamic: perception-contemplation-the living word-imagination.

One effect of this definition is to place Shakespeare foremost among the world's poets but not among the world's dramatists, and this leads us to our final concern with Goethe, what I have called his disenchantment with Shakespeare. Goethe's disenchantment is purely with Shakespeare as playwright, and its manifestations are several: the very praise of Shakespeare as poet, speaking to the mind's eye, the historical apology for Shakespeare's theater, the treatment of *Hamlet* as lying, in fact, midway between the drama and the novel and, most strikingly, the refashioning of *Hamlet* to make it dramaturgically shipshape and trim. The first of the three sections of his *Shakespeare ad Infinitum* Goethe devotes to "Shakespeare as Poet in General"—and it is all praise; the third of the three sections he devotes to "Shakespeare as Playwright"—and it is all apology, though muted. A few passages illustrate:

> Shakespeare's fame and excellence belong to the history of poetry; but it is an injustice toward all playwrights of earlier and more recent times to give him his entire merit in the annals of the theater.

> A universally recognized talent may make of its capacities some use which is problematical. Not everything which the great do is done in the best fashion.

> Shakespeare's whole method finds in the stage itself something unwieldy and hostile . . . it would only be falsehood . . . were we to say that the stage was a worthy field for his genius.

And Goethe proceeds to an exposition of the unrealistic Elizabethan stage as scholarship had then recreated it.

> Who would be content today to put up with such a stage? But amid such surroundings, Shakespeare's plays were highly

> interesting stories, only told by several persons, who, in order
> to make somewhat more of an impression, had put on masks,
> and, when it was necessary, moved back and forth, entered
> and left the stage; but left to the spectator nevertheless the
> task of imagining at his pleasure Paradise and palaces on the
> empty stage.

Shakespeare writes dramatic poems but not plays: this is one
source of Goethe's disenchantment. The other is that he writes
not plays but poetic novels. One sense of this judgment we have
seen in Goethe's remarks that *Hamlet* lies midway between play
and novel; but there is another sense. As Goethe demands that the
play be visual, he demands of it a tight economy. Loose economy
is well enough for the novel, which may wander here and there,
multiplying its places, times, persons, and incidents; but the play
requires a narrower unity and a more concentrated relation of
means to ends. When the youthful Wilhelm Meister is prevailed
upon to examine *Hamlet* with an eye to simplifying and condens-
ing it, it seems at first to him an impossible task.[14] *Hamlet* is like a
beloved in whom the lover can understand nothing defective. But
study brings Wilhelm to recognize two classes of objects: "The
first are the grand internal relations of the persons and events, the
powerful effects which arise from the characters and proceedings
of the main figures"; the second is "the external relations of the
persons, whereby they are brought from place to place, or combined in various ways by certain accidental incidents."

> Among these external relations I include the disturbances
> in Norway, the war with young Fortinbras, the embassy to his
> uncle, the settling of that feud, the march of young For-
> tinbras to Poland; and his coming back at the end; of the
> same sort are Horatio's return from Wittenberg, Hamlet's
> wish to go thither, the journey of Laertes to France, his return,
> the dispatch of Hamlet into England, his capture by pirates,
> the death of the two courtiers by the letter which they

carried. All these circumstances and events would be very fit
for expanding and lengthening a novel; but here they injure
exceedingly the unity of the piece . . .

How Wilhelm proposes to redact *Hamlet* to bring these external
relations into a true unity and economy the reader can find in
Book V, Chapter IV of *Wilhelm Meister's Apprenticeship*, or
perhaps he will prefer to work it out from Wilhelm's opening
remarks:

> After the death of Hamlet the father, the Norwegians, lately
> conquered, grow unruly. The viceroy of that country sends his
> son, Horatio, an old schoolfriend of Hamlet's, and distin-
> guished above every other for his bravery and prudence, to
> Denmark, to press forward the equipment of the fleet, which,
> under the new luxurious king, proceeds but slowly.

What Goethe proposes to do to *Hamlet*, what he does to
Romeo and Juliet when he adjusts it for the German stage, witness
to classic tendencies in a romantic mind, and testify to the
continuation in the century of bardolatry of a judicious attitude
toward Shakespeare, the humanly limited. Spiritual kin as he is to
Schlegel and Coleridge, Goethe keeps reminding one of Johnson,
he keeps preparing one for Arnold.[15]

❦ ❦ ❦

Charles Lamb, like Maurice Morgann and Johann Wolfgang
von Goethe, suffers from history's tendency to simplify. Morgann
becomes the critic who denies Falstaff's cowardice; Goethe the
critic who compares the Ghost's commissioning of Hamlet to the
planting of an oak in a delicate vase; and Lamb is the one who says
Shakespeare's plays should not, cannot be played.[16] All true, but
in all, so much less than the truth.

Part of Lamb's protest against the acting of Shakespeare, like
Shaw's at Shakespeare himself, is leveled against the kind of

staging, acting, setting, and costuming Shakespeare receives in the
theater of the day. Lamb does not say this, is perhaps ignorant that
it is so, but the things he protests exist only in certain styles of
stage representation, and it seems possible that a different theatrical experience might faintly have qualified his view. He complains
that the coronation robe in a recent production of *Macbeth*

> was fairly a counterpart to that which our King wears when he
> goes to the Parliament-house—just so full and cumbersome,
> and set out with ermine and pearls . . . But in reading, what
> robe are we conscious of? Some dim images of royalty—a
> crown and scepter, may float before our eyes, but who shall
> describe the fashion of it?

The trouble here is with theatrical realism, ostentatious and spec-
tacular. So Lamb cares nothing for the "painted trees and caverns,
which we know to be painted," when he witnesses *The Tempest*.
And when he protests that "spirits and fairies cannot be represented, they cannot even be painted—they can only be believed,"
we must, while applauding the sentiment, suspect that the acting
to which he refers had none of the stylized pretense that without
embarrassment invites to make-believe on more fortunate stages.

It seems probable, however, that the acting Lamb repudiates
had its own stylization, though of a different sort: the cheap,
popular style of simplistic gesture and grimace so that Richard III
could be rendered as "a very wicked man" who "kills little
children in their beds"—"very close and shrewd and devilish
cunning, for you could see that by his eye." Lamb reports that
those who tell him of Garrick "speak of his eye, of the magic of his
eye, and of his commanding voice: physical properties, vastly
desirable in an actor, and without which he can never insinuate
meaning into an auditory," and then demands, "but what have
they to do with Hamlet? what have they to do with intellect?"
The answer is, manifestly, whatever a good actor can make them,
but Lamb, like Hamlet with the players, is protesting an abuse of

the physical at the expense of the mental: "There is so much in [Shakespeare's plays], which comes not under the province of acting, with which eye, and tone, and gesture, have nothing to do." The same note appears in his complaint that "the practice of stage representation reduces everything to a controversy of elocution," that "every character . . . must play the orator," and in his contemptuous reference to "*that symbol of the emotion which passes current at the theater for it*" (Lamb's italics).

That the stage represents Shakespeare excessively realistically and that it represents him excessively unnaturally—these complaints frame Lamb's argument. Neither ultimately relates to the question of the fitness of the plays for a stage less limited and venal than that of London in Lamb's day. But Lamb's attack goes further. His protest about Macbeth's robe touches in fact on the whole problem of giving to airy nothing a local habitation and a name. In the reading, there is no robe, or only the faintest, indistinguishable suggestion of one. On the stage there is a robe of actual cloth and of one particular cut, drape, color, and embroidery out of all the infinitude of possibilities that may exist in the mind. So the stage imposes the material and the specific in lieu of the mind's ideal and general. Something of the same idea underlies Lamb's objection that Mrs. Siddons

> never got more fame by anything than by the manner in which she dismisses the guests in the banquet-scene in Macbeth . . .[17] But does such a trifle as this enter into the imaginations of the readers of that wild and wonderful scene? Does not the mind dismiss the feasters as rapidly as it can? Does it care about the gracefulness of the doing it?

On the stage as in actuality there must be movement and gesture which in reading the mind can forget. Lamb keeps sounding this point: "What we see upon a stage is body and bodily action; [while] what we are conscious of in reading is almost exclusively the mind, and its movements." "When the novelty is past, we find to our cost that . . . we have only materialized and brought down a fine vision to the standard of flesh and blood." How cruel it is to the mind, he says, "to have its free conceptions thus cramped and pressed down to the measure of a strait-lacing actuality."

Clearly Lamb's arguments are leveled against the theater itself, against the mimetic art with its actors imitating by look, gesture, posture, by intonation and cadence, the actions of men and women. Every play, as it goes upon the boards, takes on the specificity of actuality—this costume instead of that, this actor instead of another, this business instead of a thousand alternatives. But this process Lamb seems to repudiate in totality. Moreover, he has another complaint. He speaks of "the love-dialogues of Romeo and Juliet, those silver-sweet sounds of lovers' tongues by night; the more intimate and sacred sweetness of nuptial colloquy between an Othello or a Posthumus with their married wives," and exclaims, "by the inherent fault of stage representation, how are these things sullied and turned from their very nature by being exposed to a large assembly." Of Hamlet's soliloquies, "these profound sorrows, these light-and-noise-abhorring ruminations, which the tongue scarce dares utter to deaf walls and chambers," he demands, "how can they be represented by a gesticulating actor, who comes and mouths them out before an audience, making four hundred people his confidante at once?" Again Lamb is attacking the theater itself, this time denying to acting its initial premise, the premise of make-believe. He treats the lovers as actual lovers, Hamlet's meditations as genuine private ruminations. By this reasoning, the theater could never deal with private life, for it would always function as peep hole to an audience turned voyeur. It would only deal with communal life, public affairs.

Lamb's reasoning and his point are at odds. He is quite willing to see *The Gamester* or *George Barnwell* on the boards—their reduction to the actual does not trouble him. He is prepared to behold other lovers than Shakespeare's exchange their private endearments or listen to other heroes meditate on life, death, vanity. It is Shakespeare alone he wishes not to rule off, but to save from the stage. He has engaged with these characters, become jealous of them, regards them with a proprietary air. One of their intimates, sensitive to their sensitivities, he would defend them from the degradation they endure when made instrument to some actor's pursuit of applause. He would place them in the theater of the mind, but—and this is crucial—not of any mind. The theater of his own mind or minds like it. He would place them on that stage, both interior and infinite, tactfully and exquisitely to appreciate their ambivalent complexities.

To this appreciation, Lamb's ultimate contribution, we shall return shortly, but first, a closer examination of his quarrel with the stage and acting. Lamb speaks of acting as does Johnson when he defends Shakespeare's violation of the unities. We are always conscious of it, of Mr. C. or Mr. K. as the hero, of Mrs. S. as the heroine, of canvas and lights as trees and stars. Moreover, we cannot escape the queasy awareness that "such speeches as Imogen addresses to her lord, come drawling out of the mouth of a hired actress, whose courtship, though nominally addressed to the personated Posthumus, is manifestly aimed at the spectators, who are to judge of her endearments and her returns of love." We watch Hamlet mouthing his soliloquies *"ore rotundo,"* and know that he *"must be thinking all the while of his appearance, because he knows that all the while the spectators are judging of it"* (Lamb's italics). Watching the plays on the stage, we cannot lose ourselves in them, we cannot suspend our disbeliefs. We become judges, and, victims of "the accursed critical habit," lose the play in its playing.

Lamb defines the unhappy lot of many who in theater or concert hall can never surrender themselves to the art because of their concern with the performing artist. A reviewer's lot is not a happy one. Lamb has, moreover, a further, complementary complaint. If acting prevents the suspension of disbelief, on the one hand, on the other, it forces belief. "While we are reading any of [Shakespeare's] great criminal characters, . . . we think not so much of the crimes which they commit, as of the ambition, the aspiring spirit, the intellectual activity, which prompts them to overleap these moral fences." "The crime is comparatively nothing." But, witness the play well done on the stage, "the painful anxiety about the act, the natural longing to prevent it while it yet seems unperpetrated, the too close pressing semblance of reality, give a pain and an uneasiness which totally destroy all the delight which the words in the book convey." To oversimplify, in the study, character dominates action (a point Morgann would have applauded); in the theater, action dominates character. Similarly, and the illustration hurts,

> Nothing can be more soothing, more flattering to the nobler parts of our natures, than to read of a young Venetian lady of highest extraction, through the force of love and from a sense of merit in him whom she loved, laying aside every consideration of kindred, and country, and color, and wedding with a coal-black Moor . . . —it is the perfect triumph of virtue over accidents, of the imagination over the senses. She sees Othello's color in his mind. But upon the stage, when the imagination is no longer the ruling faculty, but we are left to our poor unassisted senses, I appeal to every one that has seen Othello played, whether he did not, on the contrary, sink Othello's mind in his color; whether he did not find something extremely revolting in the courtship and wedded caresses of Othello and Desdemona . . .

Physical and moral actualities demand in the theater a hearing they do not receive in the reading. Crime becomes blood, corpses, political upheaval and not simply the image of morbid ambition preternaturally imaginative. Miscegenation becomes black body and white in physical union, not simply the fleshless hyperbole for perfect love. Lamb cannot escape this belief. He hates the transformation, not finding it in himself to join the physical to the imaginative. For him, it is one or the other, "body and bodily action" or "the mind, and its movements." If he is wrong, as I think he is, the merit of his complaint is that it enforces on us awareness of how extraordinarily strong and rich—as well as delicate—Shakespeare's drama is. For him crime does drip blood, though from the dagger of such an imaginary colossus as Macbeth; black flesh and white do join and to a blank verse music never heard before or since.

I have spent this much space on arguments partly or totally irrelevant to Shakespeare because they evidence Lamb's own influential appreciation of the plays. His great complaint, by whatever logic he asserts it, is that the theater reduces Shakespeare. In his essay, the theater, with its inadequacy fancied or real, becomes the foil to his own sharp definitions and subtle analyses; and these, entering the tradition, invite from following Shakespeareans appreciations no less sharp and subtle. There is a very fine analysis of Hamlet's asperity to Ophelia, with a delicate feeling for the pain this gives Hamlet's admirers, and a sympathetic reading of its nature—"it is not anger, but grief assuming the appearance of anger —love awkwardly counterfeiting hate, as sweet countenances when they try to frown." There is a refined relish of the daring intellection of Shakespeare's criminals, a gooseflesh feeling that Lessing would have appreciated for Shakespeare's fairies, witches, and ghosts. There is more. But the greatest passage, and deservedly the best known, is that on Lear. Its merit, be it noted, is not in its proof that Lear cannot be played but in the enlarged awareness it gives us of the character.

So to see Lear acted—to see an old man tottering about the stage with a walking-stick, turned out of doors by his daughters in a rainy night, has nothing in it but what is painful and disgusting. We want to take him into shelter and relieve him. That is all the feeling which the acting of Lear ever produced in me. But the Lear of Shakespeare cannot be acted. The contemptible machinery by which they mimic the storm which he goes out in, is not more inadequate to represent the horrors of the real elements, than any actor can be to represent Lear: they might more easily propose to personate the Satan of Milton upon a stage, or one of Michelangelo's terrible figures. The greatness of Lear is not in corporeal dimension, but in intellectual: the explosions of his passion are terrible as a volcano: they are storms turning up and disclosing to the bottom that sea, his mind, with all its vast riches. It is his mind which is laid bare. This case of flesh and blood seems too insignificant to be thought on; even as he himself neglects it. On the stage we see nothing but corporeal infirmities and weakness, the impotence of rage; while we read it, we see not Lear, but we are Lear—we are in his mind, we are sustained by a grandeur which baffles the malice of daughters and storms; in the aberrations of his reason, we discover a mighty irregular power of reasoning, immethodized from the ordinary purposes of life, but exerting its powers, as the wind blows where it listeth, at will upon the corruptions and abuses of mankind. What have looks, or tones, to do with that sublime identification of his age with that of the heavens themselves, when in his reproaches to them for conniving at the injustice of his children, he reminds them that "they themselves are old." What gesture shall we appropriate to this? What has the voice or the eye to do with such things?

❧ ❧ ❧

In his review of Hazlitt's *Characters of Shakespear's Plays* (1817), Francis Jeffrey says of Hazlitt:

He seems animated throughout with a full and hearty sympathy with the delight which his author should inspire, and pours himself gladly out in explanation of it, with a fluency and ardor, obviously much more akin to enthusiasm than affectation. He seems pretty generally, indeed, in a state of happy intoxication—and has borrowed from his great original, not indeed the force or brilliancy of his fancy, but something *of its playfulness, and a large share of his apparent joyousness and self-indulgence in its exercise.*[18]

This is happily said. Hazlitt keeps impressing on us a feeling of exuberant delight. He likes his work. He finds pleasure in talking about these plays, these characters. He enjoys drawing passages to our attention, relishes seeking the *mot juste* for a tone or attitude. Jeffrey is also correct, in the main, when he adds,

> When we have said that his observations are generally right, we have said, in substance, that they are not generally original; for the beauties of Shakespeare are not of so dim or equivocal a nature as to be visible only to learned eyes—and undoubtedly his finest passages are those which please all classes of readers, and are admired for the same qualities by judges from every school of criticism.

Hazlitt is not one of the great seminal critics. He has no special esthetic; he explores no new metaphysic; he cares very little for theories of dramatic means—the unities, for example—and says remarkably little about dramatic ends—catharsis or instruction—though he does begin his discussion of *Othello* with a fine paragraph on tragedy as "the refiner of the species, a discipline of humanity." But he regards the plays with a robust common sense that has been disciplined by years of theater-going and reviewing and that expresses itself in a finely articulate and remarkably hard-hitting prose. He says what others have thought—perhaps not better than all others have said it, but with sufficient distinction to make his own versions heard and to stamp on the common idea his own imprint. It is Hazlitt who calls Hamlet "the prince of philosophical speculators," "the most amiable of misanthropes," who declares, "it is *we* who are Hamlet."[19] It is Hazlitt who says "Shylock is *a good hater*," Bottom is "the most romantic of mechanics," "Romeo is Hamlet in love," and Iago "is an amateur of tragedy in real life." Hazlitt speaks of Rosalind's talking "herself out of breath, only to get deeper in love," of Slender as "a very potent piece of imbecility," of Northumberland's being "caught in the web of his own cold, dilatory policy," of Petruchio as "a madman in his senses; a very honest fellow, who hardly speaks a word of truth." He speaks of "the lurking selfishness of Apemantus," of the "unshrinking fortitude in crime," of Lady Macbeth, of the witches as "malicious from their impotence of enjoyment." Coriolanus, he says, "cannot contradict the praises that are bestowed upon him; therefore he is impatient at hearing them." Falstaff's imagination, he says, "keeps up the ball after his senses have done with it." Richard III, he says, is "not a man striving to be great, but to be greater than he is."

Hazlitt's most general treatment of Shakespeare appears in his lecture "On Shakespeare and Milton"[20] wherein he reviews the topics of praise and, briefly, blame like a judicious critic of a century before, though without reference to the rules. He praises the universal and generic quality of Shakespeare's mind—

> its power of communication with all other minds . . . He was just like any other man, but that he was like all other men. He was the least of an egotist that it was possible to be . . . There was no respect of persons with him. His genius shone equally on the evil and on the good, on the wise and the foolish, the monarch and the beggar.

In a formulation that began with Rowe, Hazlitt praises Shakespeare for his power in "the fairy way of writing"—"if the preternatural characters he describes could be supposed to exist, they would speak, and feel, and act, as he makes them." He admires Shakespeare's power to create natural habitats for his characters— "the same local, outward, and unforeseen accidents which would occur in reality." He responds enthusiastically to Shakespeare's creation of a physical, mental, social context for speech and action: "all the persons concerned must have been present in the poet's imagination, as at a kind of rehearsal; and whatever would have passed through their minds on the occasion, and have been observed by others, passed through his." He pays tribute to the characters, each "absolutely independent of the rest, as well as of the author, as if they were living persons . . . By an art like that of the ventriloquist, [Shakespeare] throws his imagination out of himself, and makes every word appear to proceed from the mouth of the person in whose name it is given." Hazlitt identifies the characters as dramatic rather than narrative or epic; they are in a state of "continual composition and decomposition." Shakespeare's presentation of passion is similarly changing, fluctuating, "not some one habitual feeling or sentiment preying upon itself," but "passion modified by passion, by all the other feelings to which the individual is liable."

Shakespeare's imagination is no less plastic than his conception of character or passion, uniting the most opposite extremes, seeming "always hurrying from his subject, even while describing it," bringing into intimacy thoughts that were strangers to each other so that "they startle, and take the fancy prisoner in the same instant." Finally, Hazlitt praises Shakespeare's "magic power over words"—his language is "hieroglyphical"; it "translates thoughts into visible images"—and Shakespeare's powerful, sweet, and varied versification—"the only blank verse in the language, except Milton's, that for itself is readable." The blame Hazlitt boils down to an occasional relaxed carelessness, since Shakespeare "wrote for the 'great vulgar and the small,' in his time, not for posterity." "His barbarisms were those of his age. His genius was his own."

Much of this is commonplace; some, as on Shakespeare's "hieroglyphical" language, is not, though not new (Gray had written, 1742: "Every word in [Shakespeare] is a picture"[21]). All, I think, is well enough said to find a place in the story. And there emerge from the whole two awarenesses that seem especially Hazlitt's. One is the sense of scene. Hazlitt reads the plays like a director, quick to detect cues as to motion, gesture, costume. He cites with pleasure Ophelia's account of Hamlet's visit, Hamlet's indignant reference to the smiling of Rosencrantz and Guildenstern, and Malcolm's expostulation to Macduff, "What! man, ne'er pull your hat upon your brows." But it's not simply the physical that Hazlitt has in mind—it's the whole interrelationship of one person with another, one mind with other minds—presences both solid and psychological upon a stage. To this scenic or theatrical sense we shall return.

The second awareness that seems peculiarly Hazlitt's is of Shakespeare's plasticity. The term may not communicate at once, but Hazlitt speaks of Shakespeare's imagination as being no less "plastic" than his conception of character or passion. He sees everything about Shakespeare as flexible, not fixed, as pulsating, not steady, as speaking out of some inner principle of vitality rather than on borrowed power. Chaucer's characters, he says, are

> too much like identical propositions. They are consistent, but uniform; we get no new idea of them from first to last . . . Shakespeare's are historical figures, equally true and correct, but put into action, where every nerve and muscle is displayed in the struggle with others, with all the effect of collision and contrast.

Chaucer "answered for his characters himself. In Shakespeare they are introduced upon the stage, are liable to be asked all sorts of questions, and are forced to answer for themselves." Shakespeare's characters are independent of each other "as well as of the author." The same feeling for the plastic, the vitally unschematic and unpredictable, underlies Hazlitt's praise of Shakespeare's presentation of passion as

> passion modified by passion, by all the other feelings to which the individual is liable, and to which others are liable with him; subject to all the fluctuations of caprice and accident; calling into play all the resources of the understanding and all the energies of the will; irritated by obstacles or yielding to

them; rising from small beginnings to its utmost height; now drunk with hope, now stung to madness, now sunk in despair, now blown to air with a breath, now raging like a torrent.

From these two senses—of scene and plasticity, of the inter-relatedness of parts and of the vital independence of parts—Hazlitt arrives in his *Characters* at a larger critical awareness, a sense of the miraculous living unity of such plays as *Cymbeline, Lear, Othello*. To this we shall come.

The Characters of Shakespear's Plays, Hazlitt's principal work of Shakespearean criticism, like Schlegel's latter lectures, is something of a handbook. There is a Preface, wherein Hazlitt states his thesis about the characters, quotes approvingly a large swatch from Schlegel's general account of Shakespeare, and with the con-descension that the early nineteenth century so easily directed at Johnson, accounts for Johnson's putative failure as a Shake-spearean critic. There follow individual chapters on each of the plays (the two parts of *Henry IV* being treated as one, the three parts of *Henry VI* as one, and *Pericles* being excluded), then chapters on "Doubtful Plays of Shakespeare" and "Poems and Sonnets." With a few exceptions, the plays are grouped by genre: tragedy first, then history, then comedy. Hazlitt quotes extensively, one of the virtues of his book being the anthology of passages with comment that it provides; and he embeds in every fourth or fifth chapter a discussion, relevant to the play in question but suffi-ciently general to be considered a small essay in itself, to which one comes as to an unexpected and therefore the more delightful bonus.

There are discussions of Shakespeare's heroines in the chapter on *Cymbeline*, of tragedy as "a discipline of humanity" in the chapter on *Othello*, of the aristocratic imagination and the republican understanding (*Coriolanus*), of the differences in the genius of Chaucer and Shakespeare (*Troilus and Cressida*) of the nature of Shakespearean comedy (*Twelfth Night*) and Shake-speare as, and as not, a moralist (*Measure for Measure*)—to indicate some of the more distinguished. I doubt that Hazlitt's observations on Shakespeare's heroines achieves the perfection of Coleridge's remarks about "the sweet and yet dignified feeling of all that *continuates* society," yet he says well that the heroines

> seem to exist only in their attachment to others. They are pure abstractions of the affections. We think as little of their persons as they do themselves, because we are let into the secrets of their hearts . . . No one ever hit the true perfection of the female character, the sense of weakness leaning on the strength of its affections for support, so well as Shakespeare.

Hazlitt is blind to the quiet ironies and subtle ambivalences we have come to find in Chaucer, but the naive craftsman *he* sees in Chaucer helps him, by contrast, discover the sophisticated genius in Shakespeare—and in memorable terms:

> Chaucer had great variety of power, but he could do only one thing at once. He set himself to work on a particular subject. His ideas were kept separate, labeled, ticketed and parceled out in a set form, in pews and compartments by themselves. They did not play into one another's hands. They did not react upon one another, as the blower's breath molds the yielding glass. There is something hard and dry in them. What is the most wonderful thing in Shakespeare's faculties is their excessive sociability, and how they gossiped and compared notes together.

Even Chaucerians, I would hope, might forgive the beginning of that passage for the happiness of its end. In our own day Coghill has written pregnantly of Shakespearean comedy as deriving from the Christian rather than the classic pattern, focusing on forgiveness rather than punishment, and celebrating symbolically that comedy which is the Christian view of the world.[22] Hazlitt,

without reference to historical or religious causation, and without
fully approving, since he prefers the astringencies of Jonsonian
satire, sees nonetheless the qualities about which Coghill writes.
Shakespeare's drama, he says,

> is perhaps too good-natured for comedy. It has little satire,
> and no spleen. It aims at the ludicrous rather than the
> ridiculous. It makes us laugh at the follies of mankind, not
> despise them, and still less bear any ill-will towards them.
> Shakespeare's comic genius resembles the bee rather in its
> power of extracting sweets from weeds or poisons, than in
> leaving a sting behind it.

The chapters generally characterize the principal *dramatis
personae* with the trenchant grace and finality already illustrated;
they indicate something of the play's movement (though never by
means of a direct plot summary); quite in the eighteenth-century
fashion they draw attention to "beauties" (though avoiding that
term); and at times they seize on the ambiguity of the book's title
to speak of the distinguishing quality or "character" of the individual play.

The chapter on *Richard II* will illustrate. It begins with a
broad survey of the play as one in which "the weakness of the king
leaves us leisure to take a greater interest in the misfortunes of the
man." Carefully Hazlitt considers Richard's decline, then Bolingbroke's rise, his shift in focus according with the change of fortune
registered in the play. But as "the steps by which Bolingbroke
mounts the throne are those by which Richard sinks into the
grave," Hazlitt returns, finally, to Richard, not as a character but
as the recipient of our emotion. "We pity him, for he pities
himself . . . The sufferings of the man make us forget that he
ever was a king." The pathetic character of the play thus established, and its chiastic movement of rise and fall, Hazlitt draws
attention to two "beauties," the one a passage describing the

vastness of royal power ("such is the breath of kings"), the other a passage imaging the loneliness of exile (Mowbray's complaint).

The two passages, political in subject, open the way to a general commentary on the English history plays as set in a time "in which 'is hung armor of the invincible knights of old,' in which their hearts seem to strike against their coats of mail, where their blood tingles for the fight, and words are but the harbingers of blows." By way of illustrating "this state of accomplished barbarism," Hazlitt calls attention to the initial appeal of Bolingbroke and Mowbray and quotes in full the later appeals of Aumerle, Fitzwater, and Surrey. From this, Hazlitt proceeds to his "characters." First come Gaunt and York, "the one stern and foreboding, the other honest, good-natured, doing all for the best, and therefore doing nothing." Hazlitt quotes Gaunt's speech on "This royal throne of kings." Next comes Bolingbroke, "patient for occasion, and then steadily availing himself of it, seeing his advantage afar off, but only seizing on it when he has it within his reach, humble, crafty, bold, and aspiring, encroaching by regular but slow degrees, building power on opinion, and cementing opinion by power." Hazlitt cites Richard's cold analysis of Bolingbroke (I.iv) and, ironically, Bolingbroke's self-characterization (II.iii.46-47), "I count myself in nothing else so happy,/As in a soul rememb'ring my good friends." "We know," says Hazlitt, "how he afterwards kept his promise." Finally comes Richard: "His folly, his vices, his misfortunes, his reluctance to part with the crown, his fear to keep it, his weak and womanish regrets, his starting tears, his fits of hectic passion, his smothered majesty, pass in succession before us, and make a picture as natural as it is affecting." Hazlitt concludes by indicating certain "striking touches of pathos" in the play: Richard's wish, "O that I were a mockery king of snow to melt away before the sun of Bolingbroke"; "the incident of the poor groom who comes to visit him in prison" and tell him about Roan Barbary; and, finally, the passage, which Hazlitt quotes in full, of York's describing to his

Duchess Bolingbroke's triumphant entry into London with Richard in his train.

The chapter on *Richard II* is neither one of the best nor one of the worst in the book. Its definition of the play's character, its review of the play's movement, its comments on Gaunt, York, and Bolingbroke, and its anthology of noteworthy passages are exemplary. Its little essay on the bellicose anarchy in which the history plays are set combines brilliance with naïveté: Hazlitt sees the force but not the issues. The commentary on Richard is curiously incomplete, as though Richard were a mere figure of pathos, not a full-fledged and ambiguous character. Of the play's versification with its frequency of couplets and its archaic stiffness, especially at the end, of the paralleling of problems in Bolingbroke's kingship with those in Richard's (the appeal, the seditious cousin, the restive nobles, etc.), and of the odd tonal shift in Act V when York berates his Duchess and the two, along with Aumerle, plant their knees before the King and bicker—of these matters the chapter says nothing. Yet even such a summary of such a chapter as this may show why *The Characters* is the best handbook in its century. It says more, better, and more briefly than do the others. It speaks with an authority which its own perspicacity validates. It speaks with none of the dull anonymity of the modern handbook but vibrates with personal enthusiasm and conviction. It starts the reader very well on his way and leaves it to him—as a good teacher ought—to arrive on his own.

In the finest chapters Hazlitt arrives, as I have already indicated, at a sense of underlying unity. His scenic awareness combines with his feeling for the autonomy of the individual characters to produce such passages as this:

> as it happens in most of [Shakespeare's] works, there is not
> only the utmost keeping in each separate character; but in the
> casting of the different parts, and their relation to one an-
> other, there is an affinity and harmony, like what we may

observe in the gradations of color in a picture. The striking and powerful contrasts in which Shakespeare abounds could not escape observation; but the use he makes of the principle of analogy to reconcile the greatest diversities of character and to maintain a continuity of feeling throughout, has not been sufficiently attended to. In Cymbeline, for instance, the principal interest arises out of the unalterable fidelity of Imogen to her husband under the most trying circumstances. Now the other parts of the picture are filled up with subordinate examples of the same feeling, variously modified by different situations, and applied to the purposes of virtue or vice. The plot is aided by the amorous importunities of Cloten, by the tragical determination of Iachimo . . . : the faithful attachment of Pisanio . . . the obstinate adherence to his purpose in Bellarius . . . the incorrigible wickedness of the Queen, and even the blind uxorious confidence of Cymbeline, are all so many lines of the same story, tending to the same point. The effect of this coincidence is rather felt than observed; and as the impression exists unconsciously in the mind of the reader, so it probably arose in the same manner in the mind of the author, not from design, but from the force of natural association, a particular train of feeling suggesting different inflections of the same predominant principle, melting into, and strengthening one another, like chords in music.

For those who find the Coleridgian "imagination" too transcendent, his organic unity too mysterious, Hazlitt's explanation of unity as the product of analogy, arrived at by unconscious association, has the merit of common sense. What it lacks, in his application of it, is influence, the invitation to the reader to discover other analogies in other plays. The Coleridgian insistence on the interrelatedness of parts, *his* assumption that Shakespeare's faculties are sociable and gossip together, is, somehow, always open-ended. It pulls the reader into the pattern, makes him imitate Coleridge, and seek to discover other evidences of the judgment and the unity of genius. Perhaps because Hazlitt makes his point less often, or expresses it with less reverence and awe, or because he refers it to mechanical rather than creative aspects of the mind, or because it lacks a larger esthetic to give it meaning, the result is different. Hazlitt has no disciples; Coleridge has. Yet the demonstrations of unity in *Cymbeline* and *Othello* and *King Lear* make us see what otherwise we might not.

In listing the causes of Hazlitt's lack of critical influence in respect to the unity of Shakespeare's plays, I have omitted what I suspect is the chief: that Hazlitt's demonstrations of unity are themselves instrumental to something else, the proof of a thesis which is sound enough but without novelty or excitement. That thesis, which governs the entire book, Hazlitt quotes from Pope in his Preface. It is that "every single character in Shakespeare, is as much an individual, as those in life itself; it is as impossible to find any two alike; and such, as from their relation or affinity in any respect appear most to be twins, will, upon comparison, be found remarkably distinct." This thesis, which sets Hazlitt to demonstrating how like characters are, and how different, helps him help us see the individual characters with new sharpness.

Two things remain to say about Hazlitt. One has to do with his politics, which intrude into his criticism and which it is the custom among historians of Shakespearean criticism to decry. We have already noted his sharp analyses of Bolingbroke in *Richard II* and of Northumberland in *Henry IV*. To these we may add his remarks about the conspiracy in *Julius Caesar*: "the whole design to liberate their country fails from the generous temper and overweening confidence of Brutus in the goodness of their cause and the assistance of others. Thus it has always been." In such remarks we sense political awareness without political prejudice. But when Hazlitt treats medieval chivalry as merely accomplished barbarism, when he says that "there is neither truth nor honor in all these noble persons: they answer words with words, as they do blows with blows, in mere self-defence: nor have they any principle whatever but that of courage in maintaining any wrong they dare commit," we may well question whether early nineteenth-century liberalism has not gotten between the critic and the plays, the plays and us. Even more may we feel this when we read,

> The whole dramatic moral of Coriolanus is that those who have little shall have less, and that those who have much shall take all that others have left. The people are poor; therefore they ought to be starved. They are slaves; therefore they ought to be beaten. They work hard; therefore they ought to be treated like beasts of burden. They are ignorant; therefore they ought not to be allowed to feel that they want food, or clothing, or rest, that they are enslaved, oppressed, and miserable.

We feel the same doubt as we read that Henry V

> was fond of war and low company . . . He was careless, dissolute, and ambitious—idle, or doing mischief. In private, he seemed to have no idea of the common decencies of life . . . in public affairs, he seemed to have no idea of any rule of right or wrong, but brute force, glossed over with a little religious hypocrisy and archiepiscopal advice.

The indictment continues in terms so witheringly scornful as to have been surpassed by none, though G. B. Shaw and Wyndham Lewis have had their try.[23]

On the whole, the interpretation of Shakespeare has benefited from Hazlitt's intrusive politics. For one thing, the prejudice is so frank and evident as not to deceive even an unwary reader. For another, it forces awareness both of the political dimensions which almost all of Shakespeare's plays possess and of the delicate problems of value raised by their politics. To take a republican view of the plays, or to denounce the divine right of kings as invalid doctrine, or to assume that in history and in Shakespeare's history plays power is the only viable motive—is to go too far; but the excess forces the issues. How do the plays treat the rabble? the patricians? Does the doctrine of divine right matter in the plays? Is it tested in any way? Is it sacrosanct or moot? Do declarations by Bolingbroke or Hal or Hotspur about right and God's will mean anything more than the hypocritical tribute vice pays to virtue? Hazlitt's merit is to open such questions—with prejudice, perhaps, but frankly, passionately, so that the politics of the plays enters into the arena of interpretation in a new and dignified way.

The final point about Hazlitt comes back to his scenic or theatrical sense. Hazlitt is a drama critic both before and after he writes his *Characters*. He has seen Mrs. Siddons. He reviews Kean, Kemble, and Booth. He combines enthusiasm with acidulousness and squares them both with his own reasoned judgment of the texts in question. He can write of Kean as Macbeth, after the murder of Duncan, in this fashion:

> *as a lesson of common humanity, it was heartrending. The hesitation, the bewildered look, the coming to himself when he sees his hands bloody; the manner in which his voice clung to his throat, and choked his utterance, his agony and tears, the force of nature overcome by passion—beggared description. It was a scene which no one who saw it can ever efface from his recollection.*

He could write of Kean as Romeo in the balcony scene thus: "It was said of Garrick and Barry in this scene, that the one acted it as if he would jump up to the lady, and the other as if he would make the lady jump down to him. Mr. Kean produced neither of these effects. He stood like a statue of lead."

The habit of dramatic reviewing, the considering the plays as stage-plays, the sense of gesture and action as themselves constituting portions of the total no less significant than the script, leads Hazlitt to moments of criticism which the closet Shakespeare almost never receives.[24] In his reviews (and again in *The Characters*) he speaks of Kean's Richard III:

> His courtship scene with Lady Anne was an admirable exhibi-
> tion of smooth and smiling villainy. The progress of wily
> adulation, of encroaching humility, was finely marked
> throughout by the action, voice, and eye. He seemed, like the
> first tempter, to approach his prey, certain of the event, and as
> if success had smoothed the way before him.

The feeling here is for the acting, the manner of saying and doing.
So it is when he says that "Richard should woo, not as a lover, but
as an actor—to show his mental superiority" and when he tells of
Kean's handling of the scene of Richard's defeat:

> He fought like one drunk with wounds: and the attitude in
> which he stands with his hands stretched out, after his sword
> is taken from him, had a preternatural and terrific grandeur,
> as if his will could not be disarmed, and the very phantoms of
> his despair had a withering power.

This feeling for play as gesture, manner, appears often, too, in
descriptions of action Hazlitt does not approve. At the end of
Othello, Kean, as Iago, pointed to the dead bodies. Hazlitt
objects: "It is not in the character of the part, which consists in
the love of mischief, not as an end, but as a means, and when that
end is attained, though he may feel no remorse, he would feel no
triumph. Besides, it is not the text of Shakespeare." And candor
requires admission that Hazlitt occasionally approves gesture or
business that seems highly dubious, as when Kean is "in the midst
of the extravagant and irresistible expression of Romeo's grief, at
being banished from the object of his love, his voice suddenly
stops and falters, and is choked with sobs of tenderness when he
comes to Juliet's name." If we feel that Romeo is here, as so often
before, play-acting, it is hard to assent to Hazlitt's approval.
Similarly, when he approves of Kean's "coming back after he has
gone to the extremity of the stage," at the end of the nunnery
scene in *Hamlet*, "from a pang of parting tenderness to press his

lips to Ophelia's hand," and tells us that "it had an electrical effect on the house. It was the finest commentary that was ever made on Shakespeare"—we may have our doubts. But the contribution of stage awareness is nonetheless here as part of Hazlitt's criticism.

This contribution, we should note, Hazlitt tends to withdraw even in the offering. He dedicates his *Characters* to Charles Lamb. He writes that he "can conceive no one to play Macbeth properly." "The *Midsummer Night's Dream*, when acted," he observes, "is converted from a delightful fiction into a dull pantomime." "Bottom's head in the play is a fantastic illusion, produced by magic spells: on the stage, it is an ass's head, and nothing more." "The boards of a theater and the regions of fancy are not the same thing." At the end of the chapter on *King Lear* he quotes approvingly Lamb's great outburst on that play. Hazlitt, then, brings to Shakespeare both a drama critic's sense of the plays as theater and a closet critic's sense that the theater of the mind so far surpasses that of the stage that certain of the plays can only be acted there. Even in the closet, though, he reads as a man of the theater ought, not for the part only but for the complex of parts that make the scene. And even in the closet, I think, he feels for expression, posture, gesture. That, I take it, is one meaning of a review he wrote of Kean's *Lear*, in 1820. Speaking of "that last sublime appeal to the heavens on seeing Goneril approach" (II.iv), he writes, "One would think there are tones, and looks, and gestures, answerable to these words, to thrill and harrow up the thoughts, to 'appal the guilty and make mad the free,' or that might 'create a soul under the ribs of death!' "

Georg Gottfried Gervinus / *1805–1871*
James Russell Lowell / *1819–1891*

Contemporary influence of the Commentaries. *Gervinus's psychological penetration; his want of measure. Shakespeare's system of morality. Unifying ethical ideas of individual plays.* 🌢 *Lowell's appraisal of Elizabethan English as vital, rich, democratic. Development of older topics: Shakespeare's imagination and judgment, punning, action as evolving from character. Allegorical reading of* The Tempest. *Vindication of* Hamlet's *anachronisms and graveyard comedy;* Hamlet's *character.*

The profound and generous Commentaries[1] by Gervinus —an honor to a German to have written, a pleasure to an Englishman to read—is still the only book known to me that comes near the true treatment and the dignity of its subject, or can be put into the hands of the student who wants to know the mind of Shakespeare.

The speaker is F. J. Furnivall; the place, the prospectus of The New Shakspere Society; the time, 1873. Dowden is around the corner, Bradley around the century, but at the time, to many a Shakespearean, the judgment seems right. "To Germany," says Bunnett, Gervinus's translator,

we owe . . . the most able and systematic among the disciples of that school of Shakespearian critics who have illustrated rather his thought than his language, his matter than his manner, who have studied his writings rather as those of a moralist, a thinker, a master of human nature, and a poet of all places and of all time, than as those of an English writer of a certain epoch.

Tolstoy calls Gervinus Shakespeare's "greatest exponent and admirer."

The *Commentaries* no longer command much attention, for causes we shall examine, but in their day their influence is great. Lowell says that they are "full of excellent matter," and it seems likely that to Gervinus he owes his observation that Hamlet's character is "prophetically typical of that introversion of mind which is so constant a phenomenon of these latter days." In his *Primer* Dowden lists Gervinus first among the commentaries ("full and laborious," he calls him); and Gervinus can be seen to have anticipated and invited Dowden's biographical venture in such passages as the following:

> Let this genius of the poet be watched in its development
> . . . by comparing the abundant contents of his works and
> the scanty sources concerning his life; let even a faint image
> be sketched of the mental condition, the personal peculiarity,
> and circumstances of the great man . . . then for the first
> time we should have reached a point which would bring us
> near the poet; we should gain a complete idea of his personal
> existence, and obtain a full picture, a living view of his mental
> stature.

When Walter Pater speaks of *Romeo and Juliet* as a "perfect symphony" combining three "independent poetic forms" (sonnet, aubade, epithalamion) "which it is the merit of German criticism to have detected,"[2] the German criticism he praises is that of Gervinus. And when Bradley discourses on the painfulness of *Othello* or the primitive grandeur of *King Lear* or pays tribute to

Emilia's uttering "for us," in the terrible final act of *Othello*, "the violent common emotions which we feel," he is saying, though with the special accent of his own profound brilliance, what Gervinus has already said.

The "excellent matter" of which Lowell says the *Commentaries* are "full" is threefold: psychological, ethic, esthetic. With the ethic and the esthetic we have to do later; the psychological may be illustrated now. Gervinus sees that Northumberland is one of "the willing myrmidons" of Bolingbroke's rebellion, his hatchet man, in fact, "now smooth and flexible, and now rough and unfeeling," who first omits Richard's title, "maliciously torments King Richard with the reading of his accusation," and "would arbitrarily arrest the noble Carlisle." Henry IV, Gervinus observes, "is rather a master in concealment than in dissimulation"; his character is strangely ambiguous, private motives fusing with and undercutting the public, as in his plan for a crusade, which would both appease his remorse and distract his critics, which he both attempts to put in motion and yet prevents from coming about. Gervinus notes that Claudio, in *Measure for Measure*, "with a lively and sanguine nature . . . surrenders himself to every momentary impression"—to the Duke's persuasions of the evils of life; to his own subsequent imaginings of the evils of death; to the value Isabella places on her honor, to the value he places thereafter on his life. Among Hamlet's other attributes, says Gervinus, is the Thespian. The discussion begins thus:

> We become acquainted with Hamlet as the friend and judge of acting, as a poet and a player. He has seen the players before and has had closer intercourse with them, he inserts a passage in the piece they are playing, he declaims before them, he gives them instructions. His praise of the fragment of Pyrrhus sustained in the old Seneca-like style is perfectly serious; it distinguishes him from Polonius, whom a jig pleases better; this, as well as his instructions to the players, exhibits him as a man of cultivated mind and taste, as that judge

whose single appreciation is worth more than that of all the rest of the theater. It is, therefore, so natural that the idea should occur to him of "catching" the king's conscience in a play; he seeks, as it were, an ingenious revenge; and to accomplish this under the touching effect of the presence of his conscience-stricken mother had evidently a kind of theatrical charm for him. When this trial of the king by means of the play succeeds, it is extremely characteristic, that it is not the fearful evidence of the crime which occupies him at first, but the pleasure in his skill as actor or poet; not the result so much as his art which has effected it. "Would not this," are his first words, "get me a fellowship in a cry of players?"

Gervinus espies in Lady Macbeth the essentially feminine nature which Mrs. Siddons, in her acting, suppressed, as have so many critics since. He perceives the manner in which the appeal to Macbeth's manliness characteristically engages him either in action or in argument. And, to illustrate no further, he draws a striking series of contrasts between Macbeth and Hamlet, the effect of which is to define each the more precisely. Supernatural communication endows each with more than mortal knowledge, "but the palsied effort of the one stands in strong contrast to the spasmodic action of the other." Hamlet appears a civilized man emerging from a barbarian world; Macbeth, a barbarian in a civilized world. By his fatness and scantness of breath, Hamlet magnifies the heroic muscles of "valor's minion," "Bellona's bridegroom"; and Macbeth, by his brainsickly nervousness, his starts threatening to mar all, illuminates Hamlet's theatrical flair.

Gervinus "with his excellencies," as Johnson might have said, "has likewise faults, and faults sufficient to obscure and overwhelm any other merit." The first is the want of a sense of humor. We discover it when we find Gervinus detailing the moral shortcomings of Mercutio ("a man without culture; coarse, rude, and ugly; a scornful ridiculer of all sensibility and love," etc.) pretty much as Goddard does a century later,[3] but with nary a mention of his ebullience, his gaiety, his spark. We discover it when we realize that though Gervinus has penetrated Orsino's sentimentality and Aguecheek's imbecility, we know not whether he finds the duke absurd or the knight delightful. Gervinus has fine things to say about *Much Ado* (I am not sure that anyone has yet dealt better with the play's essential thought and structure), but his commentary almost entirely by-passes Dogberry, Verges, and their inimitable Watch.

A sense of humor is a sense of measure. Gervinus lacks measure. As Ralli devastatingly records, with dutiful apologies thereafter, "Gervinus has been called a second Dogberry who bestowed all his tediousness upon the world."[4] Alas, there's a truth here. You cannot even *skim* Gervinus quickly. The trouble is in part one of style. Gervinus goes in for parallel clauses succeeding each other in additive profusion but without gain in particularity or precision. If he employs a rhapsodic exclamation, or a rhetorical question, it is a signal that more will follow. He is wearily superlative. The chief difficulty, however, is more basic. Gervinus simply retells each play, and in such detail generally that, if you know the play and have caught his point, it can be agony.

Gervinus's want of measure betrays itself most strikingly in certain of his ethical judgments. Thus, he regards Friar Laurence as fulfilling "the part of the Chorus" in *Romeo and Juliet* and as expressing

the leading idea of the piece in all its fulness, namely, that excess in any enjoyment, however pure in itself, transforms its sweet into bitterness; that devotion to any single feeling, however noble, bespeaks its ascendancy; that this ascendancy moves the man and woman out of their natural spheres; that love can only be an accompaniment to life, and that it cannot completely fill out the life and business of the man especially.

Gervinus believes that Hamlet, musing on what I take to be the idiocy of Fortinbras's attack on Poland,

> has discovered the true principle of life, the noblest which Shakespeare has perhaps ever pronounced, and which he has pronounced alone for noble men . . .

> Rightly to be great,
> Is, not to stir without great argument;
> But greatly to find quarrel in a straw,
> When honor's at the stake.

Gervinus thinks that Othello and Desdemona should have consulted Brabantio. He might have let his antagonism to Othello die "if his daughter had not rebelled against him; and he might have given her in her new home his blessing, if not his good will. And how good had it been for the wife of the soldier . . . to have at times a refuge in her father's house!" "Why is Edgar to have a better fate" than Cordelia, demands Gervinus, "when he is just that to his father which Cordelia is to Lear?" Because Edgar evidences "wise and prudent forethought . . . in all his actions," but Cordelia does not. "His means stand ever in well-considered relation to his aims; it is not so with Cordelia's." Does the reader, then, need to be told what Gervinus thinks of Hal's repudiation of Falstaff?

Ralli considers Gervinus in error in his view that Shakespeare's art is morally based. In the light of the passages we have just examined, the point may pass without protest, yet Gervinus writes from the greatest tradition that western literature knows. Literature exists, says the tradition, not apart from man's life but in it, its test like the test of any other art, fine or useful, what it contributes to human good, and that contribution in the eyes of Aristotle, Horace, Dante, Sidney, Dryden, Johnson, is a matter of ethical content. Tragedy, says the tradition, deals with major vice and folly, comedy with minor. In their plots they show us the wages of sin and error; in their characterization they engage us on the side of virtue; in their sentiments they instruct our understandings.

Gervinus like his predecessor, Ulrici,[5] attempts to redeem Shakespeare to morality as thoroughly as Coleridge and Schlegel had redeemed him to art. He attempts as well to reveal in Shakespeare more fully than any predecessor the art they had insisted on. The two aims, it turns out, are one. As Gervinus explains it, Goethe in his famed interpretation of *Hamlet* "pointed out one single bond which linked together the apparently disconnected scenes and characters, one single thought to which every action and every figure may be traced." "It was to be expected that the example of Goethe's explanation of *Hamlet* would not be lost. What he did for the single piece it would soon be wished to see carried out for the whole. To make this attempt is my present task." Gervinus, in other words, will seek in each play, the leading idea, and the leading idea is, invariably, moral.

The success and the significance of this endeavor we shall examine shortly. First, let us abstract the ethic from the esthetic as does Gervinus himself at the end of his *Commentaries*. There he proposes that, "as the rarest judge of man and human affairs, [Shakespeare] is a teacher of indisputable authority, and the most worthy to be chosen as a guide through the world, and through life." As ethical teacher, Shakespeare "builds a system of morality upon nature and reason, a system independent of religious considerations," which may be comprised under the headings of activity, self-government, moderation, relativity.

Activity. "Man is born with powers of activity, which he is to use." "Nature only lends man his talents and gives them not." Hamlet, Richard II, Timon, and Antony waste themselves in inactivity; against them Shakespeare pits Fortinbras, Bolingbroke, Alcibiades, and Octavius: "in spite of their inferior talents, their energy in itself stands out above the inactivity of the others, no matter how beautiful the source out of which this passiveness flows, nor how base that from which this activity proceeds." "Heaven assists not the pious but indolent Richard II . . . but it helps indeed the pious Helena, who helps herself." Work is a blessing, not a curse; hence "the poet's feeling goes out against the tranquillity of the idyl," as when the sons of Cymbeline "question . . . whether repose is the best life." Shakespeare's "strong nature" delights in war:

> genuine ambition is no sin in Henry V, proud war directly makes "ambition, virtue"; the danger of resting in idleness makes war desirable in exchange for peace, whose wealth and peace induces "the imposthume that inward breaks," bringing evil and death to the age. Warlike valor is, therefore, extolled even in its exaggeration in Coriolanus, even in its criminality in Macbeth, even in its union with usurpation in John, still more when coupled with heroic calmness in Othello, with patriotic love in Faulconbridge, with that high idea of honor in Percy, with moderation and confidence in God in Henry V. Manly honor and valor are with Shakespeare one and the same idea.

Finally, "from this opinion of Shakespeare's as to man's vocation to active life springs his aversion" to systems of private or personal good instead of the common good. For Shakespeare "the common good" is "the only worthy aim of [man's] activity."

Self-government by reason and conscience. "Free self-determination is esteemed by [Shakespeare] as the most distinguishing gift of our race; mind and conscience are to be the rulers in the community of our inward being, who are to restrain the storms of passion." Shakespeare shows conscience even in such a monster as Richard III, even in such an aerial spirit as Ariel. And most particularly Shakespeare esteems "that purity of morals which has passed through struggles and temptations, not the virtue of habit but of principle, not instinctive but tested, the product of the reason and of volition." Arviragus and Guiderius must pass from the purity of ignorance to the purity of experience.

Moderation, the middle way.

> What indecision and a halfway course is Shakespeare has shown in York, what moderation and a middle-course is he has exhibited in Posthumus, who is strong even to the heroic control of his passionate and excited nature, and in Henry, in whom the middle-course is not mediocrity, but modesty in greatness.

Perhaps Shakespeare's endorsement of the middle way comes through most clearly from his explorations of excess:

> He showed in Hamlet how hesitating deliberation and fleeting sensibility mislead in action, in Coriolanus how the highest endowments by being overstrained degenerate into contrary ones, in Angelo how suppression of the senses, in Antony how suppression of the mind, avenges itself, in Romeo how excess of love is blighted, in Timon, how excess of hatred becomes powerless.

So committed is Shakespeare to the middle way that "he ventures even to oppose the Christian laws" of turning the other cheek, of going the second mile, for these "demand an overstraining of human nature." There can be, in other words, too much of a good thing. "Excessive liberality ruins Timon, whilst moderate liberality keeps Antonio in honor; the genuine ambition which makes Henry V great, overthrows Percy in whom it rises too high. Exaggerated virtue brings Angelo to ruin."

Relativity. As Friar Laurence reminds us, there is good in the basest things, vice in virtue.

> Virtue misemployed, as we have seen in Romeo, becomes vice, and vice is at times ennobled by the mode of action. . . .

Jessica innocently violate[s] childlike piety, and Desdemona truth; Isabel practices feigned sin, and Lorenzo pious deceptions without scruple; they depart from the straight line of virtue . . . because the acutest conscience and consciousness, the will to do right and to prevent wrong, directs their actions undoubtedly aright.

Pisanio's disloyalty to Posthumus in sparing Imogen's life is a case in point. "In Shakespeare's opinion . . . there is no positive law of religion or morals which could form the rule of moral action in precepts ever binding and suitable for all cases." The worth of actions depends on circumstance, on manner, on motive. "It is impossible to bring [morality] to final principles, and in the manifold collisions of duties, the balancing between man and man, between public and private duty, between case and case, is inevitable."

Faults are easy to find with Gervinus's summary. We may look askance at the high value bestowed on war or question whether Angelo's "exaggerated virtue" is not rather hypocrisy than an excess of a good thing. Is there not an undue literalness in suggesting that Desdemona "violates" truth in her last words, exonerating Othello? Is it as splendid as Gervinus makes it sound that Shakespeare opposes the Christian ideal? (And was it not in accord with the Christian ideal that Desdemona, dying, lied?) What does it mean to govern oneself by reason? Where does love fit into this ethic? Or patience? Where "the readiness is all"? We may question, too, the reasoning on which the system is founded. Does not Gervinus confuse material success in the plot—victory or life or wealth—with spiritual validation? If Gervinus can see all the endorsements of war and none, apparently, of the condemnations thereof—the horrible accounts of mangled bodies, ruptured families, orphaned children, and violated countryside, of England bleeding, France raped—on what principles of generalization has he operated to arrive at his system? Are we not, in fact, discovering in his system what he wanted to find rather than what a dispassionate and objective survey would reveal?

The faults are there, but Gervinus should be credited with a pioneering attempt to get acquainted with Shakespeare's mind, to survey his plays from end to end to discover their ethical constants, to match character against character, plot against plot, in pursuit of their author's ethical vision. Gervinus is not so much wrong, after all, as not sufficiently right. Shakespeare surely does believe in action for the common good, in rational self-government, in judicious moderation, and in the ethical force of circumstance. To be aware of so much is to read many of the plays with a quicker comprehension than many a beginner does. To discover the conflict between the actions of such fascinating villains as Richard III or Iago and the rule of reason is to apprehend something of Shakespeare's exciting ambivalence. To see that it is moot whether the elopements of Romeo and Othello, the rebellions of Bolingbroke and Hotspur, accord with or oppose reason is to become attuned to the moral and political dynamics of the plays. To discover that circumstances alter cases means to find *Hamlet* or *Antony and Cleopatra* kaleidoscopic in the changing play of their moral significances. To be sure Shakespeare believes in the marriage of true minds, in faith, patience, humility, and other qualities of which Gervinus takes inadequate account. Hubler, Stauffer, and Harbage have provided later, detailed definitions of Shakespeare's ethical vision,[6] Harbage's especially revealing how very much too simple Gervinus's is. But many a critic would have been the wiser had he read the plays with Gervinus's sense of Shakespeare's moral largeness. Shakespeare, he says, "is never Icarus with him for whom he forges the wings; he is never Phaëton with him to whom he lends the steed; but towards his unruly children he is ever Phoebus in love and Jupiter in punishment."

The ethical system we have been examining finds its source and its life in the individual plays. Its principles provide these with their leading ideas, so Gervinus believes, and it is in his demonstrating how a single ethical concern links together the apparently disconnected scenes and characters of a play that he most excitingly opens up Shakespeare to nineteenth-century wonder, delight, understanding. We can best understand his thinking by beginning with his view of the Shakespearean genres. Broadly speaking, when Shakespeare presents man at his best, "in pure, noble self-reliance, as in Henry Monmouth, Portia, or in Leonatus Posthumus," he presents him in *Schauspiele*, "dramas which have the serious turn of the tragedy and the cheerful conclusion of the comedy."

> When this self-reliance rises into egotism, ambition, and love of fame . . . tragedy appears, in which the poet, with wisely balanced admiration and caution, points out to us the greatness and the danger of this overweening nature. When, on the other hand, man's self-reliance sinks into self-love, vanity, and conceit . . . then comedy makes its appearance.

In tragedy, in short, egotism; in comedy, vanity; and in the *schauspiele* or drama, true self-reliance.

To narrow down now to individual plays:

> What we may call the leading idea, the pervading soul, in Shakespeare's plays is ever expressed plainly and simply in a single relation, in a single passion or form of character. The nature and property of love and jealousy, the soap-bubbles produced by the thirst for glory, and irresolution avoiding its task, these are the images and the ideas which Romeo and Othello, Love's Labour's Lost, and Hamlet present to us.

Gervinus develops his notion least excitingly with the histories, since he finds in both the great tetralogies a single question: "what relation the claims of the hereditary right of the incapable, however good, who endanger throne and country, bear to the claims of the merit of the capable, however bad, if they save and maintain the state." With the tragedies he is, I think, uneven, largely

from the lack of measure discussed earlier. But he invites us to
see that the Player King's speech in *Hamlet* bears on resolution
no less than Claudius's remarks to Laertes, that the king at prayer
no less than Hamlet eavesdropping fails to bring will and action
into line, that Laertes and Fortinbras are as foils to Hamlet, and,
in general, that

> the truth-loving, moral hero stands in the midst of those who
> wander on none but crooked ways in hypocrisy, dissimulation,
> and untruth; his sensible, conscientious, circumspect nature is
> opposed in strong contrast to the unprincipled conduct of all
> the others, to the heartless or thoughtless heedlessness of their
> actions and their consequences: the king and queen, Polonius
> and Ophelia, even all the subordinate figures (with the excep-
> tion of Horatio, who only observes and never acts), Fortin-
> bras, Rosencrantz, Guildenstern, and even Osric, all fall more
> or less under this aspect.

Gervinus's greatest success is with the comedies—and his
achievement, of course, is not so much the labeling the leading
idea as the showing how the parts relate to it. The leading idea of
Love's Labour's Lost, he states, is "a vain desire of fame in all its
forms." He begins by inviting us to see the "gross desire for glory"
in Don Armado and Holofernes, the braggart and the pedant
inherited from Italian comedy. These fantastics parody their
betters, and their betters *their* betters in a repetitive spiral of glory-
seeking.

> The king has chosen Armado to amuse them by his minstrelsy
> during their hermit-life; and similar to the contempt with
> which the king regards his boasting vein is the scorn with
> which Biron views the learned and ascetic vanity of the king;
> but he has himself fallen into a still lighter vanity, for which
> he incurs Rosaline's censure . . . She looks upon him as

abandoned to the same empty desire for unsubstantial applause, as he does upon those who are placed at his side.

The leading idea of *The Merchant of Venice* is man's relation to property, a relation which Gervinus apprehends as bearing on man's relation to man, "as it cannot be imagined apart from man." Gervinus develops his leading idea in respect to Antonio, Portia, Shylock, and Bassanio sanely and thoroughly, then branches out. His interpretation, he says,

> perfectly coincides with all the characters of the play, and even with the subordinate ones. The self-interested suitors of Portia, corrupted by glitter and show, choose amiss. The parasitical companions of Antonio forsake him with his fortune . . . Lorenzo and Jessica—an extravagant, giddy couple, free from restraint—squander their pilfered gold in Genoa . . . and reach Belmont like famished people . . . Launcelot also bears a relation to the common idea of the piece. Greedy and rough as he is, he also is inclined to lack economy.

These examples, all too brief, suggest the exfoliating awareness of Shakespeare's moral-esthetic as Gervinus awakens it. It is difficult in summary to convey the excitement he must have conveyed to many of his contemporaries, but I think that even now his analysis of *Much Ado* can open eyes, for he sees the folly of vanity activating character and plot most convincingly. The self-love of the youth Claudio, unstable, credulous, "is so fearfully excited even at the bare idea [of Hero's betrayal], that he forms the heartless, vindictive resolve" of shaming her at the altar. Hero's father, no less blind in his self-love, wishes Hero dead; and his brother, Antonio, "with the same unrestrained pride of family" bursts out in raging vindictiveness. Shakespeare explores the folly of this self-love in a prelude, the business of the masked ball; he enlarges and further explores it in the pair of merrier and more sophisticated lovers: "the same self-love and the same spoiling by

prosperity fall to the lot of these two characters as they did to
Claudio . . . But instead of his changeableness, we see in them
only what, with a fine distinction, we should (with Benedick) call
giddiness." All are tricked and betrayed by their vanity. All
overcome their vanity: Claudio in penance and the surrender of
himself to Leonato's wishes; Benedick and Beatrice in their commitment to Hero's cause. Even Dogberry, had Gervinus only cared
to look at him, casts a fine idiot luster on the leading idea.

❧ ❧ ❧

James Russell Lowell is the only American before the end of
the nineteenth century who requires place in this history. Before
him Emerson had lectured on Shakespeare, yet the lecture was
more on the man than the plays, more a panegyric than an
interpretation, more illustrative of its author's theory of "The
Poet" than critical of the poet's works.[7] Melville had discovered in
Shakespeare the gentleness of a Jesus, the power, too, of seeing
and saying the things "which we feel to be so terrifically true, that
it were all but madness for any good man, in his own proper
character, to utter, or even hint of them."[8] Melville's direct
criticism, however, scarcely extends beyond this; the rest lies in the
Shakespearean spirit and form of his narrative work: the vision of
Ahab, the soliloquies of the mates, the mystery of the Parsee and
the Whale, the structure of Billy Budd. Later, Sidney Lanier was
gracefully to suggest a Dowdenian scheme of Shakespeare's moral
growth, dividing it into a "Dream Period" (exemplified by A
Midsummer Night's Dream where Man is subject to Chance and
slave to Nature), a "Real Period" (where Man—Hamlet—
struggles with Fate and inquires into Nature), and finally, an
"Ideal Period" (when Man—Prospero—is superior to Chance and
Nature, is, in fact, "master of the universe").[9] Lanier's scheme
foreshadows Knight's, but unfortunately it lacks development and,
as far as I am aware, consequence. Nothing followed from it.

Lowell is an American Matthew Arnold, a scholar-gentleman,

urbane and learned, who wears his learning lightly, but so that we see it and admire the familiar citations from Greek drama, Dante, Goethe, Montaigne, each in its native tongue. He speaks to us wittily, conversationally, with a fine feeling for the best that has been thought and said in the world. His bent is classical, the Greeks providing to his mind standards that have become extra-temporal or absolute, but he is without bias. He sees Sophoclean simplicity of expression as only one of several modes of achieving tragic ends; the classicism he values is that of form, of imaginative unity, and of pleasure: "to be delightful is to be classic, and the chaotic never pleases long."

In the edition I have before me, his "Shakespeare Once More" (1868) elegantly rambles for some seventy-five pages, touching on such a multitude of topics that minute summary is difficult. From sufficient distance, however, we can see three large blocs to the essay: (1) Shakespeare's language, (2) his imaginative unity, (3) Hamlet. Lowell's Tainean thesis in the first part is that Shakespeare "arrived at the full development of his powers at the moment when the material in which he was to work—the wonderful composite called English . . . —was in its freshest perfection." Eighteenth-century critics, we recall, attributed Shakespeare's barbarism to his age: he was the wild genius of a nation emerging from savagery. Schlegel and Goethe had reversed the arguments. As Goethe said, "it is to his own country that [Shakespeare] owes his riches. For back of him is England . . . whose enterprise reaches all the parts of the earth. The poet lives at a noble and important epoch . . ." Lowell develops this perspective in relation to Shakespeare's language. Its perfection derives, first, from its vitality. It is still alive, not yet literary; its words were "ready to his use, original and untarnished—types of thought whose sharp edges were unworn by repeated impressions." This language, moreover, was rich, having

> *recruited itself, by fresh impressments from the Latin and Latinized languages, with new words to express the new ideas*

of an enlarging intelligence . . . words which, in proportion
to their novelty, and to the fact that the mother-tongue and
the foreign had not yet wholly mingled, must have been used
with a more exact appreciation of their meaning.

As Puttenham testifies,[10] this language, when Shakespeare comes
to London to use it, has already become the country's standard;
and as the comparative uniformity of usage by the popular dramatists shows, it was "already to a certain extent *established*, but
not yet fetlocked by dictionary and grammar mongers." Moreover,

no arbitrary line had been drawn between high words and
low . . . The hot conception of the poet had no time to cool
while he was debating the comparative respectability of this
phrase or that; but he snatched what word his instinct
prompted, and saw no indiscretion in making a king speak as
his country nurse might have taught him.

Shakespeare, says Lowell, "needed not to mask familiar thoughts
in the weeds of unfamiliar phraseology; for the life that was in his
mind could transfuse the language of every day with an intelligent
vivacity, that makes it seem lambent with fiery purpose, and at
each new reading a new creation." None of this, of course, is to
deny to Shakespeare himself the power of choice, of selecting,
within the capacious limits of this living language, the right terms
and the right order to express his thoughts; and Lowell conceives
of Shakespeare as conscious of his language and of its provin-
cialism no less than was Bacon:

but he knew that great poetry, being universal in its appeal to
human nature, can make any language classic . . . He had as
much confidence in his homebred speech as Bacon had want
of it, and exclaims:—

Not marble nor the gilded monuments
Of princes shall outlive this powerful rhyme.

In this discussion of Shakespeare's debt to his language,
Lowell cites no single line by way of illustration. He stops at the
generalities. The effect, then, is importantly to strengthen our
sense that Shakespeare must be understood by reference to his
historical context, but to leave the understanding itself pretty
much where it was. To strengthen that, we await the slow
digestion by criticism of the fruits of scholarship. It takes a long
time.

The essay's second section is filled with fine things yet has
about it an old-fashioned air, as though Lowell were not aware
that certain of the critical battles were over. Or perhaps it is just
that in the Victorian era the American provinces are still a decade
or two behind the continental capitals. At any rate, Lowell develops the Coleridgian distinction between primary and secondary
imagination, the one concerned with form, the other with expression, and finds, as did Coleridge, that Shakespeare is superb in
each. (At the essay's very end, when Lowell is accumulating his
perorational superlatives, he renders a final tribute to Coleridge by
saying that, wonderful as were Shakespeare's imagination and
fancy, yet more wonderful were his perspicacity and artistic discre-
tion, and "what makes him yet more exceptional was his utterly
unimpeachable judgment . . .") Lowell discusses again Shakespeare's learning ("he had as much as he wanted"); he defends
Shakespeare's word-play (by appeal to psychology, Greek example,
Shakespeare's age); he recites and develops Goethe's *sollen-willen*
distinction; and as did Schlegel and Coleridge fifty years before, he
ridicules the notion that Shakespeare was "an inspired idiot . . .
a vast, irregular genius." The topics are old, and though Lowell
speaks well on each, his own contributions are few. There is a nice
demonstration of the force of Shakespeare's secondary imagination
—his power to see everything through the peculiar mood of his

characters and make "every epithet, as if unconsciously, echo and reecho it"—as in this instance:

> The raven himself is hoarse
> That croaks the fatal entrance of Duncan
> Under my battlements.

> Lady Macbeth hears not so much the voice of the bodeful bird as of her own premeditated murder, and we are thus made her shuddering accomplices before the fact. Every image receives the color of the mind, every word throbs with the pulse of one controlling passion. The epithet fatal makes us feel the implacable resolve of the speaker, and shows us that she is tampering with her conscience by putting off the crime upon the prophecy of the Weird Sisters to which she alludes. In the word battlements, too, not only is the fancy led up to the perch of the raven, but a hostile image takes the place of a hospitable; for men commonly speak of receiving a guest under their roof or within their doors.

Further, Lowell effectively communicates his sense of the immanence and interiority of Shakespeare's imagination in his work. "One always fancies Shakespeare in his best verses, and Milton at the key-board of his organ. Shakespeare's language is no longer the mere vehicle of thought, it has become part of it, its very flesh and blood." Again, "with Shakespeare the plot is an interior organism, in Jonson an external contrivance. It is the difference between man and tortoise." And yet again:

> generally it may be said that with the Greeks the character is involved in the action, while with Shakespeare the action is evolved from the character. In the one case, the motive of the play controls the personages; in the other, the chief personages are in themselves the motive to which all else is subsidiary.

One portion of this section, however, merits attention because it does early what many and many a critic has done since. It reads

The Tempest allegorically and as illustrative of how allegory may effectively be written—

> *suggesting an undermeaning everywhere, forcing it upon us nowhere, tantalizing the mind with hints that imply so much and tell so little, and yet keep the attention all eye and ear with eager, if fruitless, expectation.* Here the leading characters are not merely typical, but symbolical—that is, they do not illustrate a class of persons, they belong to universal Nature.

The setting, Lowell, proposes, is nowhere—and everywhere— hence, "in the soul of man, that still vexed island hung between the upper and the nether world, and liable to incursions from both." Prospero becomes Imagination and Reason, Ariel the Fancy, Caliban the Understanding, Miranda "mere abstract Womanhood," Ferdinand "nothing more than Youth." "The subordinate personages are simply types." And Lowell goes on to what now seems an inevitable question: "in Prospero shall we not recognize the Artist himself"?

It is in the final section of his essay that Lowell demonstrates in a sustained endeavor his fullest critical power. His topic is Hamlet; his goal to find the heart of Hamlet, and thereby, to find the heart of the play, for in his judgment, as we have seen, Shakespeare's "action is evolved from the character" and "the chief personages are in themselves the motive to which all else is subsidiary."[11] He begins by considering two objections: against the play's anachronisms and against the low comedy of the graveyard scene. His reply to the first is to distinguish between psychological and historical truth and to argue that Shakespeare achieves psychological truth. He conveys both the rudeness of manners of an ancient past (the combat between Hamlet's father and Fortinbras, the king's wassail, the assumption that by way of royal favor England will hang Rosencrantz and Guildenstern out of hand, the notion that revenge is a religious duty) and the sophistications of a later time (Hamlet's attendance at Wittenberg, the Montaignean skepticism, the religious doubts). Shakespeare has set his play not in the barbaric antiquity of the legend, but in a "period of transition" of his own making,

> a period in which the times are always out of joint, and thus the irresolution which has its root in Hamlet's own character is stimulated by the very incompatability of that legacy of vengeance he has inherited from the past with the new culture and refinement of which he is the representative.

As to the graveyard scene, Lowell regards it as providing relief and, more importantly, as preparing by contrast for what follows. He finds

> the springs of the profoundest sorrow and pity in this hardened indifference of the grave-diggers, in their careless discussion as to whether Ophelia's death was by suicide or no, in their singing and jesting at their dreary work . . . All we remember of Ophelia reacts upon us with tenfold force, and we recoil from our amusement at the ghastly drollery of the two delvers with a shock of horror.

This combines with fascinated expectation as Hamlet stumbles "on *this* grave of all others" and "*here* . . . muse[s] humorously on death and decay."

Space prohibits any but the briefest summary of Lowell's subtle analysis of Hamlet's character. He sees it as expressing a kind of "genealogical necessity," " the resolution and persistence" of the father, "like sound timber wormholed and made shaky . . . by the [mother's] infirmity of will and discontinuity of purpose." Hamlet's mind is conscious of its own defect—of forever analyzing its own emotions and motives, of being unable to do anything because it always sees two ways to do it, of the imagination's being "so much in overplus, that thinking a thing becomes better than doing it." Hamlet

> dwells so exclusively in the world of ideas that the world of facts seems trifling, nothing is worth the while . . . He is the victim not so much of feebleness of will as of an intellectual indifference that hinders the will from working long in any one direction. He wishes to will, but never wills.

Hamlet is capable of passionate energy, not of deliberate energy— and his inadequacy is accentuated both by Laertes and by Horatio, who "is the only complete *man* in the play." Hamlet and Horatio achieve "a happy marriage of true minds drawn together by the charm of unlikeness"; "Hamlet fills the place of a woman to Horatio . . ."

To these assertions, Lowell adds others, each nicely developed —as that Hamlet is "an ingrained skeptic."

> His is the skepticism, not of reason, but of feeling, whose root is want of faith in himself. In him it is passive, a malady rather than a function of the mind. We might call him insincere: not that he was in any sense a hypocrite, but only that he never was and never could be in earnest.

> Hamlet doubts everything. He doubts the immortality of the soul, just after seeing his father's spirit, and hearing from its mouth the secrets of the other world. He doubts Horatio even, and swears him to secrecy on the cross of his sword, though probably he himself has no assured belief in the sacredness of the symbol. He doubts Ophelia, and asks her, "Are you honest?" He doubts the ghost, after he has had a little time to think about it, and so gets up the play to test the guilt of the king.

Further, Lowell sees Hamlet as perpetually inclined to irony: "the half-jest, half-earnest of an inactive temperament that has not quite made up its mind whether life is a reality or no." And "Hamlet *drifts* through the whole tragedy." To Goethe's conception of the vase shattered by the growing oak, Lowell replies that it would be adequate if Hamlet had

> actually killed himself to escape his too onerous commission . . . But Hamlet was hardly a sentimentalist, like Werther . . . It would appear rather that Shakespeare intended to show us an imaginative temperament brought face to face with actualities, into any clear relation of sympathy with which it cannot bring itself.

Lowell's analysis relates to Johnson's (in its suggestion of Hamlet's drifting), to Coleridge's, Schlegel's, Goethe's, Gervinus's, and presumably to many others; yet it is clearly his own, richly grounded in his own reading of the text, subtly informed by his own sensitivity to the philosophical, psychological, moral, and esthetic questions of the play. Its deepest critical roots are in Schlegel; it flowers in Santayana's interpretation of Hamlet and then, mordantly, in L. C. Knights's analysis.[12] One wishes there were more criticism of this sort, less of the older-fashioned and more general, in his essay.

Edward Dowden / 1843–1913
Algernon Charles Swinburne / 1837–1909
Walter Pater / 1839–1894

The labeled periods of Dowden's Primer as deriving from his Shakspere: A Critical Study of His Mind and Art, *their ultimate source in reactions to such critics as Smiles and Taine. Comments trenchant and sentimental. Shakespeare's unity. Shakespeare's objectivity and Dowden's didacticism. Dowden's excessive simplicity.* 🌿 *Critical mots from Swinburne. His inquiry into Shakespeare's artistic development: the conflict between rhyme and blank verse.* 🌿 *Pater as revealing what and how to appreciate. His elegiac tone, "esthetic" perspective, feeling for unity. Pater compared to Gervinus.*

Most of Dowden's *Shakspere Primer* (1877) has long since gone the way of other handbooks, but two and one-half of its 163 pages echo still. It is doubtful that any other exposition so brief has so plagued the history of Shakespearean criticism. The pages in question set forth an unoriginal division of Shakespeare's plays into four periods;[1] briefly they gloss each period as a forward step in Shakespeare's spiritual biography, and most importantly, they tag each period with a title which, like a political slogan, combines a maximum of suggestion with a minimum of assertion. The titles are these: "In the workshop," "In the world," "Out of the depths," and "On the heights."

Since Gorky's play, the pattern of biography Dowden attributes to Shakespeare is liable to misunderstanding. Dowden suggests no falling off of spiritual health, no surrender to riot or despair, no collapse into spiritual doldrums. The life he constructs builds steadily upward—thus:

> In the workshop. Shakespeare was learning his trade as a dramatic craftsman . . . The works of Shakespeare's youth—experiments in various directions—are all marked by the presence of vivacity, cleverness, delight in beauty, and a quick enjoyment of existence.
>
> In the world. As yet, however, he wrote with small experience of human life . . . But now Shakespeare's imagination began to lay hold of real life . . . his plays begin to deal in an original and powerful way with the matter of history . . . During this period Shakespeare's work grows strong and robust.
>
> Out of the depths. Before [the second period] closed Shakespeare had known sorrow . . . the poet now ceased to care for tales of mirth and love, for the stir and movement of history, for the pomp of war; he needed to sound, with his imagination, the depths of the human heart; to inquire into the darkest and saddest parts of human life; to study the great mystery of evil. The belief in human virtue, indeed, never deserts him: in Lear there is a Cordelia . . . Still, during this period, Shakespeare's genius left the bright surface of the world, and was at work in the very heart and center of things.
>
> On the heights. The tragic gloom and suffering were not, however, to last forever. The dark cloud lightens and rolls away, and the sky appears purer and tenderer than ever. The impression left upon the reader . . . is that, whatever his trials and sorrows and errors may have been, he had come forth from them wise, large-hearted, calm-souled. He seems to have learned the secret of life, and while taking his share in it, to be yet disengaged from it; he looks down upon life, its joys,

*its griefs, its errors, with a grave tenderness, which is almost
pity. The spirit of these last plays is that of serenity which
results from fortitude, and the recognition of human frailty
. . . In these "Romances" . . . a supernatural element is
present . . . Shakespeare's faith seems to have been that
there is something without and around our human lives, of
which we know little, yet which we know to be beneficent
and divine.*

Dowden offers, it seems, a Horatio Alger version of Shakespeare's life. We need hardly wonder at its success: it jibes neatly
with the sentimental predilections of the Victorian era—and of
the eras since; in an embarrassing way it fits the plays—though
loosely; and it has about it a well-made if superficial neatness. But
how did it come into being? And what has it to do with Dowden's
Shakespearean criticism as a whole?

I think we should see the four titled periods of the *Primer* as a
corruption, sentimental or cynical, of something Dowden had
been importantly working on in his *Shakspere: A Critical Study of
His Mind and Art* (1875). There Dowden set himself "to connect
the study of Shakespeare's works with an inquiry after the personality of the writer, and to observe, as far as is possible, in its several
stages, the growth of his intellect and character from youth to full
maturity." The language is precise. The book alternates between a
"study of Shakespeare's works" and "an inquiry after the personality of the writer," and while the one reflects on the other—while
the merits of the "study" presumably contribute to the success of
the "inquiry"—for analysis' sake, we may easily separate them.

Dowden's inquiry is the first major effort by a major critic and
scholar to discover the life of Shakespeare's mind in his works. It is
tentative—in fact, but not in style—and pragmatic. As far as I can
see, no single hypothesis embraces all of Dowden's remarks. He
explores different patterns without trying to resolve them into a
single, larger unity. In an early chapter, it seems clear that he
thinks of Shakespeare's life as having three stages—early, middle,

late—while in a later he states unequivocally that "in Shake-speare's life as artist we may distinguish four periods"—the early period of the book's beginning having been divided in two. He limits his focus in one place to Shakespeare's female characters, in another to Shakespeare's humor, and elsewhere, to the plays' presentation of success, material and spiritual. Discussing the early plays he makes inferences about Shakespeare's mind from observations about his art; but he pays scant attention to the art of the later plays. The inquiry is, then, tentative, inconsistent, and ultimately, not unified. But it is pioneering. It opens new territories to the understanding as it proceeds from the content of the plays to their causes in Shakespeare's evolving psyche.

Provocatively Dowden observes that "the changes of type which took place in the prominent female characters of Shake-speare's plays . . . would form an interesting subject for detailed study." He categorizes the females of the early comedies, the histories, the "most joyous comedies," and so on, inviting us to see that in different periods different types or pairs of types tend to dominate. And at one point he proceeds to a highly tentative explanation. He is speaking of the heroines "distinguished by some single element of peculiar strength—Helena, Isabella, Portia of *Julius Caesar*"—and observes,

> Over against these are studies of feminine incapacity or ignobleness—Ophelia, Gertrude, Cressida. It is as if Shake-speare at this time needed some one strong, outstanding excellence to grasp and steady himself by, and had lost his delight in the even harmony of character which suits us, and brings us joy when we make no single, urgent, and peculiar demand for help.

More discursively, Dowden projects a history of Shakespeare's laughter in the conviction that "if the history were faithfully made out, a good deal would necessarily be ascertained respecting the development of his whole moral nature." Here appear the four lamentable periods, but not here the slick labels or the facile generalizations. Dowden focuses on Shakespeare's evolving employment of the comic in his work. In the tentative period

> the comic and the serious, tender or sentimental, elements of the drama exist side by side, and serve as a kind of criticism each upon the other; the lover serves to convict the clown of insensibility to the higher facts of life, and the clown convicts the lover of the blindness or extravagance of passion.

The Two Gentlemen of Verona provides the illustration. Then Dowden comes to *A Midsummer Night's Dream* where

> Shakespeare's humor has enriched itself by coalescing with the fancy. The comic is here no longer purely comic; it is a mingled web, shot through with the beautiful. Bottom and Titania meet . . . an undesigned symbol of the fact that the poet's faculties . . . were now approaching one another.

Dowden pursues this notion of separate faculties coming together in his treatment of the histories.

> At first, impressed, perhaps, by a sense of the dignity of the historical drama, Shakespeare held his humor aloof. In Richard II there is no humorous scene. Had Shakespeare written the play a few years later, we may be certain that the gardener and servants . . . would not have uttered stately speeches in verse, but would have spoken homely prose, and that humor would have mingled with the pathos of this scene.

And in the two parts of *Henry IV,* Dowden sees the comic joining the serious in the corpulent wittiness of Fat Jack Falstaff attending Prince Hal. In the third period, says Dowden, Shakespeare's laughter is tragic and terrible as well as pathetic. No longer is the mirth unalloyed.

> In Hamlet, the humorous figures of the court are all a little
> contemptible and odious . . . The grave-diggers have a grim
> grotesqueness and might almost appear as figures in the
> danses macabres of the Middle Ages; each a humorous jester
> in the court of Death; hail-fellow-well-met with chap-fallen
> skulls.

Dowden approvingly echoes DeQuincey on the hell-gate humor in
Macbeth,[2] and comes to Lear as the play in which

> the interpenetration of the humorous, the pathetic, and the
> tragic has become complete . . . It is as if the writer were
> looking down at human life from a point of view without and
> above life, from which the whole appears as some monstrous
> farce-tragedy, in which all that is terrible is ludicrous, and all
> that is ludicrous terrible.

(Dowden sows a seed here variously tended in later years by
Wilson Knight, Bickersteth, and Kott.[3]) In the plays of this
period, the comic incident, when it occurs, will be "a fragment of
titanic burlesque, overhung by some impending horror, and inspired by a deep 'idea of world-destruction,' " as in the Egyptian
bacchanal on Pompey's yacht; and satire "will now be the deep or
fierce complaint against the world of a soul in its agony—the
frenzied accusations of nature and of man uttered by Lear, or the
Juvenalian satire of the Athenian misanthrope." Then, the final
period, Autolycus and Hermione in the same play:

> From its elevation and calm Shakespeare's heart can pass into
> the simple merriment of rustic festivity; he can enjoy the
> open-mouthed happiness of country clowns; he is delighted by
> the gay defiance of order and honesty which Autolycus . . .
> professes; he is touched and exquisitely thrilled by the pure
> and vivid joy of Perdita among her flowers . . . when he is
> most grave . . . he can smile most brightly, most tenderly.

What prompts Dowden to his inquiry into Shakespeare's personality? T. J. B. Spencer suggests that the brilliant and sensitive young scholar is reacting against a Victorian image of Shakespeare painted, among others, by Samuel Smiles—"Shakespeare as a keen young man of humble rank who got on; one who graduated in the university of life," and went on to prosper " 'in his business and realized sufficient to enable him to retire upon a competency to his native town.' "[4] Dowden's goal, says Spencer, is "to show that Shakespeare had a soul." This is happily said. But Dowden reacts not only against the "cheerful, self-possessed, and prudent man, who . . . wrote plays, about which he did not greatly care [and] acquired property, about which he cared much." He reacts too against Taine's picture of Shakespeare as a "man of almost superhuman passions, extreme in joy and pain, impetuous in his transports, disorderly in his conduct, heedless of conscience, but sensitive to every touch of pleasure—a man of inordinate, extravagant genius."[5] This Shakespeare manifestly has a soul but no sense. Dowden's goal is to show that Shakespeare has sense. Or, to put it in terms suitable to the Victorian scientism which clearly influences Dowden, Shakespeare shares with Bacon and Hooker, *"a rich feeling for positive, concrete fact"* (Dowden's italics).

This double concern, to endow Shakespeare with both sanity and a soul, produces the following vision, which is as close to an inclusive one as Dowden offers:

> Shakespeare lived and moved in two worlds—one limited, practical, positive; the other a world opening into two infinites, an infinite of thought and an infinite of passion. He did not suppress either life to the advantage of the other; but he adjusted them, and by stern and persistent resolution held them in the necessary adjustment. In the year 1602 Shakespeare bought for the sum of three hundred and twenty pounds one hundred and seven acres of arable land in the parish of Old Stratford. It was in the same year . . . that

Shakespeare, in the person of his Hamlet, musing on a skull, was tracing out the relations of a buyer of land to the soil in a somewhat singular fashion. "This fellow might be in 's time a great buyer of land, with his statutes, his recognizances, his fines, his double vouchers, his recoveries; is this the fine of his fines, and the recovery of his recoveries, to have his fine pate full of fine dirt?" The courtier Osric, who has "much land and fertile," is described by the Prince (who could be contented in a nutshell, but that he has bad dreams) as "spacious in the possession of dirt." Yet this dirt Shakespeare used to serve his needs.

How shall a man live sanely in presence of the small daily facts of life . . . and in presence of the vast mystery of death? How shall he proportion his interests between the bright illuminated spot of the known and the dim environing unknown which possesses such strong attraction for the soul? How shall he restrain and attach his desires to the little objects which claim each its definite share of the heart, while the heart longs to abandon itself to some one thing with measureless devotion? Shakespeare's attainment of sanity and self-control was not that of a day or of a year, it was the attainment of his life. Now he was tempted by his speculative intellect and imagination to lose all clear perception of his limited and finite life; and again he was tempted to resign the conduct of his being by the promptings of a passionate heart. He is inexorable in his plays to all rebels against the fact; because he was conscious of the strongest temptation to become himself a rebel. He cannot forgive an idealist, because in spite of his practical and positive nature he was (let the Sonnets witness) an idealist himself. His series of dramatic writings is one long study of self-control.

The thesis is moot (and such a crucial term as "fact" vague), but it provides Dowden with a way of accounting for the intensities of a Romeo or a Hamlet, for they embody tendencies within

Shakespeare's self. It provides an explanation for the rejection of Falstaff, for Falstaff denies the world of fact, which Hal, like Shakespeare, himself accepts. It accounts for the vehement out-cries of an Othello or a Lear, since Shakespeare too has stood at the moral frontiers, peering into the darkness, struggling for possession of his soul. The thesis interprets the enlarging moral, political, and spiritual horizon of Shakespeare's plays as reflecting his expanding engagement with the world. There is the young man's fanciful experimentation (the early comedies), the inescap-able concern with practical success (the histories), the mature man's concern with spiritual success (the tragedies), his commit-ment to the problem of good and evil with all of his powers at the full and in harmony. The thesis is moot but it gives to the bourgeois Shakespeare a soul and to the emotional extremist sense. It provides a springboard for biographical critics of the decades ahead—Sidney Lanier, Frank Harris, Lytton Strachey, Ernest Jones, Middleton Murry, Caroline Spurgeon, Wyndham Lewis, D. A. Traversi[6]—and, in the devastating success of its corruption in the *Primer,* a warning.

Dowden's study of Shakespeare's works contains an extraor-dinary amount of sharp and trenchant comment. Of *Hamlet* Dowden says, "Shakespeare created it a mystery, and therefore it is forever suggestive; forever suggestive, and never wholly explicable." Of *Richard III*, he observes that

> mere verisimilitude . . . becomes, at times, subordinate to effects of symphonic orchestration or of statuesque composi-tion. There is a Blake-like terror and beauty in the scene in which the three women—queens and a duchess—seat them-selves upon the ground in their desolation and despair and cry aloud in utter anguish of spirit.

> The central characteristic of Richard is not self-seeking or ambition. It is the necessity of releasing and letting loose upon the world the force within him . . . the necessity of

> deploying before himself and others the terrible resources of his will.

Dowden complains of "a certain incontinence of devout feeling" in Henry VI and writes feelingly of Brutus as "the political Girondin": "Had he lived, he would have written an Apology for his life, educing evidence, with a calm superiority, to prove that each act of his life proceeded from an honorable motive." He says that "the fascination exercised by Cleopatra over Antony, and hardly less by Antony over Cleopatra, is not so much that of the senses as of the sensuous imagination." And of Cleopatra: "in her complex nature, beneath each fold or layer of sincerity lies one of insincerity, and we cannot tell which is the last and innermost." "We feel throughout the play" of King Lear, says Dowden, "that evil is abnormal; a curse which brings down destruction upon itself; that it is without any long career; that evil-doer is at variance with evil-doer." And again,

> It is worthy of note that each of the principal personages of the play is brought into presence of those mysterious powers which dominate life and preside over human destiny; and each, according to his character, is made to offer an interpretation of the great riddle. Of these interpretations, none is adequate to account for all the facts.

These are fine comments, the last two of such excellence that Bradley echoes them. Accuracy requires admission, though, that some of Dowden's other observations are extravagantly impressionist or sentimental. "The death of Mercutio," he says, "is like the removal of a shifting breadth of sunlight, which sparkles on the sea; now the clouds close in upon one another, and the stress of the gale begins." Ophelia is "Laertes' little sister": Macbeth "stands a haggard shadow against the hand's-breadth of pale sky which yields us sufficient light to see him." In the balcony scene, Romeo "has overheard the voice of Juliet, and he cannot answer her call until he has drained the sweetness of the sound." Further illustration would be thankless.

Dowden posits unity no less firmly than do those critics who provoke his grumble: "It is somewhat hard upon Shakespeare to suppose that he secreted in each of his dramas a central idea for a German critic to discover." The unity he apprehends is mechanical at first, organic thereafter. He draws attention (following Gervinus) to the arrangement of the *dramatis personae* in *The Two Gentlemen of Verona,* where "Proteus, the fickle, is set over against Valentine, the faithful; Sylvia, the bright and intellectual, is set over against Julia, the ardent and tender; Launce, the humorist, is set over against Speed, the wit." So it was in *Love's Labour's Lost.*

> *He cannot yet feel that his structure is secure without a system of mechanism to support the structure. He endeavors to attain unity of effect less by the inspiration of a common life than by the disposition of parts. He finds he can bring forward his forces in turn, one after another, more readily when they are numbered and marshalled in definite order . . . In the plays which belong to Shakespeare's period of mastership he can dispense with such artifice. In these later plays unity is present through the virtue of one living force which animates the whole. The unity is not merely structural, but vital. And therefore the poet has no apprehension that the minor centers of development in his creation will suddenly become insubordinate. Assured that the organism is living, he fearlessly lets it develop itself in its proper mode, unicentral (as Macbeth), or multicentral (as King Lear). In the early plays structure determines function; in the later plays organization is preceded by life.*

Coleridge would have approved.

One wishes, though, that Dowden would demonstrate the point about the later plays. Instead, he assumes it. He denominates the kind of tragedy *Othello* is, say ("the tragedy of a free and lordly creature taken in the toils, and writhing to death"), or *Macbeth* ("the tragedy of the twilight and the setting-in of thick darkness upon a human soul"); and then proceeds in what is essentially a running commentary to deal with the protagonist's experience. The effect communicated is that of unity, but the effect is somewhat vague.

One final, positive virtue in Dowden's work is its insistent explicit disclaimer of didactic intent in Shakespeare. Dowden here conflicts with Gervinus, but is at one with Lowell, who regarded it "doubtful if Shakespeare had any conscious moral intention in his writings." Dowden argues that the Elizabethan drama generally is "without an ethical tendency," but along lines that Johnson would approve he says that it "produces an ethical effect. A faithful presentation of the facts of the world does not leave us indifferent to good and evil, but rather rouses within us, more than all maxims and all preaching can, an inextinguishable loyalty to good." So he can say of *King Lear* that "though ethical principles radiate through the play . . . its chief function is not, even indirectly, to teach or inculcate moral truth, but rather, by direct presentation of a vision of human life and of the enveloping forces of nature, to 'free, arouse, dilate.' "

Yet once again, accuracy requires recognition of another side. Dowden's large reading of the plays as studies of the material and spiritual success that comes with self-control gives them, individually and collectively, a clear ethical tendency. His own insistence on "fact," on Shakespeare's condemning those who neglect "fact"—Hamlet, Falstaff, Romeo—makes his readings moralistic. When he tells us that "Shakespeare would have us understand," from Iago's callousness, that there is "something more inimical to humanity than suffering—namely, an incapacity for noble pain"; or when he remarks of Kent that "Shakespeare would have us know that there is not any devotion to truth, to justice, to charity, more intense and real than that of the man who is faithful to them out of the sheer spirit of loyalty, unstimulated and unsupported by any faith which can be called theological," we know that we are once again in the presence of the didactic. He may say that Shakespeare is artist, not moralist; but he is himself so much the moralist that he imputes his own ethical weighting to the plays and, ultimately, to Shakespeare himself.

As a critic Dowden is both divided and flawed. By "divided" I mean that he seems unable to integrate or harmonize the different awarenesses he brings to Shakespeare. His inquiry into the personality and his study of the work exist side by side but scarcely interpenetrate. He sees Shakespeare's concern with success as providing the plays with unity, and he sees that Shakespeare's comic vision also provides unity; but he never brings these two awarenesses together. He has a feeling for organic unity, a feeling for character and plot, but the feelings stay apart. By "flawed" I mean not that Dowden is human like the rest of us, but that he has weaknesses of sufficient magnitude to draw unfavorable attention to themselves. Sentimentality is one, a faintly Rotarian high seriousness another, but perhaps "excessive simplicity" will serve as an inclusive term. Morally, psychologically, philosophically, Dowden, for all his addiction to the "logic of facts," sees too little of what there is to be seen. The ideas he discusses have few sides, the personalities few wrinkles, the world few alternatives.

Dowden's critical standing today is low because the influential pages of his *Primer* oversimplify the biographical approach and express their findings in an unctuously bathetic style. But it is something to have pioneered in biographical criticism. It is an achievement to have mastered enough different approaches to be divided between them. And to have important flaws can only happen to a critic who has, as I hope these pages have intimated, important virtues. Dowden deserves to be rated higher than he is.

❦ ❦ ❦

"Swinburne was a prolific writer on Shakespeare, but he dealt so lavishly in superlatives, and his inflated style is so unpalatable today, that he is sometimes regarded as more of a hagiographer than a critic. He does at least convey to the reader a sense of excitement."[7] This dourly generous comment by Kenneth Muir seems reasonably sane, though the excitement may be less about Shakespeare than about Swinburne. Can he keep heaping superlative on superlative like Pelion on Ossa? Can he keep on saying so very little and making it sonorously sound like so very, very much? Swinburne is a genius, to be sure, sailing mellifluously above the toil and muck of ordinary, mortal criticism. He is a prima donna, too, a bit of a charlatan, and every now and then he seems more of a hack writer than anything else, paid by the word or the column inch and anxiously totting up the paragraphs to see if the morning's take is enough. Very possibly he does not belong in this book—certainly he will find no place in the shorter histories of Shakespearean criticism written a century hence—but he commanded attention in his day; he contributed the general preface to the three volume *Oxford Shakespeare* for which Dowden provided the individual introductions; in the haystack of his superlatives there are some sharp critical needles; and he advances, though all too briefly, an inquiry into the development of Shakespeare's poetic art that simultaneously pays tribute to and rebukes Dowden's inquiry.

Among the sharp criticisms are such as these. "Harry Percy is as it were the true Sir Bedivere, the last of all Arthurian knights; Henry V is the first as certainly as he is the noblest of those equally daring and calculating statesmen-warriors whose two most terrible, most perfect, and most famous types are Louis XI and Caesar Borgia." To Johnson's remarks that he "could not reconcile his heart to Bertram," Swinburne adds his: "I . . . cannot reconcile my instincts to Helena." "For absolute power of composition, for faultless balance and blameless rectitude of design," he asserts, "there is unquestionably no creation of [Shakespeare's] hand that will bear comparison with *Much Ado About Nothing.*" Swinburne draws a sharp contrast between "the straightforward agents of their own destiny whom we meet in the first [quarto of] *Hamlet* and the obliquely moving patients who veer sideways to their doom in the second." "Hamlet himself," he says, "is almost more of a satirist than a philosopher." The central problem of his inner nature is neither irresolution nor skepticism, "but rather the strong conflux of conflicting forces." In *Lear* we look "from the roots that no God waters to the stars which give no man light; over a world full of death and life without resting-place or guidance." Cordelia is "the brotherless Antigone of our stage." Iago has "the instinct of . . . an inarticulate poet . . . He has within him a sense . . . of power incomparable . . . He is almost as far above or beyond vice as he is beneath or beyond virtue." "Othello has the passion of a poet closed in as it were and shut up behind the passion of a hero." *Coriolanus* is "rather a private and domestic than a public or historical tragedy . . . The subject of the whole play is not the exile's revolt, the rebel's repentance, or the traitor's reward, but above all it is the son's tragedy. The inscription on the plinth of this tragic statue is simply to Volumnia Victrix." "The hysterics of the eponymous hero and the harlotries of the eponymous heroine [of *Troilus and Cressida*] remove both alike beyond the outer pale of all rational and manly sympathy."

Swinburne's inquiry into the development of Shakespeare's art divides into periods; and though he defines three principal periods to Dowden's four, since he subdivides his third period into two, the first part containing the tragedies, the second, the romances, his division is essentially Dowden's. His titles are not. Dowden's titles imply something about the artist; Swinburne's speak only of the art: "First Period: Lyric and Fantastic," "Second Period: Comic and Historic," "Third Period: Tragic and Romance." Swinburne speaks of how foolish and fruitless it is "to hunt through Shakespeare's plays and sonnets on the false scent of a fantastic trail, to put thaumaturgic trust in a dark dream of tracking his untraceable personality through labyrinthine byways of life and visionary crossroads of characters"; and he remains faithful to his own wisdom. His design, he says, is to examine by internal evidence alone the growth and the expression of spirit and of speech, the ebb and flow of thought and style, discernible in the successive periods of Shakespeare's work; to study the phases of mind, the changes of tone, the passage or progress from an old manner to a new, the reversion or relapse from a later to an earlier habit, which may assuredly be traced in the modulations of his varying verse, but can only be traced by ear and not by finger.

The goal is clear; the method excellent—if one's ears are of the same absolute pitch as Shakespeare's. But how can Swinburne know whether there is growth, or in what direction, unless he knows in what order the plays actually came? The question concerned Dowden and received from him careful answer. Swinburne passes it coolly: "It is not, so to speak, the literal but the spiritual order which I have studied to observe and to indicate: the periods which I seek to define belong not to chronology but to art." No great damage is done, however, for the general order is well enough established for Swinburne as it had been for Dowden. There is another problem. How can Swinburne's ear instruct us about Shakespeare's artistic development in the second period if in this period, as Swinburne says, his language is most limpid, his style most pure, his thought most transparent? Where will the development show? Swinburne is equal to the question. Given the increased complexity in Shakespeare's personages, "any criticism worth attention" requires "some inquisition of character as complement to the investigation of style." In plain fact, however, Swinburne at this point drops the investigation he has undertaken. Hereafter he gives us rhapsodies about characters, and plays—and finds some fault, too, with *Troilus and Cressida*, *Measure for Measure*, and *Pericles*—but offers no new understanding about Shakespeare's style or the development of his art.

Swinburne's main contribution then, is with the plays of the first period. What his ear hears is a struggle between Shakespeare's "left hand of rhyme, and his right hand of blank verse." In *Henry VI, Part I,*

> *The left is loath to forego the practice of its peculiar music; yet as the action of the right grows freer, and its touch grows stronger, it becomes more and more certain that the other must cease playing . . . We imagine that the writer must himself have felt the scene of the roses to be pitched in a truer key than the noble scene of parting between the old hero and his son on the verge of desperate battle and certain death. This is the last and loftiest farewell note of rhyming tragedy; still, in Richard the Second and in Romeo and Juliet it struggles for awhile to keep its footing, but now more visibly in vain.*

This is not demonstration or argument, it is assertion, oracularly rendered; but Swinburne names scenes, judges their value, gives his readers something to test against their own ears and pulses. He finds the highest reaches of *Romeo and Juliet* in the blank verse of the orchard scene in Act II and the balcony scene of Act III. And he raises a fine question, why, after Marlowe's example, Shakespeare was so slow to surrender his rhyme. His answer reminds one of Dowden's explaining the mechanicalness of Shakespeare's early structures. Shakespeare, Swinburne conjectures, "had not yet the strength to walk straight in the steps of the mighty master . . . Apollo has not yet put on the sinews of Hercules." So in *Richard II*, "feeling his foothold insecure on the hard and high ascent of the steeps of rhymeless verse, he stops and slips back." Swinburne resolutely faces up to the kneeling scene in Act V, where there is a "relapse" into rhyme and "the 'jigging vein.' " He considers it worse than Marlowe's worst scene, in wretched taste, but in no worse taste than was possible to the man who wrote certain portions of *Venus and Adonis*. He refuses to posit an earlier play of which this is a surviving fragment:

It must be regarded as the last hysterical struggle of rhyme to maintain its place in tragedy; and the explanation . . . of its reappearance may perhaps be simply this—that the poet was not yet dramatist enough to feel for each of his characters an equal or proportionate regard . . . His present interest was here wholly concentrated on the single figure of Richard; and when that for the time was absent, the subordinate figures became to him but heavy and vexatious encumbrances, to be shifted on and off the stage with as much of haste and as little of labor as might be possible.

Whether this is right I do not know, but Swinburne faces up to a scene few commentators treat; he recognizes that it clashes in tone with surrounding scenes, and he offers, as conjecture, an explanation which fits into the larger pattern of Shakespeare's developing versification.

The struggle between rhyme and verse is not to a single resolution. *The Comedy of Errors* shows "that rhyme, however inadequate for tragic use, is by no means a bad instrument for romantic comedy." This play, moreover, possesses "that strange and sweet admixture of farce with fancy, of lyric charm with comic effect, which recurs so often in his later work." *Love's Labour's Lost* offers "a very riot of rhymes" yet it lets us hear "the divine instrument fashioned by Marlowe for tragic purposes alone" in a "sweet new use." For all the absurdity of its fifth act reversals and recantations, *The Two Gentlemen* has "an even sweetness, a simple equality of grace in thought and language which keeps the whole poem in tune, written as it is in a subdued key of un-ambitious harmony . . . Here too [in Launce and his dog] is the first dawn of that higher and more tender humor" which is peculiarly Shakespeare's. Swinburne brings his survey of the period to a close with *A Midsummer Night's Dream*, where "the young genius of the master of all poets finds its consummation." The blank verse is "full, sweet, and strong"; the rhymed verse is "clear, pure, and true." "Each kind of excellence is equal throughout."

This equal excellence of verse Swinburne joins in his praise with the quality "of sweetness and springtide of fairy fancy crossed with light laughter and light trouble that end in perfect music."

Swinburne takes the prosodic facts available to Dowden and fits them delicately, surely, into such a pattern as Dowden did Shakespeare's early handling of characters and character groups. To the observations he makes on style, moreover, he begins to attach others, about sweet mixtures of farce and fancy, about tender humor, about fairy fancy and light laughter. There is an analogy, he suggests, between sound and spirit, between tone as something heard and tone as a mental or moral quality. Verse and style, style and character, he assumes, exist in harmonic relationship. If one has the ear for one, he may have for the other. Unfortunately, we discover, the critic is yet to be born who can define the harmonics for us. Swinburne begins well his inquiry into the development of Shakespeare's art, but he ends too soon.

❧ ❧ ❧

Walter Pater wrote less than fifty pages on Shakespeare; would he had written a thousand.[8] Shaw's possibly excepted, his is the freshest voice between the great trio of Coleridge, Lamb, and Hazlitt in the second decade of the nineteenth century and Bradley in the first decade of the twentieth. His remarks about Biron's style, in *Love's Labour's Lost*, finely characterize his own. "What is vulgarity in Holofernes, and a caricature in Armado," he says, "refines itself with him into the expression of a nature truly and inwardly bent upon a form of delicate perfection, and is accompanied by a real insight into the laws which determine what is exquisite in language, and their root in the nature of things." His merit is the twofold one of showing us what to appreciate in certain of Shakespeare's plays and, quite as important, revealing to us by example what appreciation is. Reading Pater, we realize that reading Shakespeare is not merely a matter of holding mentally to the hundreds of bright things, small and large, we have inherited from critics from Jonson to Auden or discovered for ourselves. It is the subtle refracting of Shakespeare by our own personal sensibilities. We can echo and perhaps produce such criticism as Gervinus's or Dowden's but Pater's defies us. The stamp of his personality is upon it not intrusively, but inevitably, in his special ways of seeing, his complex patterns of feeling, his refined systems of value. It serves us, therefore, less as source or model for our criticism than as inspiration. Let us likewise truly and inwardly seek the forms of delicate perfection—in Shakespeare and in our understanding of him. Let us perceive in the nature of things the roots of the laws of the exquisite—in Shakespeare's language and our own.

Pater's most frequent tone is the elegiac. He sees the tender moment, the vivid personality, the flashing gesture against the darkness of death, the curve of eternity. Beauty and pity become for him complementary aspects of the same experience. He senses the "unutterable longing" "below the many artifices of Biron's amorous speeches," and his ear savors the "many echoes . . . awakened by those strange words, actually said in jest!—'The sweet war-man (Hector of Troy) is dead and rotten; sweet chucks, beat not the bones of the buried: when he breathed, he was a man!' " For him Claudio of *Measure for Measure* is "a flowerlike young man, whom, prompted by a few hints from Shakespeare, the imagination easily clothes with all the bravery of youth, as he crosses the stage before us on his way to death, coming so hastily to the end of his pilgrimage." All the characters of the play have to his eye something of the melancholy about them of Herbert's day—

> so cool, so calm, so bright,
> The bridal of the earth and sky,
> The dew shall weep thy fall tonight
> For thou must die.

The slightest of them is at least not ill-natured: the meanest of them can put forth a plea for existence—Truly, sir, I am a poor fellow that would live!—*they are never sure of them-selves, even in the strong tower of a cold unimpressible nature: they are capable of many friendships and of a true dignity in danger, giving each other a sympathetic, if transi-tory, regret—one sorry that another "should be foolishly lost at a game of tick-tack."*

The concern of Shakespeare's history plays, according to Pater's characteristic interpretation, is "the irony of kingship—average human nature, flung with a wonderfully pathetic effect into the vortex of great events; tragedy of everyday quality heightened in degree only by the conspicuous scene which does but make those who play their parts there conspicuously unfortunate."

This elegiac tone—*carpe diem* inside out—joins in Pater's appreciation with a viewpoint for which I know no label unless "esthetic" will serve. Customarily the critic takes the artist's imitation of nature and refers it to nature again, elucidating this episode or that character by appeal to common experience, special psychology, or some other category of actuality. Repeatedly Pater reverses the process. He keeps speaking of "lights and shades" in the plays, as if the plays were drawings or paintings. The unity of *Love's Labour's Lost*, he proposes, is

> that of a series of pictorial groups, in which the same figures reappear, in different combinations but on the same back-ground. It is as if Shakespeare had intended to bind together, by some inventive conceit, the devices of an ancient tapestry, and give voices to its figures. On one side, a fair palace; on the other, the tents of the Princess of France.

"The Duke disguised as a friar . . . and Isabella in her first mood of renunciation . . . come with the quiet of the cloister as a relief" to the lust and pride of life in *Measure for Measure*, says Pater: "like some gray monastic picture hung on the wall of a gaudy room, their presence cools the heated air of the piece." The incident of Mariana and the moated grange becomes

> a picture within a picture, but with fainter lines and a grayer atmosphere: we have here the same passions, the same wrongs, the same continuance of affection, the same crying out upon death, as in the nearer and larger piece, though softened, and reduced to the mood of a more dreamy scene.

In the history plays "as in a children's story, all princes are in extremes." "In the hands of Kean [*Richard II*] became like an exquisite performance on the violin." Pater sees the deposition of Richard as ceremonial—"as if Shakespeare had had in mind some . . . inverted rite, like those old ecclesiastical or military ones, by which human hardness, or human justice, adds the last touch of unkindness to the execution of its sentences." And Pater sees these kings not as flesh and blood only but as frozen figures on sarcophagi: "one after another, they seem to lie composed in Shakespeare's embalming pages, with just that touch of nature about them, making the whole world akin, which has infused into their tombs at Westminster a rare poetic grace."

Pater translates Shakespeare's dramatic art into other art forms—the picture, the tapestry, the children's story, the instrumental solo, the religious or military rite, the sculpture of the Abbey. His appreciation is "esthetic" in the more common sense. He seeks the structure of the individual play, its texture, the quality of its unity. And he is no idolator. He scoffs at "a dogmatic faith in the plenary verbal inspiration of every one of Shakespeare's clowns." With Jonson, he wishes that Shakespeare had blotted "a thousand hasty phrases." He finds *Measure for Measure* uneven, a redaction of an older play, often rough, often obscure, yet so structured "as to give the whole almost the unity of a single scene." The nature of this unity must already be clear, the sense of the hot-sweet haste of life coolly shadowed by the convent, coldly

shaded by death. All would live, yet some are threatened by life—
"the austere judge fallen suddenly into utmost corruption by a
momentary contact with supreme purity"; Isabella, into whose
white spirit "the swift, vindictive anger leaps, like a white flame,"
so that "stripped in a moment of all convention, she stands before
us clear, detached, columnar, among the tender frailties of the
piece"; and he in whom "the many veins of thought . . . unite,"
Claudio: "called upon suddenly to encounter his fate, looking
with keen and resolute profile straight before him, he gives
utterance to some of the central truths of human feeling, the
sincere, concentrated expression of the recoiling flesh." The quaint
unity of *Love's Labour's Lost* Pater finds in that figure of a tapestry; its leading idea, he proposes, is the "foppery of delicate
language, this fashionable plaything of [Shakespeare's] time":

> He shows us the manner in all its stages; passing from the
> grotesque and vulgar pedantry of Holofernes, through the
> extravagant but polished caricature of Armado, to become the
> peculiar characteristic of a real though still quaint poetry in
> Biron himself, who is still chargeable even at his best with just
> a little affectation. As Shakespeare laughs broadly at it in
> Holofernes or Armado, so he is the analyst of its curious
> charm in Biron; and this analysis involves a delicate raillery by
> Shakespeare himself at his own chosen manner.

Pater rejoices in the perfect symphony of *Romeo and Juliet* and
finds *Richard II* belonging with it in "a small group of plays,
where, by happy birth and consistent evolution, dramatic form
approaches to something like the unity of a lyrical ballad, a lyric, a
song, a single strain of music."

Comparisons have a habit of being unfair, but perhaps if we
put Pater's apprehensions alongside those of Gervinus, we can gain
some final measure of his mind—what he thinks and how he
thinks it. If we put Pater's description of the leading idea of *Love's
Labour's Lost*, for example, beside Gervinus's, "vain desire for

fame in all its forms," we see that Pater has narrowed the pursuit of fame down to the manipulation of language and that he recognizes both delicate raillery and appreciation in Shakespeare's half-autobiographical feeling for Biron. Gervinus is not wrong, but Pater seems more precisely and more richly right. Gervinus sees Shakespeare's "strong nature" delighting in war, and he marshals strong evidence in support of his position. To an extent, Pater agrees: "the soul of Shakespeare, certainly, was not wanting in a sense of the magnanimity of warriors. The grandiose aspects of war, its magnificent apparelling, he records monumentally enough." "Only," he says, "only, with Shakespeare, the after thought is immediate:—

They come like sacrifices in their trim.

—*Will it never be today? I will trot tomorrow a mile, and my way shall be paved with English faces.*"

And Pater proceeds to demonstrate how "this sentiment Richard reiterates very plaintively, in association with the delicate sweetness of the English fields" so that every one of the play's many references to English soil is an expression of pain felt or apprehended at the horror of civil war. Pater can see what Gervinus apparently cannot, that war has two faces for Shakespeare, one of which is chaos. A final comparison. Gervinus speaks sensitively of *Measure for Measure* as espousing punishment "not *measure for measure,* but *with* measure. Neither the lax mildness which the Duke had allowed to prevail, and which he himself condemns, nor the over-severe curb which Angelo applied, is to be esteemed as the right procedure." The Duke threatens punishment, observes Gervinus, but, in the event of crime, practices mercy. "But whilst our play first of all recommends moderation in the exercise of justice, it occupies at once a far more general ground, and extends this doctrine to all human relations." Pater draws attention to the title as "expressly suggesting the subject of *poetical justice.*" Here is what he has to say on the subject—how different from and how to be compared in value with Gervinus's remarks I leave to the reader to determine:

> The action of the play, like the action of life itself for the keener observer, develops in us the conception of this poetical justice, and the yearning to realize it, the true justice of which Angelo knows nothing, because it lies for the most part beyond the limits of any acknowledged law. The idea of justice involves the idea of rights. But at bottom rights are equivalent to that which really is, to facts; and the recognition of his rights therefore, the justice he requires of our hands, or our thoughts, is the recognition of that which the person, in his inmost nature, really is; and as sympathy alone can discover that which really is in matters of feeling and thought, true justice is in its essence a finer knowledge through love . . . It is for this finer justice, a justice based on a more delicate appreciation of the true conditions of men and things, a true respect of persons in our estimate of actions, that the people in Measure for Measure cry out as they pass before us; and as the poetry of this play is full of the peculiarities of Shakespeare's poetry, so in its ethics it is an epitome of Shakespeare's moral judgments. They are the moral judgments of an observer, of one who sits as a spectator, and knows how the threads in the design before him hold together under the surface: they are the judgments of the humorist also, who follows with a half-amused but always pitiful sympathy, the various ways of human disposition, and sees less distance than ordinary men between what are called respectively great and little things.

George Bernard Shaw / 1856–1950
Count Leo Nikolayevich
Tolstoy / 1828–1910

*Shaw's pejorative wit, reaction against contemporary stag-
ing of Shakespeare, critical perceptions. Denigrating portrait of Shakespeare; biographical criticism. Praise of
Shakespeare's "problem" plays, attack against his individualism and despair: Shakespeare compared to Bunyan.
Shakespeare's word music and imagery.* ❧ *Tolstoy as seconding and enlarging Shaw's puritan attack. His studied
obtuseness. Insistence on Lear's hyperbolic remoteness and
artificiality. Shakespeare's unnaturalness in character,
thought, and speech. His deficiency in esthetic and ethical
authority. Tolstoy's history of Shakespearean criticism.*

If Swinburne declines in his critical fortunes, Shaw ascends.
Middleton Murry says he "is a better critic than either Goethe or
Coleridge, because he is not hypnotized,"[1] which is just the kind
of extravagance Shaw himself so masterfully practices—offensive
to the communal taste but with a touch of truth to it. The truth is
that Shaw is not hypnotized. Like Dr. Johnson, he regards Shakespeare as a fellow craftsman. He views him as didactically inadequate, esthetically lazy, and, withal, consistently to be ranked

with Homer, Mozart, Michelangelo as a master among masters: "No man will ever write a better tragedy than *Lear*."

Swinburne keeps thrusting Shakespeare from earth to heaven until the head dizzies; Shaw keeps bringing him down again till the heart sinks. Shaw's critical postures vary—long-suffering reviewer, indignant defender of the public morals, eager expostulant of a social gospel—but his tongue never loses its pejorative wit. "Shakespeare is for an afternoon, but not for all time." "Much-Adoodle-do." "Thirty-six big plays in five blank verse acts, and . . . not a single hero!" "One can hardly forgive Shakespeare quite for the worldly phase in which he tried to thrust such a Jingo hero as his Harry V down our throats." "His Caesar is an admitted failure." "Othello is spoilt by a handkerchief." "To me, the wrestling is always the main attraction of an *As You Like It* performance." The temptation is to quote on and on, for Shaw supplies one endlessly, but there can be too much of a good thing. Indeed, there is too much of the reductive in Shaw as there is too much of the hyperbolic in Swinburne, and to the same effect: the leveling of every comment with every other and the wearying of the reader, who keeps sensing Shaw's presence between himself and Shakespeare. Amused at first, then irritated, he becomes bored.

Shaw, though, is too useful to be dismissed as mere buffoon or wit. He is too useful, too, to be lost in the usual way, by treating his remarks as reactions less to Shakespeare than to Shakespeare in the English theater of the 1890s. Shaw does scold Irving and Tree and Daly for their rendering of the plays. Irving, he says, "had really only one part; and that part was the part of Irving," and though it would be "an exaggeration," he suggests, "to say that the only unforgettable passages in [Tree's] Shakespearean acting are those of which Tree and not Shakespeare was the author," he makes it clear that the exaggeration is slight. Shaw opposes the star system, the obtrusive stage settings, the attempts to obtain a direct illusion of reality, the savage cutting of the plays, the rearranging of the scenes, the bringing in songs from other plays, the casting of beautiful women in the parts, say, of the two young princes in *Richard III*, the continued use of eighteenth-century alterations of Shakespeare—Garrick's *Katherine and Petruchio*, for example, instead of *The Taming of the Shrew*. Shaw cheerfully grumps at bad acting and cheap taste whenever he finds it, and find it he does in the Shakespeare they staged in his day. All of this is important, yet if we focus on it to the exclusion of his remarks directly about Shakespeare, we lose much of genuine critical value.

Shaw has sharp things to say about individual characters and plays. He sees Bertram in *All's Well* as a prototype of Helmer in *A Doll's House*, "a perfectly ordinary young man, whose unimaginative prejudices and selfish conventionality make him cut a very fine mean figure in the atmosphere created by the nobler nature of his life." "One conceives [Cleopatra]" he says, "as a trained professional queen, able to put on at will the deliberate artificial dignity which belongs to the technique of court life." The characters in *As You Like It* are not complete human beings: Rosalind

> is simply an extension into five acts of the most affectionate, fortunate, delightful five minutes in the life of a charming woman. And all the other figures in the play are cognate impostures. Orlando, Adam, Jaques, Touchstone, the banished Duke, and the rest play each the same tune all through. This is not human nature or dramatic character; it is juvenile lead, first old man, heavy lead, heavy father, principal comedian, and leading lady, transfigured by magical word-music.

The dream business of *Cymbeline*, Act V, "is not doggerel: it is a versified masque, in Shakespeare's careless woodnotes wild, complete with Jupiter as *deus ex machina*, eagle and all." "Don John is a true natural villain: that is to say, a malevolent person."

> The world being yet little better than a mischievous schoolboy, I am afraid it cannot be denied that Punch and Judy holds the field still as the most popular of dramatic

entertainments. And of all its versions, except those which are quite above the head of the man in the street, Shakespeare's Richard III is the best. It has abundant devilry, humor, and character, presented with luxuriant energy of diction in the simplest form of blank verse. Shakespeare revels in it with just the sort of artistic unconscionableness that fits the theme. Richard is the prince of Punches: he delights Man by provoking God, and dies unrepentant and game to the last.

Shaw has a good deal of this kind of criticism, the best of it in such letters as those to Ellen Terry, wherein he explores the meaning of a passage line by line and the kind of acting and staging appropriate to each segment. Shaw has, of course, the reviewer's habit, which he shares with Hazlitt, of seeing the written word as libretto to the play staged; and he records, though not, I think, with Hazlitt's extraordinary precision, the way actors and actresses handle particular passages. Thus Robert Loraine as Adam in *As You Like It*, "made a charming point by bidding farewell to the old home with a smile instead of the conventional tear." As Hamlet, Forbes Robertson "dies as we forgive everything to Charles II for dying, and makes 'the rest is silence' a touchingly humorous apology for not being able to finish his business." Mrs. Patrick Campbell makes "Ophelia really mad." She is a "wandering, silly, vague Ophelia, who no sooner catches an emotional impulse than it drifts away from her again, emptying her voice of its tone." And, speaking of a Forbes Robertson Romeo which he does not approve, Shaw writes: "Romeo was a gentleman to the last. He laid out Paris after killing him as carefully as if he were folding up his best suit of clothes. One remembers Irving, a dim figure dragging a horrible burden down through the gloom 'into the rotten jaws of death.' "

To biographical criticism, Shaw offers a portrait of Shakespeare closer to Samuel Smiles's than to Dowden's, but it is Smiles's portrait satirically denigrated:

*Everything we know about Shakespeare can be got into a half-
hour sketch. He was a very civil gentleman who got round
men of all classes; he was extremely susceptible to word-music
and to graces of speech; he picked up all sorts of odds and
ends from books and from the street talk of his day and welded
them into his work; he was so full of witty sallies of all kinds,
decorous and indecorous, that he had to be checked even at
the Mermaid suppers; he was idolized by his admirers to an
extent which nauseated his most enthusiastic and affectionate
friends; and he got into trouble by treating women in the way
already described. Add to this that he was, like all highly
intelligent and conscientious people, business-like about
money and appreciative of the value of respectability and the
discomfort and discredit of Bohemianism; also that he stood
on his social position and desired to have it affirmed by the
grant of a coat of arms, and you have all we know of Shakespeare beyond what we gather from his plays. And it does not
carry us to a tragedy.*

There's a no-nonsense sourness about all this, yet if Dowden may
react to Smiles, surely Shaw may react to Swinburne and the other
bardolaters. His comment about Shakespeare's way of treating
women touches on a point Johnson had made. Shakespeare, said
Johnson, "is seldom very successful, when he engages his characters in reciprocations of smartness and contests of sarcasm; their
jests are commonly gross, and their pleasantry licentious; neither
his gentlemen nor his ladies have much delicacy." Shaw, viewing
Shakespeare's practice through eyes no less puritan than Johnson's,
espies, however, a change in Shakespeare's later practice. He
observes that "Shakespeare did not value himself on Hamlet's
indecent jests" and proceeds thus:

*When he at last got conviction of sin, and saw this sort of
levity in its proper light, he made masterly amends by presenting the blackguard as a blackguard in the person of Lucio in*

Measure for Measure. Lucio, as a character study, is worth forty Benedicks and Birons. His obscenity is not only inoffensive, but irresistibly entertaining, because it is drawn with perfect skill, offered at its true value, and given its proper interest, without any complicity of the author in its lewdness.

Other evaluations are possible, of course, and other explanations— as that the spirit of the early comic lines is not obscene, or that Shakespeare's interests changed, or that in the later comedies he abandoned "the real conversation of his time" which he had earlier imitated. But Shaw is tenaciously holding Shakespeare to Victorian account, and before we reject his version as irrelevant, we must see how much further it extends and what its consequences are. To this we come later.

Our present concern is with Shaw and biographical criticism. His notion that Shakespeare changes his practice as a consequence of changed self-awareness suggests, of course, a view of the dramatist as changing, growing. Shaw does not elaborate this view greatly, but he recurs to it often enough to make its outline fairly certain. For him there are two periods. Shakespeare died too young to attain that third or final period in which Beethoven wrote his *Ninth*, Ibsen his *Master-Builder*, Handel his *Messiah*, and Shaw his *St. Joan*. His periods were but the juvenile and the middle. The juvenile period presumably jibes with Dowden's "In the workshop," the middle period with Dowden's remaining three. Shaw treats the middle period, however, as exhibiting change. At first Shakespeare attached himself to the taste of the times and produced "potboilers which he frankly called *As You Like It, Much Ado About Nothing,* and *What You Will,*" a Jingo hero such as Harry V, and, in general, plays romantic-commercial in nature. The change is heralded by such a play as *The Taming of the Shrew,* one of "Shakespeare's repeated attempts to make the public accept realistic comedy." Petruchio, ready to find a fortune by taking "an ugly and ill-tempered woman off her father's hands," is "an honest and masterly picture of a real man, whose like we have all met." In *All's Well*, with its adumbration of the relationship between man and wife which Ibsen explored in *The Doll's House*, in *Troilus and Cressida* with its exposure of "Homer's attempt to impose upon the world," in *Measure for Measure* with its realistic and genuinely comic obscenity, and above all in *Hamlet*, we see Shakespeare passing from early to later middle period. In *Hamlet* he

> took up an old play about the ghost of a murdered king who haunted his son crying for revenge, with comic relief provided by the son pretending to be that popular curiosity and laughing stock, a village idiot . . . transfiguring this into a tragedy on the ancient Athenian level.

As Shaw sees it,

> what happened to Hamlet was what had happened fifteen hundred years before to Jesus. Born into the vindictive morality of Moses he has evolved into the Christian perception of the futility and wickedness of revenge and punishment, founded on the simple fact that two blacks do not make a white.

That is to say, in *Hamlet* Shakespeare treats dramatically an important moral question. But Shakespeare's failure to educate his public, his own varying inadequacies (he cannot, says Shaw, solve the questions he poses), and the romantic-commercial habit lead him back to plays like *Othello*, "a play written . . . in the style of Italian opera," its characters monsters, and its plot pivoted on an accident, when it would have been "a prodigiously better play" if it had dealt seriously with "how a simple Moorish soldier would get on with a 'supersubtle' Venetian lady of fashion if he married her." Shakespeare may successfully present "the tragedy of disillusion and doubt, of the agonized struggle for a foothold on the quicksand made by an acute observation striving to verify its vain attribution of morality and respectability to Nature," in *Macbeth* and *Lear;* but he also "strains all his huge command of rhetoric and stage pathos to give a theatrical sublimity to the wretched end of [Antony and Cleopatra], and to persuade foolish spectators that the world was well lost by the twain." Of Shakespeare's final plays, Shaw has no cheerier word, and scarcely a suggestion that in them Shakespeare ventures toward any new philosophical, esthetic, or spiritual horizons.

As with Shaw's portrait of Shakespeare, so with this biography, there is much wrong—much sour and much lacking. Its slender direct value, as biographical criticism, must lie in its countering Dowden and deflating the rhapsodists generally. Its main value, though, is critical. Essentially Shaw uses the format of biography as a device for praising and blaming. He praises the plays of the middle middle period for their burden of the socially significant, the "problem" material, the Ibsenian. *All's Well* and *Troilus* he may be said to have rediscovered. And he condemns the early and late plays, not so much for the lack of this as for the alien perspective of traditional immoralities. The "well-bred" obscenities bandied by Benedick, Beatrice, Biron, and Mercutio are an obvious case in point; or the theatrical sublimation of Antony and Cleopatra at their "wretched end"; or that "altogether disgusting" business of Katherine's evangelizing for male supremacy as *The Shrew* draws to a close. Shakespeare's handling of the relations between the sexes exemplifies what Shaw finds offensive in him, but it is hardly at the center. Closer to that is Shakespeare's preaching the gospel of selfish individualism.

> *Although he was a Catholic by family tradition, his figures are all intensely Protestant, individualist, skeptical, self-centered in everything but their love affairs, and completely personal and selfish even in them. His kings are not statesmen: his cardinals have no religion: a novice can read his plays from one end to the other without learning that the world is finally governed by forces expressing themselves in religions and laws*

> which make epochs rather than by vulgarly ambitious indi-
> viduals who make rows.

In the same place that he writes this Shaw says that he has "one advantage over the Elizabethans": "I write in full view of the middle ages." They, he assumes, did not. Mid-twentieth-century awarenesses of Shakespeare's medieval heritage make Shaw's complacency about his "one advantage" seem misplaced and his judgment of Shakespeare as "Protestant" (read "anarchic individualist") seem wide of the mark. Shaw appears blind to the high politics of *King John* and *Richard II* with their questions of church and state, sovereignty and obedience; he seems blind to the political dimension of *Antony and Cleopatra, Macbeth, Hamlet* ("Something is rotten in the state of Denmark"); though he recognizes the *deus ex machina* in *Cymbeline,* it does not occur to him to ask whether, machine or not, the god means anything; and he seems deaf to the joyful reverence at the close of *The Tempest* in Gonzalo's "Look down, you gods." Shaw sees only the "Protestant," none of the "catholic." Shaw's indictment reflects, of course, on the star system of his theater, the productions focusing attention on hero and heroine to the neglect both of lesser characters and larger issues. More deeply, it reflects on the whole tradition of character criticism with its crying neglect of matters other than the personal and psychological. It proclaims the need of larger meanings which subsequent criticism has sought and found.

The heart of Shaw's indictment of Shakespeare, however, is Shakespeare's putative despair. Shaw sees the meaning of *Lear* in Gloster's "As flies to wanton boys, are we to the gods,/They kill us for their sport." He says, "The lot of the man who sees life truly and thinks about it romantically is Despair"—so Shakespeare, so his tragic heroes. For Shakespeare as for Lear "the world was . . . a great 'stage of fools.'" He "cannot balance [his] exposures of Angelo and Dogberry . . . with any portrait of a prophet or a worthy leader." He knows human weaknesses well, but not "strength of the Caesarian type. His Caesar is an admitted fail-

ure." Lacking hope, and knowledge, Shakespeare and his characters lack will. It is not Hamlet alone who is irresolute:

> *all Shakespeare's projections of the deepest humanity he*
> *knew have the same defect: their characters and manners are*
> *lifelike; but their actions are forced on them from without,*
> *and the external force is grotesquely inappropriate except*
> *when it is quite conventional, as in the case of Henry V.*

The plays offer us none of the great motive forces of faith, courage,
or conviction; instead, "nothing but death made sensational, despair made stage-sublime, sex made romantic, and barrenness
covered up by sentimentality." Shakespeare, understanding nothing, believing nothing, despairing, delivers to us the hand-me-
down immoralities of mawkish tradition.

> *All that you miss in Shakespeare you find in Bunyan, to*
> *whom the true heroic came quite obviously and naturally.*
> *The world was to him a more terrible place than it was to*
> *Shakespeare; but he saw through it a path at the end of which*
> *a man might look not only forward to the Celestial City, but*
> *back on his life and say:—"Tho' with great difficulty I am got*
> *hither, yet now I do not repent me of all the trouble I have*
> *been at to arrive where I am. My sword I give to him that*
> *shall succeed me in my pilgrimage, and my courage and skill*
> *to him that can get them." The heart vibrates like a bell to*
> *such an utterance as this: to turn from it to "Out, out, brief*
> *candle," and "The rest is silence," and "We are such stuff as*
> *dreams are made of; and our little life is rounded by a sleep"*
> *is to turn from life, strength, resolution, morning air and*
> *eternal youth, to the terrors of a drunken nightmare.*

Between the vision of Shakespeare's characters and the vision of
Shakespeare himself Shaw fails to discriminate. Macbeth's nightmare is conspicuously not Shakespeare's, and it may be questioned

whether Prospero's life-dream equation is, genuinely, his creator's. But Shaw speaks vigorously here to a point earlier critics have inadequately stressed. Shakespeare's tragic heroes are, in the main, passive rather than active; in their spiritual wanderings they enter despair and pass along the borders of madness; they die relieved to escape life's harsh inanity but without asserting a higher value, a significant hereafter. Shakespeare's powers illuminate their agonies, mute their achievements. Shaw wants something different, something better, a credo to live by rather than die by, the sense of life validated by

> being used for a purpose recognized by yourself as a mighty one; the being thoroughly worn out before you are thrown on the scrap heap; the being a force of Nature instead of a feverish selfish little clod of ailments and grievances complaining that the world will not devote itself to making you happy.

If this is in Shakespeare, Shaw does not find it.

More than most critics Shaw dissociates content from form. His complaints about Shakespeare generally focus on the former, his praise on the latter. One reason "no man will ever write a better tragedy than *Lear*" is the play's formal excellence. Shaw wishes that "Mr. Pinero, Mr. Grundy, and Monsieur Sardou could be persuaded to learn from [*Macbeth*] how to write a play without wasting the first hour of the performance in tediously explaining its 'construction.'" He delights in discovering in *Cymbeline* that the dream, which he formerly disliked, constitutes a perfect little masque. But the formal trait the sometime music critic most often celebrates is Shakespeare's "enormous command of word music." "What a pity it is," he laments, "that the people who love the sound of Shakespeare so seldom go to the stage! The ear is the sure clue to him: only a musician can understand the play of feeling which is the real rarity in his early plays." He yearns for "the Shakespearean music . . . those unrivalled grandiose passages in which Shakespeare turns on the full organ . . . the sixteen-foot pipes booming, or . . . the ennobled tone . . . the tempo suddenly steadied with the majesty of deeper purpose." "It is not enough to see *Richard III:* you should be able to *whistle* it."

This is happy praise happily put. Generally it is less precise than Swinburne's evaluation of Shakespeare's music but Shaw can make us feel his meaning exactly. He writes Mrs. Patrick Campbell about her Lady Macbeth:

> *if you get the music right, the whole thing will come right. And neither [Shakespeare] nor any other musician ever wrote music without fortissimi and thundering ones too . . . It is not by tootling to him con sordino that Lady Macbeth makes Macbeth say "Bring forth men children only." She lashes him into murder.*
>
> *And then you must modulate. Unless you can produce in speaking exactly the same effect that Mozart produces when he stops in C and then begins again in A flat, you cant play Shakespeare . . . Unless you lift that ["The raven himself is hoarse/That croaks the fatal entrance of Duncan/Beneath my battlements"] to utter abandonment, how can you drop to the terrible invocation "Come, you spirits."*

Shaw appreciates, then, and invites us to appreciate Shakespeare's richly varying music. For him as for Swinburne, moreover, Shakespeare's sound is more than sound; it is metaphor for imagery, for imaginative evocation. Shaw never says this explicitly, but it's clear enough from the passages he selects. The "first burst of true Shakespearean music" in *Julius Caesar*, he says, is the passage beginning

> Why, man, he doth bestride the narrow world
> Like a Colossus, and we petty men
> Walk under his huge legs and peep about
> To find ourselves dishonorable graves.

Surely he is responding to more than mere sound. Again, he quotes "Cleopatra's outburst at the death of Antony":

Oh withered is the garland of the war,
The soldier's pole is fallen: young boys and girls
Are level now with men: the odds is gone,
And there is nothing left remarkable
Beneath the visiting moon.

"This is not good sense," he says, "not even good grammar." The thought chaotically reflects the confusion of Cleopatra's mind. "Now it is only in music, verbal or other, that the feeling which plunges thought into confusion can be artistically expressed." But the music of "the visiting moon" is not aural. "Tested by the brain," says Shaw, Othello's part "is ridiculous: tested by the ear, it is sublime." But the passages he adduces by way of demonstration are Othello's comparison of his bloody thoughts to the Pontic sea keeping due on to the Propontic and the Hellespont, and Othello's standing over the sleeping Desdemona, musing, "I know not where is that Promethean heat/That can thy light relume."

It is, then, the music of sound *and* imagery, the appeal to the ear *and* the imagination, that Shaw praises repeatedly, discriminatingly, and with unflagging enthusiasm. This praise has, however, its negative side. Almost invariably it couples with the denial to Shakespeare of any significance other than musical or imaginary. "Tested by the brain," Othello's part "is ridiculous." Lady Macbeth has no character: "She says things that will set people's imagination to work if she says them in the right way: that is all." Iago is fabricated of conflicting sounds and images. *Much Ado* is "hopeless" in its story, "pleasing only to lovers of the illustrated police papers." Without its music "*Much Ado* becomes what *Don Giovanni* . . . would become if Mozart's music were burnt and the libretto alone preserved." "The two *Richards, King John,* and the last act of *Romeo and Juliet,* depend wholly on the beauty of their music."

With Shaw we end where we began, with exuberant belittle-ment. Frank Harris had said in the Preface to *The Man Shake-speare* that his purpose was "to liberate Englishmen . . . from the tyranny of Shakespeare's greatness." Shaw's venture is the same, but more vigorous, more lasting. It is a valiant effort, less to destroy Shakespeare than to recover the theater and, from the traditional immoralities of Shakespeare's plays and the culture for which they still speak, to redeem mankind.

❧ ❧ ❧

Coming from Shaw to Tolstoy's *Shakespeare and the Drama* (1906),[2] we may find it, with LeWinter, "unjust, wrongheaded, and wholly negative," but probably not "the most vexing document in the long history of European Shakespeare criticism." It is Shaw all over again, but now in full frontal attack. With a few notable exceptions, Shaw had stripped Shakespeare of his praises—his philosophy, his wisdom, his ethical force, his characterization, his characters, his myriad-minded genius. He had left him his magical verse-music, little else. Similarly, Tolstoy denies him everything but "the capacity of representing scenes expressing the play of emotion." Shaw's protest comes graced with joyous and ebullient wit; Tolstoy's with a wit dry, bitter, fanatic. You can imagine chatting with Shaw at a non-alcoholic cocktail party; Tolstoy you would listen to as he harangued you from the pulpit of a church.[3] But the burden of both men is the same. In Tolstoy's words: "The fundamental cause of Shakespeare's fame was and is this—that his dramas . . . corresponded to the irreligious and immoral frame of mind of the upper classes of his time and ours." The consequence —again in Tolstoy's words—is a twofold injury: "first, the fall of the drama, and the replacement of this important weapon of progress by an empty and immoral amusement; and secondly, the direct depravation of men by presenting to them false models for imitation." Like Shaw, Tolstoy would recover the stage and re-deem mankind.

Shakespeare and the Drama contains fourteen sections. Section i states the problem, Tolstoy's conviction in the face of the "universal adulation" of Shakespeare that he "cannot be recognized either as a great genius, or even as an average author." Section ii presents the principal evidence, a scene-by-scene summary of *King Lear*, which Tolstoy selects as a test case. Sections iii–vii detail a series of adverse judgments—on *Lear* as dramatic art (iii), on Shakespeare's putative perfection in character expression (iv), on Shakespeare's esthetic mastery (v), on Shakespeare's so-called "ethical authority" (vi), on Shakespeare's poetic merit (vii). Section viii presents Tolstoy's explanation of Shakespeare's fame: "it is one of those epidemic 'suggestions' to which men ever have been and are subject." Sections ix-xiii review the history of Shakespeare's fame, from its low beginnings in the seventeenth and early eighteenth centuries (ix), through its meteoric rise in Germany in the later eighteenth century (x) and its general dissemination in the nineteenth century (xi), to its present pernicious influence on the theater and on the young (xii, xiii). Section xiv presents Tolstoy's application: "the sooner people free themselves from the false glorification of Shakespeare, the better it will be." How it will be better he proceeds to explain.

Even more than Lessing on Voltaire does Tolstoy on Shakespeare sound like Twain on Fenimore Cooper. The basic device is a studied obtuseness, as of a tone-deaf man commenting on a symphony. Tolstoy plods through his summary of *Lear* unwilling to suspend his disbelief. Drily, he treats the "givens" as improbable, the conventions as literal, the dialogue as inconsequential. He regards the varying utterances of madness—actual, near, pretended—as without meaning, the fool's utterances as bizarrely irrelevant. Short illustration cannot communicate the effectiveness of this rhetoric since it depends on accumulation. Slowly one adjusts from his own position to something nearer Tolstoy's as he hears for the dozenth time that Lear looks at his trusted counselor, Kent, and does not recognize him, or that Gloucester looks at his own son, naked, and cannot recognize him—this same Gloucester who, when robbed of his eyes, can recognize Lear by the sound of his voice!—or that—but let a few illustrations indicate the rest. At the beginning, says Tolstoy, resolutely rational, "the reader or spectator cannot conceive that a king, however old and stupid he may be, could believe the words of the vicious daughters with whom he has passed his whole life, and not believe his favorite daughter." Tolstoy recounts the dialogue between Lear and the Fool at the end of I.iv in the manner of a countryman narrating a joke—

> the fool says, "Give me an egg and I'll give thee two crowns." The King asks, "What crowns shall they be?" "Why," says the fool, "after I have cut the egg i' the middle and eat up the meat, the two crowns of the egg. When thou clovest thy crown i' the middle, and gavest away both parts, thou borest thine ass on thy back o'er the dirt: thou hadst little wit in thy bald crown when thou gavest thy golden one away. If I speak like myself in this, let him be whipp'd that first finds it so."

"In this manner," says Tolstoy, "lengthy conversations go on, calling forth in the spectator or reader that wearisome uneasiness which one experiences when listening to jokes which are not witty." Repeatedly Tolstoy cites a few fragments of dialogue, then stops with a fatigued "and so forth," as though to quote more were to mean less. Of III.ii, the first of the great storm scenes, Tolstoy has this to say:

> Lear walks about the heath and says words which are meant to express his despair: he desires that the winds should blow so hard that they (the winds) should crack their cheeks and that the rain should flood everything, that lightning should singe his white head, and the thunder flatten the world and destroy all germs "that make ungrateful man!" The fool keeps uttering still more senseless words. Enter Kent; Lear says that for some reason during this storm all criminals shall

be found out and convicted. Kent, still unrecognized by Lear, endeavors to persuade him to take refuge in a hovel. At this point the fool pronounces a prophecy in no wise related to the situation and they all depart.

The merits of Tolstoy's summary, even for the unconverted, are several. He makes us feel how extraordinarily remote *Lear* is from the day-to-day actuality we know. So familiar do we become with its simplicities and sublimities, its grand passions, fractured minds, heinous betrayals, and crystalline fidelities, that we can lose sight of its extraordinary remoteness. Tolstoy forces us to recognize the problem of the play's beginning: either it is a given, an improbability accepted by convention from which the rest probably follows, or it is not. If it is not, it is probable by the same standards according to which the rest of the play coheres (a position that requires more proof than it usually receives), or it is improbable (which discredits Shakespeare). Tolstoy brings us hard up against the convention of disguise and the play's extraordinary use thereof. He forces us to recognize the rational discontinuity in the monologues of Lear and the Fool, in the dialogue of large portions of the play—so that it begins to seem fragmented, like Chekhov's *Cherry Orchard* or something later from the Theater of the Absurd. And Tolstoy makes us aware of the extremity of both speech and action in the play, its essential hyperbole. In short, Tolstoy insists on a tremendous exaggeration in *Lear* (if not a monstrous unnaturalness) which we must recognize and come to terms with as we may.[4]

The indictment implicit in his summary Tolstoy explicitly elaborates and generalizes in the following sections. He says that the persons are placed in impossible positions which neither flow from the course of events nor are appropriate to time and place, they act in arbitrary ways, out of keeping with their characters, and they speak "one and the same Shakespearean pretentious and unnatural language" ("No living man could or can say as Lear says —that he would divorce his wife in the grave should Regan not receive him"). Such characters as Shakespeare is famous for—Lear, Cordelia, Othello, Desdemona, Falstaff, Hamlet—he received from his sources and damaged in the process. The old Lear's motives were clear and natural at the beginning, as was Cordelia's offense and the King of Gaul's betrothal to her. Othello, though he is "the least encumbered by pompous volubility" of Shakespeare's famous characters, was yet more natural and lifelike in the original Italian romance: "Shakespeare's Othello suffers from epilepsy of which he has an attack on the stage." Only Falstaff is

> indeed quite a natural and typical character . . . because of all Shakespeare's characters, it alone speaks a language proper to itself. And it speaks thus because it speaks in the same Shakespearean language full of mirthless jokes and unamusing puns which, being unnatural to all Shakespeare's other characters, is quite in harmony with the boastful, distorted, and depraved character of the drunken Falstaff.

("Banish plump Jack, and banish all the world." *Tolstoy:* "I do, I will.") Shakespeare simply lacks the "feeling of measure" which lets an artist know when and how much. "From his first words, exaggeration is seen: the exaggeration of events, the exaggeration of emotion, and the exaggeration of effects." One has but to think of *Lear* for examples—"insanity, murders, plucking out of eyes, Gloucester's jump, its poisonings, and wranglings." Shakespeare "invents the events he describes and is indifferent to his characters — . . . he has conceived them only for the stage and therefore makes them do and say only what may strike his public."

Tolstoy's indictment, thus generalized, works to the same effect as his condemnation of *Lear*. It demands that attention be paid to Shakespeare's deviations from the familiar and the customary. It requires us to hear as with a fresh ear the volubility and the hyperbole of the characters' speech. It makes us recognize that in contrast to their sources and to the figures of popular fiction generally, Shakespeare's characters seem always somewhat obscure in their motivation. Why does Hamlet not act? Why *does* Iago? Is or is not Hal *using* Falstaff and his crew for selfish purposes? Why cannot Cordelia say some little word to release her father from his embarrassment? In general Tolstoy makes us conscious of the exaggeration and the discontinuity in the plays, the artificial as opposed to the "natural," the "theatrical" as against the "dramatic." With Stoll and Schücking we may celebrate the theatrical Shakespeare who plays on his audience's emotions with all the absurd conventions at his disposal; or with Bradley we may occasionally concede and in general deny that the artifice carries over to the unnatural, that the exaggeration is beyond the artistic pale, the discontinuity too broad for the imagination to overleap. But if we would gain from Tolstoy's criticism of Shakespeare's art, we must attend to the Shakespearean attributes that he identifies, the questions of esthetics and psychology that he raises.

The cynical Shakespeare Tolstoy portrays has no more ethical authority than artistic. Tolstoy proves his point by a summary of Gervinus's long last chapter, of which he cleverly catches the word and misses the spirit, somehow translating that vital balancing and blending of contrary awarenesses which Gervinus discovers in Shakespeare—his many-sided unity—into a brainless, lukewarm, conservative, British activism:

> Action at all costs, the absence of all ideals, moderation in everything, the conservation of the forms of life once established, and the end justifies the means. If you add to this a Chauvinistic English patriotism . . . according to which the English throne is something sacred, Englishmen always vanquish the French, killing thousands and losing only scores, Joan of Arc regarded as a witch, and the belief that Hector and all the Trojans, from whom the English descend, are heroes, while the Greeks are cowards and traitors, and so forth—such is the view of life of the wisest teacher of life according to his greatest admirers. And he who will atten-

tively read Shakespeare's works cannot fail to recognize that the description of this Shakespearean view of life by his admirers is quite correct.

Like Shaw, Tolstoy damns Shakespeare for writing plays romantic-commercial, cynical, as *they* liked it, the *they* being the powers that were and be, "the upper classes of his time and ours." His condemnation reaches out, finally, to include the critics who have puffed Shakespeare into greatness. Briefly he tells the history that I have been telling here, but with a difference. According to Tolstoy, Shakespeare had failed to gain any special fame in England until the end of the eighteenth century. "His fame originated in Germany." The Germans were weary of the cold French drama and charmed by the Greek drama, to the religious significance of which they were indifferent. They

> imagined they needed only reject the inconvenient law of the three unities without introducing into the drama any religious element corresponding to their own time—in order that the drama should have sufficient scope in the representation of various moments in the lives of historical personages, and in general of strong human passions.

Because of his strong scenes they selected Shakespeare as exemplar of this new drama—and because Goethe, the foremost of the group, found Shakespeare's view of life in agreement with his own. Later critics took Shakespeare's greatness on Goethe's credit, and

> to give the greater force to their praise of the whole of Shakespeare they invented esthetic theories according to which it appeared that no definite religious view of life was necessary for works of art in general, and especially for the drama; that for the purpose of the drama, the representation of human passions and characters was quite sufficient; that not only was an internal religious illumination of what was repre-

sented unnecessary, but art should be objective, i.e., should represent events quite independently of any judgment of good and evil. As these theories were founded on Shakespeare's own views of life it naturally turned out that the works of Shakespeare satisfied these theories and therefore were the height of perfection.

Shakespeare, inartistic and cynical, gratifies his times, and later times, by writing solely for effect. His drama is false to that nature which Johnson says it so superbly mirrors, and without that inner illumination, the lack of which Johnson also lamented, although in different terms, which comes from religious conviction. His plays are therefore amoral and irreligious in their impact on man. The time has come, Tolstoy believes with Shaw, to set the disjointed time aright. If men can "free themselves from the false glorification of Shakespeare," they will discover that drama unsupported by religion is trivial and will "search for and work out a new form of modern drama, a drama which will serve as the development and confirmation of the highest stage of religious consciousness in men"; they will recognize that "while there is no true religious drama, the teaching of life should be sought for in other sources."

To this challenging of Shakespeare's ethical content, in which Tolstoy joins with Shaw, some response is necessary. We may accept it and condemn Shakespeare. We may accept it and approve him: Lowell approved his objectivity, Gervinus his patriotism, Stoll his romantic-commercial values. More fruitfully, I think, we may reject and seek in Shakespeare a spiritual and ethical content to which Shaw and Tolstoy are blind. With Bradley we may analyze Shakespearean tragedy in the light of Hegelian theory to discover a larger purport; with Lily Bess Campbell, Tillyard, Harbage, Theodore Spencer,[5] we may pursue historical researches to recover the Christian humanistic elements in the plays; with Fergusson, Frye, and Barber[6] we may probe for and find anthropological patterns of deep meaning in the plays.

One last word, however, should be spoken for these doughty modern-day puritans. Both Shaw and Tolstoy are looking to the future rather than to the past. The discovery in Shakespeare of an ethical and spiritual content no less weighty than that of Dante would not satisfy them, even were they to witness the demonstration, for they see too clearly that whatever his latent meanings, Shakespeare in fact carries the virus of the contemporary values which they repudiate. Their goal is to bring in the brave new world. For them Shakespeare, even at his hyperbolic best, can only stand for the old one.

ix

A. C. Bradley / 1851–1935

*Bradley's aggregational style and rational rhetoric; his "we"
and his impressionism. "The Substance of Shakespearean
Tragedy": the tragic trait, tragic impression, tragic triumph.
"Construction in Shakespeare's Tragedies": exposition, conflict, "fourth-act problem"; Shakespeare's artistic sins; the
chief problem in interpreting Shakespeare. The world of*
Lear, *atmosphere of* Macbeth. *Character interpreted and
quickened.*

If a man were to step out of the rain into a shelter where Edmund
Burke was, five minutes of conversation would convince the man,
said Dr. Johnson, that he was in a superior presence. Five minutes
in Bradley's *Shakespearean Tragedy* (1904) has the same effect.[1]
More than half a century ago a critic wrote that Bradley's was "the
most notable piece of literary criticism that has appeared since the
day of Coleridge, Lamb, and Hazlitt."[2] The judgment remains
valid—at least in respect to Shakespeare. No work since has so
perfectly combined "the enthusiasm and vision of the romanticists
with the common sense and exactness of the scientific method,"[3]
has so perfectly fused "wide philosophic outlook with grasp of
detail, and synthetic power with analytic."[4] My own copy of the
book, dated 1932, is from the eighteenth reprinting of the second
edition, which provides some indication of its popularity. It has
since entered the public domain in the United States, circulated in

paper binding, and bids to last longer and be more popular than even Dowden's *Primer*. It remains a most popular source for student cribbing, an oblique but not inaccurate indicator of value.

It is, then, at first blush a curious fact that sharp and telling phrases from Bradley do not hang in one's mind the way they do from Coleridge, or Hazlitt. One recalls Coleridge's pinning Iago down with "the motive hunting of motiveless malignity," but though we remember that Bradley finds Iago a motive, the formulation eludes us. Hazlitt dubbed Hamlet "the prince of philosophical speculators," and said "it is *we* who are Hamlet"; Bradley, we recall, attributes philosophical genius to Hamlet and explains his inaction by melancholy, but again, the phrasing fades. The explanation is not, however, far to seek. Bradley says many things sharply and very well, and a small anthology of his remarks worthy of memory would not be hard to compile, but characteristically he expresses himself and enters our awarenesses in aggregates. His unit, like Milton's, is the paragraph. His mind is nothing if not copious.

Some indication of this fact appears in the first sentence of the first lecture, when Bradley says, "The question we are to consider in this lecture may be stated in a variety of ways." Not one way, but "a variety." Bradley proceeds to give his question four different formulations:

What is the substance of a Shakespearean tragedy, taken in abstraction both from its form and from the differences in point of substance between one tragedy and another?

What is the nature of the tragic aspect of life as represented by Shakespeare?

What is the general fact shown now in this tragedy and now in that?

What is Shakespeare's tragic conception, or conception of tragedy?

This is not garrulity. It is the thoroughness of a mind that sees truth as protean and elusive, that sees its audience as multiple and idiosyncratic, one segment to be reached by one formulation, another by another, until all are brought into union and communion. We see Bradley's aggregational style perhaps more characteristically a page later as he begins to describe Shakespearean tragedy. No single inclusive generalization comes to us, but a painstaking enumeration of separate traits, with attendant discriminations, building toward a cumulative definition—thus:

And first, to begin from the outside, such a tragedy brings before us a considerable number of persons (many more than the persons in a Greek play, unless the members of the Chorus are reckoned among them); but it is pre-eminently the story of one person, the "hero," or at most of two, the "hero" and "heroine." Moreover, it is only in the love-tragedies, Romeo and Juliet and Antony and Cleopatra, that the heroine is as much the center of the action as the hero. The rest, including Macbeth, are single stars. So that, having noticed the peculiarity of these two dramas, we may henceforth, for the sake of brevity, ignore it, and may speak of the tragic story as being concerned primarily with one person.

The story, next, leads up to, and includes, the death of the hero. On the one hand (whatever may be true of tragedy elsewhere), no play at the end of which the hero remains alive is, in the full Shakespearean sense, a tragedy; and we no longer class Troilus and Cressida or Cymbeline as such, as did the editors of the Folio. On the other hand, the story depicts also the troubled part of the hero's life which precedes and leads up to his death; and an instantaneous death occurring by "accident" in the midst of prosperity would not suffice for it. It is, in fact, essentially a tale of suffering and calamity conducting to death.

The suffering and calamity are, moreover, exceptional. They befall a conspicuous person. They are themselves of some striking kind. They are also, as a rule, unexpected, and contrasted with previous happiness or glory. A tale, for example, of a man slowly worn to death by disease, poverty, little cares, sordid vices, petty persecutions, however piteous or dreadful it might be, would not be tragic in the Shakespearean sense.

Such exceptional suffering and calamity, then, affecting the hero, and—we must now add—generally extending far and wide beyond him, so as to make the whole scene a scene of woe, are an essential ingredient in tragedy, and a chief source of the tragic emotions, and especially of pity. But . . .

And the contrasts, discriminations, enumerations, specifications, exceptions, concessions, resumptions continue, not one failing either more narrowly to circumscribe the elusive truth or more perspicuously to meet disagreement, question, or cavil latent in the mind of the audience until the definition is complete—massive, elaborate, and precise—and we have mastered it by mastering, too, all those kindred tragedies which Bradley has summoned up so that he might differentiate between them and the Shakespearean.

This aggregational style of Bradley's—calm as Coleridge's is nervous, personal as Pater's, yet far more public, so that we imagine ourselves speaking with like persuasion and authority, until we try—may seem at first an ideal instrument for philosophical abstraction but inadequate for delicate matters of esthetics or psychology. In fact, it works well wherever Bradley uses it because his sensitivities to beauty, personality, and ethics are uniformly broad and quick. Thus, he develops a wonderful paragraph on Othello, as "he comes before us, dark and grand, with a light upon him from the sun where he was born," and another on the darkness brooding over *Macbeth,* and yet another on Iago's "pluming up the will" by inflicting pain "because this pain is the unmistakable proof of his own power." His style serves superbly, to give one final example, to communicate "a very striking characteristic of *King Lear* . . . the incessant references to the lower animals and man's likeness to them":

> These references are scattered broadcast through the whole play as though Shakespeare's mind were so busy with the subject that he could hardly write a page without some allusion to it. The dog, the horse, the cow, the sheep, the hog, the lion, the bear, the wolf, the fox, the monkey, the pole-cat, the civet-cat, the pelican, the owl, the crow, the chough, the wren, the fly, the butterfly, the rat, the mouse, the frog, the tadpole, the wall-newt, the water-newt, the worm—I am sure I cannot have completed the list, and some of them are mentioned again and again. Often, of course, and especially in the talk of Edgar as the Bedlam, they have no symbolical meaning; but not seldom, even in his talk, they are expressly referred to for their typical qualities—"hog in sloth, fox in stealth, wolf in greediness, dog in madness, lion in prey." "The fitchew nor the soiled horse goes to't/With a more riotous appetite." Sometimes a person in the drama is compared, openly or implicitly, with one of them. Goneril is a kite: her ingratitude has a serpent's tooth: she has struck her father most serpent-like upon the very heart: her visage is wolvish: she has tied sharp-toothed unkindness like a vulture on her father's breast: for her husband she is a gilded serpent: to Gloster her cruelty seems to have the fangs of a boar. She and Regan are dog-hearted: they are tigers, not daughters: each is an adder to the other: the flesh of each is covered with the fell of a beast. Oswald is a mongrel, and the son and heir of a mongrel: ducking to everyone in power, he is a wag-tail: white with fear, he is a goose. Gloster, for Regan, is an ingrateful fox: Albany, for his wife, has a cowish spirit and is milk-liver'd: when Edgar as the Bedlam first appeared to Lear he made him think a man a worm. As we read, the souls of all the beasts in turn seem to us to have entered the bodies of these mortals; horrible in their venom, savagery, lust, deceit-

fulness, sloth, cruelty, filthiness; miserable in their feebleness, nakedness, defencelessness, blindness; and man, "consider him well," is even what they are.

Bradley's characteristic style is aggregational, his characteristic rhetoric is calmly rational. "Let us reason together," he seems to say, "let us examine the plays, consult our own experience, and arrive at judicious conclusions." He speaks from something of the stance and with something of the authority of a great popular preacher whose gift it is to articulate the common experience by articulating his own. I am not sure I would draw attention to this feature of his writing were it not, first, that it is extraordinarily compelling, and second, that the compulsion is furthered by two devices against which the unwary reader perhaps needs warning. One device is that very old one, the pronoun in its first person plural form. Bradley's "we" is neither royal nor editorial; it is an assertion of that collectiveness of experience which he and his audience share—during the hours of his lecturing, if not before. In *Othello*, he says,

we seem to be aware . . . of a certain limitation, a partial suppression of that element in Shakespeare's mind which unites him with the mystical poets . . . In one or two of his plays . . . we are almost painfully conscious of this suppression; we feel an intense intellectual activity . . . In other plays . . . we are constantly aware of the presence of this power; and in such cases we seem to be peculiarly near to Shakespeare himself. Now this is so in Hamlet and King Lear . . . but it is much less so in Othello. I do not mean . . .

The "I" at the end is Bradley explaining *his* diction; the earlier and repeated "we" includes Bradley and you and me—and while it may in fact, it behooves us, occasionally, to be wary.

The other device also appears in the passage we have just examined, in Bradley's speaking of our *awareness* of a limitation, the almost painful *consciousness* of suppression, the *feeling* of intellectual activity, the *awareness* of power, the *sense* of nearness of Shakespeare. The device consists in treating not the play or the character or the passage, but one's impression (generally "our" impression) of it. "What is the peculiarity of *Othello?*" Bradley demands. "What is the distinctive *impression* that it leaves?" "*Macbeth* makes an *impression* quite different from that of *Hamlet*." The mind receives "from *King Lear* an *impression* which is at least as near of kin to the *Divine Comedy* as to *Othello*." Bradley's appeal to impression reflects an esthetic which focuses on the art experience rather than the art work. It is not the play in black and white on the page that matters nor, again, the play on the boards with costumed men and women speaking the lines. It is the play as joint creation of Shakespeare and ourselves, the bright spark arcing between his cues and our responses—the play in the theater of the mind. The merits of this esthetic are obvious: it brings into relief the moral and emotionally evocative; it recognizes the rhetoric of drama as it engages our feelings, and it makes available for critical purposes the whole language of affective response. But the device threatens always to remove the matter to be interpreted from the relatively precise world of objective word and deed to the potentially murky world of subjective reaction. We have less agreement as to terms here, less copious a vocabulary, less confidence. We are likely, hence, to follow our leader, which may be all right, but to follow him without quite knowing that we are, which is not. The dangers latent in the two devices become clear as we examine Bradley's opening lecture on "The Substance of Shakespearean Tragedy."

This lecture consists of a short introduction and five numbered sections. Sections (1) and (2) deal with the story and the plot of Shakespearean tragedy, the story being one "of exceptional calamity leading to the death of a man in high estate," the plot "one of human actions producing exceptional calamity and ending in the death of such a man." Section (3) turns from the action to the hero, the tragic hero with his tragic trait who in his fall creates the tragic impression. "In almost all" the heroes, says Bradley, "we observe a marked one-sidedness, a predisposition in some particular direction; a total incapacity, in certain circumstances, of resisting the force which draws in this direction; a fatal tendency to identify the whole being with one interest, object, passion, or habit of mind. This, it would seem, is, for Shakespeare, the fundamental tragic trait." The tragic trait leads to the tragic impression, "the impression of waste." As we watch the tragedies, " 'What a piece of work is man,' we cry; 'so much more beautiful and so much more terrible than we knew! Why should he be so if this beauty and greatness only tortures itself and throws itself away?' "

Bradley's "we" and his "impressions" betray us, I think, into a melodramatic and anachronistic view of Shakespearean tragedy. The concept of the tragic trait is mechanical, like the notion of Achilles' heel, and it links with the theatrical gimmick of the "fatal moment" when character and circumstance disastrously converge. Indeed, one may feel his breath coming in short, apprehensive pants when Bradley later suggests that "under conditions of a peculiar kind, Hamlet's reflectiveness certainly might prove dangerous to him, and his genius might even . . . become his doom." About the impression of waste one may have comparable doubts, for not only do the characters not speak about it, but waste is, ultimately, a mechanical concept related to efficiency and deriving from a nineteenth-century secularism that fits Shakespeare's universe somewhat doubtfully. The same judgment extends to the rest of this opening lecture with its exploration of the ultimate power in the Shakespearean universe. Brilliantly Bradley indicates the qualities of this power that make it seem like fate; brilliantly the qualities that make it seem like a moral order. Both lines of discussion might lead him to identifying the ultimate power with Christian Providence, but on this Bradley turns his back. He gives us instead Creative Evolution:

> We remain confronted with the inexplicable fact, or the no
> less inexplicable appearance, of a world travailing for perfec-
> tion, but bringing to birth, together with glorious good, an
> evil which it is able to overcome only by self-torture and self-
> waste. And this fact or appearance is tragedy.

In his opening lecture Bradley largely omits discussing one
aspect of Shakespeare's substance that he later stresses: what might
be called the hero's triumph-in-defeat or indominability, which
gives rises, says Bradley, to a sense of reconciliation. "Why does
Cordelia die?" he asks, and supposes that "no reader ever failed to
ask that question, and to ask it with something more than pain,"
yet "with the slightest element of reconciliation" mingled with his
pain. Bradley proceeds to explain that element of reconciliation as
it relates to all the tragic heroes. We have a feeling, an

> impression that the heroic being, though in one sense and
> outwardly he has failed, is yet in another sense superior to the
> world in which he appears; is, in some way which we do not
> seek to define, untouched by the doom that overtakes him;
> and is rather set free from life than deprived of it.

In this spirit Bradley comments on Othello:

> As he speaks those final words in which all the glory and
> agony of his life . . . seem to pass before us, like the pictures
> that flash before the eyes of a drowning man, a triumphant
> scorn for the fetters of the flesh and the littleness of all the
> lives that must survive him sweeps our grief away, and when
> he dies upon a kiss the most painful of all tragedies leaves us
> for the moment free from pain, and exulting in the power of
> "love and man's unconquerable mind."

Macbeth's ruin seems complete, says Bradley,

*yet it is never complete. To the end he never totally loses our
sympathy . . . There remains something sublime in the defiance with which, even when cheated of his last hope, he
faces earth and hell and heaven. Nor would any soul to whom
evil was congenial be capable of that heart-sickness which
overcomes him . . . In the very depths a gleam of his native
love of goodness, and with it a touch of tragic grandeur rests
upon him.*

Such reading seems to me sentimental. Grandeur all the
heroes have in their lives and in their deaths, but there is no
"native love of goodness" in the "tomorrow and tomorrow and
tomorrow" speech, nor is there triumph. Cordelia surely is not
seen freed from life—she is murdered; and though Lear is released
from the rack of existence, his final crying out that a dog, a horse,
a rat has life but Cordelia will never come again sounds no note of
superiority to the world. Othello is lofty and self-possessed in his
death, the ironic master of those around him as he was long before
in the Senate scene, but he has just glimpsed what will happen to
him on Judgment Day:

> This look of thine will hurl my soul from heaven,
> And fiends will snatch at it.

He is superior to those around him in the sense that he no longer
values life, not that he has bested it.

If Bradley, as I think, misinterprets the substance of Shakespearean tragedy in respect to the tragic trait, the tragic impression, and the tragic triumph, his remarks on "Construction in
Shakespeare's Tragedies," his second lecture, remain the most
useful we have on the subject. With a master craftsman's sensitivity he sees the parts of the plays as characteristically posing
problems and Shakespeare's dramaturgy as so brilliantly realizing
solutions as to veil both problems and achievements from our
awareness.

Bradley begins with the Exposition. Its "main business," he says, "is to introduce us into a little world of persons; to show us their positions in life, their circumstances, their relations to one another, and perhaps something of their characters; and to leave us keenly interested in the question what will come out of this condition of things." From definition of the part, Bradley proceeds to statement of the problem—"to impart to the audience a quantity of information about matters of which they generally know nothing and never know all that is necessary for [the playwright's] purpose." This problem raises another: "he must conceal from his auditors the fact that they are being informed." And then Bradley shows us how Shakespeare does it: "His usual plan in tragedy is to begin with a short scene, or part of a scene, either full of life and stir, or in some other way arresting. Then, having secured a hearing, he proceeds to conversations at a lower pitch, accompanied by little action but conveying much information." Bradley supports his generalization with liberal documentation: *Romeo and Juliet* opening with a street fight, *Julius Caesar* and *Coriolanus* with a crowd in commotion, *Hamlet* and *Macbeth* with the supernatural. As Dryden observed, suspense is initially generated if others discuss the hero while the dramatist holds him off-stage. This is another of Shakespeare's devices. Yet a third, to which Bradley draws attention, is the allotting to sub-plots or important subgroups, as the Gloucester plot in *Lear*, the family of Polonius in *Hamlet*, clearly separated expository scenes so that the appropriate information may be communicated cleanly, the appropriate interest aroused free from interference. Bradley proceeds to a fourth device, as when Iago begins *Othello* or the witches *Macbeth*: "We are made conscious at once of some power which is to influence the whole action to the hero's undoing." This power of doom Shakespeare reinforces, Bradley makes us see, "by some expression that has an ominous effect"—for example, Hamlet's "The time is out of joint. Oh cursed spite,/That ever I was born to set it right."

As the middle part of a play is larger than its beginning, so

Bradley's analysis of the conflict expands beyond his treatment of the Exposition. Shakespeare alternates scenes of high and low tension, he observes, short scenes and rapid changes being possible on the Elizabethan stage as they are not on the modern. Moreover, Shakespeare presents us with alternating fortunes from beginning to end, now the King ahead, let us say, now Hamlet, then the King, then Hamlet, etc. Further, though these independent rhythms of tension and fortune continue to the catastrophe, there is a turning point or crisis in the action, generally in the play's middle, at which point the chances of victory or success reach their flood and thereafter begin to ebb. Bradley's solution of the peculiar problems posed by *Lear* and *Othello* to this scheme of analysis I shall by-pass to focus on his handling of the conflict as it develops between the crisis and the catastrophe.

> But when the crisis has been reached there come difficulties and dangers, which, if we put Shakespeare for the moment out of mind, are easily seen. An immediate and crushing counteraction would, no doubt, sustain the interest, but it would precipitate the catastrophe, and leave a feeling that there had been too long a preparation for a final effect so brief. What seems necessary is a momentary pause, followed by a counteraction which mounts at first slowly, and afterwards, as it gathers force, with quickening speed. And yet the result of this arrangement, it would seem, must be, for a time, a decided slackening of tension. Nor is this the only difficulty. The persons who represent the counteraction and now take the lead, are likely to be comparatively unfamiliar, and therefore unwelcome, to the audience . . . Possibly, too, their necessary prominence may crowd the hero into the background.

Bradley makes us see this "fourth-act problem," makes us realize how ticklish it is, then lets us appreciate how Shakespeare solves it. The wealth of his illustration I omit. Here are his headings: (1)

"A reverse or counterblow not less emphatic and in some cases even more exciting"—Antony's funeral oration, for example, following the assassination in *Julius Caesar*. (2) A reminder, by parallel action, "of the state of affairs in which the conflict began" —for example, the reappearance of the Ghost in *Hamlet*. (3) The exhibition in the hero of some "inner change," as when Hamlet moralizes on his irresolution after missing his chance in the prayer scene. (4) The appeal "to an emotion different from any of those excited in the first half of the play"—the pathos of the reconciliation of Brutus and Cassius, Lear's waking from insanity in Cordelia's presence. (5) Occasionally, humorous or semi-humorous passages—Lady Macduff and her boy, Coriolanus among Aufidius's servants. (6) Scenes of battle, as in *Richard III, Julius Caesar, King Lear*. (7) The awakening of false hopes, as with Edgar's victory in *Lear* or Hamlet's apology to Laertes. (8) The expansion of the catastrophe to reduce the fourth-act pause, as in *Othello* and *Antony and Cleopatra*.

No one before Bradley communicates such a sense of entering the Shakespearean workshop and seeing there the tools and patterns by which the master craftsman makes his plays. When one hears, as one does, that Bradley treats the plays as history, the characters as actual, one should remember this second lecture. And one should remember, too, its conclusion, where Bradley considers Shakespeare as artist, and as artist who "frequently sins against art." Here is his list of the sins: (1) A certain choppiness from stringing together a number of short scenes, as in *Macbeth*, V. (2) "The introduction or excessive development of matter neither required by the plot nor essential to the exhibition of character: for example, the references in *Hamlet* to theater-quarrels of the day." (3) A failure to conceal the expository intent of certain soliloquies, a weakness incident to the early plays but evident, too, in Edgar's soliloquy in *Lear*, II.iii. (4) "Inconsistencies and contradictions, and . . . questions . . . which it is impossible . . . to answer with certainty," as with time in *Othello* or Hamlet's situation at the time of his father's murder. (5) Language "obscure, inflated, tasteless, or 'pestered with metaphors.'" (6) Passages dramatically inappropriate, as "when the player-king discourses for more than twenty lines on the instability of human purpose." (7) A superfluity of "gnomic" passages, usually rhymed, of the sort one finds in Polonius's advice. What are the sources of these flaws? "Nine-tenths of [Shakespeare's] defects," says Bradley, in a formulation with which Johnson and Coleridge would have agreed, "are not . . . the errors of an inspired genius, ignorant of art, but the sins of a great but negligent artist."

Out of this sense of Shakespeare as extraordinary artist, with his art resembling nature, organizing and vitalizing its product outward to the minutest marking on the surface, and out of his sense of Shakespeare as negligent artist, overworked, perhaps, or inattentive, self-contradictory and rough, Bradley arrives at a statement of "the chief difficulty in interpreting his works"—the difficulty of determining whether skill or negligence is the source of what perplexes us. "We know well enough what Shakespeare is doing when at the end of *Measure for Measure* he marries Isabella to the Duke—and a scandalous proceeding it is; but who can ever feel sure that the doubts which vex him as to some not unimportant points in *Hamlet* are due to his own want of eyesight or to Shakespeare's want of care?"

From the days of Johnson critics have differentiated between the special qualities of the great tragedies. For Johnson, the distinguishing feature of *Hamlet* was its variety; of *Othello*, the monumental perfection of the characters; of *Lear*, its torrential power; of *Macbeth*, its grand solemnity. For Schlegel *Hamlet* was a tragedy of thought, *Lear* of compassion, *Macbeth* of terror. Coleridge said that "*Lear* is the most tremendous effort of Shakespeare as a poet; *Hamlet* as a philosopher or meditator; and *Othello* is the union of the two." On another occasion, he remarked that "of all Shakespeare's plays *Macbeth* is the most rapid, *Hamlet* the slowest, in movement. *Lear* combines length with rapidity." According to Hazlitt, "*Lear* stands first for the profound intensity of the passion; *Macbeth* for the wildness of the imagination and the rapidity of the action; *Othello* for the progressive interest and powerful alternations of feeling; *Hamlet* for the refined development of thought and sentiment."

Now Bradley does something like this when he comments on the splendor and popularity of *Hamlet*, the painfulness of *Othello*, and when he discriminates now one way, now another between the various plays; *Julius Caesar* and *Hamlet* are tragedies of thought; *Othello, Lear,* and *Macbeth* tragedies of extreme passion, *Antony and Cleopatra* and *Coriolanus* tragedies wherein reconciliation plays an especially strong role. But in his treatment of *Lear* and *Macbeth* he goes further. He seems to see the play as occurring in a unique *world*, as possessing a unique *atmosphere*. The world of *Lear*, he says,

> is dim to us, partly from its immensity, and partly because it is filled with gloom; and in the gloom shapes approach and recede, whose half-seen faces and motions touch us with dread, horror, or the most painful pity . . . This world, we are told, is called Britain; but we should no more look for it in an atlas than for the place called Caucasus, where Prometheus was chained.

This is not simply a passing impression. Bradley substantiates this insubstantial world by drawing attention to the vagueness of the play's locale, its bulk of material, its extraordinary "number of figures, events and movements," its double action, which suggests

> that in that dark cold world some fateful malignant influence is abroad, turning the hearts of the fathers against their children and of the children against their fathers, smiting the earth with a curse . . . blinding the eyes, maddening the

brain, freezing the springs of pity, numbing all powers except
the nerves of anguish and the dull lust of life.

He points to the radical division of the characters into two groups
in whom either love or self-seeking finds extreme expression, as
though mankind were somehow reduced to its elements. He points
to the play's insistence on monstrosity in "beings, actions, states of
mind," and to that "striking characteristic of *King Lear*," which
we have already examined, "the incessant references to the lower
animals." No less striking than this definition of the world of *Lear*
is Bradley's extended description and analysis of the atmosphere of
Macbeth—of a horrid "darkness, the lights and colors that illuminate it, the storm that rushes through it, the violent and gigantic
images" and the Witches and the Ghost and the repulsive in-
gredients of the caldron, the owl's clamoring, the cannibal horses,
the raven's croaking, the voice crying "Sleep no more" and a
hundred other things as well.

In Bradley this atmosphere is the air the characters breathe,
the murk through which they stumble, the haze through which we
see them and apprehend their desperation. Pater had sensed something like this in the special combination of the pride of life and
the chill of death in *Measure for Measure*. Lowell sensed it in that
"period of transition" in *Hamlet* when "the times are always out
of joint." But Bradley makes us conscious of it as had no critic
before. He adds it as an element to that unity of impression
Coleridge and Schlegel had discussed. He prepares the way for
Wilson Knight with his view that atmosphere is not only the
environment of the characters but a function of them as they are a
function of it. For this organicism Bradley is not quite prepared.
When he speaks, as he often and usefully does, of a character from
one play confronting the problem faced by the character of
another—Macbeth, for example, and Hamlet's problem, or Hamlet and Othello's—he shows that he basically considers the characters independent of their worlds. Indeed, the concept of the tragic
trait, with its suggestion that under other combinations of circum-

stance the hero would have escaped his entrapment and destruction, operates in the same way to separate the character from his world. But by thus clearly defining the worlds of the plays, and by indicating the contribution thereto of the passions, values, and thoughts of the characters therein, Bradley prepares for Knight, for Mack, and for those who follow.[5] He plants the seed, though he is not there to reap it, of a concept of organic unity which both expresses character and subsumes it.

With Bradley we come at last, as so many do at first, to character. These pages have tried to make clear that he does not deal with character alone. He responds to impressions of the plays. He explores their atmospheres. He apprehends in all the tragedies a universe of which characters are the expression. He sees art in the plays as well as the life, the failure as well as the success. In short, Bradley did not write *The Girlhood of Shakespeare's Heroines* nor does he ask *How Many Children Had Lady Macbeth?*[6] Yet it is what he has to say about character that occurs to most people when they speak of Bradley. Why? There are two answers. One is Muir's. Bradley, he says, "attempted to analyze each play as though he were an actor studying all the parts, not as a producer to whom the characters are creations subordinated to a poetic conception and existing only in relation to that conception and to each other."[7] Exactly. In the minor characters as in the major, Bradley seeks the secret of life—as did Johnson with Polonius, Morgann with Falstaff, Coleridge with Hamlet. Claudius attracts his sympathetic attention no less than Hamlet, Emelia as well as Desdemona. This is one answer. The other is that he does this job incredibly well. He does it so well that, as Muir says, "Bradley's conception of the characters is still an orthodoxy to be questioned."[8] Bradley's achievement is not in capsule characterization nor in that notion of tragic trait which is both power and weakness. It is, simply, the bringing the characters to life. Under his criticism they pulse and breathe, intricate miracles of significant vitality. Bradley quickens every character, every incident, every speech. He catches the trick of Hamlet's voice, its repetitions, its ironies; he detects the note of Claudius's agonized praying for God's grace at the moment he has set in motion Hamlet's assassination. As a member of the Senate, even as young Desdemona, he hears the resonances of Othello's wanderings.

Bradley's interpretations of character and the life he quickens in character are functions one of the other. He makes us understand the characters by his thorough, discriminating, closely articulated and repeatedly tested reasoning, and in the process he makes them breathe for us, in their habits as they lived. Sometimes his method, as with Hamlet, is to approach the character by way of various theories. With each theory for Hamlet's inaction—that of external difficulty, that of internal difficulty (conscience, unconscious moral repulsion, delicate sensitivity, reflection)—stated, tested, fitted into the play as far as it will fit, rejected as far as it must be rejected, we seem to approach closer to the real Hamlet, until we come to Bradley's theory of melancholy. Then, finding it fitting the evidence of character (nervous instability, moral idealism, intellectual genius) and finding it fitting the evidence of conduct (Hamlet's inaction, his energy, his special satisfactions, his pleasure at meeting his old friends, his irritability, his callousness, his bursts of passion, his bestial oblivion, and, finally, his incapacity to understand his delay)—then we seem to see Hamlet as he is, alive and suffering, and this sense of his living reality grows in us, as Bradley leads us through the play, pointing out, episode by episode, how Hamlet's actions and reactions accord with the vision he has given us.

Usually character requires exegesis nowhere near as thorough as this—needs, perhaps, less exegesis than sympathetic understanding so that we can feel it truly in its situation. And to his logic and psychologic Bradley then adds swift sympathy and appreciation. Consider this sentence on Lear as evidence, and as a final illustration of Bradley's power to hold the mirror up to Shakespeare's nature:

The old King who in pleading with his daughters feels so intensely his own humiliation and their horrible ingratitude, and who yet, at fourscore and upward, constrains himself to practice a self-control and patience so many years disused; who out of old affection for his Fool, and in repentance for his injustice to the Fool's beloved mistress, tolerates incessant and cutting reminders of his own folly and wrong; in whom the rage of the storm awakes a power and a poetic grandeur surpassing even that of Othello's anguish; who comes in his affliction to think of others first, and to seek, in tender solicitude for his poor boy, the shelter he scorns for his own bare head; who learns to feel and to pray for the miserable and houseless poor, to discern the falseness of flattery and the brutality of authority, and to pierce below the differences of rank and raiment to the common humanity beneath; whose sight is so purged by scalding tears that it sees at last how power and place and all things in the world are vanity except love; who tastes in his last hours the extremes both of love's rapture and of its agony, but could never, if he lived on or lived again, care a jot for aught beside—there is no figure, surely, in the world of poetry at once so grand, so pathetic, and so beautiful as his.

Robert Bridges / 1844–1930
E. E. Stoll / 1874–
Levin L. Schücking / 1878–

*Bridges' indictment of Shakespeare: consistency of charac-
ter vs. surprise, new characters for old stories.* ❦ *Stoll as
historian and theater-goer. The topicality and unreality of
Shakespeare's characters. Gains and losses from the Stollian
perspective: restoration and reduction.* ❦ *Schücking's historical objectivity. Primitive conditions of Shakespeare's
theater: Shakespeare's art as literal and fragmented. Schücking's obscurations of his own theory.*

In his famous essay on Shakespeare's audience, Bridges defines an
achievement in the tones of one making a complaint.[1] The
achievement is Shakespeare's art in rendering his characters lifelike; the basis of the complaint is, ultimately, that art and not
nature accounts for the result. Bridges resembles Voltaire and
Rymer in this, that he points to inconsistencies and contradictions
in Shakespeare; but, whereas they focus on matters of decorum,
Bridges focuses on matters of psychology, and where they say,
"How absurd! How destructive of delusion!" Bridges says (though
in *their* tones), "How plausible! How persuasive! How contributory to the illusion!" Such mismatching of tone and statement can
be explained by referring to the success of such critics as Morgann,

Coleridge, and Bradley. Their brilliant demonstration of rich, deep life in Shakespeare's characters rests finally on their persuasion that the conduct of the characters is consistently referable to the laws of psychology, the laws of life. Bridges, finding inconsistency in the characters—and inconsistency not to be explained by contradictions between unconscious and conscious, or by ambivalence, or by changes of mood or situation: in short, not to be explained by natural causes—Bridges cries "Foul!" The cry is against Shakespeare. Quite as fairly it might go against his critics, and Bridges might say of Shakespeare, as by the end of his essay one half suspects he feels inclined, "Eureka! What a triumph of art!"

"If fault-finding were good criticism," begins Bridges, "it would be easy to criticize Shakespeare well; for his faults are like the prickles on a rose-bush"—rather more frequent than the blooms. And Bridges will attempt to sort out the prickles so that he may contemplate the pure blooms remaining. He begins with "mere foolish verbal trifling," "bad jokes and obscenities," brutality, both physical and in manners, and "the readiness with which offenses of the first rank are sometimes overlooked and pardoned." As Hamlet's speech to the Players makes clear, the explanation of these flaws, is that Shakespeare "deliberately played false to his own artistic ideals for the sake of gratifying his audience." The complaint and the explanation are old, but treating Shakespeare's easy pardon of offenses, Bridges opens up a new charge. If Shakespeare's audience "could forgive Proteus and Angelo, it would be on the ground of their own indifference to the crimes, and because of a moral bluntness which does not discriminate." "Shakespeare took advantage of this, and where his plot demanded a difficult reconciliation, he assumed its possibility, and accomplished it by a bold stroke." This is the grand new charge:

> we have passed away from mere concession to the audience, and are come to discover Shakespeare taking advantage of their stupidity, and admitting inconsistencies . . . for the sake of

dramatic effect or convenience, where he knew that the liberty would be well tolerated.

To the exploration and definition of this point Bridges devotes the rest of his essay.

Angelo provides the first illustration. Shakespeare presents him, says Bridges, as heartless and overly regardful of his reputation: "he deems himself a saint: he is consequently a self-deceiver." The old rupture of his affair with a lady on her losing her dowry and his defaming her character constitute an enormity irreconcilable with the sincerity of his purpose, but with this sole exception Shakespeare presents him consistently "till the end of his first interview with Isabella; after which he is, in a few hours, completely changed from a high-principled, stoical self-deceiver, to a licentious hypocrite trafficking in crime." Such a change might occur in a man either unprincipled or passionate, but Angelo is neither. Further, he shows no remorse at his fall: "He is now just like Borachio: and how should the disgrace of exposure remodel such a villain in fifteen minutes?" Looking forward into the play from its beginning we saw Angelo a Pharisee; looking back, we see him a hypocrite. Looking forward, we saw him fall; looking back, we find "no virtue to fall from." Between these perspectives no middle ground is possible.

Bridges sees "in Macbeth the same kind of inconsistency." There is the contradiction between the man—of "magnificent qualities of mind, extreme courage, and poetic imagination"—and his crimes. There is a blurring of motives: "whether Macbeth's ambition had preconceived and decided on the murder of Duncan; or whether the idea was chiefly imposed upon him by a supernatural devilry; or whether he was mainly urged to it by his wife." Even if we say that the last two motives dominate, and that Macbeth had just sufficient ambition for witches and wife to work on, even that much ambition "is still contradictory to the picture of nobility impressed on us by Shakespeare, and essential to his drama." "This veiled confusion of motive," says Bridges, "is so well managed that it must be recognized as a device intended to escape observation." (Moralistically he calls the device a " 'dishonesty.' ") The device works, seems natural, because "in nature we cannot weigh or know all the motives or springs of action"; but it is unnatural because the motives or springs of action are not ultimately susceptible of rational, coherent analysis.

Bridges has proceeded from outrageous inconsistency barely veiled, in Shakespeare, to a muted inconsistency most carefully veiled and from the veiling to the explanation of its success. But why the device at all? The question opens a striking new way of seeing Shakespeare. "The interest in a Shakespearean tragedy lies chiefly in the hero's conduct, and is greater as his conduct surprises while it satisfies: and from the constitution of things it is difficult to imagine a character or personality whose actions shall be at once consistent and surprising." Shakespeare gains surprise from extreme villainy in Richard III and Iago; from "monstrous forms of special qualities" in Timon and Coriolanus; but "to sustain surprise in a worthy hero" he risks, even sacrifices, consistency.

> Having found a story the actions of which were suitable, Shakespeare adopted them very much as they were, but remade the character of the actor. In the original story the actor would be known and judged by his actions: this, Shakespeare reverses by first introducing his hero as a man superior to his actions; his art being to create a kind of contrast between the two . . . and his success depends on the power and skill with which this character is chosen and enforced upon the audience; for it is when their minds are preoccupied with his personality that the actions follow as unquestionable realities.

Bridges applies his analysis to Antonio's unexplained melancholy and to "all that is unsatisfactory in the character of Bassanio," to Leontes' "senseless" jealousy, to Othello's jealousy, and finally, to Hamlet's madness, real or feigned.

Bridges relates in many ways to the history of Shakespearean criticism. As already indicated, he echoes and inverts neo-classical complaints. He speaks out against the great Morgann-to-Bradley tradition of Shakespeare's characters as true-to-life. Usefully, he catalogues critical trouble spots. He reinforces Tolstoy's indictments, provides Stoll with sanction and stimulus for his reduction of character to convention, and establishes the archetypal pattern for Harbage's *As They Liked It*, a book treating just such inconsistencies as Bridges identifies. Bridges puts the characters, if rather grumpily, back into the theater, on the boards, before an audience. And finally, in his formula of new characters for old stories, characters contrasted to their actions,[2] their surprise achieved at the expense of their consistency, and their inconsistency veiled, he finds a way of defining Shakespeare's achievement in language this side idolatry and extraordinarily suggestive.

❧ ❧ ❧

The most exuberant of the no-nonsense school of Shakespeare criticism in America, E. E. Stoll combines a firm historical approach, an exciting theatrical awareness, and a simplistic way of thinking, feeling, and judging.[3] His rhetoric is that of the polemicist: black and white without intermediate gray, assertion and reassertion and saying it yet again. He projects a Shakespeare who looks remarkably like himself: prodigal, exuberant, impatient of rules, guided by healthy instincts, taking "to himself new virtues, but put[ting] from him few faults or defects."

Stoll is historian and theater-goer. He argues against those who take Shakespeare out of his time or off the stage. To him, most Shakespeare criticism seems anachronistic. Shakespeare's ghosts have been turned into projections of the unconscious, his Shylock made pathetic, his criminals metamorphosed into modern "cases," Henry V degraded, Falstaff ennobled, and Hamlet subtilized. Stoll replies by going to the record. He argues that in creating Shylock, for example, Shakespeare enlisted the prejudices of his day against miser, money-lender, and Jew. That these were in fact the prejudices he demonstrates by examining in fair detail Marlowe's *Jew of Malta* and other Elizabethan plays in which the Jew is baited: an anonymous *Timon, Jack Drum's Entertainment, Englishmen for My Money,* and *Travels of Three English Gentlemen.* In all "are to be found, in various combinations, usurer and miser, villain and butt, devourer of Christian blood and coin, and limb of the devil,—all big-nosed, or (in accordance with the vulgar error) foul of breath, in some fashion or other egregiously 'Jewy.' " Stoll explores further. He glances at the Jew in the English mysteries, in medieval mysteries elsewhere, in the German Carnival plays, in the Italian *carri,* and finds in these "a similar spirit of rude caricature and boisterous burlesque." Having examined the literary tradition, Stoll proceeds to opinions about Jews in Shakespeare's time and both before and after. His documentation is rich and painful. It includes the Lopez trial and execution, Prynne's raking up the charges against the Jews in his *Short Demurrer,* Coke's abuse in his *Institutes,* and scores of other sickening testimonies. By the time one has finished reading them, it is hard indeed to believe that Irving's dignified Shylock, more sinned against than sinning, has much to do with Shakespeare's creation.

But if Shakespearean drama reflects the actualities of history, Stoll says, it does so not by being true to life, but by being true to art. This is the dominant note of his criticism. He agrees with Bridges that Shakespeare jettisons psychological consistency for "contrast, clear and unbroken." Shakespeare reduces Macbeth, "unpsychologically," "to the murderer and his conscience," the conscience by convention external and opposed to the man. He presents Othello as without the seed of jealousy in him, and then, following the convention of the slanderer believed, as fully, terribly jealous. Shakespeare "seems not to have been much inclined to analysis . . . or to mixed and ambiguous characters or situations . . . He presents no studies of love, ambition, pride, or jealousy, though he presents characters powerfully animated by such passions."

And everything else in situation or characterization suggestive
of a subtle contradiction or paradox . . . he eschews. For
him no honor rooted in dishonor; no Falstaff of the critics,
with the constitutional instincts of courage, but without the
principles which ordinarily accompany them; no Othello with
such confidence in Iago, who is not his friend, that he can
naturally distrust his innocent friend Cassio, and the wife of
his bosom; no Macbeth . . . prompted by fear of his own
courage; no Hamlet . . . endowed (or afflicted) with a
"double consciousness," who, the more he tries to force
himself into action, the more his unconscious self invents
pretexts to keep him from it.

According to Stoll, the critics are misled by taking literally the
conventional devices which in Shakespeare's day served to simplify, compress, and contrast: the devices of deception and slander,
of feigning or playing a part, of mistaken identity, of disguise, of
contracting time, of self-description. Confused by conventional
devices, critics are confused as well by conventional characters.
Stoll devotes an essay to Shakespeare's criminals to show how
untrue to actuality, how faithful to convention they are. Aaron,
Richard, Iago are Machiavels, self-conscious, self-confessed, self-
delighting; they are not men but men "turned upside down, or
wrong side out, and thrust beyond the pale of the species."
"Richard is but the voice of poet and people concerning him. In
accord with their sentiments he looks upon his deformity as . . .
setting the seal on his depravity instead of explaining and extenu-
ating it." Richard briefly, Macbeth at length, experiences "the
horrors," but the effect is "purely technical":

like most Elizabethan and many Shakespearean characters,
Macbeth often comments on his feelings instead of uttering
them. He dwells on the misery and hideousness of his situa-
tion rather than on his own purposes and the end in view. As
he approaches the royal chamber, it is a dagger that he sees

before him, not the crown. And he dwells on the circumstances and consequences of the crime—punishment, public indignation, the deep damnation of violating the laws of hospitality and of killing a king so virtuous and meek. He is preoccupied with all the scruples of pit and poet. Likewise he has a curious eye, as critics have remarked, for what poetically befits the occasion.

For Stoll Shakespeare is a man in a theater, a man with a vitalizing sense of detail, to be sure, and with a marvelous ear for the music of speech, but most especially a man playing with conventions to achieve surprise and delight. So Shakespeare gives us Falstaff, a compound of traditional or conventional characters—coward, *miles gloriosus*, clown, wit. And so Shakespeare has Falstaff do things—because the tradition and the expectation require it. Why does Falstaff go to the wars? "It is on the stage—it is in a comedy . . . And Falstaff goes to the wars to say his catechism, brandish a bottle for a pistol, fall dead, joke, cheat, and lie . . . Falstaff goes to war to furnish matter for comedy." He sleeps while the watch search for him, he carries a bottle instead of a pistol—because these are among the conventions of comic cowardice. (At this point Morgann's Falstaff turns into thin air: he is such stuff as critical dreams are made on.) Falstaff reveals himself to the gibes of Prince and Poins, "simply that the dramatist may secure a telling and immediate comic effect, that of the scorner scorned, the enemy of love fallen in love, the boaster and liar as a coward laid bare." "Not psychological consistency but dramatic effectiveness is Shakespeare's aim, and like every other dramatist he will sell, if not his own soul, at least a character's, for a contrast."

When we first come to Stoll, he refreshes and emancipates us. He releases us, perhaps, from the pain of hearing Hal muse so coldbloodedly on his roistering friends ("I know you all") or the shame at Portia's drawing out to such length her judgment on Shylock. The characters, says Stoll, speak not as they are, but as convention requires. He frees us, perhaps, from the embarrassment we feel when Iago, for all the world like the mustachioed monster of a horse opera, demands which of us would call him villain or when Othello pauses over his sleeping wife to instruct us in the pathos of his situation: "This sorrow's heavenly,/It strikes where it doth love." Again, says Stoll, not character but convention speaks here. And we begin to grasp that Stoll has taken Bridges' direction, gone far, far along it, not in the mood of complaint, though, but of rejoicing. "A merry heart goes all the day/Your sad tires in a mile-a."

Only Stoll almost never examines a speech line by line or image by image. His approach avoids discovering the psychological subtleties that close reading might produce. Moreover, his studies both of the ideas current in Shakespeare's day and of the conventions available to him in his theater are invariably reductive. Their purpose is to discover wherein Shakespeare is like his fellow, not wherein he differs.[4] Is Shakespeare's Jew big-nosed like Barabbas? Does Barabbas suffer, like Shylock, a long-drawn-out humiliation before the audience while the resonances of the Lord's Prayer echo in his ears and theirs? Such queries Stoll does not make. Further, he seems not to ask whether the conventions which abound in Shakespeare may not in fact express inner truths. Perhaps such invocations as Lady Macbeth's exist as conventions because people did believe, and do, that dark powers confer upon man for the price of his peace of mind immediate gifts of position, wealth, or success. And even if the convention is purely mechanical, the device of a dramaturgy still crude, might it not, one wonders, in skilled hands, begin to carry its old weight and new weight too? Perhaps Hal's soliloquy means that he *is* calculating as his father and good Queen Bess were, as a good political leader must be.

Our doubts about Stoll flourish most as we behold him confronting *Hamlet,* for here the evidence of ambiguity or enigma seems staggeringly evident. But Stoll sees it not. "Neither [in Hamlet's final soliloquy] nor anywhere else, whether by Hamlet himself or by Horatio, is it suspected that there is any mystery about him or within him," says Stoll, but in that final soliloquy

Hamlet himself says, "I do not know/Why yet I live to say, 'This thing's to do.'" Stoll says, "to no one in the play is Hamlet known to have a defect; and no one ventures to speak of him or to him either slightingly or critically." But Hamlet speaks of himself slightingly, critically in the tremendous soliloquy at the end of Act II, and the Ghost comes in Act IV explicitly to whet his "almost blunted purpose." Stoll lists a series of ironies in the play only to deny them:

> The hero receives the command of the paternal ghost but feigns madness; he upbraids himself for failure to act but resolves upon a play; he undertakes the play, but next appears soliloquizing on suicide and saying not a word of play, ghost, or revenge; he gives the play at last, but after it, though now convinced, spares the king at prayer and "goes softly to his mother"; and thereupon he upbraids and exhorts himself in soliloquy once more, but embarks for England. Yet it is merely as we edit and gloss the dramatic text . . . that any such effect of contrast can be attained. Here is no sharpness, no speciousness, no bleak ironic light, nor the repetition that we think to find. For the Elizabethans . . . familiar with the old story, the old melodrama which Shakespeare was re-writing, and with popular Senecan tragedy on their stage, these motives and conduct, so queer to us, were natural enough, in those uncritical days.

I do not believe it. The age of Shakespeare's sugared sonnets and Donne's metaphysical conceits, of Hooker's *Polity* and Bacon's *New Organon* and Spenser's enormous allegory had its pop-eyed, open-jawed primitives, of course, but it had eyes and ears for subtleties. As Harvey said, Shakespeare's "*Lucrece*, and his tragedy of *Hamlet, Prince of Denmark*, have it in them to please the wiser sort."[5]

Stoll sells Shakespeare short. Most of the time he opens our eyes neither to wonder nor wisdom. If he saves us a Falstaff, he loses us a Hamlet, and in his hands other characters and plays

dwindle painfully. Nonetheless, the corrective value of his criticism is enormous. From Morgann through Bradley the tradition
paid inadequate attention to history. It came to impose Victorian
moralities upon Shakespeare, and post-Darwinian metaphysics. Its
poorer representatives sentimentalized Shakespeare in some ways,
sophisticated him in others. They laid his ghosts, sweetened his fat
man, softened his Jew. Stoll helps restore Shakespeare to the
Elizabethan and Jacobean age. No less damaging to Shakespeare
was the tradition's tendency to lose sight of the stage, its realities
and pretences, its limitations and conventions. In a curious way,
the tradition, having accepted Shakespeare's art as equal to his
nature, tended to lose sight of his art all over again. Stoll brings it
back. In Siegel's fine image, Stoll is like the restorer of the paintings of an old master.[6] Bringing to his task both the special
knowledge of the historian and the taste and judgment of the art
critic, he removes from the works the incrustations of centuries.

❦ ❦ ❦

Schücking is a phlegmatic Hamlet in a world made rank and
gross by the weeds of subjective criticism.[7] "Whoever has looked
with horror at the endless caprices to be found in this field," he
says, "will perhaps regard this attempt as not having been made in
vain." The attempt is to restore Shakespeare to objective criticism,
which is to say, to historical criticism, which means for Schücking
to a feeling for the primitive elements and principles in Shakespeare's plays. "Shakespeare's art-form," he says, "is in fact a
mixture of the most highly developed with quite primitive elements: on one side an inexpressible delicacy and subtlety in the
portraiture of the soul, on the other aids and props to the understanding of the most antiquated description, as well as elements in
the plot uncritically adopted and never properly fused into the
play of character." Shakespeare's nature, in other words, is highly
developed, his art is primitive—which sounds like the eighteenth-
century only Schücking develops the argument in a modern or
Stollian fashion.

Schücking begins with the conditions of the theater in Shakespeare's day. As its practice of collaborative authorship shows, he argues, it was little concerned with the individual expression of the individual artist. It catered to the public taste, giving them what they wanted—plots according to the current fad, whether histories or tragedies of blood; the indecorous devices of proven success, such as the severed and gory head, armies conflicting on stage, trials by combat; spicy topicalities at the price of anachronism; the clown ad libbing though some necessary question of the play got muted or lost; the mixture of comic and tragic whatever the learned might say of classical practice. It was a popular theater, and its dramaturgy was molded by the mentality of an audience which, while not always the vulgar, had generally a good portion of the vulgar in it.

From these conditions, says Schücking, comes Shakespeare's art, which is primitive in two ways: in literalness and in fragmentation. The literalness appears in the monologues and in the private reflections of characters on one another. The rule is that these speak true. Not only does an introspective character directly explain himself, as he might in today's realistic theater, but all kinds of characters do the same. Falstaff speaks true of himself (as witty and cause of wit in others, as youthful in spirit) no less than does Hamlet. The villains declare their villainy (Aaron, Richard, Don John, Iago, Edmund), and quite as unrealistically, with no suggestion of arrogance or self-conceit, the heroes proclaim their virtues—Prospero his mastery of the liberal arts, Cordelia her sincerity and candor, Brutus his honesty, Henry V his graciousness. Similarly, reflections by characters are accurate—obviously and realistically, as when the populace describes Coriolanus as proud and mighty; obviously but unrealistically when Iago speaks of Othello's nobility and Cassio's "daily beauty."

The fragmentation appears in a lack of harmony between character and expression, between character and action. Although Shakespeare at times endows a figure with consistent traits of speech, as he does Shylock with Biblical references, repetitions, and rhetorical questions, he generally ignores this practice. He considers effect without regard to character. Thus he has Lady Capulet comparing Juliet's contemplation of Paris to a scholar's perusal of an annotated manuscript and he makes Macduff speak of "most sacrilegious murder breaking ope the Lord's anointed temple and stealing thence the life o' the building" not to show them as learned or oddly formal, but to make the lines more powerful. Similarly he has Macbeth speaking of Duncan's "silver skin lac'd with his golden blood" not by way of revealing unnaturalness or hypocrisy, but simply to make the audience sit up. Shakespeare's willingness to divorce speech from character is especially evident in episodes where characters change their usual way of speaking for the sake of immediate effect: booby Bottom speaking like a courtier to Titania's retinue, the coarse Mercutio exquisitely celebrating Queen Mab, the doting Polonius speaking solid wisdom to his son.

Between character and action a similar disharmony obtains, says Schücking. Shakespeare tends to build his plays step by step, giving individual scenes or episodes a measure of independence from character and plot no longer esthetically tolerable—Richard III's wooing of Anne, for example, or Hamlet's discussion of the London theater-wars or the vignette of Edward the Confessor's touching for the King's evil in *Macbeth*. Schücking agrees with Goethe that Shakespeare worked for immediate effect at the expense of consistency; he instances Iago's reference to Othello's brother's being shot from his side, Prospero's speaking of having opened graves, Lady Macbeth's claim to having given suck. The same kind of fragmentation occurs when Shakespeare changes his conception of a character from one scene to another: Cleopatra is mere trollop at first, marble-constant at the last. "The contradiction," says Schücking, "is astonishing." Moreover, Shakespeare at times seems mechanically to follow his history or his plot so as to produce matter not harmonious with the rest, as with Cleopatra's connivings with her treasurer, which come from history but are out of keeping with her character, or Hamlet's melancholy, which derives from the *Ur-Hamlet* but has nothing to do with Shakespeare's prince.

I have been at pains to set forth Schücking's line of reasoning because it is useful, I think, and because he himself repeatedly obscures it. He obscures it by engaging in endless arguments with other critics, and by forcing particular positions against the grain. Perhaps others will agree with him that Caesar's speeches about himself—as not fearing, as amazed that other men fear death, as born with, and elder brother to, danger, as unsusceptible of flattery, as not like other men, as Olympian—are to be taken literally without suggestion of inflated self-esteem. Few, one imagines, will agree that Lear undergoes "not a development, but a decadence," that his words to Cordelia, "Come, let's away to prison./We two alone will sing like birds i' the cage," show "not a purified Lear . . . but a nature completely transformed, whose extraordinary vital forces are extinguished, or about to be extinguished." Schücking, having established that the private reflections of characters on one another are always valid, finds an exception to the rule in Lady Macbeth's declaration that there is too much of the milk of human kindness in her husband. If, as Schücking argues, there is *not* too much milk, one wonders what his rule is worth. And one doubts that all is fragment that seems fragment to him. Perhaps Hamlet's feigned madness and his melancholy do harmonize; conceivably Cleopatra tried to protect her investments as well as her love.

If we can by-pass Schücking's interminable debates, if we can put aside his own special interpretations, we have left more systematically than in Stoll a definition of the primitive, popular, Elizabethan dramatics which is, if not Shakespeare's, as Schücking argues, then that from which his own emerges. This definition is least dubious in its postulates about monologues and reflections, least certain in its assumption that the evidences of separate scenes cannot and should not be resolved into harmony. But in any instance, it provides a hard test of interpretation that conflicts with it. If Schücking cannot completely rend and deracinate the subjectivism he detests, he does, one hopes, subdue it a trifle.

xi

Frank Harris / *1856–1931*
Ernest Jones / *1879–1958*
Wyndham Lewis / *1884–1957*

Harris as redeemer: his Shakespeare.

Harris as redeemer: his Shakespeare. The dark lady. Limitations and merits of Harris's esthetic. ❧ *Jones compared to Harris. Hamlet psychoanalyzed. "Tragedy and the Mind of the Infant." "The Theme of Matricide." The Oedipal in Shakespeare. Merits and limitations of Jones's approach.* ❧ *Lewis's Shakespeare as public executioner, as "shamanized" man, contemptuous of king and multitude. His master-subject: past vs. present, The Lion and the Fox. Styles appropriate to each world. Shakespeare's ambivalent implication in both worlds. Coriolanus. Shakespeare's nihilism. Lewis's Shakespeare an anti-Shakespeare.*

Frank Harris's Shakespeare criticism is restorative in intent, reductive in practice, rude and extravagant but, as Ernest Jones says, displaying "considerable insight."[1] Harris tries to redeem Shakespeare from the hero-worshippers. "It is begging the question," he asserts,

> to assume that whatever Shakespeare did was perfect; humanity cannot be penned up even in Shakespeare's brain. Like every other man of genius Shakespeare must have shown himself in his qualities and defects, in his preferences and

prejudices; "a fallible being," as stout old Dr. Johnson knew, "will fail somewhere."

Harris tries to redeem Shakespeare from the scholar-dullards whom he contemptuously lumps under such names as Dryasdust and Gradgrind. He tries, finally, to redeem Shakespeare from the prudish sentimentalists. He sees Shakespeare as marrying of necessity and against his will, deserting his wife early, failing to support her, denigrating her in his portraits of shrewish wives, humiliating her with his bequest of "the second-best bed," and guaranteeing by the rubric over his tomb that she be excluded from her eternal resting place beside him. Then he finds Halliwell-Phillipps telling "us how on the morning of the day [Shakespeare] died 'his wife, who had smoothed the pillow beneath his head for the last time, felt that her right hand was taken from her.' "[2] The proper Victorians would keep Shakespeare's marriage tidy and sweet, his eroticism cold. Harris tries to right the record.

His redemptive esthetic is an uncomplicated expressionism. "As it is the object of a general to win battles," he says, "so it is the life-work of the artist to show himself to us." He imagines that Shakespeare "has painted himself twenty times from youth till age at full length"—in Romeo, Hamlet, and Macbeth, in Duke Vincentio and Posthumus, in Arthur and Richard II, in the impatient Hotspur (but not the militant), in Henry VI, Orsino, Falstaff, Biron, Valentine, Antonio the Merchant, Brutus, Troilus, Antony, Lear, Timon, Prospero.

> It is time to speak of him frankly; he was gentle, and witty; gay, and sweet-mannered, very studious, too, and fair of mind; but at the same time he was weak in body and irresolute, hasty and wordy, and took habitually the easiest way out of difficulties; he was ill-endowed in the virile virtues and virile vices. When he showed arrogance it was always of intellect and not of character; he was a parasite by nature. But none of these faults would have brought him to ruin; he was snared

again in full manhood by his master-quality, his overpowering
sensuality, and thrown in the mire.

Harris identifies the dark lady as Mary Fitton, but what he has to
say of her derives not from the identification but from female
figures in the plays and sonnets. Harris sees her as proud, dark,
beautiful, daring in speech and deed, taking Shakespeare by
storm.

> She was his complement in every failing; her strength
> matched his weakness; her resolution his hesitation, her bold-
> ness his timidity . . . He forgot that humble worship was
> not the way to win a high-spirited girl. He loved her so
> abjectly that he lost her; and it was undoubtedly his over-
> powering sensuality and snobbishness which brought him to
> his knees, and his love to ruin.

Shakespeare's passion for her, says Harris, lasted twelve years.
"Again and again he lived golden hours with her like those Cleo-
patra boasted of and regretted. Life is wasted quickly in such
orgasms of passion; lust whipped to madness by jealousy." As
Shakespeare so often painted himself, so he painted her—in
Rosaline, Cressida, Cleopatra.

> All his other women are parts of her or reflections of her, as
> all his heroes are sides of Hamlet, or reflections of him. Portia
> is the first full-length sketch . . . taken at a distance: Bea-
> trice and Rosalind are mere reflections of her high spirits, her
> aristocratic pride and charm: her strength and resolution are
> incarnate in Lady Macbeth. Ophelia, Desdemona, Cordelia,
> are but abstract longings for purity and constancy called into
> life by his mistress's faithlessness and passion.

The notion that an author's heroes are projections of himself,
his heroines impersonations of the woman in his life, fits Heming-
way more neatly than Shakespeare but neither as neatly as Harris

supposes. It suggests a one-to-one relation between fact and fiction which ignores the molding influences of story, plot, theme, genre, convention, company, and audience, to say nothing of an author's own reticence. It imagines the artist dashing out his works, as a Richardson heroine her letters, in the white heat of the experience being described. In Brutus, says Harris, Shakespeare shows "no murderer, no conspirator, no narrow republican fanatic, but simply gentle Shakespeare discovering to us his own sad heart and the sweetness which suffering had called forth in him." "Forced to see other men as they were, [Shakespeare] tried for a moment to see himself as he was"—in Hamlet. He puts the young aristocrat who stole the dark lady's love into the play as Laertes; he puts in the dark lady herself as the faithless and sensual Gertrude. *Othello* shows "that Shakespeare's nature gave itself gradually to jealousy and revenge." *Troilus and Cressida* "shows us the poet's mistress painted in a rage of erotic passion so violent that it defeats itself and the portrait becomes an incredible caricature—that way madness lies: *Troilus and Cressida* points to *Lear* and *Timon.*"

If Harris's esthetic is naive, his application of it often seems arbitrary and without humor. It may well be that Rosaline's description of Biron portrays Shakespeare as he would like to be seen—as of becoming mirth, witty, apt, sweet, and voluble in his discourse; but it is doubtful (pray God) that Shakespeare is completely and characteristically confessing his feelings, as Harris says he is, in the comically sentimental lines that open *Twelfth Night*:

> If music be the food of love, play on;
> Give me excess of it, that surfeiting
> The appetite may sicken, and so die.
> That strain again;—it had a dying fall . . .

It is doubtful that Shakespeare "preferred Arthur to the Bastard" in *King John*, as Harris says, nor does Jaques' being "a melancholy student of life" make him much resemble Hamlet. Harris considers the unseen Rosaline of *Romeo and Juliet* to be a "picture taken from life" of the dark lady, for she is described as possessing scarlet lips, high forehead, white skin, and black eyes. One wonders whether the description is not rather conventional, and whether, since she is described as chaste, the portrait can rightly be said to fit. Harris says that Portia is a "full-length" sketch of the dark lady; Portia, though, is both chaste and blonde. Harris asserts that Portia's remarks on mercy are in fact directed to Queen Elizabeth on behalf of Essex, and what seems equally far from the mark, he doubts that most men would have condemned Gertrude's lechery: "certainly," he says, they "would not have suffered their thoughts to dwell on it beyond the moment."

The weaknesses of Harris's criticism are evident, the merits perhaps are not. The effort to bring Shakespeare from the clouds down to man, from the libraries out to the marketplace, and from the Sunday Schools into the streets is valuable. The truth sets us free. If the method is manifestly too simple, and erratically applied, it expresses a truth good to be reminded of: a man writes out of himself; he walks, as Raleigh puts in, on his own shadow.[3] Beneath the dazzling variety of Shakespearean surfaces, Harris recalls what Coleridge noted long before, that Shakespeare's characters are not, after all, so many. Harris invites us to attend to the likenesses instead of the differences so that we begin to get at the common ground, the unchanging Shakespeare. And by way of helping us, he draws attention to matters little attended to before though much mentioned since—what has come to be called the sex nausea running through the tragedies and Shakespeare's insistent focus on passivity rather than activity, on failure rather than success. His Shakespeare comes closer to breathing than Dowden's. Shaw is in his debt, and Ernest Jones, and Wyndham Lewis—and through them, the rest of us.

❦ ❦ ❦

Ernest Jones gives us in polished and elaborate depth the psychology of Hamlet and his creator.[4] Jones's range is narrower than Harris's, his analysis more profound, his findings more complex, but he relates to Harris more nearly than either do to Dowden. He too finds in author and character a thwarted sexual drive expressing itself in dreams of revenge, murder, and death. "Harris may well be right," he observes, "in saying that behind Queen Gertrude stands someone like Mary Fitton," though he goes on to say that "behind that lady certainly stands Shakespeare's mother." And Jones sounds Harris's own note when he suggests that Shakespeare, "unable to express [his resentment] towards either the faithless friend or the faithless mistress," responded by composing "a tragedy whose theme was the suffering of a tortured man who could not avenge his injured feelings."

Jones is no less aware than Bradley's critics that the characters of a play are just that and not "real people"; ultimately, like Harris, he views the characters as projections, more or less distorted, of the author's psyche; but his initial position is the pretence that the characters are actual. He puts Hamlet on his analyst's couch, as it were, and after performing the critical equivalent of listening to him free associate in blank verse arrives at this hypothesis:

How, if, in fact, Hamlet had in years gone by, as a child, bitterly resented having had to share his mother's affection even with his own father, had regarded him as a rival, and had secretly wished him out of the way so that he might enjoy undisputed and undisturbed the monopoly of that affection? If such thoughts had been present in his mind in childhood days they evidently would have been "repressed," and all traces of them obliterated, by filial piety and other educative influences. The actual realization of his early wish in the death of his father at the hands of a jealous rival would then have stimulated into activity these "repressed" memories, which would have produced, in the form of depression and

other suffering, an obscure aftermath of his childhood's con-
flict . . .

    The explanation, therefore, of the delay and self-frustra-
tion exhibited in the endeavor to fulfil his father's demand for
vengeance is that to Hamlet the thought of incest and
parricide combined is too intolerable to be borne. One part of
him tries to carry out the task, the other flinches inexorably
from the thought of it.

This is the hypothesis which comes at the end of the chapter,
"The Psycho-Analytical Solution." The demonstration takes the
two following chapters, "Tragedy and the Mind of the Infant"
and "The Theme of Matricide." "Tragedy and the Mind of the
Infant" sets forth the essential dynamics of the Oedipus complex,
then examines Hamlet in its light. Among the chapter's findings
are the following. The Queen's "markedly sensual nature and her
passionate fondness for her son" accord with the idea that "as a
child Hamlet had experienced the warmest affection for his
mother, and this, as is always so, had contained elements of a
disguised erotic quality, still more so in infancy." Contrasts between Ophelia's character and Gertrude's suggest that Hamlet
"had unknowingly been impelled to choose a woman who should
least remind him of his mother," but, "a case might even be made
out for the view that part of his courtship originated . . . in an
unconscious desire to play [Ophelia] off against his mother." The
Oedipal drives aroused to new life by the death of his father, the
marriage of his mother, have as one of their first manifestations
Hamlet's "reaction against Ophelia" in which sexual revulsion and
jealousy combine. Ultimately, says Jones, the infantile unconscious
splits "the mother image . . . into two opposite pictures," the
saint and the sensualist, and "when sexual repression is highly
pronounced, as with Hamlet, then both types of women are felt to
be hostile: the pure one out of resentment at her repulses, the

sensual one out of the temptation she offers to plunge into guiltiness. Misogyny . . . is the inevitable result." Hamlet's attitude toward Claudius is complex:

> He of course detests him, but it is the jealous detestation of one evil-doer towards his successful fellow. Much as he hates him, he can never denounce him with the ardent indignation that boils straight from his blood when he reproaches his mother, for the more vigorously he denounces his uncle the more powerfully does he stimulate to activity his own unconscious and "repressed" complexes.

> In reality his uncle incorporates the deepest and most buried part of his own personality, so that he cannot kill him without also killing himself. This solution . . . is actually the one that Hamlet finally adopts.

Among the findings of "The Theme of Matricide" are these. Hamlet's first soliloquy reveals his own repressed incestuous proclivity. He is

> more concerned about putting an end to the incestuous relationship [between Gertrude and Claudius] than about avenging the murder, though he never doubted it was his duty to do so. His difficulty was what to do about his mother, and he was by no means so inclined as his father to let her off lightly; in fact, he keeps reminding himself to be careful not to injure her, as if that was a dangerous propensity he had to keep in check.

It is indeed, says Jones. The unfaithful or lascivious mother, "particularly if she is unduly sensual with the boy himself," arouses unendurable drives toward incest. "Were she to proceed even further, and commit incest itself, then she has broken down the barrier so valuable to the boy in coping with his own impulses." "There is only one hope left"—matricide.

Having thus meshed evidence from the play with the dynamics revealed by psychoanalysis, Jones turns from prince to poet. "It was a living person who imagined the figure of Hamlet with his behavior, his reflections, and his emotions. The whole came from somewhere within Shakespeare's mind." About the external events of Shakespeare's life Jones has little to say. The deaths in the year of *Hamlet's* composition of Shakespeare's father and of Essex, "an obvious father-substitute," and the experience detailed in the sonnets of "some overwhelming passion that ended in a betrayal in such circumstances that murderous impulses towards the faithless couple were stirred but could not be admitted to consciousness" account for the Oedipal eruption in him as the death and betrayal account for it in Hamlet. But Jones finds further evidence in Shakespeare of the Oedipal surfacing, as it were, by looking at another play. He agrees with Otto Rank[5] that in the tragedy preceding *Hamlet* "Caesar represents the father, and Brutus the son, of the typical Oedipus situation." In fact, filial attitudes are divided among three "sons": "Brutus represents the son's rebelliousness, Cassius his remorsefulness, and Antony his natural piety." But where Hamlet divides his feelings toward his father, according to the memory of his father "pious respect and love" and to his father-substitutes, Claudius and Polonius, "hatred, contempt, and rebellion," Caesar is "both loved and hated at once." Polonius, Jones reminds us parenthetically, "did enact Julius Caesar: [he] was killed i' the Capitol; Brutus killed [him]."

Jones's exposition of his thesis contains considerably more than this summary indicates but perhaps this adequately suggests his line. Clearly Jones escapes Harris's brashness. His interpretation complexly accommodates the text. It helps account for the play's genesis, its workings, and its inveterate appeal (for Oedipus, he reminds us, is in us no less than in Hamlet and Shakespeare).

Although it runs the risk of confusing the fictional with the factual, Jones shows himself aware of the dangers and is tactful in his presentation. The past he imagines for Hamlet is generic rather than specific: what happens to him happens by and large to infants everywhere. Of course, those who regard psychoanalysis as fol-de-rol have no use for Jones, but their number diminishes. There are, however, important limits to his analysis of the play. As Fergusson observes, "the Oedipus complex does not account for the fact that Hamlet, besides being a son, is also a dispossessed prince; nor that Claudius, besides being a father symbol, is also the actual ruler of the state."[6] Moreover, Jones's analysis is secular; the play is not. To Hamlet comes a figure from another world, and this at once makes his experience unique. Further, heaven and hell are dimensions of Hamlet's universe, though not of the analyst's; they engage in the affairs of men whose ultimate concern is less with the here than the hereafter. Hamlet acknowledges the Everlasting's canon 'gainst self-slaughter; Claudius bends his stubborn knees to ask for Heaven's mercy; Gertrude will confess herself to Heaven while her son, who sees himself as scourge and minister of the powers above, discovers that "there's a divinity that shapes our ends, rough-hew them how we will." Oedipal Hamlet may be, then, but there is more to his mystery than that. And there is, of course, the poetry. Though the rest of us were to slay our fathers and marry our mothers, as Jones well knows, no such miracles of wit and passion would come from our lips as come from Hamlet's.

❧   ❧   ❧

Wyndham Lewis, like Gervinus, concerns himself with the content of Shakespeare's mind, but he is expositor rather than advocate and of a system not generally transferrable, but uniquely expressive of Shakespeare's own nature.[7] Lewis is hard to read at first, for his style is jumpy and obscurely belligerent, like a blindfolded man's in a battle royal; but after you catch his essential method—a steady beating forward, one step at a time—and begin to realize how alive his Shakespeare is and emancipated from the clichés of the English social and religious establishments, then Lewis becomes enormously exciting.

"Shakespeare," says Lewis, "was the poet of kings, and to the pathos of this function he was peculiarly susceptible, and technically the *pathos* or death of a king or hero was a subject he treated constantly in the course of his trade." Pater dwelt on the irony of kingship; Lewis focuses on its anthropology. The king is the one in the society of the many, the principle of the ego in the world of the community, and so he is hated, guarded, set off, used. "Behind his lonely, spectacularly egotistic, eminent figure a thousand equally intense, cosier, privileged egotisms could subsist." Further, he was quartered on his people like a small god,

> giving a personal form to all the anonymous outer power of the universe, against which it was impossible to fight, but against which—on usurious terms and in exchange for service and taxes . . . —he agreed to protect them. He was their enemy, a representative of the outer hostile world, between whom and themselves the terms of propitiation and sacrifice had been systematized.
>
> To see this semi-divine person, even in effigy and in play, exposed to the vulgarest misfortune, disgraced, humiliated and killed, must have been in most times an extraordinary sensation. This man masquerading as a god was suddenly confronted with powers superior to himself: the delight in the spectacle of this confrontation was one of the great assets of tragedy.

Lewis asks that we see the tragedy as "of the same nature as a public execution." You and I are the audience, watching the king die, hated by us, perishing for us; and the executioner, "a quiet and highly respectable man," wearing his impassibility like the professional mask of a hangman, he is the tragic dramatist, he is

Shakespeare—"but actually the mask was incessantly convulsed with the most painful unprofessional emotions; and it was apt to be tear-stained and fixed in a bitter grimace as he left the scaffold."[8]

Lewis turns to the executioner. What sort of person was he?

> The character of his genius was responsive and not active: he was not a philosopher himself at all, so much as a very great and accommodating artist—accommodating himself, with great suppleness, but not slavishly or without bitter comment, to the life, art and ideas around him.

He was "a transformed or *shamanized* man," by which term Lewis means one who has attained magical power (a *shaman* is a medicine man) by taking to himself the attributes of the female sex. Generations have "marvelled at the truth and delicacy of 'Shakespeare's women'"; Lewis finds in their portrayal that "understanding of the female nature, so characteristic of the 'unmanly.' "

> In Antony and Cleopatra, . . . the author of the play, if in love with anybody, is in love with Antony . . . The mysterious and unreasonable change [of which Schücking makes such a point] occurring in the character of Cleopatra, at the end, culminating in her death . . . is a female self-immolation to the man-god of whom she has made a cult.

Those marvelous speeches Cleopatra makes in her dying "are really the afterglow of Antony; it is the last warmth of *him* that we are invited to taste."

Shakespeare, then, is public executioner, wearing the mask of impassibility, feminine in his sexual and emotional organization. He has (*contra* Gervinus) "the poorest opinion both of the action and the actors" in his plays. Though his blank verse endows his heroes with a specious glory, "most if not all had come to a violent and stupid end, clamoring about their divine right and their kingly ways, defiant or idiotically remorseful. He probably did not think much more of these kings that passed through his hands than Gibbon did of his gallery of despots." He accepted them for what they were, human and politically necessary—"but with a much worse grace than is generally believed." He accords the many-headed multitude no greater honor. When his kings come to their pathos, Shakespeare enters their bodies and speaks his own views and often enough this is to curse the many who have betrayed the king and brought him to his destruction. Shakespeare, with little regard for the one, with little for the many, condemns action and so selects tragedy as his form of literature—tragedy, which tells not of the success of action but of failure.

The "master-subject" of Shakespeare's plays was, "immediately and historically, the reflection of the struggle between chivalry, 'Celtism,' Christian mysticism, on the one hand, and the 'scientific spirit' of the Renaissance mind and of the modern world on the other." Lewis sees "the Hamlet-problem" as conspicuous evidence of Shakespeare's interest in this subject, but it manifests itself as well in the Machiavellian opposition that gives his book its title, *The Lion and the Fox:* "the contest or the tragedy arising from the meeting of the *Simpleton* and the *Machiavel*, the Fool and the Knave," the one functioning as king and representative of the past, the other functioning as the instrument of the many, as representative of the modern world.

> The great spectacular "pugnacious" male ideal is represented perfectly by Othello; who was led out to the slaughter on the Elizabethan stage just as the bull is thrust into the Spanish bull-ring. Iago, the taurobolus of this sacrificial bull, the little David of this Goliath . . . is for Shakespeare nothing but Everyman, the Judas of the world, the representative of the crowds around the crucifix, or of the ferocious crowds

at the corrida, or of the still more abject Roman crowds at the mortuary games. Othello is of the race of Christs, or of the race of "bulls"; he is the hero with all the magnificent helplessness of the animal, or all the beauty and ultimate resignation of the god.

The two opposing worlds and their representative figures have their appropriate style in Shakespeare. For the heroes, it is the grand style, which is the actual source of their grandeur, according to Lewis. Wherever the grand style enters the conflict, "the chivalry substitutes itself for the self-interest, a mystical religion for a 'scientific truth,' the Lion for the Fox. But the moment the drums stop beating the appeal of art weakens; the Fox resumes the center of the stage, and the Lion withdraws." The Fox's style is that of the "man of the world" "with its 'knowingness,' its smartly advertising cynicism, herd-reclamation, mechanical snobbery." Iago is one exemplar of this tribe; Falstaff is another, of the subspecies "man of wit and pleasure." Iago is the Italian Fox, but "if the Machiavel were an Englishman he would be like Falstaff. This laziness, rascality and 'good fellow' quality, crafty in the brainless animal way, is the English way of being a 'deep-brained Machiavel.' "

Shakespeare has little enough regard for his Foxes, says Lewis, but he is implicated with them. They destroy the Lions; he destroys the Lions. His implication has another dimension, for he endows his Foxes with attributes of his own. The "man of the world," "like the woman, or the jesuit . . . if we erect him into a figure, is one of abnegation. His is essentially a system of defence and not of attack. He is a man who is himself small and weak, but who has acquired, who lives in the midst of, a powerful defensive machinery." And Falstaff's humor "which served him better than any suit of armor could in the various vicissitudes of his life," like the *shamanizing* faculty, enables "its possessor to escape the inconveniences and conventional disgrace of being feminine—at the same time it provides him with most of the social advantages of the woman."

Shakespeare possesses a similar ambivalence toward his Lions. In general, he little values them except for Antony, Othello, perhaps Hector—figures of action whose glory somehow transcends the stench of mere slaughter. But he has among his heroes a Quixotic group—Timon, Coriolanus, Brutus, Hamlet: these he regards coldly "save when something like a sexual excitement seems to take possession of him, and he begins caressing and adoring his hero as though he were a woman—like another Antonio in front of a Sebastian, in *Twelfth Night*." Lewis chooses Coriolanus by way of illustration. He

> is of course the super-snob. Of all Shakespeare's heroes he is the coldest, and the one that Shakespeare himself seems to have felt most coldly towards. He was the child of Volumnia, not of Shakespeare, and one that never became anything but a schoolboy, crazed with notions of privilege and social distinction, incapable of thinking (not differing in that from the rest of Shakespeare's nursery of colossi), but also congealed into a kind of machine of unintelligent pride.

Shakespeare no more supports his politics than he does that of the Foxes, Sicinius and Brutus. "For him *l'un vaudrait l'autre* . . . For it was human nature about which Shakespeare wrote, and he did not write on a tone of morals, nor on one of class-prejudice or class-illusion."

> It is a play about a conventional military hero, existing as the characteristic ornament of a strong aristocratic system. Shakespeare was neither for or against him, on propagandist, feudal or non-feudal grounds. He was quite ready to curse the crowd with him: and he was equally ready to examine with as little

pleasure the child of a harsh practical system, abusing his many advantages, and showing to perfection how the top, as likewise the under, dog is unsatisfactory and foolish, the one very nearly worthy of the other—the violent, dull, conceited leader, and the resentful but cowardly slave. Meantime the play is charged with a magnificent rhetoric, as wherever any character utters Shakespeare's blank verse. Coriolanus speaks frequently like a god: also the altofronto tone is adopted by him from time to time, as by most Shakespeare heroes—his banter and bitterness being often just the same as that of Hamlet, Timon or Lear. But that is Shakespeare's own voice and manner that you hear, the central surge, that, wherever the music he is making excites him, comes out and is heard.

"Shakespeare's own voice"—is nihilistic. He is "the adversary of life itself . . . and his works a beautifully impersonal outpouring of fury, bitter reflection, invective and complaint." "When the misfortune arrives, [the heroes] automatically become Shakespeare," which is to say, they speak with the bitterness, the outrage, the madness of Hamlet, say, or Lear.

And madness accounts for the nihilism that surges up in every tragedy of Shakespeare, once the characters have become 'mad' enough with suffering. Their 'madness' is for an Englishman the necessary excuse. Such wildness would have seemed unnatural if it had not been labelled pathologic.

Pathologic or not, it expresses Shakespeare's own views, says Lewis: "there is a voice that is Shakespeare's and there is a character that is his. His greatest heroes gibe like Thersites (the *altofronto* type), and his most embittered chorus-work is grandly direct and stings like truth."

Trying to do justice to the complex harmonics of Lewis's argument, I have quoted much, expounded little. But Lewis has seemed his own best expositor, as he does, one last time, in this passage from "Some Concluding Observations":

> In spite of the placid and "gentle" surface of this mirror of a man, we know the storms that raged beneath it; and we know that he must, personally, have suffered as much from the world about him as any of his heroes. If we take one of his great tragedies, Timon of Athens, for instance, and see what happens, in reality, in the progress of the play, the point of this protracted argument will be apparent. The Timon that a dispassionate observer would see (without the intervention of Shakespeare's poetry) would be the Timon seen by Apemantus. Shakespeare saw that one also—as he shows by means of the discourse of Apemantus. But Timon has to be sacrificed, to become nothing in a worldly sense, from having been everything; he has to suffer heroically and have a pathos. This does not happen to most men of the world—they know too much, are too prudent, or merely sufficiently lucky, in ordinary circumstances, to escape this degradation. In Timon's case, or Lear's, it was due expressly to some violent or child-like kink. It is when these figures fall to abjection that they reach the region of the Christs. But what is not so readily admitted is that that is also the region of the Shakespeares. If these figures had no pathos and humiliation they would never be clothed, as they are invariably by Shakespeare, for these occasions, in the most grand and mournful rhetoric . . . Antony and Cleopatra, Othello, Lear, Timon, and the rest, are all splendid masterpieces, all reproducing the same music of extinction and unbounded suffering. They are a gallery of sunsets: they are dream-storms in a single soul, with a piling up of vaster and vaster burdens with ever more colossal figures to carry them.

Lewis's Shakespeare is more "real," more completely individual, than the Shakespeare of his predecessors. The plays, as he views them, more intricately and immediately express their author's temper and person. And his comments on individual characters—Iago, Falstaff, Coriolanus, Timon—are more excitingly appreciative. Lewis's Shakespeare is, in a sense, an anti-Shakespeare, a creature the obverse of the image held up for adoration by the critical establishment. The established Shakespeare is moral, Lewis's is esthetic. The established Shakespeare is conservative, aristocratic, feudal—or somewhat less commonly, liberal, democratic, modern; Lewis's is a-political, damning both one and many and implicating himself in both—in the heroes whom he creates, invests with the glory of his blank verse, and speaks through in their hours of pathos; in the destroyers whose defences resemble their creator's, whose destructiveness exemplifies his own. The established Shakespeare is either impersonal or gentle; Lewis's is vibrantly personal and savagely bitter. He is feminine in temperament rather than masculine, and nihilistic rather than Christian or optimistic.

Two contradictory impulses operate in Lewis's criticism. One is an open-minded willingness to consider all the evidence, to follow where it leads, whatever the consequences. This, combining with a rich anthropological, historical, and literary understanding, contributes to the anti-Shakespeare we have been examining. Equally contributory, however, is an advocate's prejudice that selects only such evidence as speaks to his purpose. I am not speaking of the attribution to Shakespeare of a feminine sexual organization. Harris and Jones agree with Lewis here, but each reader must satisfy himself. I refer to the undemonstrated assumption that Shakespeare's values are esthetic rather than ethic and the cognate conclusion that the nihilism in the plays expresses Shakespeare's own view. Lewis treats the insanity of the tragic heroes as the mask for Shakespeare's truth. Why? Why not consider what they say in their madness as in fact mad? Othello's outpourings receive the lie in Desdemona. Lear's ravings find their repudiation in Cordelia, Kent, the Fool. Macbeth's "Tomorrow and tomorrow and tomorrow" is the swansong of a spiritual suicide. The plays may present life as a tempest, but they repeatedly assert too that there "is an ever-fixed mark that looks on tempests and is never shaken." Curiously Lewis hears nothing of love. His Shakespeare, then, may seem an anti-Shakespeare not only in opposing the tradition, but in refusing to express alongside the curses and the rantings, the ultimate affirmations.

xii

G. Wilson Knight / 1897-

*Taints. Boldness and freshness. "Interpretation." Bradley
and Knight on* Macbeth. *Visionary unity of individual
plays, of entire Shakespearean corpus. Seminal comparison.
The axis of Shakespeare's great plays.*

"His taints and honors/Wag'd equal with him," says Maecenas of
Antony. We might apply the comment to G. Wilson Knight.[1] As
Siegel observes, Knight's works "have had a more profound influence than the work of any other critic of our generation."[2] He
is one of the great seminal critics whose remarks, like Coleridge's,
open the way to new discoveries and appreciations. Yet no major
critic writes so cloudily as he, none so muddies his morality and
metaphysics, none so wearies by trying to do our feeling for us. In
the interests of accuracy we must glance at this side of Knight; in
the interests of charity we may do it swiftly, trusting that the
taints are the excesses and deficiencies of his honors, manifestations of the same impulse, the shadows that define his sunlight.

    Knight's amorality can stun. He says that, granting the fact of
his original crime, "Claudius can hardly be blamed for his later
actions." He says that "we must not be repelled by Pandarus' lax
morality in helping [Troilus and Cressida] to illicit love." In
general, he appears not to distinguish the sensual from the spiritual in human relations. His metaphysics similarly jar, as when he
says that "Timon, at the end, is pure essence of significance,

beyond the temporal, in touch with a conquering knowledge of his furthest destiny. Nothing will be proved the largesse of all things." And perhaps the following passage on *Lear* will suggest Knight's occasional crudity of critical diction and the flamboyance of his emotionalism:

> There are thus two primary qualities in King Lear: the panoramic view of good and bad people working out their destiny; and the fiery-passionate, grotesque Lear-theme which the pangs of this cold world bring to birth. The naturalism of the play travails to produce out of its earthly womb a thing of imaginative and miraculous splendor, high-pitched in bizarre, grotesque, vivid mental conflict and agony: which in turn pursues its rocket-flight of whirling madness, explosive, to the transcendent mystic awakening into love, dropping bright balls of silent fire, then extinguished, as the last tragic sacrifice claims its own, and the darkness closes. This is the sweeping ascent of the Lear-theme, rushing, whistling in air, a sudden visionary brilliance, and many colors across the heavens, expanding petals of jewelled flame . . .

From the beginning, as even these "taints" suggest, Knight has been bold. He has freshly asserted the uncommon and unconventional. His first work, *Myth and Miracle*, authoritatively sets forth a Dowdenian conviction that the plays in their order trace Shakespeare's spiritual progress, that the final plays reveal a triumphant culmination rather than the exhaustion attributed to them by such as Strachey,[3] that their meaning is to be found in their symbols, and that "*The Tempest* is at the same time a record of Shakespeare's spiritual progress and a statement of the vision to which that progress has brought him." Knight comes to Hamlet refreshingly convinced that "we have done ill to sentimentalize his personality." Coleridge and Schlegel sounded that note long before; L. C. Knights will sound it hereafter.[4] But Knight focuses in his own way on the point. "Hamlet's soul is sick," he says. His "disease is mental and spiritual death." "His consciousness, functioning in terms of evil and negation, sees Hell but not Heaven." He is, in an important manner of speaking, the something rotten in the State of Denmark, "the ambassador of death walking amid life." Knight turns confidently to *Troilus and Cressida*. "When once we see clearly the central idea . . . from which the play's thought and action derive their significance, most of the difficulties vanish," he asserts, and he proceeds to unravel and define the play's "philosophy":

> Envenomed cynicism [Thersites], with its food, ignorant stupidity [Ajax], are thrown into relation with the profound philosophy of the Greek leaders: both contrast with the romantic chivalry of Troy and the humor of Pandarus. The symbolic setting for the main theme is, indeed, masterly. Two views of human life are pitted against each other in the opposing armies, and in the continual and lengthy discussions. Always we find it to be fundamentally the same dualism of (i) immediate and personal experience, intuition, the infinite, the timeless; and (ii) the concepts of order and social system, intellect, the finite world, the time-concept. Between these two modes the consciousness of Troilus is wrenched, divided. There is no rule in unity itself.

Knight approaches *Measure for Measure* parabolically, finding its central idea in the prayer, "Forgive us our debts as we forgive our debtors." The play's structural technique he considers exquisite, its unity profound. Isabella is "self-centered" in her saintliness, her fall deeper than Angelo's: "she knows now [when Claudio appeals to her] that it is not all saintliness, she sees her own soul and sees it as something small, frightened, despicable, too frail to dream of such a sacrifice." "The Duke, like Jesus, is the prophet of a new order of ethics," who discovers, by his machinations, that his "original leniency" was "right, not wrong." "The Duke knows his tolerance to be now a moral imperative: he sees too far into the nature of man to pronounce judgment according to the appearance of human behavior." Knight approaches *Othello* by way of its style. "The dominant quality is separation," he says, "not, as is more usual in Shakespeare, cohesion." Image stands aloof from image, that is to say, word from word. When Othello cries out that there should be a huge eclipse of sun and moon, or that the moon in her error comes more near the earth than she was wont, he establishes contrasts between the vast night sky with its moving planets and the passions of men. These things

> remain vast, distant, separate . . . something against which the dramatic movement may be silhouetted, but with which it cannot be merged. This poetic use of heavenly bodies serves to elevate the theme, to raise issues infinite and unknowable. These bodies are not, however, implicit symbols of man's spirit, as in King Lear: they remain distinct, isolated phenomena, sublimely decorative to the play.

Knight develops his definition of *Othello*'s style by contrasting it to the styles of *Lear* and *Macbeth*, observes, then, that the Othello music crashes into dissonance at certain points in the play when the Moor loses his self-control, and works toward an inclusive, symbolic interpretation of the play on the basis of this stylistic development.

The purpose of these brief paragraphs is not to do justice to Knight's expositions but to suggest something of his extraordinary freshness and to provide background for discussion of his critical approach. He dubs this approach "interpretation" to distinguish it from "criticism." The latter suggests

> a certain process of deliberately objectifying the work under consideration; the comparison of it with other similar works in order especially to show in what respects it surpasses, or falls short of, those works; the dividing its "good" from its "bad"; and, finally, a formal judgment as to its lasting validity.

Interpretation, by contrast, is non-judicial and passive: it submits itself to the work and attempts to reconstruct its vision. It operates in a certain, very definite way:

> One must be prepared to see the whole play in space as well as in time. It is natural in analysis to pursue the steps of the tale in sequence, noticing the logic that connects them, regarding those essentials that Aristotle notes: the beginning, middle, and end. But by giving supreme attention to this temporal nature of drama we omit what, in Shakespeare, is at least of equivalent importance. A Shakespearian tragedy is set spatially as well as temporally in the mind. By this I mean that there are throughout the play a set of correspondences which relate to each other independently of the time-sequence which is the story: such are the intuition-intelligence opposition active within and across Troilus and Cressida, the death-theme in Hamlet, the nightmare evil of Macbeth . . . Now if we are prepared to see the whole play laid out, so to speak, as an area, being simultaneously aware of these thickly scattered correspondences in a single view of the whole, we possess the unique quality of the play in a new sense.

Interpretation by this definition means concern with the "spatial" as well as the temporal. In Knight's practice, it means concentration on the spatial to the neglect of the temporal. More precisely, in his practice it means the following: (1) Neglect of the conventional analytic categories of character and plot. Knight speaks of character, of course, but not as personality or as psycho-ethical organism, replete with motive and reaction; for him individuals are embodiments or experiencers of theme. (2) Suppression of the moral imperatives by which we usually live. "Ethical terms, though they must frequently occur in interpretation, must be allowed in so far as they are used in absolute obedience to the dramatic and esthetic significance: in which case they cease to be ethical in the usual sense." (Here, perhaps, lies the explanation of

Knight's attitudes toward Claudius and Pandarus.) (3) Focus on theme as indicated by "poetic symbolism," by parabolic style, and by correspondences of action, attitude, imagery, spectacle—especially as these cross over the boundary lines of conventional analytic categories. As characters share images or tones, these emerge as thematic (and the characters as individuals diminish in significance). (4) Concern with the ultimate "statements" of the plays, as about death in *Hamlet* or evil in *Macbeth*. (5) Assumption of a unity highly organic, the play being seen, in effect, as "an expanded metaphor" in which, as in a dream, the varying elements are functions one of another and of a central, inclusive meaning.

Quite obviously, Knight's interpretation is a far cry from Bradley's, though he conceives himself as following in Bradley's steps: "he it was who first subjected the atmospheric, what I have called the 'spatial,' qualities of the Shakespearian play to a considered, if rudimentary, comment." We can recognize Knight's accomplishment if we put his essay on "*Macbeth* and the Metaphysic of Evil" beside Bradley's two lectures on the play.

Bradley's first lecture begins with *Macbeth's* special atmosphere, under which heading fall the darkness of the play, the lights and colors that illuminate it, the storm and violence rushing through it, the witches and the ghost, the pictures called up by the witches, the actions of nature sympathetic to human guilt, the omens, the emphasis on the obscure regions of man's being (sleep, dreams), and, finally, the play's insistent and extraordinary use of irony (a point first made and documented by Hazlitt). Bradley turns next to the witches, to the "perverse" view that they are goddesses or fates, and to the "inadequate" view that they are "merely symbolic representations of the unconscious or half-conscious guilt in Macbeth itself." Finally, he turns to Macbeth and Lady Macbeth, who "are never detached in imagination from the atmosphere which surrounds them and adds to their grandeur and terror." They share, says Bradley, ambition, a high, proud, and commanding disposition; they possess no love of country, no altruism. But in most respects they differ. Here Bradley focuses on

Macbeth's character, his physical courage, his ambition, his sense of honor, his possession, however slight, of humanity and pity, and his "poetic" imagination, which expresses the torment of his conscience in terrifying images. Macbeth, he proposes, commits his crime "as if it were an appalling duty" and, the instant it is finished, recognizes its futility. Thereafter, and Bradley pursues him through the incidents of the plot, Macbeth feverishly plunges into guilt. "What a frightful clearness of self-consciousness in this descent to hell, and yet what a furious force in the instinct of life and self-assertion that drives him on!"

The second lecture begins with Lady Macbeth's character, seen statically and then as it develops (or deteriorates) in the actions of the play. Next it examines Banquo's character, which Bradley conceives as falling prey to the temptation of the witches and Banquo's own ambition, the evidence being his remaining silent about the prophecies of the witches and his acquiescence in Macbeth's accession and in the official theory of the guilt of Duncan's sons. Bradley proceeds to the minor characters, the lightness of whose sketching he tentatively attributes to Shakespeare's desire to present his play with "a certain classical tinge." Next Bradley examines three passages (the Porter's monologue, Lady Macduff with her son, and Macduff's receiving the news of his family's slaughtering); and finally he discusses the relative absence of prose in *Macbeth* and the effect thereof.

Clearly this summary obscures Bradley's customary richness of documentation, nor does it do much more than point to topics which he develops with his habitually elaborate and precise discrimination. Yet it may serve as contrast for Knight's essay, the contents of which we may examine in slightly more detail.

Knight begins by asserting his theme. In other plays (*Hamlet, Troilus, Othello, Lear, Timon*) there is gloom; "in *Macbeth* we find not gloom, but blackness: the evil is not relative, but absolute . . . The nature of this evil will be the subject of my essay." But Knight will not concern himself with Macbeth and Lady

Macbeth, their natures, their histories: "The whole play is one swift act of the poet's mind, and as such must be interpreted, since the technique confronts us not with separated integers of 'character' or incident, but with a molten welding of thought with thought, event with event." This being so, Knight will "start by noticing some of the more important elements in this totally imaginative effect." He draws attention to the baffling obscurity of the *Macbeth* world. "Probably in no play of Shakespeare are so many questions asked." "All the persons are in doubt, baffled." "Surprise is continual." "This blurring and lack of certainty is increased by the heavy proportion of second-hand or vague knowledge reported during the play's progress." "We, too, who read, are in doubt often. Action is here illogical." "Darkness permeates the play." To obscurity the play joins abnormality: "this world of doubts and darkness gives birth to strange and hideous creatures . . . not only are animals of unpleasant suggestion here present: we have animals, like men, irrational and amazing in their acts." "We are confronted by mystery, darkness, abnormality, hideousness: and therefore by fear . . . Fear is predominant. Everyone is afraid . . . The impact of the play is thus exactly analogous to a nightmare." This is the point to which Knight's initial discussion leads. The impact of the play is that of a nightmare. The experience of the characters is nightmarish.

> *The Weird Sisters are nightmare actualized; Macbeth's crime nightmare projected into action. Therefore this world is unknowable, hideous, disorderly, and irrational. The very style of the play has a mesmeric, nightmare quality, for in that dream-consciousness, hateful though it be, there is a nervous tension, a vivid sense of profound significance, an exceptionally rich apprehension of reality electrifying the mind: one is in touch with absolute evil, which, being absolute, has a satanic beauty, a hideous serpent-like grace and attraction, drawing, paralyzing.*

In the nightmare world of *Macbeth* Knight has emphasized the irrationalities and the horrors. "These two elements repel respectively the intellect and the heart of man. And, since the contemplating mind is thus powerfully unified in its immediate antagonism, our reaction holds the positive and tense fear that succeeds nightmare." We are forced "to a consciousness . . . exquisitely unified and sensitive."

Knight proceeds to examine the human events "to which the atmosphere of unreality and terror bears intimate relation." Banquo, like Macbeth and his wife, "succumb[s] to the evil downpressing of the *Macbeth* universe"; Macduff too, and Malcolm.

> Not that the persons are "bad characters." They are not "characters" at all, in the proper use of the word. They are but vaguely individualized, and more remarkable for similarity than difference. All the persons are primarily just this: men paralyzed by fear, and a sense of evil in and outside themselves . . . Neither we, nor they, know of what exactly they are guilty, yet they feel guilt.

So Lady Macbeth "is not merely a woman of strong will: she is a woman possessed . . . To interpret the figure of Lady Macbeth in terms of 'ambition' and 'will' is, indeed, a futile commentary . . . She is an embodiment—for one mighty hour—of evil absolute and extreme." Macbeth, similarly, has neither will nor ambition: he "is paralyzed, mesmerized, as though in a dream . . . He is helpless as a man in a nightmare." He is, in effect, propelled to crime by the evil within him. He "undertakes the murder, as a grim and hideous duty . . . Throughout he is driven by fear—the fear that paralyzes everyone else urges him to an amazing and mysterious action of blood. This action he repeats, again and again." Eventually, he overcomes his fear, and the hypocritical secrecy that has attended his crimes.

He has won through by excessive crime to an harmonious and honest relation with his surroundings. He has successfully symbolized the disorder of his lonely guilt-stricken soul by creating disorder in the world . . . He now knows himself to be a tyrant confessed, and wins back that integrity of soul which gives us:

I have lived long enough: my way of life
Is fallen into the sere, the yellow leaf . . .

. . . the delirious dream is over. A clear daylight now disperses the imaginative dark that has eclipsed Scotland. The change is remarkable . . . There is, as it were, a paean of triumph as the Macbeth universe, having struggled darkly upward, now climbs into radiance.

The experience of the play, thus suffered by Scotland, Macbeth, Lady Macbeth, and the others, thus caught up in that atmosphere at once irrational and horrible, is the experience of evil absolute. This is what the play gives us, says Knight.

Bradley's treatment is fuller than Knight's, though it should be said that Knight has written other discussions of *Macbeth*. And Knight's indebtedness to Bradley is clear—in the awareness of atmosphere, the notion that Macbeth proceeds to his crime as to an appalling duty, the conviction of Banquo's implication in the general guilt, the feeling for the lightness of the sketching of the "minor" characters. But Knight's contribution to Shakespearean criticism is defined by his differences. As I have suggested before, he neglects the conventional analytic categories of character and plot, suppresses the moral imperatives, focuses on theme, seeks the ultimate statement or significance, and assumes a unity highly organic, like that of an expanded metaphor or a dream. Everything in Knight's analysis proclaims the visionary unity of Shakespeare's play, its expression and communication of the experience of evil. Bradley catalogues the elements composing that play's atmosphere;

Knight classifies them under two headings, relates these to the mind and emotions of men, and explains how they operate first on the characters, then upon us. Bradley treats the atmosphere as the backdrop against which the characters move or, at its most immediate, as the air within which they move; but always, in his discussion, the characters are apart from it. Knight makes us see atmosphere and characters as in fact simultaneous expressions of the inclusive nightmare. He makes the witches more significantly participate in the play's meaning: they are neither subject for debate nor merely malign old women with hellish powers. They speak more nakedly from the heart of evil; they engage more horrifically the fear of character and audience. Knight refers the sketchiness of characterization to the dominant theme: the paralysis, the will-lessness of men possessed by evil without and within. And if he sentimentalizes Macbeth at the end, attributing to him a victory over fear which I do not see that he achieves, and an integrity of soul which I fail to discover within the play, Knight nonetheless relates the play's ending to its beginning, its new atmosphere to its old, its final vision to its former nightmare more satisfyingly than does Bradley.

Knight's chief seminal contribution to Shakespearean criticism is this insistence on organic or "poetic" unity, this invitation to discover functional relationships between all parts of a play and its meaning, all parts of a play and the impression it creates. He opens the door to a renewed sensitivity to imagery and symbolism and vision. And having opened the door, Knight himself, with Murry, Traversi, Mack, and a host more, has walked through.[5]

Knight insists on the unity of the individual play only slightly more than he insists on the progressive unity of the whole body of Shakespeare's writing from *Julius Caesar* to *The Tempest*. His biographical theory—of a "progress from spiritual pain and despairing thought through stoic acceptance to a serene and mystic joy"—is more sophisticated than Dowden's; I think it is more valid. Nothing, however, follows critically from its acceptance or rejection. But the process by which Knight arrives at his theory is seminal (though not original). It is the old process of comparison and contrast, putting the imagery, incidents, or characters of one play beside those of another to discover the likenesses and differences. Knight uses this method frequently both to discriminate between things similar, thus more precisely defining the item under discussion, and to discover the underlying identities, thence to infer the abiding concerns and expressions in Shakespeare's art.

Knight makes us grasp *Timon* by looking at *Othello*. The earlier play is story where the later is parable, particular where the later is universal, artistic where the later is philosophic. Timon generalizes the Moor; the men of Athens—or, more broadly yet, mankind—replace Desdemona; Apemantus substitutes for Iago. Is the equation valid? Partly, perhaps, partly not. But there is imagination in making the comparison, and a suggestion of archetypal pattern as we meditate on the parallels.

Knight asks us to see *Lear* in the light of *Othello* and *Timon*: Lear's unjust distrust resembles Othello's, his disillusionment resembles Timon's. Lear, Cordelia, and Edmund replay the relationships of Othello, Desdemona, and Iago, of Timon, Athens, and Apemantus. Further, Knight urges, *Troilus and Cressida* focuses on the same theme of love disillusioned we find in these other plays, though it examines the theme "from a more purely intellectual, metaphysical standpoint" than does *Lear*. But "as in *King Lear*, the hero's mind is distraught by a knowledge of incompatibles that leave no 'rule in unity itself.'" Thersites clearly links with Apemantus, Iago, and Edmund in cynicism. In *Measure for Measure*, says Knight, we find in the Duke, Isabella, and Lucio something of the familiar pattern. "In each of these plays we see the same three figures recurring. They are representative of (i) noble mankind, (ii) the supreme value of spiritual love, and (iii) the cynic." From such comparisons, Knight turns us again to *Hamlet*, "the first of the plays to express vividly that mode of cynicism and hate which I have called the hate-theme . . . Hamlet is nauseated by Gertrude's unfaithfulness—justly; he cynically rejects Ophelia—unjustly. Hamlet thus contains the germ of

Troilus and Cressida, Othello, and *Timon of Athens.*" But where is the cynic in Hamlet, the figure analogous to Iago, Thersites, Lucio? In the prince himself.

> Hamlet is both hero and villain in his own drama . . . He torments himself as well as others. The poet's mind, aware of a certain rhythm of human life associated with love, disillusion, and despair, in the later plays splits these forces of his own consciousness into appropriate figures, playing them off against each other . . . But in the single figure of Hamlet he has attempted to reflect the totality of his creating mind.

All the great plays of Shakespeare, says Knight, *Macbeth* excepted, turn on the same axis. Within the framework of a love-convention, partly personal, partly the general possession of the modern world, Shakespeare gives us a "free-hearted hero" who is ultimately representative of mankind; a villain, a creature of cynicism, who is no less than the Devil; and a beloved, like Dante's Beatrice, the divine principle. The symbols remain, reappearing in *Timon* though in transformation, in *Antony and Cleopatra* (where Enobarbus is but a pale reflex of Apemantus), in *Cymbeline* (where Posthumus, Imogen, and Iachimo reassert the old triangle); and "finally, in the all-inclusive statement of *The Tempest,* the three figures are seen to be three modes of the poet's mind: there Prospero has mastered, and controls, both Ariel and Caliban."

Strain though one may at equations too facile, at parallels more athwart than aligned, Knight's comparisons compel one toward a feeling for the plays as visions rather than as histories. He makes us see them as expressions of the poet's own concerns rather than accounts of the concerns of others. He invites us to discover their meaning less from the English language they share with other dramatists than from the Shakespearean tongue they share, uniquely, with one another. Seeing the plays this way we lose interest, momentarily, in those old Bradleyan concerns of character and plot structure. Instead, we seek and with growing sensitivity react to the newer concerns of image and symbol and archetypal pattern. We pulse to life-themes and death-themes. We juxtapose characters and incidents. We listen for the roaring of storms, the restorative notes of sweet harmonies. For a moment, or longer, we read Shakespeare afresh and derive from that experience the power to find new meanings in the plays individually, which is the immediate goal of "interpretation," and new meanings in the plays collectively, which is its ultimate goal.

xiii

Caroline F. E. Spurgeon / 1869–1942
John Middleton Murry / 1889–1957
Edward A. Armstrong / 1900–

Whiter's Specimen. *Spurgeon's thesis: Shakespeare's imagery as self-revealing. "The Subject-Matter of Shakespeare's Images." "Shakespeare's Senses." Outdoor interests. Thought. "Shakespeare the Man." Spurgeon's focus on figure at the expense of thought. Other limitations. Contributions. ❧ Murry's Shakespeare as Nature's spokesman. Personal experience in the imagery. The Bastard as Shakespeare's Adam; Henry V as the Bastard legitimized, the problem of kingship solved. The Shakespearean Man and the Shakespearean Woman. Hamlet the final embodiment and catharsis of the Shakespearean Man. Lear the work of a divided Shakespeare. Bridgean perspectives. Rhapsody on Antony and Cleopatra. ❧ Armstrong on "Linked Images": the dynamics of Shakespeare's imagination. Shakespeare's dualistic awareness: related imagery, unity, puns, ambivalence. Freedom of his associative powers: meanings below consciousness. Inspiration. Attacks against biographical and psychoanalytic criticism. "The Structure of the Imagination."*

In 1794, in *A Specimen of a Commentary on Shakspeare,* Walter Whiter undertook "to explain and illustrate various passages . . . on a new principle of criticism, derived from Mr. Locke's doctrine of the association of ideas." By *association* he understood the combination of ideas "which have *no* natural alliance or relation to each other, but which have been united only by chance, or by custom." He meant such idiosyncratic linkings as Shakespeare's of a lover and a book or of candy and a fawning dog. His method was to seek for recurrences of such irrational linkings, and he tried, by exploring the contexts of the different passages, to throw light on them all. Whiter's *Specimen* pioneered the exploration of Shakespeare's imagination, and by a method the essential utility of which seems pointless to question. His researches, however, had no consequence. The path he made stopped where he stopped. In time it grew over, and when the exploration was to be made again, by a similar method, Caroline Spurgeon had to begin from scratch.[1]

Spurgeon believes that

> the imagery [Shakespeare] *instinctively uses is* . . . *a revelation, largely unconscious, given at a moment of heightened feeling, of the furniture of his mind, the channels of his thought, the qualities of things, the objects and incidents he observes and remembers, and perhaps most significant of all, those which he does not observe or remember.*

In this belief she collects and sorts, classifies and counts all the images in the plays—not simply those linked irrationally—checks her findings against comparable classifications and tabulations performed on the images of Bacon, Marlowe, Jonson, Chapman, Dekker, and then proceeds to draw, as it were, Shakespeare's mental portrait.

In her chapter "The Subject-matter of Shakespeare's Images," she observes that Shakespeare's images fall mainly "into two groups, those from nature, and those from indoor life and customs." "By far the greatest number" of the images of nature "is devoted to . . . the gardener's point of view, showing intimate knowledge and observation of growth, propagation, grafting, pruning, manuring, weeding, ripeness and decay." The next largest group is of images of weather and its changes. Shakespeare "notes with loving accuracy the sound of the different winds."

> He revels in delicate changes of light, especially at dawn . . . and he so loves the swift play of sun and shadow that when he seeks a comparison for the most exquisite of human experiences, young love, he can find nothing more beautiful in nature than "the uncertain glory of an April day."

Shakespeare knows and loves birds, but what especially "attracts him is their *movement*."

In her chapter on "Shakespeare's Senses," which is, in fact, a description of the apparatus of Shakespeare's sensibility, Spurgeon draws attention to and documents such matters as the following: "that what [Shakespeare] notices about color and what attract him supremely are *change* and *contrast*"—especially in the human face; "that the spectacle of the rising sun seems ever peculiarly to inspire and delight Shakespeare," whereas "the sight of the setting sun . . . depresses him"; that Shakespeare's ear is sensitive and his musical knowledge, "both theoretical and technical," real; that he shrank "from discord and harshness" and was greatly susceptible "not only to 'sweet airs,' but to sounds of every kind"; that he constantly and exquisitely discriminated in the quality of voices; that "next to the human voice, there are three classes of sound which seem specially to interest or affect Shakespeare—echo and reverberation, the toll of passing or funeral bell . . . and the song of birds"; that for Shakespeare "heaven is hushed stillness with 'touches of sweet harmony,' and hell is a place of noisy strife, discord and clamor." "Shakespeare has clearly a very acute sense of smell, and is peculiarly sensitive to bad smells; the two he specially names and dislikes being the smell of unwashed humanity and of decaying corpses." His touch is sensitive to the textures of skin. His palate is delicate and discriminating, responsive to seasoning, and quick to feel the queasiness of excess.

Exploring Shakespeare's outdoor interests, Spurgeon develops his knowledgeable fondness of gardening, his sense of the power of seeds, his interest in the new process of grafting, his Frostian sensitivity to the uncertainties of spring weather. She finds evidence of Shakespeare's deep reaction to the Avon in flood, his fondness for swimming, his relative ignorance of fishing, his not caring for deer hunting. There is a strong zest for the chase in the mouths of his characters, to be sure, but "if we look at his *images* only, we get an entirely different picture. We get the picture of an extremely sensitive man, whose sympathy is scarcely ever with the hunters, but consistently and obviously on the side of the hunted or stricken animal." "What he did like was to watch the deer, unseen by them, in their native forest."

> He liked watching the dogs almost as much . . . and knew all about their skill and shortcomings, on a hot or cold scent "keeping" or "recovering" the wind, crying on a "false trail" or, in their eagerness, outpacing the other dogs and having to be restrained, to be "trashed for overtopping."

I pass by Shakespeare's indoor interests to come to evidences of Shakespeare's thought, which Spurgeon treats under the headings of Love, Hate, Fear, Evil, Goodness, Time, and Death. Her remarks under the first heading include these: In Shakespeare's imagery, "love is a food, but it is also a hunger." It is a bitter-sweet food, but " 'Love surfeits not, Lust like a glutton dies.' " Shakespeare's images "bring out four qualities or aspects of love: its wayward, uncertain and consequently attractive character, its swift and soaring nature, its shaping and transforming power, and its infiniteness." As to Shakespeare's thought about death, Spurgeon grants that Hamlet, Claudio, and Timon expatiate on the subject, and "Shakespeare himself may have felt and believed" as they do, "but we do not know that he did." "What we do know," says Spurgeon, "is that when he thought of death certain sets of pictures flashed into his mind, and these we can look at with him, and by virtue of his own genius, we can see them almost as vividly as he did." Shakespeare gives us pictures of death as warrior, as skeleton, as "carrion monster," as repellant tyrant. Again, Shakespeare gives us death as antic or mummer, and, "when death takes toll of youth and beauty," as lover, husband, bride.

> The power of death, and man's helplessness in his grip, are constantly kept before us, and Shakespeare shows us death as a wrestler, a tilter, an antagonist against whom we fight a losing game, and whom we can at most hold "awhile at the arm's end"; a hound dogging us at the heels, a hunter, a fowler and an archer, with an ebon dart; a fell sergeant, "strict in his arrest"; a soldier, laying seige to the mind, pricking and wounding it, a king boldly keeping his court within the very confines of the crown of a mortal king; a jester scoffing and grinning at the pomp with which he humors a monarch's vanity, while, at his own time, with a little pin he bores his castle wall and claims him for his own; and life itself is seen but as death's fool or dupe, ever vainly trying to escape him, while ever irresistibly drawn towards him.

From these pictures can we infer Shakespeare's own thought of death? From these, and from his images of life, Spurgeon thinks we can. He thought of death as "a journey's end, sometimes a shipwreck, but never a haven or harbor." He thought of it as "the sure physician" to life's fitful fever, as a sleep, as the extinction of life's light, candle, lamp, fire, or spark, as the frost killing life's spring flower, as the release from life's prison, as the untying of life's knot, as the cutting of life's thread. "In general it would seem Shakespeare does not rebel against death, but accepts it as a natural process . . . on the whole, most often, . . . an end wholly peaceful, merciful and restful."

In her chapter "Shakespeare the Man," which sums up part I of her book, Spurgeon stands back from the portrait, the parts of which she has been developing, and shows us the whole. She offers, in far more detail than I can present, a man "extraordinarily well-coordinated, lithe and nimble of body, quick and accurate of eye, delighting in swift muscular movement." "He was healthy in body as in mind," as Goethe long ago suggested, "clean and fastidious in his habits, very sensitive to dirt and evil smells." He was physically alert, intensely vital, "incredibly sensitive and amazingly observant." He was a countryman, with the outdoor interests already noted, and, indoors, most interested in the routine occupations of eating, drinking, sleeping, the busy kitchen, like the garden, filling his mind with its varied activities. "For the rest of him, the inner man, five words sum up the essence of his quality and character as seen in his images—sensitiveness, balance, courage, humor, and wholesomeness." "He is indeed himself in many ways in character what one can only describe as Christ-like; that is, gentle, kindly, honest, brave and true, with deep understanding and quick sympathy for all living things."

So strikingly different is Spurgeon's Shakespeare from those of Harris and Lewis, so peculiarly unturmoiled, so very far from "the expense of spirit in a waste of shame," that it has been met with some gently masculine scoffing. "Miss Spurgeon was a Lady," observes one critic, "and naturally, certain areas of experience were closed to her." "Miss Spurgeon has studied Shakespeare and found him to be—a Victorian gentleman." The comments have their validity. Spurgeon's Index has no entry for "Sex." Although there is an entry, "Woman, idea of wantonness of," which refers to Shakespeare's "instinctively" expressing disgust at woman's wantonness "in terms of physical appetite and food," one looks in vain for clear, confident treatment of those hundreds on hundreds of items Eric Partridge catalogues in his *Shakespeare's Bawdy.* One thinks of Iago's beast with two backs and suspects Spurgeon filed it under "Animals, Fabulous," or of Leontes' Sir Smile fishing in his neighbor's pond and wonders, fascinated, whether it is filed under "Daily Life, Sport."

A similar reticence confronts us as we consider Spurgeon's

treatment of Religion. The Index has an entry, "Religion and Superstition," and the "Chart Showing the Range and Subjects of Shakespeare's Images in their Exact Proportion" has a category "Learning" *under* which comes "Religion." This sub-heading is sterilely subdivided into "Various" (60 images), "Simple Beliefs" (40-odd), "Biblical" (40), and "Superstition" (30-odd). There is no heading, "Faith." Appendix IV offers a detailed analysis of the subject-matter of the images in *Romeo and Juliet* and *Hamlet*. Under "Religion and Superstition" it lists five in the earlier play (including "wide as a church door" and "round worm pricked from the lazy finger of a maid"), and under "Religion, Biblical and Superstition," it lists six in the later: "Hell 2 (black as hell, loosed from hell to speak of horrors), temple, Jephthah, wheel bowled down hill 2." Where, one wonders, are Hamlet's meditations, early and late, on suicide, where the Ghost's revelations of purgatorial suffering, the King's prayer and Hamlet's soliloquy thereat, the son and mother's discourse on confessing and the stained soul, Hamlet's musings on why God made man, on the divinity that shapes our ends, on the graveyard, Horatio's "flights of angels sing thee to thy rest"?

Blindness to the sexual and deafness to the religious may ultimately reflect the prejudices of a gentlewoman reared in the tradition of nineteenth-century secularism, but immediately they derive from Spurgeon's approach to images, and were her prejudices entirely different, the approach would still yield the present result. For Spurgeon considers only the "vehicle" in an image, never the "tenor," only the figure, never the thought it embodies. According to this approach, Christ's parables of the kingdom of heaven would find no placement under "Religion" but would be variously accommodated under "Nature, Gardening, Growth" (the sower and his seed) or "Domestic, Fire & Light, Light & Darkness" (the ten virgins), or "Daily Life, Money" (the talents). "God the Father" would be *sub*sumed under "Domestic, Human Relations, Men." The thought, however, the informing passion, matters no less than the figure—is, in fact, its excuse for being. To neglect it, as Spurgeon does, is to miss, repeatedly, the creative essence for the figurative accident, the generative power for its mere manifestation. It is to give us a secular gentleman but hardly a Renaissance genius.

Certain other aspects of Spurgeon's approach contribute to the thinness of her Shakespeare, though these seem to me less failings than recognized limitations. Thus she focuses on the content rather than the form of Shakespeare's images, which means that she gets at the furnishings of his imagination but not at its dynamics—concerns that exercise Knight, Jones, and Armstrong. She focuses on Shakespeare's sensation but not upon his experience, as do Harris, Murry, and Traversi.[2] Although she sees growth in Shakespeare's images about sickness, the later images possessing deeper feeling, and in his orientation toward good and evil—"the kindling and reverberating quality of goodness is more present in Shakespeare's mind in the later plays, the 'infection' of evil in the earlier"—Spurgeon draws what is essentially a portrait, not a biography. And since her method is statistical, one image counting exactly as much as another, the strokes of her portrait are necessarily broad and general.

Spurgeon's principal contribution to our understanding of Shakespeare comes in her study of "The Function of the Imagery as Background and Undertone in Shakespeare's Art," the latter half of her book, which we shall examine later. Her contributions in the chapters we have examined are several, I think, and real. She does show us in an orderly way the furnishings of Shakespeare's imagination. She describes for us the apparatus of his sensibility. She gives us one kind of portrait of the man—in water rather than in oils, perhaps, but with the tint of life upon it. She invites us to respond sensitively to the images which we, running readers as we so often are, too easily overlook in our pursuit of the gist. And, awakening our sensitivity to the imagery, she alerts us too to its personal dimension, to an eye seeing sharply and a mind recalling freshly to put life upon the London boards. A single final illustration lets us see how Spurgeon awakens us both to the imagery of the plays and to the vital sentience behind them.

Shakespeare's intense interest in the human face has never, I think, been adequately noticed: its frowns and wrinkles, smiles and tears, the tint and shape of the nose, the tension of the nostrils, the eye, its color and character, "in flood with laughter," sparkling, sun-bright, quick, merry, fiery, mistful, dim, lack-lustre, heavy, hollow, modest, sober, sunken or scornful; the peculiar beauty of the eyelid, the betrayal of the gnawing of a nether lip, the dimples on a child's chin, and, above all, the way in which he continually makes us see the emotions of his characters by the chasing changes of color in their cheeks.

These he conveys through every kind of metaphor, which in each case carries with it the particular atmosphere of emotion which gives rise to the change, making it quite unnecessary, for the most part, to mention any specific color at all. Thus we see the traitors whose "cheeks are paper" as they glance at the documents handed them by their king; the fair high color of Richard quickly coming and going, and in anger turning pale, as when Gaunt's outspoken words chase

the royal blood
With fury from his native residence;

we realize how flushed will be the faces of the soldiers on the "gaudy night" when Antony promises he will

force
The wine peep through their scars;

we watch Bassanio, dumb with emotion before Portia's surrender, the color suffusing his face as he stammers,

Madam, you have bereft me of all words,
Only my blood speaks to you in my veins;

and we feel with Macbeth the horror and fear gripping the servant who, with "linen cheeks" and "whey face," rushes in to report disaster.

� 🌿 🌿

Middleton Murry is the most level-headed of Shakespeare's major biographical critics[3]—which is not to deny him either a delicate and elaborate sensitivity or a propensity for high piled hyperboles when he comes to *Antony and Cleopatra*; and though he invokes none of the psychological and anthropological mysteries to which Wyndham Lewis appeals, his readings of the plays similarly challenge habitual notions. His Shakespeare is one of Keats's men of power rather than of character, a creature of negative capability, "capable of being in uncertainties, mysteries, doubts, without any irritable reaching after fact and reason," peculiarly selfless, though the history of Shakespeare criticism has been that of the attempt to give him a self, a character, a morality. His Shakespeare refuses to "become a man of principle . . . He remains at the end what he was at the beginning: Nature uttering herself through a human being as completely as we can imagine."

Seeing Shakespeare in this Emersonian way, Murry fails to discover in him Lewis's shamanized executioner, Jones's Oedipal sufferer, or Harris's tormented lover. He finds, in fact, no personality at all, and relatively little personal history. That little, however, illuminates Shakespeare's work.

Murry views the evidence and the traditions about Shakespeare's life undogmatically, but certain images from the plays ring uniquely true for him. He senses personal experience, for example, in the image of the offending wife's holding up her child to ward off her husband's correction in *Henry IV, Part II* (IV.i.210–214) and in the extended simile of house-building in the same play (I.iii.41–62), and in the old shepherd's lament in *The Winter's Tale* that between sixteen and three and twenty youth does nothing "but getting wenches with child, wronging the ancientry, stealing, fighting" (III.iii.58–62). From such evidence as this Murry hypothesizes Shakespeare pretty much as Aubrey and Rowe presented him[4]—a young man trapped into marriage with a nagging wife, humiliated by Lucy, proceeding to London, pursuing a patron during the plague years, becoming successful as an actor-writer in competition with Greene and the university-writers. With Wordsworth, Murry regards the sonnets as keys to Shakespeare's heart.[5] They record the experience of the years 1593–1595, which "both forms and fills a hiatus in Shakespeare's dramatic career." This

> period of intoxication, hesitation, despondency, passing finally into secure confidence, . . . was probably accompanied at the beginning by a momentary wild surmise on Shakespeare's part that he was to be liberated by a miraculous conjuncture of his poetic genius and an aristocratic deus ex machina from the drudgery of the popular theater. From this disturbance Shakespeare emerged with the conviction that his destiny lay in the theater, and a determination to prevail.

Shakespeare becomes the "professional," holding up the mirror to England's nature, himself "a force of Nature, accomplishing its hidden purpose amid and through a welter of practical exigencies."

Murry attends to the young professional in much the same way as Swinburne. He detects "in the early histories . . . an individual verse-style emerging." It has two main elements: "one, the more striking, a formal patterning employed to bring variety into the blank-verse on every appropriate occasion; the other a simple and lovely periodic *flow* of verse, liquid and almost naive." He sees Shakespeare as carrying the formal patterning to its extreme development in *Richard III*, then retracing his way, in *Richard II*, and seeking "—instinctively, not deliberately—a fusion between the lyricism of *The Two Gentlemen of Verona* and the substance of history."

This retracing of his way after the years of plague and sonnets, finds Shakespeare coming toward a new mastery of his material, a new relationship with his audience. "One has only to allow one's fancy to substitute a figure like the Bastard for Bolingbroke in *Richard II*, and as it were to blend *Richard II* and *King John* into a single play . . . to see the nature of the advance made by Shakespeare's genius." The advance is in the direction of mirroring to England its own features: the Bastard "represents England against the vagaries and the viciousness of its titular king. His is the native royalty, while the King is the shadow." The Bastard evolves into Falstaff and, another way, into Hotspur.

> *At this point, and in this form, Shakespeare's genius made a new and more creative contact with the people. Precisely this combination of Falstaff and Harry Hotspur was prodigiously popular. It outrivalled* Richard III . . . *Shakespeare has found his way back to the people by exploring his own genius.*

Back in *Richard III* Shakespeare used an extraordinary number of metaphors from the theater, but they are "metaphors of an abstract stage; the audience is not included in them." For example, "Plots have I laid, inductions dangerous"; "Had you not come upon your cue"; "I can counterfeit the deep tragedian,/Speak and look back . . ." In *King John* and *Richard II*, on the other hand, in the metaphors of the theater "it is the audience which matters." Thus the Bastard compares the citizens of Angiers to an audience comfortably gaping at the "industrious scenes and acts of death" of the players. Thus Richard's cold reception by the citizenry of London is likened to the contemptuous reception accorded the actor who comes on "After a well-graced actor leaves the stage." Such images suggest Shakespeare's own experience of humiliation, says Murry. But Shakespeare is resilient. And when he comes to write the induction of *Henry IV, Part II*, he exhibits a kind of retaliation that would be impertinent except that it is true:

Enter Rumour, *painted full of tongues.*
RUM.: Open your ears; for which of you will stop
The vent of hearing when loud Rumour speaks?
                    . . . Rumour is a pipe
Blown by surmises, jealousies, conjectures
And of so easy and so plain a stop
That the blunt monster with uncounted heads,
The still-discordant wavering multitude,
Can play upon it. But what need I thus
My well-known body to anatomize
Among my household?

"That Shakespeare meant to please his audience if he could," thinks Murry, "is certain; but it is equally certain that he meant to please himself in doing so."

This professional, finding the voice of England, resiliently accommodating himself to his audience, and it to him, borrowing his plots because "he did not believe that his unaided inventions would be dramatically effective enough to fill the house; and he could take no risks for the company"—this professional is, for Murry,

> a man who has won a victory, of which he had momentarily despaired, who has fused not merely the poet and dramatist in himself, but established a unique creative relation between himself, his dramatic material, his audience and his actors. He has conquered his necessities by submitting to them.

The event in Shakespeare's life to which Murry attributes highest importance is Shakespeare's "second plunge into the social humiliation out of which he had struggled." Out of this experience

> the Bastard emerges . . . He is the Adam of the Shakespearean earth . . . He is the first imaginative outcome of the particularity of Shakespeare's conditioning which was the ground of his universality. Out of an experience which was a

quintessence of *Elizabethan England,* came the figure of this insular, magnificent and universal hero.

If I follow Murry aright, the Bastard reflects his creator's necessity, suffering, and triumph and his nation's as well. His attributes become those which author and audience recognize or seek within themselves.

> He is realist and idealist at once, yet he is not divided. He is the natural Man, in whom the gift of consciousness has served only to make nature more truly itself. He is detached from the world only to be more effectively a part of it . . . He is conscious, as no Shakespearean character has been conscious before.

"He can afford to be cynical about himself, because he knows he cannot do anything base. He has no need of virtue, because he has no vice to conceal." The Bastard's function

> is to embody England, to incorporate the English soul: that indefinable reality of which the anointed king is but a symbol. This figure of the Bastard Shakespeare . . . sets at the beginning of his sequence of histories. And his last addition to the series, *Henry V,* is a play in which he presents an anointed king, who is not merely, by virtue of his office and his function, a symbol of the English spirit, but also an embodiment of it. In *Henry V,* so to speak, the Bastard becomes the legitimate King of England.

Out of the professional's experience, then, the Bastard, and from him, in legitimate line, Falstaff, Hotspur, Harry—the voices of England. Out of the Bastard and his inheritors, further, the solution to the problem of kingship. In *Richard II* Shakespeare had deliberately, philosophically, propounded the doctrine of the divine right of kings, which he found imaginatively unsatisfactory

and hence counterposed to it in the Duke of York the divine
principle of order. The first gives way to the second.

> But Order alone is not enough. Order must be organic and
> creative. This organic and creative order is embodied in Harry
> the king. It is an order which grows out of the nation and is
> reflected back upon it again, through the person and by the
> will of the king. He gives utterance to the dumb striving of
> the nation towards a higher order . . . an order in which
> nobility is the reward of those who of their own free-will are
> ready to hazard their lives and their all for the common weal.
> This is Shakespeare's answer to the problem of kingship.

To Murry, the Bastard and his line constitute varying embodiments of "the Shakespeare Man" as Rosaline, Portia, Beatrice,
Rosalind embody "the Shakespeare Woman." They

> become his nature; or his nature has become them. They
> accommodate themselves to the necessities of the stage . . .
> but they are not confined in them . . . Nature is behind
> them, and about them, and in them—the Nature of which
> Shakespeare is, and now knows himself to be, the instrument
> and the voice.

The Shakespeare Man appears in some plays, not in others, not in
Midsummer Night's Dream, for example, or *The Merchant of
Venice*, or *Julius Caesar*, or *Twelfth Night*. "Speaking roughly,
where Shakespeare is most in control as an 'artist,' there the
Shakespeare Man is absent." "He is the utterance of something
which seeks to be uttered less personally more diffusedly; when he
appears he tends to sap the life which should be impersonally
spread through the whole drama." The Shakespeare Woman
continues to the end—in Desdemona, Imogen, Miranda. But the
Shakespeare Man finds his final embodiment in Hamlet. And
Murry accounts for this, for his having an entire play to himself

and then appearing no more, by inferring in Shakespeare two drives: (1) to embody "this Shakespeare Man, and by complete embodiment to get him out of his system"; (2) to bring his artistry and his liberty, his restraint and his power, into union. "Beyond all this," says Murry, "there is a crisis in realization: a dying into life."

> *Prince Hamlet dies. The Shakespeare man has run his course. He will not revisit the glimpses of the moon; he will neither relieve creative inertia, nor vex creative control. He will not take the burden, when Shakespeare is tired, ·nor divert his energy when he is full of power. When Shakespeare fails henceforward, he will fail; when he succeeds he will succeed. He will be diffused throughout his creation, or will not be alive in it at all.*

Hamlet's experience is, then, inferentially, Shakespeare's. What it amounts to is, in one sense, an awakening fear of death, in another, the discovery that one's "universe has been suddenly emptied of God." "The revelation of his mother's animality, his dreadful doubt concerning the manner of his father's death—these have already meant the shattering of a whole moral universe." Then comes the Ghost, shattering the spiritual universe.

> *And suddenly a new and awful terror is added to death. Death may be the entrance, as it were, to a realm of hideous reality (like Svidrigailov's dusty room with a spider in the corner) corresponding to that which in the actual world his prophetic soul surmised and the Ghost confirmed.*

Hamlet consequently "has to teach himself, as it were all over again, to make a mouth at the invisible event; and to do it calmly and deliberately with all that is veritably God-like in reason working purely within him." He must achieve again, what he has lost, the ability "to remember himself and forget himself at the same moment." He must achieve within himself and his universe, "a new Order, a new Law and a new God." And he does. He moves in suffering, and then in serenity, from "the dread of something after death" to the beatitude of "Absent thee from felicity awhile."

Murry's explanation of *Hamlet* caps his biographical reading of the plays. He sees in *King Lear* "the work not so much of a tired, as of a divided man . . . intermittently possessed by a vision that is inimical to the spontaneity of Imagination"—a work "to be understood somewhat as Shakespeare's deliberate prophylactic against his own incoherence." He sees Prospero as "to some extent, an imaginative paradigm of Shakespeare himself in his function as poet . . . in part embody[ing] Shakespeare's self-awareness at the conclusion of his poetic career"; and he reads the great speech on our being such stuff as dreams are made of thus: "At the moment when [Shakespeare] understood that Imagination was the world in which Innocence grew to ripeness, its blossom unshattered by Experience, his mind was turmoiled by the thought that Experience might be the Imagination of Another Power." These analyses aside, Murry's reading of the plays after *Hamlet* is interpretive but not biographically. Critically, he belongs in Bridges' camp. He sees Shakespeare as "appropriating tried and foolproof action, and creating persons and poetry" so that "insoluble psychological problems" inevitably develop. The problem plays show Shakespeare not as "the supreme and ideal romantic poet" Coleridge hypothesized, but as an Elizabethan playwright working within certain limitations of theater, audience, and material and, in fact, not always bringing it off. Murry has a fine discussion of Shakespeare's "Imagery and Imagination," in which he suggests a progress from "a discrepancy between his poetic technique and his dramatic necessities, into a condition in which they are really fused together." Clemen among others has since traced that progress in technical detail. Among Murry's observations is this: that just as clusters of images exist in Shakespeare's mind, having a life of their own "until one part . . . can suggest any other by no logical connection at all" (as with the famous cluster of fawning spaniels, sticky sweets, flattery, humiliation, greyhounds, the kitchen, and melting) so character exists for Shakespeare. "Cleopatra is, for Shakespeare, a 'sensation' as immediate, as incontrovertible, as independent, as natural, as the 'sensation' of the hounds." And Murry has a rhapsodic chapter on *Antony and Cleopatra* which takes something of Wyndham Lewis's perspective. Antony's last supper analogizes with *the* Last Supper, Enobarbus is a repentant Judas. Antony's death mysteriously transfuses his royal spirit into the mind and heart of his fickle queen.

> And all this we have watched, not merely with the bodily, but with the spiritual eye; we have heard it, not merely with the bodily, but with the spiritual ear. The prime instrument of this sustained and deepening enchantment has been a peculiar quality of poetry, of such a kind that it is the reverberation of the noble deeds which our bodily eyes have seen enacted; and more than the reverberation of them. This quality of poetry conditions those acts; gives them a quality of significance, over and above and distinguishable from the declared intention of the acts: so that the quality of "inspiration," which our dividing minds would attribute to the poetry alone, envelops and suffuses the acts which it accompanies. The poetic utterance passes, without jolt or jar, into the dramatic deed, as though utterance and act were but a single kind of expression.

Many a critic would disagree, but the romantic view of the play has rarely received a more profound vindication than this.

Murry's hypothesis about Shakespeare's life—of the birth of the Shakespeare Man in a humiliation that was also a union with Nature, the stage, and the English people; of the death of the Shakespeare Man in a union of self with creation—this seems to me sanely to jibe with the awarenesses of other critics. They too have seen certain figures recurring in the plays between *King John* and *Hamlet*; they too have sensed that Hamlet is peculiarly marked with Shakespeare's own lineaments. Bradley observed that of all Shakespeare's characters, only Hamlet might have written his plays. Murry's hypothesis usefully and excitingly articulates the works of the first half of Shakespeare's career in a pattern other than temporal. His Shakespeare is less glandular than Harris's but more English, less sick than Lewis's, less neurotic than Jones's. All of which may suggest that he is more "true" or, conversely, that he is more "false." The reader will decide, but two points might be made on Murry's behalf. He avoids the Shakespeare-can-do-no-wrong approach of one kind of rhapsodist; he acknowledges failures; he is willing to challenge the admiration for *King Lear* that, Tolstoy excepted, seems to be universal. He does not write, then, as apologist or rhapsodist. And insistently, in a way that such a treatment as this necessarily fails to communicate, he grounds his inferences in passages in the plays. His reading is sensitive, tactful, unoracular. Murry's insistent and delicate reference to particular passages has a special virtue. Now faintly, now fully, it makes us hear notes other than those of plot and character. It quickens our senses to the personally immediate in the objective realm of the plays, to the pulse therein of Elizabethan England and the English countryside, of the author's moods and the nation's musings and the interplay between the man and his audience. For a moment, when Hamlet speaks of the play that was caviar to the general, we may think we hear, too, Shakespeare recalling an early failure—one, perhaps, that led him to borrow plots since his own wouldn't do. We may let the notes die. We need not affirm that all are truly there. But as we respond, they deepen and enrich the plays, suggesting something about their source and their vitality.

🌱 🌱 🌱

Shakespeare's images tell Spurgeon about the poet's fancy. They tell Armstrong about his imagination.[6] And since "we cannot explore the complexities of one man's mind without learning truths of general application," they tell us about every man's imagination. In Armstrong's book we see Shakespeare and ourselves as well.

Armstrong speaks of himself as a "plodder," perhaps with some legitimacy. His style has a one-foot-before-the-other quality, sturdy, regular, suggesting that the traveler's gaze is downward rather than aloft. Occasionally we feel ourselves mired in particularities or anxiously suspect we have lost our way. Armstrong, however, knows where he is going. He gets us there. And like Morgann, though less ecstatically, he enjoys the "rich, beautiful, picturesque, and perhaps unknown country" through which we go.

The first part of the journey consists of ten chapters on "Linked Images." Here we follow Whiter's old trail of image clusters, as of "Kites and Coverlets" (Chapter I), "Birds and Beetles" (II), or "The Eagle, the Weasel, and the Drone" (III). Armstrong's clusters, however, contain images naturally as well as "unnaturally" linked. They are therefore larger and more inclusive than Whiter's and more significantly reflective of the workings of Shakespeare's imagination. Armstrong's customary procedure may be seen in the chapter on "Kites and Coverlets." He begins by inviting us to think of the kite as it was in Tudor times, a common predator swooping down on drying linen for nests, on chickens for food, a scavenger and a devourer of carrion. "In spite of the toleration with which the bird was regarded in his time," says Armstrong, "Shakespeare's kite is a despicable creature symbolic of cowardice, meanness, cruelty and death." For Antony, Lear, Hamlet, "kite" is a term of opprobrium. "Shakespeare by a natural process of association pictured this carrion feeder flying over battlefields, and . . . he commonly connected it with sickliness and disease"—as in "kite of Cressid's kind" for the venereally afflicted prostitute. Moreover, in eight out of fourteen contexts in which Shakespeare names the kite, he names an article of bed furniture. For example, *"Henry V* gives us 'bed,' 'sheets' and 'warming-pan.'"* Further, Shakespeare associates with the kite thoughts of "man's last restingplace, the tomb," and "in every context there is some image connected with feeding." Autolycus's first song with its following monologue nicely illustrates the unconscious "association thinking" Armstrong is here defining:

> "When daffodils begin to peer,
>   With heigh! the doxy over the dale,
> Why, then comes in the sweet o' the year;
>   For the red *blood* reigns in the winter's *pale*.
>
> The white *sheet bleaching* on the hedge,"

. . . .

> "My traffic is sheets; when the kite builds, look to lesser linen. My father named me Autolycus; who, being as I am, littered under Mercury, was likewise a snapper-up of unconsidered trifles. With die and drab I purchased this caparison, and my revenue is the silly cheat. Gallows and knock are too powerful on the highway: beating and hanging are terrors to me: for the life to come, I sleep out the thought of it. A prize! a prize!"

Pick out the significant words and we find—sheets—kite—linen—die—hanging—life to come. See what has happened! Once the kite came on the scene—evoked by blood, pale, sheet and bleaching—thought veered round to death and the hereafter—and, incidentally, bed-linen suggested sleep.

Armstrong concludes his chapter with the observation that

> an image in Shakespeare's mind tended to acquire associates which became, at least in some instances, almost inseparable from it. Failing pressure from another set of associated images they tended to recur again and again, grouping themselves about a central image with the alacrity and pertinacity of chicks responding to a clucking hen.

After the chapter comes the table (see below).

THE KITE IMAGE CLUSTER

CONTEXT	KITE	BED	DEATH	SPIRITS	BIRDS	FOOD
Henry VI Part 2 3.1.249	kite[249]		death[245]	soul[247]	chicken[249] eagle[248]	empty[248]
3.2.193	kite[193, 196]	sheets[174]	dead[188] dead[192]	ghost[161]	partridge[191]	feast[184]
3.2.196		bed[212]				
5.2.11	kites[11]		deadly-handed[9]	soul[18]	crows[11]	empty[4] carrion[11]
Richard III 1.1.133	kite[133]	bed[142]	die[145]	soul[119]	eagle[132] buzzards[133]	diet[130]
Taming of the Shrew 4.1.198	kite[198]	bed[203] pillow, bolster[204] coverlet, sheets[205] canopy[98]	kill[211]	soul[197]	falcon[108] haggard[106]	empty[198] full-gorged[194] eat no meat[200]
Julius Caesar 5.1.85	kites[85]			ghost[89]	ravens, crows[85] eagles[81]	gorging[52] feeding[52]
Henry V 2.1.80	kite[80]	Tearsheet[51] bed[87] sheets[88] warming pan[88]	death[65]	spirits[72] devil[65]	crow[91]	couple a gorge[78] pudding[61] food[67]
Hamlet 2.2.607	kites[607]	(John-a-dreams[595])	murdered[612] blench[626]	soul[620] devil[628]	pigeon[604]	offal[603]
Lear 1.4.284	kite[284]	(sleep[229])	marble-hearted[281]	devils[273]		epicurism[265]
Macbeth 3.4.73	kites[78]		monuments[72] die[70] murders[51]	devil[159] (ghost[78])		feed[68]
Antony and Cleopatra 3.13.89	kite[89]	pillow[106] canopy[42]	dying[505]	devils[59]		feeders[109]
Coriolanus 4.5.45	kite[45]				crows, daws[45]	batten[35]
Winter's Tale 2.3.186	kite[186]		death[184]	soul[151]	ravens[186]	nurses[187]
4.3.23	kite[23]	sheets[28] linen[23]	bleaching[5] die[27]	soul[57]	lark, thrush, jay[10]	dish for a king[8]

The small figures refer to the number of the line in which the image occurs. They are placed above the image when it is on the same line as, or earlier than, the context image, and below the image when it occurs later than the context image.

Each of the ten chapters on "Linked Images" develops a separate cluster, and cumulatively they develop a rich and complex body of assertions about Shakespeare's imaginative processes. In Chapter II, "Birds and Beetles," Armstrong finds that "there is one conception characteristic not only of the beetle contexts but also of the kite contexts of the previous chapter. It is death. Death is the Master Image . . . the image category to which they are all in less or greater degree relevant."

In Chapter III, "The Eagle, the Weasel and the Drone," Armstrong opens a further inference:

> *The adventures of the kite, beetle and drone . . . suggest that we may postulate below the level of consciousness an active and subtle organizing principle . . . It is evident that when [Shakespeare] concentrated on the development of the main theme and directed his attention to attaining his dramatic purpose he was able, to a considerable extent, to leave the ordering of the images to his subliminal mind.*

Armstrong sees the grouping of images into clusters as the work of this principle "linked in some degree with emotion." And he sees Shakespeare's mind as possessing "the useful twin capacities—retentive memory and vigorous powers of association. He obtained many of his most striking effects by new combinations of the old. *Plus ça reste la même chose, plus ça change!*"

Chapter IV, on "Hidden Images," proceeds to identify the powers that activate Shakespeare's memory. These are (1) mood; (2) master imagery, "as Pride or Darkness"; (3) "natural" association, as of one member of a group with another; (4) irrational association, one member of an image cluster calling forth its old but odd acquaintance; and (5) contrast, "an image frequently call[ing] forth its opposite." Chapter V, "Pinch's Partners," (the title refers to the clustering of beetle and pinching images) explores yet further the ordering principles in Shakespeare's imagination. It finds Life and Death to be the supreme or master images, discovers subordinate categories under Life, such as Love and Light, and, under Death, Hate and Darkness, and recognizes that richly ambivalent imagery develops when images inhere in more than one group:

> love has groups of partner-images in both camps [Life and Death]; with Life by virtue of associations with light, with Death because lovemaking takes place at night. It is by his masterly use of these associations, juxtaposed and contrasted, that Shakespeare builds up with overwhelming effectiveness the sense of tragedy in his plays.

Thus, for *Romeo and Juliet*, "the nightingale is the symbol *par excellence* of the whole play, epitomizing the conflict of the powers of Light and Darkness."

Chapter VI, "The Gestation of Caliban" demonstrates that

> the conjunction of imagery in one play is sometimes a step towards the evolution of characters and situations in later plays . . . Imagery may generate further imagery. What began its manifest life as a group of images may evolve into a character or a plot . . . It seems that an image may, as it were, call the tune which sets its companions dancing in strange new figures.

Chapters VII and VIII, on "The Unsavory Goose" and "The Painted Jay," raise the question whether Shakespeare's images derive from personal experience. Does the goose image cluster with its insistent reference to venereal disease point to the poet's suffering? Does the painted jay cluster with its suggestions of a dark and deceitful lady reveal the poet's passion? Armstrong opens the problem in these chapters, and without solving it, proposes

> that while many image clusters are not relics of specific personal emotional upheavals, neither are they simply colloca-

tions of images independent of emotion. They may owe their being to an emotional factor without originating in experience of great emotional stress or revealing repressed disagreeable experiences.

Chapter IX, "Birds of a Feather," surveys some of the associations that birds, beasts, and flowers have for Shakespeare. Their meaning for him, Armstrong finds, was "strictly determined by their human reference. Man was the center of his world." Shakespeare's mind, "molded by medieval doctrines of the hierarchies of being," tended to place birds, beasts, and flowers "in the category 'sub-human' or 'quasi-human,'" a category which, like Love, "contains elements which belong both to the Life and Death" master images. The resulting ambivalence helps Shakespeare heighten his tragic effects. Chapter IX replays Chapter V in a way, both chapters developing the rich ambivalence of Shakespeare's imagery. Chapter X, "Firearms, Fish, Fleas and Fowl," similarly replays Chapter VI, the controlling notion being that later plays resuscitate and modify earlier imagery. The particular focus of this chapter is on Shakespeare's "bring[ing] together in later plays images which first occurred scattered throughout a scene or even a whole play."

Such a review as this fails to do justice to the richness of Armstrong's presentation, to the arabesque intricacy he makes us see in the trails images follow from work to work, to the startling discoveries he keeps making. Nor can it do justice to the meticulous construction of Armstrong's argument in the second portion of his book, "The Psychology of the Imagination." The following paragraphs garner some of his more striking observations.

Shakespeare's imagination plays between the poles of a dualistic awareness that sets life against death, light against darkness, and arranges its findings in such opposing categories, major and minor. From this inter-playing derive "the numerous related images," in such a play as Romeo and Juliet,

> acting like the hundreds of images mediated by the facets of a
> fly's eye, cumulatively impos[ing] one distinctive but multi-
> tudinously constituted impression of Life-Love—Death-
> Hatred conflict. Thus the author's dominant idea, the inspir-
> ing conception of a whole play, is recreated in the mind of the
> spectator or reader with such masterly subtlety that the
> apparatus of imagery by which the effect is achieved is more
> or less unwittingly accepted as "natural."

From the interplaying, too, derive such ambivalent symbols as the
nightingale and what so troubled the seventeenth and eighteenth
centuries, the puns. Hence, further, the image clusters, held by
Shakespeare's "remarkably efficient and systematic" memory.

In 1833 Coleridge observed that "in Shakespeare one sentence
begets another naturally; the meaning is all inwoven. He goes on
kindling like a meteor through the dark atmosphere." Armstrong
agrees. Shakespeare's work shows his associative powers shackled
by neither emotional stress nor concentrated attention. The
powers are free in him as "the citizen of an ideal state is free."
And so the associations stream after one another, naturally, and
seem natural to us. Other causes contribute to this "naturalness."
Shakespeare

> employs the full potency of his word symbols by integrating
> them into the context and awakening chains of not fully
> conscious associations which cooperate in the reader's mind to
> give emotional tone. Much of Shakespeare's poetic genius lies
> in the capacity of his subconscious thought to arouse har-
> monics in our minds.

Shakespeare's "thought oscillates from the abstract to the concrete
and carries our minds with it in its movement," never losing our
attentions in abstraction. His images "transform and reciprocally
augment each other's power and content." He uses words "in such
a way that secondary meanings of which our minds are dimly
aware bridge the gap between the units of speech." In short,

"Shakespeare in a supreme degree employed secondary and associated meanings to achieve an effect which is felt by the reader or hearer to be masterly because levels of consciousness lower than that of conscious attention respond to the undertones of the poet's song."

Memory "contributes materials for association [and] emotion troubles the waters in which they lie immersed so that there float up from the depths products of startling beauty." With this image Armstrong opens his discussion of Shakespeare's inspiration, the end product of the process, "Concentration, Incubation, Inspiration."

> He saturated his ideas and images in the 'well of unconscious cerebration.' The 'sleeping images' lay submerged, and after sojourning in the depths were called forth again, altered in shape or tint and linked with partners, some new, some old.

Hence, in part, the testimony of Heminge and Condell, that Shakespeare's mind and hand went together so that "what he thought he uttered with that easiness we scarce have a blot in his papers."

Armstrong argues that image clusters cannot be trusted to reveal personal experience. Experience may contribute, but so may memory of source material or of one's own earlier writing, so may other associative drives. The presence of elements in a cluster resembles the presence of students at a lecture—some there to maintain their attendance record, some to watch the opposite sex, some to learn. It is hard to determine which is which.

Armstrong likewise attacks psychoanalytic methods of literary criticism. Freudian theory assumes that art sublimates unconscious and internally censored wishes. Armstrong denies the theory's adequacy. Many authors are aware of the wishes they express in their art. More importantly, the imagination has available to it enormous ranges of material "unconnected, or connected very remotely, with any moral or social censorship."

If most of the subliminal processes involved in imagination
are independent of ethical relevance, we cannot assume that
the symbols and phantasies in which they manifest themselves
are related to an ethical universe of discourse at all, and to
regard them as emanating from "prohibited sources," or
interpret them as being disguised expressions of morally ille-
gitimate and therefore relinquished sources of gratification, is
gratuitous.

What then do the image clusters teach us? As Spurgeon has
indicated, they show us much about Shakespeare's feelings. And,
negatively, they show us that Shakespeare's imagination is peculiarly impersonal. (This is, perhaps, one aspect of the almost
universal sense that Shakespeare is a natural genius.) "His imagination achieved a high degree of autonomy." "There is, indeed,
reason to believe that Shakespeare's imagination was more harmonious than his personality." Armstrong sees a "peculiar obses-
siveness" in Shakespeare's clustering imagination, which lends
support to the hypothesis of Harris and others "that the poet
depicted himself most clearly in Hamlet."

This is not to say that I believe Hamlet is a portrait of Shakespeare. Neither Frank Harris nor any of his supporters have
produced convincing evidence of this, but those who believe,
with Coleridge, that Shakespeare evolved characters by the
exaggeration of his own characteristics, can hardly doubt that
the constant harking back to circles of ideas which cluster-
thinking involves, indicates that in himself Shakespeare found
the nucleus of Hamlet. Hamlet is cluster-thinking come to
life.

To be fair to Armstrong's final chapter, "The Structure of the
Imagination," I can only refer the reader to it. It sets forth a
closely reasoned and meticulously schematized model of the imagi-

nation, considers the optimum relations therewith of reason, emotion, and memory, and suggests that in Shakespeare this ideal balance and harmony developed. Ariel, suggests Armstrong in a fine peroration, is Imagination: in himself and in his relations with Prospero's god-like reason and with Caliban's libidinous brutishness he bears out the Armstrongian hypothesis. He is the flying spirit of fire, air, and music, "but he can transform himself alike into the lightning or a mermaid." "He is full of pranks," which often mask a deeper meaning. Once he was enslaved by the evil and sensual Sycorax, but Reason freed him. "Ariel continually aspires after freedom . . . In the measure that Ariel is in thraldom to emotion or reason he is less a sprite than a servant. Few there are sufficiently spacious-minded to hold Ariel so lightly that he is most his independent self."

Armstrong has yet to receive just recognition. This may be because of the particularities mentioned before; it may be that he fails to bring out the structure of his argument as surely as he might. Certainly, though he has occasional felicities of expression —as in the image of emotion stirring the waters of memory or of the elements of image clusters shifting partners as in an elaborate dance—his style rarely explodes with Coleridgian illumination. Yet no one since Coleridge has so taken us into the dynamics of Shakespeare's composing. Armstrong shows us how Shakespeare's imagination works and why it works on us. He brings home to our understandings that naturalness of Shakespeare which our feelings never doubted. He corrects our tendencies to view the plays as naked reflections of personal experience or as the deliberate constructs of prudent rationality. They are something else, and more mysterious. Like a good cleric, Armstrong takes us into the presence of this mystery. In little and in large he describes it, defines it, engages us in its operations. The result is that we admire Shakespeare the more and reverence him the more wittingly. And since our own imaginations find in his their enlarging and idealizing reflection, perhaps we more clearly recognize and revere the creative powers within ourselves.

Caroline F. E. Spurgeon / 1869–1942
Wolfgang Clemen / 1909–

Spurgeon's limitations. Her pioneering exploration of "iterative imagery." Dominating images of individual tragedies. Reinforcement and contradiction of traditional views. Impetus to modern study of imagery: Brooks's criticism of Macbeth. ❧ *Clemen's analysis of Shakespeare's mechanical style in* Titus. Love's Labour's Lost *as showing gain.* Henry VI *as revealing Shakespeare's early uses of imagery.* Richard III: *imagery formal but integrated.* Richard II *a step forward. Shakespeare's middle period as revealing new techniques of associative and fully harmonized imagery.*

"*Shakespeare's Imagery* remains, as a first survey, indispensable to students of the subject," writes M. C. Bradbrook. "Its chief contribution was the concept of imagery as undersong, seen at its most potent in the main tragedies, but traceable throughout Shakespeare's work."[1] This is just, especially if we recognize that Spurgeon's work is not only a first survey but was *the* first survey of its subject. We look back at it now as upon a pioneering mechanism, a first Ford, say, or a Wright brothers plane, rapt both by the simplicity of the original and by the stupendous alteration it has brought about in our world.

The simplicities and crudities are clear enough to a modern eye: the card indexing, the statistical egalitarianism, the rigid classifications, the cataloguing by figure to the exclusion of idea, the failure to explore the dynamics of images. Spurgeon's critical vocabulary is presumably more precise than I have been able to determine—she confidently counts 95 "poetical" images out of the 114 images in *Midsummer Night's Dream*, and 18 "poetical" images as against 27 images that are "vivid, quaint, or grotesque" in *Measure for Measure*—but she uses it loosely nonetheless. A short passage on the functions of iterative imagery will illustrate:

> In the comedies, this imagery contributes chiefly atmosphere and background, as well as sometime emphasizing or re-echoing certain qualities in the plays. In the later plays, the romances, this symbolism becomes . . . more subtle, and illustrates an idea rather than a concrete picture; while in the tragedies it is closely connected with the central theme, which it supplements and illuminates.

Her practice is uneven and inconsistent. She discusses the distribution of images by speaker and scene in *The Merchant of Venice* but in no other play. To *Twelfth Night*, on which most critics would expand, she gives but a perfunctory page and a half of comment—there are only fourteen "poetical" images, "but these are either peculiarly beautiful . . . or they are vivid and unforgettable . . . or inimitable pictures"; and there are "an unusual number (sixteen) of 'topical' images"—while to *King John* she gives eight pages.

Surely, though, the pioneer must be allowed some vagaries in the excitement of discovery. And what Spurgeon discovers, when she is not touching-in the portrait of Shakespeare, is the fact that in addition to the normal range and proportion of images in every play, there are "certain groups of images, which, as it were, stand out in each particular play and immediately attract attention because they are peculiar either in subject, or quantity, or both." By "standing out," be it understood at once, Spurgeon means, as one pores over her statistical charts, not as one reads or sees the plays. But the consequence of the first, for the sensitized reader is, of course, the second. Eyes opened one way see another. This individuating pattern or group of images Spurgeon variously calls "floating," "leading," "dominating," "running," "iterative," "recurrent"—and sometimes she speaks of it not as "image" or "imagery" or "images" but as "note," "motive," or "theme." She speaks, too, of "undertone" and "undertone of running symbolic imagery." The varying terms point, I think, both to her excitement at what she has found and her uncertainty about it—at least, she finds no single way to convey it all. She sees the imagery as a picture in the poet's mind. Again, she sees the separate images as dramatic figures competing, like Shakespeare's kings, for dominance. Anon she thinks in musical terms and speaks of images as motifs, as in a fugue or opera. Then images become for her like illuminations in a medieval manuscript, as when she considers the personification of emotions in *King John*. And when she considers the role recurrent images play in the tragedies, they are, she decides, analogous to

> Blake's illustrations to his prophetic books. These are not, for the most part, illustrations in the ordinary sense of the term . . . they are rather a running accompaniment to the words in another medium, sometimes symbolically emphasizing or interpreting certain aspects of the thought, sometimes supplying frankly only decoration or atmosphere, sometimes grotesque and even repellent, vivid, strange, arresting, sometimes drawn with an almost unearthly beauty of form and color.

Spurgeon finds the explanation of iterative imagery in Coleridge's idea that original genius modifies by its predominant passion the images it uses. In her own apt formulation, "the poet's mind, unlike the dyer's hand, subdues to itself what it works in, and colors with its dominating emotion all the varied material which comes its way." If the emotion is slight, there will be no floating image at all, as in *Julius Caesar*—"one feels it was not written under the particular stress of emotion or excitement which gives rise to a dominating image"—or it will be slack, as in *Coriolanus*, "where certain functions or persons in the state are rather wearisomely and perfunctorily compared with various parts of the body." If the emotion is strong, the iterative imagery becomes powerful, as in *King John:* "Here one feels . . . that the poet's imagination was intensely and brilliantly alive, dancing with fire and energy like Philip Faulconbridge himself." And if the emotion has heated the imagination to white heat, as in *Lear* or *Macbeth*, then the images "become one with the movement and characters pictures in the mind's eye of the poet? The dominating image and could be no other than they are."

What, then, are the iterative images, the floating symbols, the Spurgeon finds in *Romeo and Juliet* "is *light*, every form and manifestation of it: the sun, moon, stars, fire, lightning, the flash of gunpowder, and the reflected light of beauty and of love; while by contrast we have night, darkness, clouds, rain, mist and smoke." "Shakespeare saw the story, in its swift and tragic beauty, as an almost blinding flash of light, suddenly ignited, and as swiftly quenched." The dominating image in *Hamlet* is "the idea of an ulcer or tumor, as descriptive of the unwholesome condition of Denmark morally." Images of food dominate *Troilus and Cressida*. "The main image in *Othello* is that of animals in action, preying upon one another, mischievous, lascivious, cruel or suffering." "One overpowering and dominating continuous image" runs through *King Lear*—"of a human body in anguished movement, tugged, wrenched, beaten, pierced, stung, scourged, dislocated, flayed, gashed, scalded, tortured and finally broken on the wrack."

Spurgeon's exposition of Shakespeare's iterative imagery bears importantly on our understanding of the plays. Carried no further than she carries it, it helps us, anew or afresh, to apprehend many things. In the history plays we see the rise and decline of England's health in gardening imagery which, "in *Richard II* gathers strength and volume, until it becomes the leading theme." We discover King John's moral inadequacy the more painfully evident from this fact, that in a play filled with personifications, the king himself "is always pictured as a *portion* of a body only"—a bloody hand, a bloody foot. We recognize how the moon contributes to our sense of woodland beauty in A *Midsummer Night's Dream*, and how, though *Much Ado* is laid in Sicily, its imagery provides a sustaining background of English country life. The music in the words as well as in the air at Bassanio's choosing of the casket we hear with sharpened ears, and the sound that thunders and sighs and hums through *The Tempest*. We blink at *Romeo and Juliet* as at a lightning flash, our palates and gorges react to the appetitive in *Troilus and Cressida*, our bodies wince to the anguish of *Lear*.

Spurgeon does more than reinforce traditional awarenesses. In certain important instances she runs counter to the common view. Her enthusiastic response to *King John* puts her beside Middleton Murry and against the pack. Her analysis of *Hamlet* counters Schlegel, Coleridge and their multitudinous train:

> To Shakespeare's pictorial imagination . . . the problem of Hamlet is not predominantly that of will and reason, of a mind too philosophic or a nature temperamentally unfitted to act quickly; he sees it pictorially not as the problem of an individual at all, but as something greater and even more mysterious, as a condition for which the individual himself is apparently not responsible, any more than the sick man is to blame for the infection which strikes and devours him, but which, nevertheless, in its course and development, impartially and relentlessly, annihilates him and others, innocent and guilty alike.

Spurgeon's analysis of the running imagery in *Macbeth* likewise leads her to oppose "the view emphasized by some critics (notably Coleridge and Bradley) of the likeness between Macbeth and Milton's Satan in grandeur and sublimity." For the play's imagery, she discovers, keeps dressing Macbeth, like Charlie Chaplin, in clothes unsuited to him—

MACBETH:
The thane of Cawdor lives: why do you dress me
In borrow'd robes?

(I. iii. 108)

BANQUO *of Macbeth:*
New honors come upon him,
Like our strange garments, cleave not to their mould
But with the aid of use.

(I. iii. 144)

LADY MACBETH *to Macbeth:*
Was the hope drunk
Wherein you dress'd yourself?

(I. vii. 35)

MACDUFF *of Macbeth's coronation:*
Well, may you see things well done there: adieu!
Lest our old robes sit easier than our new!

(II. iv. 37)

CAITHNESS *of Macbeth:*
He cannot buckle his distemper'd cause
Within the belt of rule

(V. ii. 15)

ANGUS *of Macbeth:*
Now does he feel his title
Hang loose about him, like a giant's robe
Upon a dwarfish thief.

(V. ii. 20)

"Undoubtedly," says Spurgeon,

*Macbeth is built on great lines and in heroic proportions . . .
[but] there is an aspect in which he is but a poor, vain,
cruel, treacherous creature, snatching ruthlessly over the dead
bodies of kinsman and friend at place and power he is utterly
unfitted to possess. It is worth remembering that it is thus*

> *that Shakespeare, with his unshrinking clarity of vision, re-peatedly sees him.*

Since Spurgeon criticism has had either to *rebut* such judgments as these or to accommodate them; it cannot blink them.

The principal importance of Spurgeon's work, however, lies less in the propositions she sets forth about the individual plays than in the impetus she has given to the study of Shakespeare's imagery. More than any other critic in the twentieth century she has opened up this dimension of dramaturgy for critical explora-tion and assessment. In the process, she has, of course, played into the hands of spatial criticism, and her work gives aid and comfort, or a point of departure, to the so-called new criticism generally. She helps L. C. Knights regard the plays as metaphors.[2] She supports C. S. Lewis in focusing on *Hamlet*, the poem, at the expense of Hamlet, the prince.[3] She provides Armstrong grist for his examination of Shakespeare's imagination, and of our own. But her influence is confined to no one critical school. And its range is extraordinary. More than a thousand books and essays already find their roots in her work (to say nothing of the tens of thousands of exercises on Shakespeare's imagery in schools and colleges), and thousands are surely to come.

At the beginning of this discussion I spoke of Spurgeon as a pioneer, and having treated her pioneering crudities and simplici-ties, I passed on to her achievements and attempted to suggest something of the shape of these: the reinforcing of old aware-nesses about individual plays, the inaugurating of new ones, the stimulating of spatial criticism, new criticism, and Shakespearean criticism generally; the giving this stimulus lavishly across the decades. We should see, finally, that this enlarging criticism is also progressively sophisticated and that as in all such matters, the refinement of today pays genetic tribute to its ancestry, however simple. Mack's sensitive exploration of the imagery of *Hamlet*, Heilman's studies of *Lear* and *Othello*, repudiate Spurgeon's immediate conclusions, or go way beyond them, but they celebrate her initiative and example.[4] The same is true of Cleanth Brooks's famous essay, "The Naked Babe and the Cloak of Manliness,"[5] one part of which I shall briefly digest by way of illuminating Spurgeon's work the better—in its simplicity and in its potential for sophistication.

Brooks summarizes Spurgeon's commentary on the clothes imagery in *Macbeth* and objects to the conclusion. That Macbeth's enemies, Caithness and Angus, see him "as a poor and somewhat comic figure" does not mean that *Shakespeare* sees him that way. More important, though, "the crucial point of the comparison . . . lies not in the smallness of the man and the largeness of the robes, but rather in the fact that . . . these are not *his* garments." Hence Macbeth is uncomfortable in them. Further, "the oldest symbol for the hypocrite is that of the man who cloaks his true nature under a disguise. Macbeth loathes playing the part of the hypocrite." "The series of garment metaphors which run through the play is paralleled by a series of masking or cloaking images which . . . show themselves to be merely variants of the garments which hide none too well his disgraceful self." For example, "False face must hide what the false heart doth know"; "Scarf up the eye of pitiful day"; and yet more striking:

> Come, thick night,
> And pall thee in the dunnest smoke of hell,
> That my keen knife see not the wound it makes,
> Nor heaven peep through the blanket of the dark,
> To cry, "Hold, Hold!"

In one sense the keen knife is that in Lady Macbeth's hand, but in another, it is Macbeth himself, and the meaning of the plea is that the deed be concealed both from the eye of heaven and "from the hesitant doer." "The imagery thus repeats and reinforces the substance of Macbeth's anguished aside uttered in the preceding scene:

> Let not light see my black and deep desires;
> The eye wink at the hand; yet let that be
> Which the eye fears, when it is done, to see.

"Blanket" is the clothing of sleep, "pall" of death. "They are the appropriate garments of night; and they carry on an important aspect of the general clothes imagery." Yet another instance occurs, on the discovery of Duncan's corpse, when Banquo speaks of hiding in clothing "our naked frailties," and Macbeth replies, "Let's briefly put on manly readiness." "It is ironic," says Brooks, "for the 'manly readiness' . . . is, in his own case, a hypocrite's garment." And "manly" is ironic yet another way, for he, under Lady Macbeth's reproaches, has attempted to do more than man and has become less, "a beast." The "manly readiness" that he must put on, then, is the hard hypocrisy of the "resolved murderer."

Brooks finally returns to a passage he has examined earlier (as illustrative of the play's difficult style), to come to some new conclusions about the clothes imagery therein:

> Here lay Duncan,
> His silver skin lac'd with his golden blood;
> And his gash'd stabs look'd like a breach in nature
> For ruin's wasteful entrance: there, the murderers,
> Steep'd in the colors of their trade, their daggers
> Unmannerly breech'd with gore.

The clothes imagery runs throughout the passage; the body of the king is dressed in the most precious of garments, the blood royal itself; and the daggers too are dressed—in the same garment. The daggers, "naked" except for their lower parts which are reddened with blood, are like men in "unmannerly" dress—men, naked except for their red breeches, lying beside the red-handed grooms. The figure, though vivid, is fantastic; granted. But the basis for the comparison is not slight and adventitious. The metaphor fits the real situation on the deepest levels. As Macbeth and Lennox burst into the room, they find the daggers wearing, as Macbeth knows all too well, a horrible masquerade. They have been carefully "clothed" to play a part. They are not honest daggers, honorably naked in readiness to guard the king, or, "mannerly" clothed in their own sheaths. Yet the disguise which they wear will enable Macbeth to assume the robes of Duncan—robes to which he is no more entitled than are the daggers to the royal garments which they now wear, grotesquely.

Whether Brooks is articulating the mysteries within Shakespeare's play or merely verbalizing his own highly patterned responses may be a question, but I hold for the former. The difficulty, if the reader feels any, comes in part from the lurch inevitable when translating the dynamic into the static, the dramatic into the analytic, the passional into the cerebral. Brooks stops the play at various points, as it were, holds up to its palpitating form a high-powered lens, and descants learnedly on the elements interacting within the immediate field of his vision. It is all there, all true, but not the way we see it in the theater or read it in our closets. Or perhaps we should say, much of it is there, perhaps most—but some of it is in Brooks too. Spurgeon could never write thus. Nor could Brooks, without her.

❦ ❦ ❦

In *The Development of Shakespeare's Imagery*[6] Wolfgang Clemen has the merit of attempting, early on in the imagery-is-king movement, to chart one line in the growth of Shakespeare's art. His important precursors include Swinburne and Dowden and, far back, Coleridge. Like them he speaks most fruitfully of the early Shakespeare whose works, pupil-like, submit yet to our analysis. I find the chapters on the romances mechanical and perfunctory, the discussions of the tragedies uneven and, given G. Wilson Knight's antecedent accomplishments, of uncertain importance. But the portion of his work that chronicles Shakespeare's maturing illuminates its subject nicely and helps us apprehend, if only by contrast, the miracle by which Shakespeare's images became the very pulses of his creating thought.

Clemen starts us with *Titus Andronicus* where the speech is unindividuated, bombastic, and often dramatically unfunctional— a play where Shakespeare talks, not too well but certainly too much. To show off his knowledge and his mastery of "fashionable stylistic devices," he uses a language that "adds and accumulates and would seek to replace clarity and definiteness by multiplicity." With the adhesive of "like" or "as" he sticks images onto passages from which they might without loss be dropped. He uses epic similes, undramatic in their length and, by their pictorial completedness, tending to declare their independence of context. He arranges a series of line-long, syntactically parallel images so that one can be stitched on after another as long as the comparisons occur—

> The birds chant melody on every bush,
> The snake lies rolled in the cheerful sun,
> The green leaves quiver with the cooling wind.

His characters he endows with an unusual frequency of rhetorical questions so that they may pretend to be engaging in dialogue, like persons in a play, though they are in reality "delivering pompous orations to the audience." And to add one more to this amused bill of particulars, Shakespeare can so far overlook the occasion for his imagery that he gives Marcus forty-seven high-flown lines on finding the mutilated and ravished Lavinia: Marcus compares the blood gushing from Lavinia's mouth " 'to a bubbling fountain stirr'd with wind,' her cheeks 'look red as Titan's face,' and of her lily hands he says in retrospect that they 'tremble like aspen-leaves upon a lute, and make the silken strings delight to kiss them.' "

Love's Labour's Lost marks a slight organic gain in that, though its taffeta phrases "veil and adorn, but . . . do not yet elucidate," they are here native to their environment. Further, the play's elaborate punning trains the author in "finding words and turning a phrase." It also helps him to tighten his dialogue and prepares for the more organic tightening that comes when continuity of image-themes takes over from mere word-play. In both *Love's Labour's Lost* and *The Two Gentlemen of Verona* a vein of "keen wit and frank realism" develops a tension with the elegance we have noted and heralds the art of Falstaff and the fools of the comedies to come:

> Speed, in an amusing series of comparisons, describes to Valentine the behavior of the enamoured: ". . . to weep, like a young wench that had buried her grandma; to fast, like one that takes diet; to watch, like one that fears robbing; to speak puling, like a beggar at Hallowmas."

Although the *Henry* VI trilogy still evidences little organic relation between imagery, characters, and situation, it lets us see more clearly into Shakespeare's early use of imagery. In argumentative speeches he reaches for proverbs, as when Suffolk would dissuade Henry of Gloucester's loyalty—"Smooth runs the water where the brook is deep . . . The fox barks not when he would steal the lamb." In soliloquies Shakespeare is more apt to use imagery than in dialogue, "the retarding quality of the monologue leav[ing] more time for the elaboration of images," and the images therein "appear to be more direct, more 'expressive.'" He invents obtrusive programmatic similes "by means of which a detailed survey of the state of affairs is given"—as when Margaret compares Warwick to the anchor, Montague to the topmast, slaughtered friends to tackle, Edward to the ruthless sea, etc. The later Shakespeare will subdue such imagery as he will the imagery of natural description, which here stands out—as introductory and external in the scene preparatory to Suffolk's murder: "The gaudy, blabbing and remorseful day/Is crept into the bosom of the sea . . ."

The maturing art of Shakespeare's imagery shows itself in a

growth from multiplicity to unity, from the mechanical and exterior to the interior and organic. Clemen finds evidence of this growth in *Richard III*. The images "become briefer." "There are no more lengthy conceits and digressions, no long general reflections spun out in detailed simile." "We have not a single case of image-aggregation, and the similes introduced by 'as' and 'like' have largely disappeared." The play is, of course, "still in the formalistic and artificial manner . . . But all [the] rhetorical devices . . . are employed . . . in a more appropriate way than was earlier the case." "The conventional stylistic figures, by being suited to the occasion, possess a new vitality," as in the great laments and curses. "The metaphorical element gradually pervades the language," as in the lines, "now prosperity begins to mellow/ And drop into the rotten mouth of death."

> This passage marks the commencement of Shakespeare's peculiar art of expressing abstractions metaphorically; it also shows how Shakespeare, refining and extending his technique of foreboding and anticipation, no longer only relies on the use of omen and prophecy but resorts to new devices.

Like Spurgeon, Clemen draws attention to the animal imagery by means of which Richard III is repeatedly characterized—"*Richard III* is Shakespeare's first play in which the chief character is delineated by symbolical images recurring as a *leitmotif*."

Richard II—and with this play we shall cease our step-by-step retracing of *Wilhelm* Shakespeare's *lehrjahre—Richard II* carries us forward. It has "many scenes in which imagery has [the] function of enhancing and deepening the symbolic meaning of what occurs on the stage"—for example, the garden scene to which Spurgeon likewise draws attention. But the exciting thing is that now

> imagery becomes the characteristic manner of expression of the chief character. To talk in similes, to make use of metaphors, is indeed a natural quality of the king's mind and

temperament. Richard II *is the first instance of Shakespeare's habitual manner of endowing his heroes with unusual imagination and the poetic gift.*

Richard, of course, is given to imagery instead of action, a point Clemen develops by analyzing the scene wherein Richard commands Bolingbroke to seize the crown he holds forth and then moralizes upon the emblem they compose:

> Now is this golden crown like a deep well
> That owes two buckets, filling one another,
> The emptier ever dancing in the air,
> The other down, unseen and full of water:
> That bucket down, and full of tears am I,
> Drinking my griefs, while you mount up on high.

This simile . . . grows out of the scene on the stage . . . So strong is [Richard's] desire for significant imagery that even the outward action must serve this end. This image marks the climax of the scene, but at the same time it sums up the whole substance of the play: the tragedy of kingship which demands that the parting king must wane in the same proportion as the new king waxes.

In Shakespeare's early plays, the images are "ready-made." "In the middle period," according to Clemen, "a new technique is evolved, . . . the technique of the associative rise of the image. The images are formed in the very act of composition; one word engenders another." Lamb suggested this a century earlier when he wrote that "Shakespeare mingles everything, he runs line into line, embarrasses sentences and metaphors; before one idea has burst its shell, another is hatched and clamorous for disclosure."[7] Images no longer seem to interrupt. Further, they are often merely suggested, having penetrated beneath the surface of discourse, as it were. Metaphors now mix, images cluster, the concrete continually mingles with the abstract, and ambiguity burgeons. I cite conclusions without evidence—a tendency to which Clemen himself occasionally succumbs—because Armstrong has since provided us with ample illustration, but the conclusions point the way Shakespeare has come, the way he will go. A few words about the latter.

In the tragedies "every element of style . . . becomes dramatically relevant, . . . the images becoming an inherent part of the dramatic structure." They help prepare for coming events; they "emphasize and accompany the dramatic action, repeating its themes"; they participate importantly in a style increasingly oblique, suggestive, polyphonically ambiguous, and dramatically ironic.

> In the tragedies, it is through the imagery that the cosmic and superhuman powers enter into the drama . . . [and] the world of nature also—animals, plants and flowers . . . not merely to provide background or atmosphere but to take part in the action and to express symbolically correspondences and interrelations which underlie the real action and often contain the essential meaning of the play.

And in the tragedies, finally, the imagery becomes almost a "key," helping "to create an organic unity which makes us forget the lack of the classical unities of time and action."

In the light of modern sophistication about imagery, Clemen's book may seem naïve, but it is modest, quietly stimulating, pioneering. It enlarges our understanding of Shakespeare's growth and achievement by pitting the awkwardnesses of his early writing against the reasonable unity of his middle writing, against the miraculous unity of his greatest work. Simultaneously, by focusing on the image, by seeing the different ways it participates in character and occasion and plot, in background and atmosphere, in the whole chain of dramatic meaning, it joins the work of Knight and Spurgeon. It helps open up the critical highway down which a succeeding generation has traveled.

Theodore Spencer / 1902–1949
and E. M. W. Tillyard / 1889–1962
Alfred B. Harbage / 1901–
Edward L. Hubler / 1902–1965

Spencer and Tillyard as illuminators of the "Elizabethan World Picture." The optimistic view: man's end, God's law, geocentric universe, hierarchy of souls, powers of man's mind, kinds of law; correspondences. The pessimistic view. Spencer's thesis; Tillyard's. 🌷 *Harbage as historian. His felicitous style. "The Dignity of Man": affirmed in public theaters, undercut in coterie theaters; Shakespeare's aversion to humiliation, his affirmative characterization. "Sexual Behavior": the popular drama chaste, the coterie not; Shakespearean broadness analyzed. Limitations and merits of Harbage's approach.* 🌷 *Hubler's analysis of sonnets and plays in the light of each other. His rhetoric, sympathy. Shakespeare's wholeness. His healthy, unromantic view of sex. Belief that the heart must give itself away. Secular frame of reference of his tragedies: importance of reputation.*

Recently I asked a colleague who had just begun teaching a Shakespeare course whether he had not found useful Theodore Spencer's book, *Shakespeare and the Nature of Man* (1942). "No," he said. He had looked at it, "but it was old hat." Others of his generation condescend with similar negligence to E. M. W. Tillyard's *The Elizabethan World Picture* (1943), and I am reminded of Dr. Johnson's sage remarks explaining why Dryden's *Essay of Dramatic Poesy* seemed old hat in Johnson's time. "Learning once made popular is no longer learning," he said; "it has the appearance of something which we have bestowed upon ourselves, as the dew appears to rise from the field which it refreshes."[1] It is so. Who now reads Ulysses' speech on degree without failing to perceive therein the Elizabethan doctrine of hierarchy, the Elizabethan feeling for correspondence? Yet who remembers that it was Spencer or Tillyard or one of their scholarly predecessors who discovered and published these meanings?

Perhaps neither Spencer nor Tillyard belongs in this short gallery of critics, though their works would guarantee them a place in a longer, more comprehensive history. Indeed, the *New York Herald Tribune*'s reviewer praised Spencer's book as "the most distinguished contribution to our understanding of Shakespeare's mind and purposes" since Bradley;[2] and Harold Jenkins, in his "Shakespeare's History Plays: 1900–1951,"[3] gives special length and prominence to Tillyard. But neither man inaugurates a new critical approach or develops an old one with particular distinction. For a man writing in the 1940s, Spencer is old fashioned. He asserts that Shakespeare's "greatness consists . . . in his ability to create characters in whom we can believe, and it is only in so far as we are helped toward an understanding of how he does this, that a study of the conventions of his time is really useful." And he finds Shakespeare's career "divided into three stages: a period of experiment and adaptation, a period of tragic vision, and a period of affirmation." Tillyard writes with rather a fuller consciousness that Wilson Knight and Caroline Spurgeon have come to pass. If at times he speaks overconfidently about the genuineness of a character's emotion or analyzes a character for all the world as if he were an historical individual—as when he asserts that Hal, "while admiring his father and sympathizing with his difficulties, hates him for holding up Hotspur as a model"—he is usually happily sensitive to mode or style as it bears on interpretation, and he recognizes that metaphors possess levels of meaning that transcend the psyches of the speakers who use them. But as a critic Tillyard is an enthusiast, seizing on whatever argument comes to hand, and repeatedly marring his case by relying on ambiguous evidence.

It is not as critics but as illuminators of criticism that we must recognize Spencer and Tillyard, and through them the hosts of those who by patient exploration of the history of ideas have opened the literature of the Elizabethan era to us in a new way. They are the expositors of a perspective. They have mediated to us, in Tillyard's formulation, "a mass of basic assumptions about the world" which even such opposed groups as the puritans and the courtiers never disputed. "Our aim," says Spencer, "is to describe the point of view . . . the framework that gave Shakespeare his terms and his values."

Tillyard's table of contents provides a tidy overview of this "Elizabethan World Picture":

1. Introductory
2. Order
3. Sin
4. The Chain of Being
5. The Links in The Chain
    (i) Angels and Ether
    (ii) The Stars and Fortune
    (iii) The Elements
    (iv) Man
    (v) Animals, Plants and Metals
6. The Corresponding Planes
7. The Correspondences
    (i) Celestial Powers and Other Creations
    (ii) Macrocosm and Body Politic
    (iii) Macrocosm and Microcosm
    (iv) Body Politic and Microcosm
    (v) General Significance

8. The Cosmic Dance
9. Epilogue

Spencer develops the same material in much the same way, his chapter on "Man in Nature: the Optimistic Theory" roughly corresponding with Tillyard's chapters on order, chain of being, correspondence, and cosmic dance, his chapter on "Man in Nature: the Renaissance Conflict" paralleling Tillyard's chapter on sin.

"In the sixteenth century," says Spencer (whose formulation I shall let stand for both), "the combined elements of Aristotelianism, Platonism, Neo-Platonism, Stoicism, and Christianity were almost indistinguishably woven into a pattern which was universally agreed upon, and which, in its main outlines, was the same as that of the Middle Ages." Man's end was "to know and love God." The knowledge of God was available through the book of His works no less than through the Bible. The works of God revealed "an eternal law, a general order—in the universe, in the ranks of created beings, in the institution of government," discovery and contemplation of which engaged man in the knowledge and the love of his creator.

The universe was the great geocentric one of Ptolemaic astronomy, created in the six days' work narrated in *Genesis* and with a life span of 6,000 years, some 5,000 of which had elapsed in Shakespeare's time. Its sublunary part was variously and mutably composed of four elements, earth the lowest, then water, then air and fire. Its celestial part, immutably composed of some stuff superior to the four elements, lay outward in eight concentric spheres: the moon, Mercury, Venus, the sun, Mars, Jupiter, Saturn, and the fixed stars. These spheres, revolving at different speeds, each making its own musical note, governed each by an angelic intelligence, are

bounded by the Primum Mobile, the first mover, the outer rim of the created universe. It makes a complete revolution

> every twenty-four hours from west to east, and by doing so,
> sets the eight spheres below it whirling in the opposite
> direction. It is the direct cause of all heavenly movement,
> and . . . the indirect cause of all earthly movement as well.

Within this world of Nature "everything had its function, from
the humblest mineral and plant to the most splendid constella-
tion, and for each created thing the function was the same; it
existed to work for man." Outside lay "the Empyrean heaven,
eternal and infinite, the abode of God, and, after the Last Judgment, the dwelling of the blessed."

In the sublunary realm, all living things participate in a
hierarchy of souls.

> At the bottom are objects which have no soul at all, like
> stones; they have merely being, but not life. In the next rank
> are plants, which possess the most rudimentary kind of soul,
> the vegetative or nutritive soul which takes care of growth and
> reproduction; in the rank above plants are animals, which in
> addition to possessing a nutritive soul or faculty, also possess a
> sensitive soul or faculty; they can not only grow, they can also
> feel, and hence they have the power of motion and, to some
> extent, the faculty of imagination. Above the animals comes
> man, who in addition to possessing a nutritive and sensitive
> soul, possesses also a rational soul. Above man come the
> angels, who are pure intellect, and who are able to apprehend
> universal truth without the medium of the senses. Above the
> angels is God, who—in Aristotelian terms—is pure actuality.

In this scheme man is crucially placed. As in the cosmos there is a
celestial and a sublunary region, so in the domain of living things
there is an intellectual and an animal or sensual realm. "Man is
the essential link between them. He is the highest of the animals,
and the lowest of the intellectual beings." It is his duty to rise. To
help him he has three powers of the mind. Reason abstracts from

"sense-data the immaterial forms which they contain. These forms are then apprehended intuitively by the understanding or intellect, which is akin to the pure intellect of the angels . . . And finally there is will," which stirs man to mount upward through a knowledge of to a love of God. "Thus man, for whom all the rest of the world was created, stands in the center of the second of Nature's domains, the world of living beings, his head erect to contemplate the heavens, his soul able to rise from the realm of sense to apprehend the God who made him."

But "man must do more than contemplate the world that was created for him, he must govern it." As there is order in the universe and in the ranks of created things, so here, in the institution of government, there is order, manifest in a hierarchy of three kinds of law. "There is the law of Nature itself, there is the law of Nations which derives from it, and which is generally applicable to all countries, and there is civil law, which applies to the customs of particular communities." Under civil law comes the question of the form of government. The civil law of England provides that government be a monarchy, the king no despot but representative of "a universal principle of justice, as firmly established as the order of the heavens." Society itself, like the spheres of the heavens, exists in a hierarchy of ranks: " 'gentlemen, citizens, yeomen artificers, and laborers.' "

The central truth about creation is that it is a single unity, each part informed by the same principle of ranked order. To understand any one part of this unity, then, man may compare it to the other parts. He finds the king set in the middle of his realm as the sun is, "in the middle of the heavens, and as man's heart is placed in the middle of his body." Man's body is, in truth, the microcosm, "a little world made cunningly." His soul is the center of his sinful earth. "Nothing is more striking in serious sixteenth-century literature than the universal use of analogy: the cosmos is explained by the body, and the body is explained by the state; all three hierarchies are parallel—as they had been for centuries."

These paragraphs have set forth the central content of

Spencer's chapter, "Man in Nature: the Optimistic Theory." Tillyard explores the details of the various hierarchies rather more fully in his two chapters on "The Chain of Being" and "The Links in the Chain," and he expands and reinforces Spencer's point about analogical thinking in his chapters, "The Corresponding Planes" and "The Correspondences." But the two think—and write—almost as one in setting forth the affirmative world view that Spencer summarizes in these words:

> Thus the whole universe, which was made for man, found in man its reflection and its epitome; man was the center of the ideal picture which optimistic theory delighted to portray. Nature's order was shown in the elements, in the stars, in the hierarchy of souls, in the ranks of society. Everything in the world was part of the same unified scheme, and the body and soul of man, each a reflection of the other, and both an image of the universal plan, were the culmination and the final end of God's design. "Homo est perfectio et finis omnium creaturarum in mundo"—man is the perfection and the end of all the creatures in the world.

Complementing this affirmative view the Elizabethans inherited from the Middle Ages a negative. In his fall man had damaged the powers of his mind, subjugated his will to his passions, and so upset the original and ideal hierarchy that his body now ruled his soul. With man Nature had fallen—many of its creatures now at enmity with man, its stars all too often evil in their aspects. Beneath the moon all was mutable and mortal. The earth itself could now be seen not so much as center and apex as " 'the place farthest removed from the Empyrean, the bottom of the creation, to which its dregs and baser elements sank.' "[4] And, given its life span of a mere 6,000 years, Nature could be seen to be in its old age, running down. This pessimistic view of man, however, "did not at all decrease his immense importance to the universe. He was, in fact, so necessary that God himself, after man's fall, had taken on man's shape in order to set things right again."

Tillyard develops these same points in his chapter on "Sin," but Spencer goes a step further. Even the pessimistic view of man's nature has, it must be seen, its optimistic center. Even to its eye God is in His heaven and His justice reigns. But Spencer sees the total system under triple attack as the sixteenth century draws to a close. "Copernicus had questioned the cosmological order, Montaigne had questioned the natural order, Machiavelli had questioned the political order." "The new philosophy," Donne wrote, "calls *all* in doubt":

> 'Tis all in pieces, all coherence gone,
> All just supply, and all relation.
> Prince, subject, father, son, are things forgot,
> For every man alone thinks he hath got
> To be a phoenix and that then can be
> None of that kind of which he is but he.

It is Spencer's particular thesis that these attacks on the traditional perspectives, reinforced as they were by religious and political uncertainties, by the growing cult of melancholy, and by the popularity of realism and satire in literature—encouraged the pessimistic view of man, made the conflict between the bright ideal and the dark actuality yet more striking, and so provided the playwright Shakespeare with a model and a vision: "It was because Shakespeare, as he developed his art, was able to see individual experience in relation to the all-inclusive conflict . . . that his great tragedies have such wide reverberations and give us so profound a picture of the nature of man."

It is not Spencer's thesis, however—nor Tillyard's, that Hall provides Shakespeare with the philosophical overview for his tetralogies—that matters so much here. It is that these two set forth common Elizabethan assumptions about the world and reveal the extraordinary extent to which these enter into the fabric of Shakespeare's imagery. When Prospero speaks of taking part with his nobler reason 'gainst his fury, when Hamlet says that a beast that wants discourse of reason would have mourned longer than his mother, we now perceive that the human psyche itself is conceived as a hierarchy (reason-passion), that its hierarchy analogizes with the hierarchy of created things (angel-man-beast), and that behind all there is a sense, a dream, of order wherein man has his special, crucial, and precarious place. When Falstaff speaks of sherry illuminating the face, "which, as a beacon, gives warning to all the rest of the little kingdom, man, to arm; and the vital commoners and inland petty spirits muster me all to their captain, the heart, who, great and puffed up with this retinue, doth any deed of courage," we now apprehend the body physical conceived in terms of the body politic, and both subsumed in the single, inclusive vision these pages have described. So it is when Albany demands of Goneril,

> What have you done?
> Tigers, not daughters, what have you perform'd?
> A father, and a gracious aged man,
> Whose reverence the head-lugg'd bear would lick,
> Most barbarous, most degenerate! have you madded.
> Could my good brother suffer you to do it?
> A man, a prince, by him so benefited!
> If that the heavens do not their visible spirits
> Send quickly down to tame these vile offences,
> It will come,
> Humanity must perforce prey on itself,
> Like monsters of the deep.

The animal imagery, [as Spencer says], the interweaving of relationships, the rapid shift of thought from man as an individual to man as a prince and from man to the heavens, the reinforcement of the degeneracy in one hierarchy by the degeneracy in another, the doubt concerning divine control of man's affairs, the monstrous chaos and destruction into which man's unassisted nature will lead him—all these things which form the macrocosm of the play are woven in a typical fashion into the microcosm of a single speech.

We had seen these things before—and a thousand others—but we had seen them, not seeing. Now, thanks to Spencer and Tillyard, we see. And now, thanks to the luster with which they perform their expository function, we forget, analogy by analogy, metaphor by metaphor, that it is they who have made us see.

❧ ❧ ❧

As I wish to consider him here, Alfred Harbage, like Spencer and Tillyard, is less a critic than an illuminator of criticism.[5] He is an historian whose researches into the repertories of the public and coterie theaters of Shakespeare's time provide clear perspectives on the systems of value to which the public dramatists adhered in respect to the divine plan of the universe, the dignity of man, sexual behavior, wedded love, and the commonweal. Harbage's findings possess the same general relevance to Shakespeare that Spencer and Tillyard's have; and if, as G. B. Harrison has said in a wrily appreciative review, "these matters have long been known and understood by anyone who has intelligently studied Elizabethan drama," it is also true, as he adds, that "they have not hitherto been worked out with such detail or erudition; and, as might be expected of the author, the selection of facts is skilful and the passing comment felicitous and at times brilliant."[6]

The style is indeed easy, engaging, quietly witty, and humanely wise. "Jonson," says Harbage, "fluctuated as dramatist between the public and private theaters on the principle of repulsion from the company where his latest play had failed." "It is strange," he says, "how often the speech of Ulysses in *Troilus and Cressida* is quoted to illustrate the conservatism of the past, as if the newer ideal were chaos." "Any of Marston's plays may be defined as a five-act lapse in taste." "The sexual jesting upon articles of religious faith that is fairly endemic in sophisticated circles," he observes, "can be taken less seriously as sacrilege than as cultural vandalism." Illustration of this sort can continue indefinitely, but it catches the wit more than the wisdom and conveys the author's irony without adequately indicating his humanity. Perhaps this can emerge—and his breadth, and the sanity of his method—from a survey of two of his chapters, "The Dignity of Man" and "Sexual Behavior."

"The conception of human character in [popular] Elizabethan drama," says Harbage, "is so closely integrated with the cosmological and ethical system as to render somewhat artificial a segregate discussion." We owe such tragic heroes as Faustus and Macbeth

> to underlying assumptions about universal order and the abnormality of evil. And we owe such creations as Simon Eyre and Falstaff . . . to underlying assumptions that we all share family traits in a brotherhood of man. Characters like these did not appear, and could not have appeared, in the coterie drama. Its philosophical dissidence denied man the dignity for the truly tragic and the complexity for the truly humorous, however horrendous, comic, or theatrically effective its dramatis personae might sometimes be.

Harbage finds the coterie dramatists (Jonson, Marston, Chapman, Middleton, Beaumont and Fletcher) indulging themselves in fashionable melancholy and reviving—at times "orgiastically"— the pre-humanist tradition of "contempt for the world and those who infest it." "Always there is a compulsion to degrade," a compulsion which Harbage illustrates abundantly. "The select dramatists painted corruption with a gusto unknown outside their circle": "allusions to excrement, human odors, and physical disease are rife." And their general attitude toward man is suggested by the census of the good and the evil in the *dramatis personae* of the coterie plays. Whereas in Shakespeare and his colleagues the good outnumber the evil seven to three, according to Harbage's count, in the writers for the private theaters "the ratio is more than reversed . . . In Jonson and Middleton the servants and other background characters are as defective as the principals, and among the principals the winners are cleverer rather than better than the losers."

Among the popular dramatists, faith in man's essential virtue

> is manifested in the way it was presumed to be communicable. Exposure to it converts erring characters . . . Evil, on the other hand, is neither contagious nor hereditary . . . Rogues and villains are plentiful, but the sky line is kept steady by the background characters.

"The popular impulse was always to elevate." Even witches and wizards are presented as tending to employ their powers virtuously. Generally speaking, the popular dramatists censor their sources and cleanse them as they translate them to the stage. And whereas "coterie plays delight in cruel punishment and scenes of humiliation," the popular plays tend "to expose and lecture rogues and then pardon them, and to give villains swift, clean deaths."

I have neglected Harbage's abundant illustration, but some of the loss may be made up as we come to his treatment of Shakespeare. "Human dignity was a quality so prized by Shakespeare," says Harbage, "that he denied it to no more than a handful of his hundreds of characters. Even the most ridiculous of them are permitted to retain their own self-evaluations, and even the most vile are never made to whimper or crawl." Harbage develops this general thesis in a series of interesting ways. To begin with, he observes that " 'coward' and 'villain,' not 'liar' or 'bastard,' are the epithets most commonly used as the insult direct, intended to provoke combat." "But cowardice," he proceeds, "so often mentioned, is rarely portrayed." Thurio is a minor character and not amusing in his cowardice. The other indubitable cowards—Aguecheek, Trinculo, Parolles—are minor comic figures: "the trait . . . is never displayed in anyone presumably self-respecting." "The worst of the villains—Aaron, Richard II, Edmund, Iago—are at least brave men."

Similarly, drunkenness, which finds frequent condemnation in Shakespeare's plays, finds rare exhibition. "Christopher Sly, Sir Toby Belch, Stephano, and the Porter in *Macbeth* provide the few instances of amusing drunkenness, and all but the Porter are subjected to reproof." We never see King Claudius in his cups and though Falstaff presumably grew great from sack, he is never shown "reeling-drunk."

Shakespeare seems averse to the scenes of humiliation that gratify the coterie audiences. We see neither Shylock's frenzy over his daughter and his ducats nor the hard-hearted citizens of London throwing dust on King Richard's head. "We hear of harsh sentences upon villainous characters but we do not see them carried out. When a character is no longer able to resist, he is no longer displayed. No body of literature ever offered fewer opportunities to gloat." Sparing his characters thus much, Shakespeare spares them more—"the ignominy of the deathbed," and the exposure of suicide when it is, as with Ophelia, Goneril, Lady Macbeth, "a symptom of psychological collapse."

Harbage finds Shakespeare portraying characters after their kind, his barbarian aristocrats barbarians indeed, yet noble too, like Hotspur, his grooms and peasants rude and hard-headed, perhaps, but "as dauntless in their fashion as his noblemen. They are never servile, and are frequently jaunty and impudent." "Of workingmen we get only glimpses—the staff in Capulet's kitchen, the carriers at a wayside inn, the sailors who work the ships of Pericles and Alonso; but they are cheerful, sturdy, independent." Bottom holds his own, as does Dogberry, and "Michael Williams comes off well at the end of his tiff with the disguised king." Feeble may be but a ladies' tailor, yet his are the words, "A man can die but once; we owe God a death."

"Often the way in which characters are permitted to state their case seems purely gratuitous"—as when the Prince of

Morocco defends his color in *The Merchant of Venice* or Poins his reputation. "The comic butts are always given the last word—a bit of final face-saving bluster"—Armado, Malvolio, Sir Oliver Martext, even Parolles and Pistol.

> *Falstaff is the gamest of all. The most majestic snub in literature, "I know thee not, old man," is followed by the most magnificent recovery, "Master Shallow, I owe you a thousand pounds." It is a credit to the human species, even though the species is represented by one "so surfeit-swell'd, so old, and so profane."*

"The victims of tragedy meet the last disgrace with equal resilience." Suffering and death are real for them, but they endure them with dignity—"even the children." And "even among the villainous there is no groveling. The last we hear from a Goneril or an Iago is a defiant snarl." Macbeth goes out with "Lay on, Macduff."

Harbage begins his chapter on sexual behavior by setting forth the ideal of Shakespeare's day, which is also the ideal he finds in the popular drama.

> *The new orthodoxy was concerned with properly channeling the sexual impulse, not anathematizing it, and the answer was marriage . . . The code was quite simple. Both man and woman should be virginal at marriage, and should cohabit with each other alone until parted by death. Deviations from the pattern were assumed to be personally improvident, socially dangerous, and sinful in the eyes of God. Fornication was weak and contemptible, adultery a crime akin to murder.*

Both popular and coterie drama endorse chastity, of course, but Harbage finds the popular drama chaste, the coterie drama " 'sexy.' " Coterie drama holds clearly to a double standard of sexual morality, popular drama to a single. In Shakespeare's plays "we are informed that the young men have had no guilty relations with women. Romeo is 'stainless' as Orsino is 'stainless.' The very 'ice of chastity' is in the kiss of Orlando. Young Malcolm affirms that he is 'unknown to women.'" So it is with Florizel and Ferdinand, and Laertes accepts "Ophelia's precept that chastity is as important in him as in herself."

> There is never any heroic libertinage among Shakespeare's men . . . Those specified as lecherous—Falstaff, Shallow in his youth, Lucio, Patroclus—are either comic or contemptible . . . Those perhaps not lecherous in a comic way but so infatuated as to become lawlessly involved—Claudio, Cassio, Troilus, Antony—are all viewed as pitiable.

Shakespeare's married men are as committed to chastity as his young lovers, and a rather large number of characters in Shakespeare are concerned with maintaining the sexual code: "Friar Laurence worries about Romeo's relations to Rosaline, Bassanio feels responsible for Gratiano's good faith to Nerissa, Camillo is more willing to abet his Prince's marriage to a peasant than his seduction of her."

Coterie drama treats prostitution tolerantly, often providing the wenches with marriage at the end. Conversely, "prostitutes do not win husbands or plead their cause in plays of the public theaters: they are more apt to make their exit like Shakespeare's Doll Tearsheet, cursing the beadles who drag her to Bridewell." Shakespeare generally scores prostitution: "the courtesans who hover in the half-light in *The Comedy of Errors* and *Othello* are the only ones used with even a modicum of gentleness." Moreover Shakespeare accords to women who have shifted lovers the traits of common prostitutes—Cressida and Cleopatra, of course, but Helen too. Panders receive an "awesome indictment"—in Pandarus himself, in Marina's speeches in *Pericles*, in the common hangman's refusal in *Measure for Measure* to have a pander as an assistant. In Shakespeare, commercialized vice carries with it the certain mention of disease and the threat of destruction.

Coterie drama abounds in suggestive language and in sensual display—Harbage's illustrations are almost embarrassingly to the point here, yet the audiences at the private theaters presumably responded to verbal and visual excitation with decadent aplomb. Public drama, by contrast, "in both comedy and tragedy . . . not only failed to cultivate chances for erotic treatment but took considerable pains to avoid it." "In Shakespeare the most sensual lines are Troilus's when he is about to have his assignation with Cressida" and these are "exceptional." Mariana and Helena play the bed trick, but with "consummate modesty." Romeo and Juliet may palpitate for each other, "but their speeches, like those of all the young lovers, are neither luscious nor coy." "Cleopatra's seductiveness is a matter of record rather than of demonstration in the play." "The 'seduction' of Diana by Bertram is the most chaste in literature, and the dialogue between Lysander and Hermia, when resolving to sleep apart in the wood as a concession to the proprieties, is the most competely delicate."

But popular drama is broad in its "sallets," and Shakespeare is "the most fertile of the popular dramatists" in the practice. Harbage ends his long discussion of sexual behavior on this old question of Shakespeare's "indecencies." First, he observes that "the amount of the ribaldry is about in proportion to the prominence of the love interest in the various plays"—large in *Romeo and Juliet*, where Mercutio and the Nurse provide a lusty commentary, absent entirely in *Richard II*, *Julius Caesar*, and *Coriolanus*, "where the theme of courtship does not figure." Next, he recognizes that "the wanton jests are not distributed indiscriminately among the characters," except for clichéd horn jokes, but are usually limited either to young men, not the lovers, or to clowns and servants, or to "the women who are courted and their ladies in waiting." "No lewdness ever issues from the lips of

Valentine, Lucentio, Romeo, Bassanio, Lorenzo, Orlando, Fenton, Orsino, Sebastian, Florizel, Ferdinand, or even Troilus." And if their ladies are "more practical and humorous in their attitude toward sex than the men," their jests are mild and uttered, usually, in feminine privacy. Finally Harbage comes to the nature of the ribaldry itself. It is, he says, "the least esoteric in the world," and though the jokes "certainly indicate in Shakespeare a satisfaction with the facts of life, they suggest that he was a man of humor rather than one inveterately lickerish." The sallets come invariably as puns—indirectly, that is, rather than expressly. And they have the uniform quality of "normality and candor." The ribaldry

> consists solely of the whisking away of fig leaves, so that the sexual act or organs are unexpectedly imaged—there is no more to it than that. In spite of the puns, the humor is not sly but remarkably frank, and the imagery though concrete is not particularized. The perverted and bestial are completely barred, and the scatological almost so. The jokes do not necessarily, in fact do not usually, predicate sexual relationships that are illicit.

All of which is not to say that Shakespeare is spotless, but that, compared to the coterie dramatists, he comes off remarkably well: indecent at times, perhaps, but not immoral. Coleridge would agree.

The merit of Harbage's comparative method is obvious. By exploring the coterie drama he finds a means of throwing the popular drama into relief, and by treating Shakespeare as one of the popular dramatists, he confers on Shakespeare's practice—as it bears on the divine plan, the dignity of man, sexual behavior, etc.,—the definition and meaning derived from the group. This is clear, and clearly Harbage applies his method with a broad feeling for similarities, a fine sense of differences, and a lively delight in the matter he contemplates. Yet there are dangers in the method.

It runs the risk of reducing Shakespeare to the common pattern, of neglecting his subtleties and ambiguities in the interests of accommodating his attitudes to those of his fellows. If we recall that Romeo had apparently tempted the virtue of Rosaline with "saint seducing gold," and that he prays that Juliet refuse to be the maid of the "envious moon"—"Her vestal livery is sick and green,/And none but fools do wear it"—we may grant that he is not the libertine of coterie drama and yet doubt that he is quite so "stainless" as Harbage suggests. We may grant that Shakespeare does not seem compelled to degrade man in the manner of a Marston, yet as we think on the loathing which Hamlet, Lear, and Timon express toward the human species, we may wonder whether in Shakespeare there is not "a compulsion to degrade." It is true that Shakespeare's plays lack the prurience Harbage so abundantly illustrates from the coterie drama, yet when we remember the love-drugged Cleopatra musing on Antony, standing, sitting, walking, perhaps mounted on his horse—"O happy horse, to bear the weight of Antony!"—we may doubt that Shakespeare is quite so erotically unsuggestive as claimed. And, to take one final instance, though we may agree that cowardice of the cringing, craven variety finds little exposure in Shakespeare—and that gaily comic, as when Aguecheek and Cesario meet in mortal combat—still, cowardice of a sort makes Antony flee at Actium and then bitterly upbraid himself, and surely it may be asked whether Hamlet is so far off the track when he keeps demanding whether he is not, in some way he cannot fathom, in his inaction cowardly.

Let us grant the risks the method runs and accept gratefully what it offers. It does not tell us how to interpret this play or that. But it offers us, with the confidence of abundant demonstration, that basic "philosophy" of Shakespeare's plays which Gervinus and Shaw and Tolstoy and many another so strikingly misread. It makes available to our reading of the individual plays the systems of value and feeling to which they most closely relate, which they broadly embody or subtly challenge. And, as Harbage practices the method, it does this engagingly, wisely, in the tradition of Christian humanism in which he places Shakespeare himself.

❦ ❦ ❦

To catch the special cast of Shakespeare's individual thought, Hubler proposes to examine it "against the background of his time *and* the poetic personality which his works reveal." The result is a book modestly entitled *The Sense of Shakespeare's Sonnets* (1952). Almost as accurately it might have been *The Sense of Shakespeare's Plays*, for it helps us see that in themes, characters, plot, and the personality that created them, the lyric verse comments on the dramatic, the public upon the private. Both give the same values to the same topics—sex, love, the closed heart and the open, fortune, the knowledge of good, reputation, mortality and immortality. The dark lady illuminates the shadowed recesses of Gertrude's nature—and Cressida's, and Cleopatra's. Rosencrantz, Guildenstern, and the Northumberland who is Bolingbroke's hatchetman help bring out the self-possessed incompleteness of the young man to whom most of the sonnets are addressed. The poet of the sonnets undergoes with friend and mistress and rival an articulated series of experiences—of infatuation, suspicion, discovery, fury, enslavement, moral struggle, renunciation—that relates to the stories of Hamlet and Troilus, Gertrude and Lear. As Hubler says at one point,

> the sonnets depict a progress on the poet's part which is parallel to the spiritual progress of Lear. Lear's journey from arrogance to a knowledge of his own unworthiness shows, near the beginning, an attempt to lighten the growing burden by the assertion that although he has erred, the wrongs of others are greater: "I am a man more sinned against than sinning." In the sonnets the poet repeats that although he is forsworn, the lady is twice forsworn. Can she condemn him when her errors are more than his? This is a familiar attempt

at the maintenance of illusion, but in Shakespeare it does not work. Their rationalizations failing, both Lear and Gertrude move on to self-knowledge. The poet of the sonnets comes to think of his love as a thing without health, as a fever always longing "for that which longer nurseth the disease." He comes to loathe his passion, and his loathing swells until it includes both himself and the dark lady:

For I have sworn thee fair and thought thee bright,
Who art as black as hell, as dark as night.

The sonnets of deepest revulsion present an agony which cannot contain itself . . . It is an awareness which must change because it cannot bear to be itself. With Shakespeare it moved to a magnification of the spirit and a renunciation of the flesh.

To Shakespeare's "sense" and poetic personality we shall come shortly, but first a word on Hubler's rhetorical stance, which is neither single nor simple. At times he is merely expositor, the competent instructor guiding us through obliquities of syntax and modes of thought no longer current. At times he is Johnsonian pragmatist, regarding Shakespeare as a professional writer whose "technical practice in the sonnets is of a piece with that of his plays. It is sometimes perfect, often brilliant, too often impatient and content to let well enough alone." This strain of no-nonsense evaluation combines oddly with a pietistic formula, which crops up from time to time, "It was Shakespeare's way"—as though the manner, being the master's, were somehow free of our question. Often Hubler is Shakespeare's champion, defending his perspectives by deprecating those the moderns have substituted for them —the romanticizing of sex, for example, or the view that evil in man is merely deviant or privative—and his voice ranges from the quietly ironic to the boldly forthright until, as he contemplates Eliot's judgments that *Hamlet* fails and that Othello, in his last words is "cheering himself up,"[7] it becomes stridently sarcastic. At times, the device of enlarging one thing by diminishing another palls, and the passion expended on the moderns deflects attention, at times, from Shakespeare. But Hubler's characteristic posture is one of broad sympathy. He finds in Shakespeare what had first to be in himself, what Keats called "negative capability," what he himself calls "simultaneousness"—the power to forego the gains derivable from a particular vantage point in the interests of an inclusive view. It is this wholeness which places Hubler in this history. Nowhere is it more evident than in his treatment of Shakespeare's treatment of Doll Tearsheet:

> Doll Tearsheet, the girl on call at Mistress Quickly's tavern, is so minor a character that everything she says and everything which is said about her could be printed on a page or two. Commentators and actresses alike prefer to think of her as pure trollop, thus simplifying the act of comprehension and making the task of the actress easier than Shakespeare intended it to be. I hope that I do not seem to bestow on Doll Tearsheet any considerable dignity. She is, of course, the most common of mortals; but she is not simply a type. Shakespeare establishes her commonness in the beginning. "What pagan may that be?" asks the Prince when she is first mentioned. And the Page replies, "A proper gentlewoman, sir; and a kinswoman of my master's." The Prince is not deceived: "Even such kin as the parish heifers are to the town bull." Nothing that follows belies the guess, and the estimate of her character is confirmed on her first entrance, made after having drunk too much canary, "a marvelous searching wine" which "perfumes the blood e're one can say, 'What's this?'" Her conversation demonstrates that in all truth she is as "common as the way between St. Alban's and London." Shakespeare never pampers her. When we last see her she is being dragged off to prison for being what she is. Nor does he patronize her. He allows her a kind of wit and abundant animal spirits (the whore in modern literature is generally anemic) and although

her tact is not what it should be, she means well: "I'll be friends with thee, Jack: thou art going to the wars; and whether I shall ever see thee again or no, there is nobody cares." It is comedy, but it is not farce. There is a humanity which the actress would do well to remember. Shakespeare's feeling for Doll is written in the lines. It cannot be abstracted, and it must not be ignored. She is the embodiment of warm and tawdry humanity, and she is also a trollop. If in our love of categories we think of her as only a trollop and fail to distinguish her from her sisters, we shall reduce Shakespeare's sketch to a stereotype.

There is no word for the point of view embodied here. "Rabelaisian" will not do, for the gusto it implies suggests a commitment absent from Shakespeare. "Elizabethan" and "Shakespearean" indicate but do not define the view so free from both bravado and apology. Sometimes we read that Shakespeare's view is naïve, but nothing could be further from the truth. Shakespeare is not naïve; it is simply that he is not sophisticated. He is not afraid of the commonplace, and he can accept the simple without condescension. In one of his sonnets he lists the things which displease him most, and among them he places "simple truth miscall'd simplicity." He is not Olympian, though no writer ever had more reason to be. He is not neutral. One understands the temptation to find him so, but it will not do. No writer's view of life was ever less a priori than Shakespeare's. He came to conclusions about life, but first he saw it. And what is more remarkable is that there are so many areas of his observation which his point of view does little to color. His tenderness does not trap him into sentimentality; his wit never serves as protective coloring, sophisticating the thrust of emotion to an easy obliquity. In the sonnets to the dark lady he accepts the passion, and, later, the remorse. "Everyone," wrote Aldous Huxley long ago when his wit was without solemnity, "feels a little Christian now and then, especially after an orgy." This is precisely the sort of awareness Shakespeare did not have; it diminishes both the Christianity and the orgy. One of the greatest aspects of Shakespeare's art (no other writer has it to a like degree) is his ability to give us contrasting things without the slightest diminution of either. It was a gift which found its fullest expression in Antony and Cleopatra.

The simultaneousness which this passage both celebrates and reveals, this wholeness or totality of engagement with life, is the central fact of Shakespeare's mature art, as Hubler explores it, and of Shakespeare's mature personality. That it bears upon his ideas will become increasingly evident as we sample Hubler's discussions of Shakespeare's views on sex, the heart closed and open, and reputation.

As to sex, Shakespeare's view in sonnets and plays is unromantic. On the night of his love's consummation, Troilus can tell Cressida what one imagines few lovers in literature or life to have communicated on the threshold of bliss, that in love "the will is infinite and the execution confined . . . the desire is boundless, and the act a slave to limit." Sonnet 129, "The expense of spirit in a waste of shame/Is lust in action," speaks with the same open-eyed candor. Sex is a drive deep in man, irrational, of course, and able to turn men into the fools at whom Puck laughs, but more than that, it is an incalculable potential for both good and evil. It is part, always, of love, which in Shakespeare "does not deny the body." Juliet yearns "to lose a winning match/Play'd for a pair of stainless maidenhoods"; Perdita sees one aspect of Florizel's love as a desire to breed by her. Sex leads to procreation, which Shakespeare repeatedly images in terms of tilling and ploughing. Hubler quotes approvingly Harbage's observation that "the characters seem to desire children simply because children are a good thing to have." He adds: "Shakespeare assigns the belief in the goodness of propagation impartially to his characters. It is urged by such diverse persons as the clown in All's Well, Venus, and the heroine of *Twelfth Night* . . . Parenthood is presented not only as good but as urgent"—both for the young man of the sonnets and for the lovers in the plays. And the abrogation of parenthood is the greatest evil that Hamlet or Lear can conceive. Shakespeare's convictions here derive from beliefs in plenitude and stewardship. The glory of God is the fulness of the world, and by propagation man, like the beasts of the field, adds to the fulness. Further, man does not own what he has; it is his only for use: "Nature's bequest gives nothing, but doth lend." The young man of the sonnets, like Olivia, owes it to the world to leave the world a copy of his graces. And, of course, the continuity of graces, generation by generation, is a kind of fleshly and secular immortality, a victory over time and mutability.

The sexual drive offers these goods; it threatens as well great evils, which is why, especially in his later years, Shakespeare treats it as both attractive and repulsive. Unless governed, it rebels and usurps upon the reason as Hamlet, appalled, discovers in his mother. It enslaves man, as the writer of the sonnets knew no less than Antony. Hubler writes finely of Shakespeare's range of attitudes here:

> He sometimes regards sexual indulgence as an evil excess of something which is good in itself. He is most stern with libertinism in which habit has worn away the sense of transgression, or in which there is no indication that it ever existed —Lucio in Measure for Measure, Paris and Helen, and, in the sonnets, the dark lady. He is not very tolerant of sexual freedom erected into a principle, nor is he generally cordial to unprincipled transgressors, unless they are people of whom not much could be expected, and such characters—Doll Tearsheet, for example—are at last overtaken by their past . . . His greatest sympathy is for the intelligent man who cannot in spite of himself "Shun the heaven that leads men to this hell." The most striking instance of this is Antony.

The sonnets that proclaim Shakespeare's friendship recognize as well the faults that threaten the friendship, the central one of which Hubler calls the closed heart.

> In Shakespeare's view the open heart must give itself away in order to maintain its existence. It is confronted with a perpetual dilemma: it can know of its being only through self-loss. The alternative is to conserve itself until it has withered away. Both courses of action are illustrated in the plays; both are observed in the sonnets.

The open-hearted suffer—Hamlet, who gives himself to mother, love, friends, only to be betrayed; Othello, who gives himself to Iago; Lear, who gives himself to his daughters.

> There is not a character giving his heart wholly—and it does not matter how imprudent the giving may be—who does not in a large measure win Shakespeare's admiration. Whole-heartedness is not only for Shakespeare's lovers; it is for husband and wife, father and daughter, mother and son, brothers, sisters, friends.

And obviously, as the sonnets reveal, it was for Shakespeare himself who gave himself to friend and mistress, imprudently indeed as became evident, yet discovering his own heart in the process. The alternative would have been "the economy of the closed heart."

> The closed heart may be poor, but it is at ease. Those men are most content who, though they inspire affection in others, have no need of it themselves. They are the men "in hue, all hues in their controlling." They have the power to hurt, but they are not hurt. Their happiness is the ignorance of their incompleteness.

They are Rosencrantz and Guildenstern, prudently self-interested; Goneril, Regan, and Cornwall, fiercely self-assertive; Northumberland, aggressive to the cost of his king, cautious to the cost of his son; the coldly acidulous Antonio of *The Tempest* and his companion, the dreamy, would-be fratricide, Sebastian.

For Shakespeare, says Hubler,

> the horror of mutability, the love of earth, the regard for the good opinion of his peers—these stand together and support each other. His tragedies, though Christian in point of view, have a secular frame of reference. They find their good in the world, as the regard of Hamlet and Othello for their good name among men testifies.

The concern for reputation which Shakespeare's characters so often have—Hal as well as Hotspur, Antony in his dying and Enobarbus in his—is particularly difficult for moderns, who mentally oppose reputation to character as the appearance to the reality. For Shakespeare, says Hubler, though reputation may be false, as with Hal or Angelo, it tends to be something like consensus—the competent and valid moral assessment of the community. To be sure Hamlet speaks momentarily for moral relativism when he says that nothing is good or bad but thinking makes it so, but the axiom is at odds with the play, which is anything but relative in the values it places upon fratricide, regicide, adultery, and incest; and though Troilus argues that nothing "is aught but as 'tis valued," Hector puts him down. Shakespeare, says Hubler, is no relativist. With his age he believes that "divine law was the will of God made manifest by revelation. Natural law was the will of God made manifest in nature. Human law was law as discovered by mankind, and it was agreed that human law was valid in proportion to its approximation of natural law." The test of that approximation was "the agreement of competent men . . . It is to this reliance on agreement that Shakespeare's faith in reputation is related." The heroes concerned even in their dying with the reputations they leave upon earth acknowledge and testify to a principle of value neither superficial nor transitory. They expose no last infirmity of their noble minds but reveal instead one of the first evidences of the nobility itself.

Hubler's book is small. As it seeks to illuminate Shakespeare's sense it is suggestive rather than definitive. Its values are in this suggestiveness, which reaches out further than these pages can indicate, in the wholeness or largeness of its treatment, and in the more precise definition it gives of Shakespeare's sense. Spencer and Tillyard place that sense in the broad tradition of Elizabethan thought. Harbage places it much more precisely within the rival traditions of the Elizabethan and Jacobean theater. Hubler yet more precisely fixes it in the body of Shakespeare's own work—his plays and his sonnets.

Harley Granville-Barker / 1877–1946
Alfred B. Harbage / 1901–
Bernard Spivack / 1911–

Granville-Barker's stances, his Pirandelloism. Shakespeare as "genius of the workshop." Granville-Barker as returning Shakespeare to the platform stage. Preface to Antony and Cleopatra: *the central focus—character in action in the theater; running commentary; "The Verse and Its Speaking." Final estimate.* ❦ *Harbage's freshness. His thesis: Shakespeare's exciting then reassuring his audience through moral notions. Moral paradoxes, enigmas, unreliable spokesmen to excite. Gratification of our sense of justice to reassure—in the fables, in the histories. Reservations. Accomplishments.* ❦ *Spivack's thesis: Iago both Iago and evolving Vice. Spivack's scholastic style. "Iago": the contradictions in his motives, emotions, goals. "Iago Revisited": Shakespeare's dramaturgy in the service of moral sentiment; the natural Iago and Iago-as-Vice. Synthesis of Stoll and Bradley.*

A surprising amount of what I have said about Hazlitt applies with equal if not superior force to Granville-Barker. A man of the theater, he too sees gesture and tone, grouping and effect, as dimensions of a play's meaning; and the script is, to him, until acted, but the libretto to the symphony, not the music itself.

Hazlitt, though, writes more as a reviewer; Granville-Barker is variously actor or director, producer or playwright. In his ten prefaces (to *Hamlet, Lear, The Merchant of Venice, Antony and Cleopatra, Cymbeline, Othello, Coriolanus, Romeo and Juliet, Julius Caesar,* and *Love's Labour's Lost*)[1] we see him in shirt-sleeves, as it were, vigorously and passionately communing with his company. He is sketching out in the present tense, as if it were happening here, before and with them, the main lines of the story. The story may have a unifying idea, some principle fixed and out of time, but for him in the theater, it is essentially a series of events, each with its own shape and feeling, a part of a continuum of action which must be seized, sensed, articulated. On this he lavishes himself. His mind races, now asserting, now questioning, mobile, flexible, and above all, alive. The interpretation, given his compelling manner, is just so, yet tentative too, an hypothesis to be tested for its rhythm on the company's pulse as on the speaker's. He pauses to take up some general point—as to the nature of the verse key within which individual speakers must find their proper melodies, or the location on the stage of some particular business—and then he comes to the actors, taking them over their roles, starting sometimes with the minor parts, sometimes with the star. The parts, as he sees them, though they may be formulated in a phrase, are essentially dynamic. In Hazlitt's terms, the characters are in a state "of continual composition and decomposition." So it is that his analysis of character as of plot is by running commentary.

Hazlitt has the happy image of Shakespeare's characters' being "present in the poet's imagination, as at a kind of rehearsal." Granville-Barker has the same kind of Pirandelloist view. He attributes to the characters—at times, at least—a prior, independent existence. Shylock, he says, "steps into the play, actual and individual from his first word on." "Shakespeare can only allow [Bassanio and Portia] a few lines of talk together, and that in company." Gratiano "missed by only a little the touch of magic

that would have made something more of him." For Granville-
Barker, though, it isn't characters in search of an author so much
as it is characters (*and* author) in search of a play:

> It is always instructive to watch Shakespeare getting his play
> with its crew under way, to see him stating his subjects,
> setting his characters in opposition. Some lead off, fully
> themselves from the start, some seem to hang on his hands,
> saying what they have to say in sound conventional phrase,
> some he may leave all but mute, uncertain yet, it would seem,
> of his own use for them. Not till the whole organism has
> gathered strength and abounds in a life of its own is the true
> mastery to be seen.

This Pirandelloism expresses a live, practical feeling for
Shakespeare as a "genius of the workshop." The workshop idea had
been used by Moulton in his *Shakespeare as Dramatic Artist*
(1885) and by Quiller-Couch in his *Shakespeare's Workmanship*
(1918). The approach is to see Shakespeare as a craftsman attempting, with the tools and materials at hand, to solve particular
problems—the problem of keeping the audience mindful of Cleopatra during the stretch when she has no active part in the plot,
the problem of keeping *King Lear* going after "the exhaustion of
[the king's] impetus to action with the play's end barely in sight,"
the problem of keeping the casket-theme drawn out through three
acts of *The Merchant of Venice* or of keeping Bassanio sympathetic or of creating "a sense of time passing in Venice while the
bond matures." The approach is obviously fruitful, though it can
be irritating when the critic presents as a problem what one does
not feel to be one. And of course, it can be used melodramatically
—"here's the problem, great enough, and how Shakespeare will
solve it perhaps not even he can tell. There is this Charybdis to
avoid, that Scylla to beware. And not for a moment must the
audience be allowed to sense . . ." If Granville-Barker uses the

approach in this way—and he does—the reason is that it engages that imaginary company of his, and us, too, in his explorations of character and action. There are, however, workshops and workshops. The striking things about the one Granville-Barker conceives are its placement and its empiricism. Its placement is the theater, with all the hot bustle and noise of live actors and old conventions and audiences who have paid their penny and demand satisfaction. And its empiricism is that of the green room and rehearsal. No theorist, Shakespeare. He writes his plays as Frost his poems, finding their meanings, solving their problems, even as he writes:

> We should never, probably, think of Shakespeare as sitting down to construct a play as an architect must design a house, in the three dimensions of its building. . . . He was liker to a musician, master of an instrument, who takes a theme and, by generally recognized rules, improvises on it; or even to an orator, so accomplished that he can carry a complex subject through a two-hour speech, split it up, run it by divers channels, digress, but never for too long, and at last bring the streams abreast again to blend them in his peroration. Clarity of statement, a sense of proportion, of the value of contrast, justness of emphasis—in these lie the technique involved; and these, it will be found, are the dominant qualities of Shakespeare's stagecraft.

Every critic, painting Shakespeare, paints himself. Granville-Barker's style, imitating the speaking voice and the vital mind behind it, feeling its way confidently, according to familiar principles, to unforeseen conclusions, and Granville-Barker's view of plot as dynamic sequence and of character as process, and Granville-Barker's Pirandelloist sense of Shakespeare in the workshop, holding this character back, letting this one step forth, Shakespeare ad-libbing his way to a masterpiece—all this paints the critic. It may paint Shakespeare too. The portrait is kin to that of Heminge and Condell, Jonson, Coleridge, and Armstrong, and the portrait gains in credence from the manifest technical competence of the painter—one to the manner born. The first two critics paint their picture of the flowing Shakespeare by way of praise; Jonson by way of blame. Armstrong uses it to understand the creative imagination but not the individual plays. Coleridge uses it simultaneously to find the idea behind or at the heart of the play and to discover its working out in character and incident, scene by scene, in such running commentaries as we have examined. Coleridge, though, addresses a lecture audience, people who read the play, not see it. Granville-Barker does what Coleridge does, but for an acting audience, first, and with a feeling for theater that Coleridge does not have. And if we may distinguish between the idea and the process, the Platonic realm of absolutes and the realm of passing time, Coleridge's Shakespeare and his personal affinities are for the first, Granville-Barker's for the second.

Before we illustrate this theatrical immediacy of Granville-Barker's, a word about another aspect of his criticism. Especially in his introduction to the collected Prefaces, he speaks in the accents of the reformer. "The Procrustean methods of a changed theater deformed the plays," he asserts, "and put the art of them to confusion; and scholars, with this much excuse, have been apt to divorce their Shakespeare from the theater altogether." Now, however, we know much about Shakespeare's theater, its great platform, its conventions of place, its verse as its chief means of emotional expression, its boy-actors and soliloquy and anachronistic costuming; and Granville-Barker writes his prefaces with this Shakespearean theater in mind. From the deformities of the realistic picture-frame stage as well as from the aridities of the scholar's closet he will recover Shakespeare and seek "to discover, if possible, the production he would have desired."

The Preface to *Antony and Cleopatra* will illustrate these points. In the collected edition it is 92 pages long, shorter than the prefaces to *Hamlet, Coriolanus,* and *Othello,* longer than the others. Its divisions are as follows:

4 pp. [Untitled introduction]
8 The Play's Construction: The Main Problem and Some Minor Ones
2 The Question of Act-Division
9½ A Digression, Mainly upon the Meaning of the Word "Scene"
9½ The Play's Construction, *Continued:* The Three Days' Battle
4 [The Play's Construction, *Concluded:*] Cleopatra Against Caesar
4 The Staging
2½ Costume
1 The Music
12½ The Verse and Its Speaking
35 The Characters

The "Digression" focuses on the fluidity of the Shakespearean stage which modern editorial separation into scenes (13 in Act III, 15 in IV) obscures. This section reflects the reformational aspects of Granville-Barker's criticism. The terms "construction" and "problem" reflect the idea of the workshop, Shakespeare as craftsman. And collectively the headings reflect a basic view of drama as characters in action in the theater—characters receiving 35 pages, action or plot 21½ pages, and matters of intermission (act-division), staging, costume, sound effects, and speaking 22½ pages. One other statistic is indicative. In the course of his preface the critic quotes roughly 725 lines of the play, one-fourth of the total. His manner of explicating his play, of making it live for us, is, clearly, to live it himself.

Antony and Cleopatra, says Granville-Barker in his introduction, "is the most spacious of the plays . . . a play of action . . .

not of spiritual insight . . . a large field of action too . . . the
whole range of the Empire."

> A tragedy of disillusion . . . As to the lovers, from the
> beginning they have little to learn about each other . . . And
> that industrious apprentice Octavius, as he nears his reward,
> grows under our eyes ever colder of heart, more meanly
> calculating, more deliberately false . . . Towards the play's
> end comes a very procession of generals, soldiers and dutiful
> servants, their fidelity abused, their valor wasted.

And the Roman people, once so important as "friends," "country-
men," are now to both Caesar and Antony "slippery," worthless.
This is Shakespeare's unhopeful picture of the Empire. In it, "the
love-tragedy . . . is not made the main question till no other
question is left, till the ruin wreaked by Triumvir and Queen is
accomplished. And the action of the play is schemed throughout
for the picturing of this wider ruin."

How?—this is the "main problem" of the first heading. The
answer is, by reducing

> the actual story to simplicity itself. Antony breaks from
> Cleopatra to patch up an insincere peace with Caesar, since
> Pompey threatens them both; he marries Octavia, and deserts
> her to return to Cleopatra; war breaks out, Caesar defeats
> them and they kill themselves. This is the plot; every charac-
> ter is concerned with it, hardly a line is spoken that does not
> relate to it; and much strength lies in this concentration of
> interest.

"For a broad picturesque contrast," however, "Roman and Egyptian are set against each other; and this opposition braces the
whole body of the play." That it braces the play through III.iv the
critic proceeds to demonstrate, concluding that Shakespeare "has
told his story, woven his pattern, kept conflict alive and balance

true, character prompting action, and action elucidating character, neither made to halt for the other. This really is the be-all and end-all of his stagecraft."

For his company—and, through them, for us—Granville-Barker elucidates these matters of theme and movement. He gives us the pattern into which the separate parts must fit. But he has more to reveal. The appearance of Ventidius, he reminds us, follows the debauch on Pompey's yacht. The alert reader catches "the contrasting of the soldiers at their duty with the rulers at their drinking bout," but the Shakespearean stage—and this is the point—the Shakespearean stage gave the spectator

> the quick shift from singing and dancing and the confusion of tipsy embracings to the strict military march that brings Ventidius as in triumph upon the stage. There was no pause at all . . . there was no distracting of mind or eye, a unity of effect was kept, and the action flowed on unchecked.

Similarly, as Cleopatra leaves the Shakespearean stage at the end of III.iii saying "All may be well enough," "*Enter Antony and Octavia.*" In this section Granville-Barker also defines the problem of keeping "Cleopatra pretty constantly in our minds" though "all the story asks is that she should be left by Antony and then sit waiting." Shakespeare's solution he finds in the expansion of the play's opening impulse, "abundant in life and color, . . . till he has his story's master-motive made fertile in our minds." Then Shakespeare gives us Cleopatra feeding herself with most delicious poison, thinking of Antony en route to Rome, so that though we travel with him, it is through her eyes. Then he has Cleopatra receiving the news of her lover's treachery—"first the savage and suffering Cleopatra; next, on the rebound, the colder, baser-natured woman, feeding on flattery and deceit—and well aware of their worth."

I do not propose to pant after Granville-Barker as he runs through the story, but it should be noted that he does far more than simply tick off successive scenes or fit them into the Rome-Egypt matrix or adjust them to the platform stage or define the playwright's problems. He conveys a sense of the kind of action the play gives us. "The first day's fighting," he observes, "is compressed into . . . symbolism"—"a sort of variation upon the old dumb show," marches and countermarches.

> The stage empties again, and its emptiness holds us expectant. Then, of a sudden, comes the climax, the significant event; the noise of a sea-fight is heard. Then, actual drama reasserting itself, Enobarbus, with alarums to reinforce his fury, bursts upon us, tongue-tied no more, to interpret disaster.

The critic conveys the emotional life of the scenes as well as their kind of action. He has a fine passage on Antony in his rage, "glutted and appeased by the sight of the wretch [Thidias] half-slaughtered at his feet." He writes sensitively of the scene-painting of the sentries as they hear the music of hautboys and sense that Hercules is leaving Antony. And to make an end on it, he has a superb realization of the duel between Caesar and Cleopatra when she is captured. It ends thus:

> She is beaten. Even Seleucus can withstand her scoldings now; it is Caesar, contemptuously considerate, who orders the man off. She is helpless in his clutches, but for the one sure escape. And he thinks, does he, to lure her from that with his lies? She fawns on him as he leaves her; let him think he has!

> He words me, girls, he words me, that I should not
> Be noble to myself!

Matters about intermission, staging, costume, sound effects are for the producer and we may pass them by, as well as any further comment on the flexible ubiquity of the Shakespearean

stage. But the discussion of "The Verse and Its Speaking" demands a special attention. Six of the prefaces have such sections.
They testify to the conviction that Shakespeare's verse was his
chief means to emotional expression and that, "when it comes to
staging the plays, the speaking of the verse must be the foundation
of all study." By verse the critic means style. The term includes
imagery and attitude quite as much as meter and the varying
concerns of prosody. In a general way Granville-Barker considers it
as something like a musical key, or perhaps range of voice is a
better figure. He cites three passages—Antony's "Sir,/He fell upon
me ere admitted: then/Three kings I had newly feasted"; Caesar's
"Let's grant it is not/Amiss to tumble on the bed of Ptolemy"; and
Pompey's "To you all three,/The senators alone of this great
world,/Chief factors for the gods"—all extensively, and observes
that these "may be taken as the norm of the play's poetic method,
upon which its potencies are built up. And it is upon this norm,"
he continues, "that the actors must model their own style."
Variations on or within this norm he invites his company to
respond to—"Caesar's calculated indignation" in one passage,
Cleopatra's "shrill arrogance," in another, "the violence of
Antony's anger when he finds Thidias kissing Cleopatra's hand."
His method is to cite the passage, then to describe (or act out) its
emotion in technical or semi-technical terms. For example:

> Approach there! Ah, you kite! Now, gods and devils!
> Authority melts from me. Of late, when I cried "Ho!",
> Like boys unto a muss, kings would start forth
> And cry "Your will?" Have you no ears?
> I am Antony yet. Take hence this jack and whip him.

*Long lines, giving a sense of great strength. Exclamatory
phrases, prefacing and setting off the powerful center-phrase,
with its ringing "kings" for a top note. The caesura-pause of
two beats that the short line allows is followed by the repeated
crack of two more short phrases, the first with its upward life,
the second with its nasal snarl and the sharp click of its*

ending; *the last line lengthens out, and the business finishes
with the bitten staccato of*

Take hence this jack and whip him.

Note the deadly flick of the last two words!

At first this may seem the old fallacy of reading the sense into the
sound. Read it over, though; read the passage as the commentary
requires, and we see that Granville-Barker has provided for the
verse what amounts to the dynamic markings by which a composer
instructs the instrumentalist how to play the music. We may
disagree, of course, but the point is to see that here, as everywhere,
he treats the play as character in action *in the theater*.

The final long section on the characters (Antony 12½ pages,
Cleopatra 13, Octavia 1½, Octavius 2, Enobarbus 2, Pompey,
Lepidus and the rest 4½) engages us in the same minute savoring
of attitude, gesture, and speech. When Cleopatra says,

> See where he is, who's with him, what he does:
> I did not send you: if you find him sad,
> Say I am dancing: if in mirth, report
> That I am sudden sick: quick, and return,

Granville-Barker comments: "Here is actuality; and forged in
words of one syllable, mainly. This is the woman herself, quick,
jealous, imperious, mischievous, malicious, flagrant, subtle; but a
delicate creature, too, and the light, glib verse seems to set her on
tiptoe." He describes her next with Antony—pouting, plaintive,
ironic, petty, and then—

> *For a moment in the middle of it we see another Cleopatra,
> and hear a note struck from nearer the heart of her. She
> is shocked by his callously calculated gloss upon Fulvia's
> death. Vagaries of passion she can understand, and tricks
> and lies to favor them. But this hard-set indifference! She*

takes it to herself, of course, and is not too shocked to make capital of it for her quarrel. But here, amid the lively wrangling, which is stimulus to their passion, shows a dead spot of incomprehension, the true division between them. They stare for an instant; then cover it, as lovers will.

The commentary runs on. "Tiresome" it may be, the critic proposes, but "though the reader be teased a little, it cannot hurt him to realize that this close analysis of every turn in the showing of a character and composing of a scene—and much besides— must go to giving a play the simple due of its acting."

Granville-Barker is undoubtedly too rich for some critical stomachs. The nervous copiousness, the mannered slipping in and out of roles, the having a word for absolutely everything—all this can seem intrusive. The interpretations of individual characters and incidents must often enough rub us the wrong way. (It may be doubted, for example, that Cleopatra's response to Antony's lashing in III.xiii is "easy lies.") The treatment of verse gets fairly rarified when the critic speaks of consonants as "tense" or "pinched" or when he says that "there is dread and hate in the very vowels" of a speech. More profoundly, we may find Granville-Barker so caught up in the particular that we sense in him some inadequacy of the general, the philosophical. He has made us pulse to the characters and conflict of Antony and Cleopatra, perhaps, but there are larger meanings still to be articulated.

With all such reservations I find myself in sympathy. They are legitimate complaints which lose none of their force though we add to the critic's achievements dozens of excellent passages I have not mentioned—on *The Merchant of Venice* as a fairy tale, for example, its "unlikelihood of plot" being "redeemed by veracity of character," or on the device of reiteration working through *King Lear* from the echoed "nothings" of the first scene to the despairing "nevers" of the last. The catalogue could grow but it would not alter the reservations. These, on the other hand, do not deny the central fact that Granville-Barker, as no one else in the history of Shakespearean criticism, helps us to a sense of the stage actuality of a Shakespearean play. One cannot follow him and remain quite so contentedly in the Bradleyan closet or on the Freudian couch or in the anthropologists' realm of ritual and myth or in the new critical world of metaphorical analysis. Granville-Barker takes us back to the place where Shakespeare began, to "the play's acting in a theater."

❧ ❧ ❧

As They Liked It (1947) is Harbage's favorite among his several books on Shakespeare. One can see why. Gracefully exciting and brief, it pays delighted tribute to Shakespeare's moral artistry. Respectfully, it turns Bridges' complaints back upon themselves. Handsomely, it faces up to Johnson's regretful discovery that the plays, though moral, do not moralize. Generously, it opens to us some of the hidden causes of Shakespeare's power to engage our passions and restore our souls. I speak elsewhere of Harbage's style, but this book has a special springtide freshness which comes in part perhaps from this, that Harbage is not so much proving points here—about Shakespeare's audience or the rival repertories—as communicating a discovery. He is letting us see what he has come to see, and the mood is less "because" and "therefore" than "lo!" and "behold!"

The assumption upon which Harbage's discovery rests is of a solidarity between Shakespeare and his audience; and the discovery is that Shakespeare pleasurably excites and then pleasurably reassures his audience by means of moral notions. The exposition proceeds thus: poetic loveliness in Shakespeare "is always infused with ethical sentiment." Even the flowers that Perdita celebrates have their qualities of pride and humility. "Each lyrical passage has its ethical infusion or its ethical setting."

> In Shakespeare a little candle shining in the night suggests "a
> good deed in a naughty world" . . . And a Roman cobbler,
> of all people, puns upon salvation, "A trade, sir, that I hope I

may use with a safe conscience, which is indeed, sir, a mender of bad soles."

And these are but moral gleams. "In most of Shakespeare's lines the moral infusion is evidenced . . . by a constant and powerful glow," for actions which have consequence are moral actions, and these are the substance of drama. Further, Shakespeare intensifies and renders yet more complex the moral potential of his sources, witness Shylock, King John, Prince Hal as against their originals.

By the moral qualities of his characters Shakespeare stimulates and engages us. We argue about Hamlet and Falstaff, Angelo and Brutus because the characters are "*foci* of moral interest," and "our concept of character in the drama is largely a matter of moral partisanship." The various critics deny the reality of character but these characters "are *real* enough, in the moral world, more real than actual people." And morality is of the essence. "Although Stoll and Kittredge differ over whether Falstaff is cowardly or courageous, neither of them doubts for a moment that in Shakespeare courage is a good thing and cowardice a bad, and that the bad things always are distinguishable from the good."

The moral notions in the plays engage us in moral response—but to what end? Harbage sets forth his answer in a chapter entitled "Highroad Leading Nowhere." "On every point that is in the least degree debatable," he asserts, Shakespeare's "plays argue both sides." As a consequence, critics from Johnson to Bridges have lamented his immorality, irresponsibility, irony, levity. Not Harbage. Moralizing for him is a road that leads somewhere, but—

Shakespeare's drama is a highroad leading nowhere. It is designed as an amusement, a recreation, and therefore has no destination. It is a quality of journeys taken for amusement, by excursion boat, Ferris wheel, roller coaster, or carrousel, that they return us after their excitements to the point of departure. Shakespeare's highroad is circular. The point of departure in a particular play is the moral nature of spectator or reader. Each of us begins the circuit at a slightly different point, but when the stimulating journey is over, each finds himself at his place of departure. The play is as moral as the person who traverses its course, and exercises the good in that person to the limit of his capacities, but it intensifies his moral convictions rather than alters or extends them. The distinction between Shakespeare's plays and most modern fiction is that the plays are artistry whereas modern fiction is morality. The serious work of our time entices us on a journey that leads somewhere.

Stimulus, response, and a circular journey, moral in nature but not in end—this is Harbage's start. He proceeds in chapters on "Involvement," "Paradoxes," "Enigmas," and "The Unreliable Spokesman" to show how it all works. Shakespeare puts good and evil "side by side in a single play, a single situation, a single person"—not because he is imitating life, for he departs from life in scores of ways, but to engage us.

Pictures of Christian struggling with Apollyon are interesting only for their composition. They have no moral interest. Christian is good, Apollyon bad, and that is the end of it. But Claudius, Gertrude, and Hamlet require constant evaluation on our part. We have to keep weighing them on our scales. Always in Shakespeare we perceive that the good might be better and the bad might be worse, and we are excited by our perceptions. The virtuous seem to need our counsel, and the vicious seem capable of understanding our censure. We are linked to the former by sensations of solicitude, and to the latter by moments of sympathy and understanding. We are constantly involved.

The moral paradox is an extreme case of this jostling together of the morally incongruous. As Falstaff attacks honor or water-drinking, as the bravo in *Richard III* attacks conscience for making man a coward, as the clown in *All's Well* defends cuckoldry and Parolles attacks virginity—the paradox "reduc[es] for the moment our values to mere coruscations." So, too, do characters who embody paradoxes—Juliet's morally imbecile Nurse or Dame Quickly or, best of all, Jack Falstaff himself. Moral dilemmas, to which Shakespeare responds with enigmatic silence, similarly tease us. Isabella's choice between her chastity and her brother's life provides an extreme instance. "Sometimes the moral dilemma and its enigmatical treatment is absorbed, so to speak, in the character. The character himself then becomes an enigma"—Brutus, Hector, King Lewis, Faulconbridge, Angelo, Hamlet. Operating to the same effect of engaging us and involving our moral sympathies and antipathies, Shakespeare develops the commentator whose comments are false or askew—Apemantus and Thersites, Jaques, the Bastard—satirical chaps whose words must be sifted; or Shakespeare puts wisdom into the mouths of fools and knaves, as when Polonius and Claudius utter general truths; or he presents suffering humanity listening to wisdom and paying no attention thereto: "the poet who is inimitable at framing moral maxims never portrays them as doing the slightest good." And Harbage comes to this conclusion, that the various terms sometimes used to characterize Shakespeare—*indifferent, impartial, ironic*—miss the point, implying as they do some attitude on the poet's part incompatible with the effects he produces. "The word *accommodating* would be preferable to any of them were it not for the ignobility of its suggestions. The best word of all, obvious but inevitable, is simply *artistic*. These plays are deft. We are the instruments, and Shakespeare knows our stops."

One part of Shakespeare's art reveals itself in the pleasurable excitation of his audience by moral means; another part in the pleasurable reassurance—again, by moral means, by appealing to or gratifying our sense of justice. How? By "remov[ing] the onus from agents and plac[ing] it on the thing itself: he does not punish evil persons and reward virtuous ones [which is the way of 'poetic' justice], but condemns evil and praises virtue by portraying their contrasted effects." More fully to explore Shakespeare's justice, Harbage divides the plays into two groups: fable and histories. "The distinguishing mark of the fables is that," whatever actual happenings they may reflect, "those events have no final authority in determining the dramatist's version of them." Titus, Timon, and Macduff are figures with some pretensions to historical authenticity but Shakespeare's treatment of them is fabulous. The distinguishing mark of the histories is that past happenings, real or reputed, do have final authority. "Shakespeare could alter the [story of Lear] to let Lear die, but he could not alter the [story of Troilus and Cressida] to let Hector live." In the fables "the relationship among the characters is mainly personal and domestic, not political; and vice and virtue operate on individuals directly, not [as in the histories] through the intermediary of national programs or party platforms."

In Shakespeare's plays based on comic fables, Harbage finds that the weak or vicious get off with brief humiliations, and are, in fact, egregiously rewarded—Proteus with Julia, Claudio with Hero, Bertram with Helena, Angelo with Mariana. The justice that Shakespeare here invokes has these elements, according to Harbage. First, the criminals have been ineffectual, and "in Shakespeare's plays as in our courts, offenders are punished in the degree that their offenses have taken effect." This is, to be sure, a pragmatic scheme of justice, as the plays themselves acknowledge, but they remind us, too, that such a scheme operates in this our world, else who should 'scape whipping? Second, the sinners are required to exhibit "a token portion of the full schedule of open confession, repentance of sins, and amendment of life." That their exhibitions are incredibly brief, Harbage grants, but argues that the brevity of repentance, like the ease of impenetrable disguise, is a convention: "In *The Two Gentlemen of Verona*, 'Sebastian' takes off a cap and becomes Julia again; her lover puts on penitence and becomes Proteus again." Third, "the happy endings . . . are the result of the triumph of virtue over vice"; and fourth, "the happiness that follows the elimination of evil, the triumph of good, consists in the Shakespearian world of reunion of kindred, the end of strife, and, above all, the mating of lovers." "We must not miss," says Harbage, "the *moral satisfaction* conveyed by these matings . . . *The story has come out right.*"

"Shakespearean tragedy," says Harbage, "does not deal with the punishment of sinners or provide spectacles of personal retribution." "The villains are not important enough to be permitted much share in our final emotions." What, then, of the villain heroes like Macbeth? "The distinction of Macbeth derives not from the vice in him that meets retribution but from the virtue in him that suffers." And the other tragic heroes "are not evil ones, but ones in whom evil has found its mark." "The defects of these tragic personages leave in us no residue of satisfaction with their fates. It was Shakespeare's way to dwell upon the suffering of the victims and to end his stories with their deaths—the most affecting thing he could do." Evil in the tragedies has different faces— "human unkindness" in *Lear*, "senseless strife" in *Romeo and Juliet*, "earthly venality" in *Hamlet*, "egotism" in *Macbeth*, "envious malice" in *Othello*, "greed and ingratitude" in *Timon*. "But these are only words. The enemy is always unkindness behind the familiar visage of one of the seven deadly sins." "These plays all treat of *sad particular instances* in which evil bore its bitter fruit. What can be identified can be avoided. Plays which make us look at the thing, hate it, and pity its victims do not offend our sense of justice."

In his history plays, Shakespeare is manifestly partisan when he deals with England, otherwise "there is an unsparing treatment of the mixed good and evil on both sides of partisan divisions." The endings of his histories lack the universal joy or sorrow of the fabulous endings. "The fable represents elliptically the whole of existence in either of its two aspects; the history . . . represents— obviously—a segment of existence." The Greek and Roman plays are "not tragedies but segments of a larger tragedy—the fall of an ancient civilization. His English histories, in contrast, may be considered segments of a comedy, and some such conception underlies the common impression that no individual king but England itself is always their hero." By way of summing up these points, Harbage says:

> It is thus, then, that Shakespeare reckons with the craving for justice in moral mankind. In some of his plays evil misses its mark and is disarmed: the result is happiness. In others evil finds its mark: the result is sorrow. In still others the issue is undetermined: such plays present single acts in the larger drama of history which is always unfolding and in which mingled good and evil bring in their train mingled joy and sorrow. There is justice in all these plays in the largest sense, a satisfying concatenation: unhappiness is never the product of good, and happiness never the product of evil.

There is more to Harbage's book. A chapter on "The Safe Majority" observes that "in the plays as a whole, the morally sound people compose a comforting majority." A fine chapter on "The Sense of Solidarity" explores yet more fully the sense of kindness and unkindness, of belonging to or of being alien to the human race: "What gives the term 'gentle Shakespeare' its lasting authority and draws concessions of 'endearing qualities' even from Bernard Shaw is the spirit of compassion shown by the characters and for the characters to a degree unequaled elsewhere." And a final chapter on "The Attainable Goal," has among its happy sentences, these:

> The endings are always the same: the feast and dancing, the reunion of kinsmen or restoration of concord among them, the marriage of lovers—Shakespeare's definition of happiness. The goal is the enjoyment of life in the simplest and most available ways. In the Shakespearean world . . . there are no stopping places or substitutes. Nothing but living itself will do. The goal, unlike fame or wealth or power or position, is the

one thing the spectators as a whole have some hope in achieving.

Harbage's distinction between the fables and the histories is manifestly arbitrary, for the tragedies have a clear political, as the so-called histories a clear personal, dimension. The state of Denmark suffers the same rottenness that afflicts its prince, and the division Antony experiences within himself mirrors that which afflicts his entire world. The critic is trying, of course, to exculpate Shakespeare from the sin of leaving our craving for justice unsatisfied. He had to, argues Harbage, because he was not free of his material. But perhaps he was quite as free as he needed to be. Perhaps *Richard II* or *Troilus and Cressida* ends as it does because the story has come to an end—the story of a kingship, the story of a love affair—and the story, not the slaking of an audience's thirst for justice, was the poet's aim.

More importantly, we may question whether in his treatment of evil Harbage has not separated crime from criminal in a way contrary to the common experience. Shakespeare externalizes evil, Harbage proposes, so that we hate it but not its agents. Evil is something out there that finds its mark in the sinner, the rankling dart around which the flesh reddens and putrifies. But if evil is part of the flesh itself, an imbalance of physical claims and thrusts, a tumor—then we need a different theodicy. Let each reader satisfy himself, but for some, part of Macbeth's distinction *is* the monstrosity of his greed. For some, Hamlet's suffering is less the result of evil coming into him than of evil coming *out*, his nature engaged in mortal combat with itself. And so, for the tragic outcome, some may feel genuine satisfaction—moral, not malicious—in the fates that overtake Hamlet and Othello and Lear. What happens to them affirms the large, general laws of psychomoral causation, and their deaths release them from sufferings which, their stories being done, they need no longer endure.

In short, the pleasurable reassurance that Harbage credits Shakespeare with providing his audience may seem in some instances doubtful, in others, rather bland, even sentimental. This is not to say, of course, that the reassurance is not there; it is to question the definition. A more serious objection to Harbage's study would attack its fundamental proposition, that the varying kinds of moral contradiction within the plays are devices whereby Shakespeare plays upon his audience. The objection is not to the effect these things have upon the spectator (our own moral-emotional engagement in character and speech will testify, I believe, to Harbage's soundness in this respect), but to the notion that the moral ambiguities are means to the end of engagement. With equal logic they might be regarded as means to the end of truth. Was Shakespeare being artistic or honest? The question is embarrassing in its simplicity, for presumably art and truth can become dimensions of one another, and presumably, too, the conscious dedication of the artist (to art or nature) matters less than the way the whole current of his life molds the matter before him. But the question points to the distortion inescapable in Harbage's choice to present his case one way, the artistic way, rather than both.

Against these objections—and putting aside entirely the sheer pleasure that comes from watching a felicitous performance—we may pit certain accomplishments. One is to have taken Bridges' indictment of Shakespeare and to have turned it the other way about, so that the ambiguities and contradictions may be seen as laudable accomplishments, not irresponsible shenanigans. Harbage accomplishes this by the appeal to art we have just questioned; Bridges, of course, appeals to nature. Another accomplishment is the brilliant definition of the area of investigation. In catalogues of paradoxes, enigmas, and unreliable spokesmen, which this review has scarcely begun to indicate, in interspersed analyses of such figures as Falstaff and Hamlet, Harbage makes us see how much of the morally contradictory there is in Shakespeare and how it arouses and holds our interest. Further, his open-mindedness as he contemplates Shakespeare's contradictory beings invites his readers to a comparable humanity. He offers release from the felt necessity of passing simplified moral judgments and of taking sides. A final accomplishment is the direction he offers toward discovering the reassuring vision the plays provide. I say "direction," for it is not until his *Shakespeare and the Rival Traditions* that Harbage finds an adequate statement of the vision, but the discussion here of justice in the comedies is exceedingly happy. The stress on an ethics of effect, on a convention of brevity in repentance, and on a morally satisfactory outcome in which strife ends, kindred reunite, and lovers mate is all to the good. It jibes with what Frye and Barber discover.

❧ ❧ ❧

Unless Northrop Frye or Arthur Sewell claims the honor, Bernard Spivack is the most sophisticated of the modern Stollians. His *Shakespeare and the Allegory of Evil* (1958) focuses on four confusing characters—Aaron, Richard III, Don John, and pre-eminently Iago—whom he regards as essentially the same figure, and his thesis is that "this figure . . . is confusing because he is the hybrid product of two conventions that met and merged in him." The one convention, to which succeeding centuries of dramatic practice have habituated us and by which, according to Stoll, our criticism of the older drama has been vitiated, is that of naturalistic imitation: the character as live. The other, older, still evolving convention in Shakespeare's day, far removed from naturalism, is that of the Vice, whose stock function over two centuries "was to confound his human victims by playing upon their gullible honesty and human frailty, and particularly to confound them in respect to those values that governed any play in which he appeared."

Since the thesis can be stated so briefly—that Iago is both Iago *and* evolving Vice, human *and* changing convention—it may be asked why Spivack takes almost 500 pages to establish his thesis. The answer is in part the thoroughness with which he explores Iago's ancestry. He goes back to the Psychomachia of medieval allegory, the war of good and evil for the possession of man's soul, then comes forward through the flourishing of the many separate vices upon the morality stage until the Vice himself emerges, changes, and declines. Next he explores the hybrid play that comes into being as this figure of homily and allegory enters the new environment of history or legend, where individual men and women inhabit in place of the older type figures. And thus he brings us to Shakespeare's contemporaries and their hybrid plays, to Shakespeare himself and his *Titus, Richard III,* and *Much Ado,* and finally, to the point from which he started, to *Othello* and Iago. The thoroughness of the history is part of the answer, but there is as well a matter of style.

The style is extraordinarily repetitive though not repetitious. Spivack's gift is to be able to keep saying the same thing so brilliantly that it is ever the same yet ever different, and his reader makes haste slowly by happy pulses of recognition and discovery. What is true of sentence and paragraph is true too of section and chapter: compendious introductions and comprehensive summaries abound as if from a compulsive need to keep the reader (or the writer) oriented. The compulsion may be there but the cause, I think, lies deeper. It lies in a scholastic cast of mind, a vision in which ends are implicit in their beginnings. So in the style, subject contains predicate, predicate subject, in a minutely exhaustive, steadily enlarging circularity of thought. The first chapter is "Iago," the last, fitly, "Iago Revisited." We see again what we saw first, but with an understanding enormously enriched, and that enrichment a function of Spivack's having narrowly explored and largely set forth his own abundant vision.

By way of particular we may glance at the chapters which frame the book. The first begins with the question, "What is Iago?" "He is a soldier, a liar, an adept at dissimulation and intrigue, a cynic, an egotist, a criminal," who destroys a pair of wedded lovers and a pair of warm friends. "His crimes, he explains, are motivated by his resentment over the denial of an office to which he aspires and by his desire to recover it, by his suspicion that he is a deceived husband and by his desire for revenge, and by his need ultimately to cover up his previous malefactions." The literalists accept this explanation, which Spivack develops at length, but it will serve, he says,

> only until we read the play and find ourselves entangled in the mystery to which an enormous literature of conjecture pays tribute. The problem that confronts lay reader and scholar-critic alike . . . arises from the inescapable impression that a profound ambiguity vitiates each of Iago's motives individually, and divorces all of them together from his dramatic personality and his actions. Adequate enough in the abstract as motives theoretically sufficient . . . they are invalidated by the way they are expressed and by their failure to conform with the dominant impression Iago makes as a character in a play. Lifted from the play and paraphrased, they point the ancient human way of sensible injury and passionate retaliation; but in the play itself Iago goes a very different way, dragging his motives backward, as it were, in spite of themselves. The result has been more than one hundred and fifty years of perplexed speculation over a problem that can be illustrated as three-fold.

(This passage strikingly illustrates both the forward-inching repetitiveness I have pointed to and the compendious introduction that holds several sections of a chapter together as parts of a single, elaborated statement.) The sections immediately following develop the three folds of the problem, which are those just specified: (1) the ambiguity of Iago's motives, (2) the disjunction between the emotions Iago says he feels and those he in fact reveals, (3) and the divergence between the revenge he seeks and the non-retaliatory goals he seems simultaneously and by the same means to achieve. The discussion of the ambiguity of motive will suggest the recurrent brilliance of Spivack's style and the cataloguing copiousness of his analysis:

The force of [Iago's] provocations is dissipated by the very texture of the language in which he expresses them, by a literal and formal frivolity that resides in the vocabulary and syntax of his statements.

Not only do his suspicions . . . lack objective support in the play, they do not even possess the quality of hallucination, but are studiously voiced by him as the flimsiest hearsay and conjecture. And once so voiced early in the play, they are forgotten.

The very number of his motives augments their ambiguity. They come crowding in frivolous profusion and jostle each other off into oblivion. They sound like parenthetical remarks, postscripts, marginalia—like a clutter of opportunisms for an action that was inevitable before they were ever thought of.

The grounds for revenge which Iago advances, he says,

are fantasies stabbed to death in the very moment of their birth by equivocation as deliberate as a jest, and as invariable as a formula:

'Tis thought abroad
I know not if't be true
I do well believe it
'Tis apt and of great credit
I fear Cassio with my nightcap too
I do suspect the lusty Moor.

More important than the frivolity of Iago's motives to Spivack's argument (to which, from this point, we shall confine ourselves) is another kind of equivocation between two different levels of motivation. The motives that Iago advances, and which the literalists accept, are paired with "explanations that do not have intelligible reference to the human situation inside the play, or, for that matter, to the conventions of human behavior outside it." Iago's specific and natural fear of adultery combines with a vague, general enmity against the Moor; his pointed aim of getting Cassio's place joins with a general desire to plume up his will; his need to destroy Cassio lest Cassio learn of his plotting links with an unfocused desire to destroy the daily beauty in Cassio's life. These general motives suggest the older, stock figure whom Shakespeare is naturalizing into his Renaissance play.

Spivack's analysis of Iago's actual emotions, as opposed to those he declares himself to feel, produces anew an old discovery, that Iago's essential passion is jocularity. By the end of II.i "he is completely done with [his professed motives], and nothing competes with his intense pleasure and single-minded concentration upon the felicity of his intrigue." This ambiguity of emotion jibes with a curious ambivalence about Iago's victims. To him Othello is both "lusty Moor" and "the middle-aged man of 'weak function.' " "Cassio, who is a precocious amorist and faithless friend, is also an 'honest fool' who 'hath a daily beauty in his life.' " "Of Desdemona he believes it likely that she loves Cassio in adulterous violation of her marriage vows; yet she is also a woman who inclines to 'any honest suit,' whose 'virtue' he intends to turn into pitch, out of whose 'goodness' he will weave a net to enmesh them all." In short, "at one moment all his victims are guilty of moral turpitude and devious faithlessness; at another they are all exemplars of virtue, all honest fools whose simple-minded rectitude and credulity render them his natural prey." These anomalies join with "the astonishing fact" that the cuckolded husband, though he treats Emilia "with amiable contempt, reflecting the easy familiarity of a settled marriage and his inveterate cynicism toward the feminine sex," against all the practice of Elizabethan and Jacobean drama seems emotionally oblivious of her guilt. The critic is directing us to the awareness that Iago's specific motives reflect the "naturalized" Iago, the general motives, the archaic original; the cuckold's fury points to Renaissance if not more general humanity, the cuckold's oblivion to the allegorical figure of homiletic tradition.

The third aspect of the problem about Iago Spivack finds in the goals the non-retaliatory Iago so ebulliently pursues—deceit, temptation, conniving, destruction, knavery, villainy, the advancing of the banners of Hell and night. All reveal behind the surface image of the vengeful ancient the grinning agent of the Devil, the vivacious enemy of man, the Vice.

If Spivack will have none of the literalist's reduction of Iago to his stated human motives, neither will he accept the subjectivities of motive-hunting or rudimentary conscience as advanced by a Bradley or a Coleridge. Spivack is, for the moment at least, an uncompromising disciple of Stoll whose words on the Elizabethan soliloquy as "truth itself" he quotes. For him the answer to the problem of Iago, as we already know, lies in the dramatic archaeology to which he devotes the great central portion of his study. When he returns to Iago in his final chapter he is still the Stollian, but, as we discover, with a difference.

His first concern here is with Shakespeare's dramaturgy and the limitations that the theater, the stage, impose. He deprecates as "sentimental fallacy" Swinburne's explanation of Shakespeare's unchilding of Iago. "In Shakespeare's world as in nature's," said Swinburne, "it is impossible that monsters should propagate." For Spivack this is poor eugenics to start with, irrelevant morality at best. "Shakespeare's reasons for deleting the ancient's daughter were not moral, they were dramaturgic." In the play she would have been "incidental," "essentially meaningless," and, in a theater where children were either infants in arms, represented by dolls, or young lads of seven or eight, she would have been hard to come by. By the "omission of the meaningless, impossible child," Spivack continues, "Shakespeare was able to dramatize another object very much to his purpose . . . the handkerchief." "Through forty-four lines of the play the attention of the audience is fixed upon the little square of cloth as it moves from hand to hand, its initial triviality swelling into the portent of its ultimate operation. It has not only been introduced, it has been staged, animated, transformed." Progressively Spivack discloses Shakespeare's stagecraft operating—to unmarry Cassio ("the blunt theatrical fact [was] that with two respectable wives already inside a play dealing with matrimony a third would have had no dramatic virtue at all compared with the opportunity to stage a harlot"), to curtail the sprawling narrative of the source, "to rid the story of its original element of chance" (as in Cassio's original quarrel while on guard, or in Desdemona's originally unprompted intercession on Cassio's behalf). "Such revisions . . . deepen the organization of the intrigue and, therefore, of the play; [and] they emphasize the villain by augmenting and ramifying his villainy."

Dramaturgic efficiency might make merely for the well-made play, but Spivack sees it in Shakespeare as in the service of moral sentiment. "Romantic love," he asserts, "dominates the values that organize the moral meaning of the play," and he defines that love in both moral and esthetic terms:

The feeling between [Othello and Desdemona] scales love's loftiest romance and expresses more acutely than anywhere else in the English drama, the refinement of sexual love in the sentiment and literature of Renaissance Europe, the evolution of l'amour courtois to its richest spiritual possibilities. For the realization of such an effect the poet's means lie in the formidable disparity he places between them and in its resolution through the characters he gives them: in her the initial refinement and modesty, the admiration growing to love for character and achievement, the spirited rejection of convention and parental constraint, the depth and constancy of her feeling; in him the sheathed power and heroic largeness, the rich past instinct in every present word and act, the tenderness, the frankness, the noble ingenuousness. In a sense their union is a proposition and the play their battlefield, testing whether love so conceived and dedicated can long endure. But poetry is at work upon the proposition to transform it into sensation, and commentary at its best can only hint at the immediate experience the play gives us of gentle Desdemona and the noble Moor.

(Critics *do* write well about *Othello*.)

One of the most remarkable of Spivack's advances upon Stoll is the place he gives to moral sentiment as a principle governing Shakespeare's dramaturgy. Not only does it permit him to see characters as moral functions of one another and of the values organizing the play—the spiritual Desdemona in a sense creates the material Iago as the credulous Moor creates the cynical Italian, as the friendly Lieutenant the egotist Ancient—but it allows him a view of character as subtly appreciative as Bradley's. Whereas Bradley views the characters as "actual," Spivack's view, like Harbage's, is of the character as a moral-esthetic construct, though the construct walks with all the individuality of an historical person.

> The high art that wrought [Iago] into the dense and exclusive design of his own play does not allow him to remain an undifferentiated specimen of villainous humanity according to the commonplace Elizabethan formula of the Machiavel. He is matched and specialized against a theme, and his evil refined into something rare through the ironic felicity of its polarization and the dramatic felicity of its operation within that theme.

Spivack speaks richly of this Iago, the natural man. "Before he is through," he says, "his nimble logic has roped everyone in the play, including himself, into his sexual syllogism"—that love "is merely a lust of the blood and a permission of the will." "His separate suspicions bewilder us less and seem less absurd . . . when we see them for what they actually are—related local disturbances moving out from the broad weather front of his sexual doctrine." His motives, as we see them, are two: "his cynical Machiavellianism toward sex, which hovers over everyone in the play and creates his personal provocation when it lights on his wife and 'black Othello,' " and his resentment at being passed over for the lieutenancy.

Spivack accepts such a portrait of Iago, "because it exists," but rejects it also "because it does not exist alone." With it, the Vice. His succeeding discussion explores this figure as it has become modified in Iago, Richard III providing a useful measure of its evolution:

> For one thing, the bravura image of multiple deceit, though ramifying upon as many victims as before, is no longer tandem and episodic, but deftly organized into a single complex intrigue within a comprehensive dramatic plot. For another, the amoral humor of the moral personification, having ceased to be explosive, has become pervasive—a mood and a tone penetrating Iago's role throughout. In the third place, the homiletic dimension of the role, its didactic voice and naked moral display, is relatively subdued and fragmentary, modified by indirection and mainly limited to sentences and half-sentences that twist in and out his more relevant phraseology. Finally, while the stark antinomy of the Psychomachia remains, supplying for his aggression an explanation that contradicts his motives, it has suffered attrition, and of the original formula only part survives: "I hate the Moor."

This is the outline for an extended and illuminating analysis of Iago-as-Vice which we have no space to rehearse. Nor in glancing at these two chapters has there been room for a good many of Spivack's good things, and of course, in the chapters we have not examined, there are many more. We can see, though, that Spivack's criticism escapes from Stoll's simplism while paying full obeisance to the twin principles of history and art which guided his predecessor. Moreover Spivack's awareness of convention has a delicacy of calibration his master never achieved: he can see in

Iago not merely the conventional if archaic role of Vice, but he defines that role in a particular one of its permutations, neither the simple Vice of the far past nor the layered Vice-human of a more recent past, but "the contrary elements of the conflation" now "relatively merged and granular, with the older image recessive and diminished." Spivack tends, especially at first, to oppose archaeology to psychology, stagecraft to philosophy, in a way reminiscent of Stoll in his no-nonsense moods, yet his final estimate of character and play impresses by its binocular inclusiveness. Stoll *and* Bradley inhere in his vision, their largeness in his research and application, their felicity in his style. He provides one of the central models for the Shakespearean criticism to come.

xvii

C. L. Barber / 1913–
John Holloway / 1920–
Northrop Frye / 1912–

Barber's analogy of Shakespeare's plays to holiday entertainments: "through release to clarification." Love's Labour's Lost. *Barber compared to Gervinus and Pater.* ❦ *Holloway's view of Shakespeare's plays as literature of power, not knowledge.* King Lear *as relating to the legend of world's end, its imagery, society, and characters descending toward the brute; comparison to* Job*—the common moral vision; personal bonds. Holloway's larger view: tragic pattern as ritual sacrifice of scapegoat hero. Reservations. Appeal of scapegoat role.* ❦ *Frye's view: Shakespeare's comedies as self-contained conventions, deriving from or working toward myth. The New Comedy formula of Renaissance and Shakespearean comedy: an old society giving way to a new, with detached spectators at the end. Shakespearean romance to the contrary. Larger meanings of the endings of Shakespearean romance. Frye's criticism assessed.*

C. L. Barber is the most compelling of the anthropological critics and his book, *Shakespeare's Festive Comedy* (1959), is to my mind far and away the most illuminating yet to appear on its subject. He is compelling for many reasons—a mind both intricate and deft, a sensitivity quick to the accommodations of esthetic form to the intricacies of psychological function, a humanity benignly tolerant and inclusive—but most immediately, here, because the analogy he perceives between Shakespeare's plays and the realm of ritual and myth is more "available," as it were, than the analogies Fergusson sees or Frye.[1] When Fergusson suggests that the play of *Hamlet* celebrates and secures the "welfare of the whole, of the monarchy, and of the 'lives of many' that depended on it," we may see what he means but not particularly feel it. The same, I think, is true of Frye's analogy of the winter-spring movement in nature and the trouble-joy movement in comedy: we see the comparison but don't in our bones truly sense the seasonal change. For many of us Portia triumphs over Shylock, not over winter. But when Barber analogizes Shakespeare's plays to holiday entertainments, the characters caught up in patterns of festive release from which they return, enlightened, to an everyday world —just as we still may do come May Day or Halloween, New Year's Eve or Twelfth Night or any time we choose to attend Shakespeare's comic theater—then we both see and feel the likeness. What went on in ritual, what goes on in the play, goes on still in us.

This thing that goes on is caught in Barber's formula, "through release to clarification." In the plays in question Shakespeare expresses release "by making the whole experience of the play like that of a revel." The "events" of the narrative put the

persons in the position of festive celebrants: if they do not seek holiday it happens to them. A tyrant duke forces Rosalind into disguise; but her mock wooing with Orlando amounts to a Disguising, with carnival freedom from the decorum of her identity and her sex. The misrule of Sir Toby is represented as personal idiosyncrasy, but it follows the pattern of the Twelfth Night occasion; the flyting match of Benedict and Beatrice, while appropriate to their special characters, suggests the customs of Easter Smacks and Hocktide abuse between the sexes. Much of the poetry and wit, how-

> ever it may be occasioned by events, works in the economy of
> the whole play to promote the effect of a merry occasion
> where Nature reigns.

Praising nature, mocking fortune and the drab restraints of worka-
day actuality, the characters of the plays, like festive celebrants
anywhere, release the energies customarily devoted to maintaining
inhibition. And in the release, they achieve clarification, "a heightened awareness of the relation between man and 'nature'—the
nature celebrated on holiday." "The plays present a mockery of
what is unnatural which gives scope and point to the sort of scoffs
and jests shouted by dancers in the churchyard or in 'the quaint
mazes in the wanton green.' And they include another, complementary mockery of what is merely natural, a humor which puts
holiday in perspective with life as a whole." The plays make butts
of the kill-joys, the Malvolios and Shylocks who deny or are
inadequate to the natural pleasure which gives the others solidarity. At the same time, they mock the romantic idealism which
confuses the springtime of love with eternity. The festive comedies
celebrate present mirth and present laughter but acknowledge,
too, the rain that has rained since the world began. They *place* the
holiday moment in the rhythm of the seasons, in the calendar of
the years.

The especial merit of Barber's criticism lies in its sensitive
exploration of the individual working out of the release-clarifica-
tion formula in five separate plays. Each, he discovers, "tends to
focus on a particular kind of folly that is released along with
love—witty masquerade in *Love's Labour's Lost*, delusive fantasy
in *A Midsummer Night's Dream*, romance in *As You Like It*, and,
in *The Merchant of Venice*, prodigality balanced against usury."
Twelfth Night, to complete the list, focuses on misrule and its
complementary folly of time-serving. A review of the chapter on
Love's Labour's Lost will let us examine Barber's performance
more closely.

The chapter comprises seven sections. The first of these, an

untitled introduction, sets the play in the confluence of two traditions, that of aristocratic festivity on the one hand, that of the
public theater on the other. If the occasion were some special
aristocratic entertainment,

> Shakespeare's professional interests naturally led him to pro-
> duce a piece which could be used afterward in the public
> theater. So . . . he needed to express holiday in a way that
> would work for anybody, any day . . . And there had to be
> protagonists whose experience in a plot would define the
> rhythm of the holiday, making it, so to speak, portable.

Shakespeare satisfies the demands of both traditions by going for
the model of his action neither to theatrical nor literary sources
but to pastimes and games.

In the second section, captioned " 'lose our oaths to find
ourselves,' " Barber grants that the story of the play "is all too
obviously designed to provide a resistance which can be trium-
phantly swept away by festivity," but insists that "story interest is
not the point: Shakespeare is presenting a series of wooing games,
not a story. Fours and eights are treated as in ballet, the action
consisting not so much in what individuals do as in what the group
does, its patterned movement." The comedy that comes in such
scenes as IV.iii, where each lord enters, reads his sonnet, and
retires to witness the next lord do the same, "is at the opposite
pole from most comedy of character," Barber observes.

> Character usually appears in comedy as an individual's way of
> resisting nature: it is the kill-joys, pretenders, and intruders
> who have character . . . But with Shakespeare, the cele-
> brants are at the center. And when merrimakers say yes to
> nature, taking the folly of the time, the joke is that they
> behave in exactly the same way . . . The festive comedies
> always produce this effect of a group who are experiencing
> together a force larger than their individual wills.

The release, then, is collective, a surrender or loss of identity as the individuals give themselves to the communal impulse. But even in *Love's Labour's Lost*, Barber observes, Shakespeare discovers that there may be variety in the ways individuals accept nature: Berowne reveals a consciousness and an articulateness different from those the others possess.

The third section, " 'sport by sport o'erthrown,' " defines the folly in which the lords find their release, and though in a general sense this might be called "the impulse to love," "the particular form that it takes for them," says Barber, is

> what one could call the folly of amorous masquerade, whether in clothes, gestures, or words. It is the folly of acting love and talking love, without being in love. For the festivity releases, not the delights of love, but the delights of expression which the prospect of love engenders—though those involved are not clear about the distinction until it is forced on them; the clarification achieved by release is this recognition that love is not wooing games or love talk. And yet these sports are not written off or ruled out; on the contrary the play offers their delights for our enjoyment, while humorously putting them in their place.

" 'A great feast of languages,' " the fourth section, grants that

> if all we got were sports that fail to come off, the play would indeed be nothing but labor lost. What saves it from anti-climax is that the most important games in which the elation of the moment finds expression are games with words, and the wordplay does for the most part work, conveying an experience of festive liberty.

Barber quickly recognizes the different kinds of artificial prose and verse the various groups employ, but he sees that something other than satire on overelaborate language is going on. Armado

and the schoolmaster do make ridiculous two main Elizabethan vices of style. But each carries his vein so fantastically
far that it commands a kind of gasping admiration—instead
of being shown up, they turn the tables and show off, convert-
ing affectation and pedantry into ingenious games.

"In a world of words, the wine is wit." So Barber begins his
fifth section wherein his concern is to show that in wit the festive
principle operates. His argument is that in social festivity we are
exhilarated by receiving something for nothing—some food, drink,
warmth or beauty—that signals our belonging in the universe.
Wit, he argues, works the same way. "In wit, it is language that
gives us this something for nothing; unsuspected relations between
words prove to be ready to hand to make a meaning that serves
us." Space prevents following Barber's illustrative analyses, but his
generalization appeals: "When wit flows happily, it is as though
the resistance of the objective world had suddenly given way. One
keeps taking words from 'outside,' from the world of other systems
or orders, and making them one's own, making them serve one's
meanings as they form in one's mouth."

This section focuses on release; the next, "Putting Witty
Folly in Its Place," focuses on "clarification about what one sort of
wit is and where it fits in human experience." The "one sort of
wit" has no identifying name but it is the wit that expresses the
galvanizing of the whole sensibility by love. Characteristically,
descriptions of the process of being witty in the play "go with talk
about brightening eyes": as the eye brightens, the wit turns its
observations to jest, and these the fair tongue

> Delivers in such apt and gracious words
> That aged ears play truant at his tales
> And younger hearings are quite ravished,
> So sweet and voluble is his discourse.

Berowne's great speech justifying folly similarly focuses not on
"love as an experience between two people" but "on what happens

within the lover, the heightening of his powers and perceptions," the addition of "a precious seeing to the eye," a precious hearing to the ear, a precious feeling to the touch. Vital this self-centered absorption is, but foolish too, and Shakespeare's comic form reveals the vitality *and* the folly. Moth parodies the lordly lovers. The ladies drybeat them with pure scoff. Berowne repudiates his taffeta phrases and silken terms precise. But the elaborate games with languages are not, in fact, ultimately denied:

> The lords' trusting in speeches penn'd, with three-piled hyperboles, has been part and parcel of trusting in the masquerade way of making love, coming in a vizard, in a three-piled Russian habit. And these pastimes are not being dismissed for good, but put in their place: they are festive follies, relished as they show the power of life, but mocked as they run out ahead of the real, the everyday situation.

Berowne's control and poise permit him to help place these follies in the larger economy of life. The commoners, too, "contribute to placing the festivities"—by telling comments, for example, but these "are less important than the sense Shakespeare creates of people living in a settled group," a group that "functions together to represent 'his lordship's simple neighbours.' Through them we feel a world which exists before and after the big moment of the entertainment, and we see the excitement of the smaller people about the big doings." Of course, the ladies' moratorium on further wooing, the penances they mete out to the lords, similarly place the holiday folly they have all participated in.

Barber's final section, " 'When . . . Then . . .'—the Seasonal Songs," invites us to see that the group singing at the play's end expresses communal solidarity and that the songs of summer and winter "evoke the daily enjoyments and the daily community out of which special festive occasions were shaped up. And so they provide for the conclusion of the comedy what marriage usually provides: an expression of the going-on power of life."

Barber's especial merit, I have proposed, lies in the rich yet delicate exploration of his formula's working out in the individual plays. What he sees about release and clarification at one point is uniquely different from what he sees at another. Always he seems close to the play in question, attuned to its individual text and complexion. And if one puts his interpretation of *Love's Labour's Lost* beside those of Gervinus and Pater, we find it more precise, more elaborately fitted to the action of the play. Gervinus saw the play focusing on the vain desire of fame in all its forms; Pater saw the play focusing on the foppery of delicate language. The first is not wrong, the second is finely right, but Barber sees more—sees the connection of language with love, the connection of both with festivity and the mornings that stretch out thereafter. Comparison of his treatments of the other plays with the criticisms of his predecessors would result I believe, in similar judgments. He does not render character for us so much as role, nor plot so much as festivity, but his criticism is never reductive. If it invites us to see behind the fantasy of *A Midsummer Night's Dream* the ritual of a Maying or behind the repudiation of Falstaff the scapegoating of saturnalian ritual, it does so with a tact that treats the ritual more as backdrop or analogy than as present ceremony. Always it acknowledges the particularities of the plays no less than the general patterns contained therein. Frank Kermode has objected of Frye's criticism that it sacrifices the plays to generalization.[2] Barber's criticism does not. Satisfyingly, it celebrates both.

❦ ❦ ❦

John Holloway's *The Story of the Night* (1961), says Philip Edwards, "is contentious and choleric; it is not well planned, and has the air of being hastily written. If Holloway had delayed publication for five years, we might perhaps be welcoming the first real successor to Bradley."[3] Holloway's choler and contentiousness are most evident in an introduction that restively shoulders aside the dispensers of the "current coin of Shakespeare criticism." Under such formulae as of Shakespeare's "explicating themes" or "elaborating conceptions" or "obstinately questioning" or "defining, asserting and clarifying values," Holloway charges that they present the plays as literature of knowledge rather than as literature of power. For him a Shakespearean play "is not a statement or insight or special kind of informativeness—not these things essentially, though it may be all of them incidentally—but is a *momentous and energizing experience*." And from this perspective he undertakes analyses of *Hamlet, Othello, Macbeth, King Lear, Antony and Cleopatra, Coriolanus,* and *Timon of Athens.*

These analyses function at two levels. They are, first, explorations of the individual plays, shaped to the questions the plays and the history of their interpretation have raised—as of Hamlet's "character" or Othello's jealousy—and attempts to define the experience, particularly that of the tragic protagonist, in which each play engages us. Holloway's instruments here combine a fine feeling for the macro-architecture of the plays—for the great outlines and principal patterns of their actions—and a firm historical awareness. These work together to produce individual chapters of great power. Kermode calls the chapter on *Lear,* "like the play, incomparable."[4] At the second level, the explorations gradually discover beneath the experiences of the individual plays an archetypal pattern, that of the ritual sacrifice of the scapegoat hero. Holloway explores *Coriolanus* and *Timon* solely as they reveal this pattern, and he devotes the final chapter of his book to "Shakespearean Tragedy and the Idea of Human Sacrifice." Recognizing, moreover, that anthropological or archetypal awarenesses trouble many a modern as Freudian awarenesses once did, Holloway gives an appendix to "The Concepts of 'Myth' and 'Ritual' in Literature" in which he attempts to explain how literature of the variety to which Shakespearean tragedy belongs works upon us. Such literature, he proposes, offers us what rituals offer the members of other societies, "and has come to do so through being in some respects the same kind of thing." It is "a source not of pleasure, not of insight . . . but of experience: an experience peculiarly comprehensive and demanding, an experience unified, ordered and imposed." In this appendix, Holloway brings us back to the position of his Introduction—to his attack on the "current coin of Shakespeare criticism" which values the plays for their informativeness, to his assertion that it is as experience, as power, that the plays most matter.

The chapter on *King Lear* exemplifies Holloway's analyses of individual plays. The play is set "in the legendary pre-history of Britain," in "a world which is remote and primèval," and the play's "permanent relevance is what follows from having the quality of legend, and the primeval as subject." The legend contains at its center "an event which today has largely lost its meaning": the end of the world—"not the Day of Judgment, but the universal cataclysm which was to precede it."

> For Shakespeare's time collapse into universal chaos was not merely a permanent possibility in a fallen (though divinely created) Nature: it was a foreordained part of created Nature's route to salvation; and to envisage it, to dwell on it, to comprehend what it could be like, was part of what went to make up a comprehension of God's governance of the world.

The idea of the end of the world finds expression in various of Shakespeare's plays—by the guards in *Antony and Cleopatra* who speak of the star's falling and time's being at his period, by Macduff's speaking of "the great doom's image" and of rising up from graves, by Kent and Edgar's speaking of Cordelia dead in Lear's arms as either "the promis'd end" or "image of that horror." Gloucester's interpretation of "these late eclipses of the sun and moon" "reechoes the words of St. Luke on the end of the world" (xxi. 25–6). "The storm on the heath recalls what the Book of Revelation says of Armageddon" (xvi. 18). "How *Lear* is in part a rehearsal of" the end of the world "becomes plainer, if one bears in mind that what the descent into chaos would be like was delineated by tradition"—in Mark xiii, for example, or the Homily of 1574 *Against Disobedient and Wilful Rebellion*, with their language of nation against nation, subjects against sovereign, brother against brother, and parent against child.

Extraordinarily realistic though *Lear* at times is, our sense of the play's generic quality and decisive pattern derives less from its fidelity to "the complex and individualized movements of minds vehemently working and intently engaged" than from its stylization. The division of the kingdom is stylized both in itself and in its suggestion of the evil to come. "It is the established sign or first step in a movement which threatens chaos or actually brings it.

Holloway takes up points raised by earlier critics but develops them in new ways. He associates the primitiveness on which Bradley had expatiated with the quality of legend and the event of world's end. He sees the division of the kingdom, on the probability of which discussion has frequently raged, as stylized, conventional, formulaic. He brings similar new vision to the animal imagery of which Bradley and Knight had said good things. The repeated likening of the humans to the beasts, says Holloway,

> gives no mere general or pervasive tinge to the work, and embodies no merely general idea about humanity at large. It cannot be found in the opening scene. It arrives as the action begins to move, and becomes dominant as the quality of life which it embodies becomes dominant in the play.

The great and horrifying images that "burst upon the audience all together" matter less in their general suggestion about humanity than "how they qualify the phase of the action which comes at that point, crowding the audience's imagination, surrounding the human characters with the subhuman creatures whose appearance they are fast and eagerly assuming." As the characters descend toward the brute, they do so in a context of imagery that defines their fall to our understandings and to our feelings.

The sense of descent finds reinforcement from "the progressive transformation, as Act II advances, of the settled society of men, with their fixed abodes, into a confusion of people constantly leaving their homes, constantly on horseback and riding recklessly from place to place." But the quality of the descent goes beyond what can be conveyed by the imagery of beast and confusion. Lear elects to be "recreant against Nature and outcast among its creatures," wandering on the heath when even the beasts seek shelter, until he comes finally to the extreme—"Is man no more than this? . . ." "Regan and Goneril also seem to pass down through, and out of, the whole order of Nature; though they are its monsters not its remnants."

Holloway explores Lear's descent and his part in the whole transformation by comparing his condition with Job's. Sharp, local resemblances warrant the comparison as do "passages in *Job* that seem to resume whole sections of the play," as in this extraordinary lament, which Holloway quotes from the Bishops' Bible (1568)—the Bible on which Shakespeare presumably drew:

> *Myne owne kinfolkes haue forsaken me and my best acquaynted haue forgotten me. The seruantes and maydes of myne owne house tooke me for a stranger, and I am become as an aliant [-alien] in theyr sight. I called my seruant, and he gaue me no answere . . . Al my most familiers abhorred me: and they whome I loued best are turned agaynst me.*
>
> (xix. 14–18)

Holloway observes that both *Job* and *Lear* are extraordinarily protracted. By the middle of Act IV, Lear has had his eyes in a sense opened. He has learned some humility, some self-knowledge. He has recovered "the central and traditional lessons that good kings must know" about poor naked wretches and rascal beadles. But Lear's sufferings continue, as do Job's. Why? Holloway's explanation is that we customarily think of Nature as an order of justice. Men who sin suffer and suffering derives from sin. Suffering, moreover, atones for sin—rights the balance—so finally ends, replaced by good. But Job suffers in his innocence and suffers protractedly. Instead of good replacing evil, "evil returns twofold and is prolonged far beyond its proper span." *Job* opens to us the experience of a world wherein the natural, moral order no longer operates. *Lear* does the same. Edgar thinks that he is at the bottom and therein finds cause for hope, only to come a moment later upon his blinded, outlawed father. Lear has sinned and suffered, yet when the Captain hurries to restore him, *"Enter Lear, with Cordelia dead in his arms."* In *Lear* as in *Job*, suffering "tops extremity." "We that are young," says Edgar, "Shall never see so much nor live so long."

> The ordeal has been unique in its protraction of torment, and the note is surely one of refusal to hide that from oneself, refusal to allow the terrible potentialities of life which the action has revealed to be concealed once more behind the veil of orthodoxy and the order of Nature. If there is such an order, it is an order which can accommodate seemingly limitless chaos and evil. The play is a confrontation of that, a refusal to avert one's gaze from that.

The personal bonds on which the play focuses at its close Holloway believes to be something other than those of love alone. Cordelia speaks of her aged father's right. Her concern throughout is with rights and duties, bonds, service. Edgar has nursed and tended his father. Kent will serve his master still—"I have a journey, sir, shortly to go./My master calls me." Albany calls on Kent and Edgar to rule and sustain the "gor'd state." Suffering may "renew itself unremittingly until the very moment of death," but "the forces of life," though "persistently terrible and cruel . . . have also brought men back to do the things it is their part to do . . . To follow the master, to sustain the state, to bless one's child, to succor the aged and one's parents—this idea of being brought back to rectitude is what the play ends with."

In effect the essay on *Lear* ends at this point although a few pages follow in which Holloway brings the play into the anthropological perspective. The freshness of his interpretation is surely evident. He reviews the topics of former critics but places on each his own definition. The parts of his analysis are distinguished by their fidelity to the text, and the whole is cumulative and compelling. Like the other anthropological critics, Holloway turns his gaze from character to focus on pattern, but his criticism is not reductive. For him *Lear* is not simply another exemplification of an archetype; it is apocalyptically huge, violent, affirmative. And Holloway interprets the play in accord with his initial conviction, that it is a work of power rather than of knowledge. It acts upon us. He shows us how and why it does.

We turn now to Holloway's larger, anthropological view. He sees the protagonist of the tragedies as undergoing an ordeal which means more than mere fall "from the top of Fortune's wheel to the bottom."

These tragic protagonists occupy the pinnacle of Fortune in a special way. They are not merely at the height of prosperity or greatness. They are "the observed of all observers," the man sought by everyone, the savior of the state, the center of its ceremony, the central figure of the court, the senate, the battlefield, the throne in the marketplace. Nor is their progress one merely of declining fortune. It is one of progressive isolation, in the course of which real deference becomes nominal, empty, and even hostile (Hamlet with Rosencrantz or Polonius, Lear with his cruel daughters, Cleopatra with her steward), or is replaced by open estrangement. Moreover, the end of this change is as distinctive as the change itself. The protagonist does not simply die, by violence or otherwise, as the last of his misfortunes. To a greater or lesser extent, his case is presented as one in which ceremonial and deference turn into a pursuit, a hunt; in the course of which there comes a point when, fleeing from disaster, he can flee no

> further. At this point, he turns and faces destruction; and his
> death is made to seem like an execution, or a sacrificial rite, or
> something of both.

This external process Holloway sees as the counterpart of "what
might be termed a mental history undergone within the protagonist's own consciousness."

With much of this it is foolish to quarrel. Shakespeare's tragic
heroes *are* cynosures. The deference they are accorded does become sick. They suffer isolation. And their deaths are not the last
of their misfortunes—are not, indeed, misfortunes at all. Hamlet,
Othello, Antony, Cleopatra, Timon seek death as a consummation
devoutly to be wished. There is some question, however, as to
what extent their communities isolate or drive out their heroes. It
may be that the Venetian state, by relieving Othello of his command, loosens the bonds that knit him to his community, but it is
questionable whether, as Holloway says, Horatio becomes one of
those who "in one way or another are on the side of [Hamlet's]
opponent." There is, clearly, a sense in which deference turns into
pursuit in all of the tragedies, and a sense in which the protagonist, bayed, faces destruction; yet it may be questioned
whether some sort of moral distinction is not to be recognized
between the baying of the more or less "good" man by the more or
less "evil" (Hamlet by Claudius, Othello by Iago, Lear by Edmund) and the converse (Macbeth by Malcolm, Antony, perhaps,
by Octavius)—unless the shooting down *of* an outlaw and the
shooting down *by* an outlaw are comparable in their meaning to a
community. To the deaths of his protagonists Shakespeare gives a
fine formality, and there is a sense, of course, in which these
resemble executions and rites of sacrifice; again, however, distinctions may be made. Hamlet is not executed but murdered, and if
he is a sacrifice, it is not the community that sacrifices him but
providence: he was born to set the time right. Othello is his own
executioner, and in what sense he may be regarded as a sacrifice for

or by the community I cannot determine. Shortly, we know, Venice will execute and sacrifice Iago. Lear dies of a broken heart, Cordelia of the executioner's noose; both are, in Lear's terms, such sacrifices as the gods throw incense on—but to suggest that the "community" sacrifices them makes sense only if Albany and Kent and Edgar and their forces be excluded from the community. It is ungrateful to protest in this way, but Holloway stretches his pattern, I think, to fit more than it rightfully ought. His remarks superbly apply to *Macbeth* and to *Coriolanus*, to *Antony and Cleopatra* and to *Timon*—to plays Shakespeare wrote late in his career, in the years immediately before the final romances. They fit the earlier tragedies and *Lear* at times, but only at times.

Holloway's "discovery" of the role of scapegoat and sacrifice in Shakespeare's tragedies is one part of his anthropological contribution; the other is his attempt to understand why the role matters. Though his answers here are tentative, they open a hopeful way into the dynamics of such tragedy as Shakespeare customarily wrote. The role of scapegoat, which characters elect as embodying one of the major standing possibilities of life, engages the attention, emotion, and sympathy of an audience for three reasons. First, the scapegoat's experience engages man with "the world of unseen and holy powers"; it turns an audience's mind "towards an apprehension of life seen in the context of what goes beyond life . . . not . . . in the sense of advancing a doctrine about these matters, but at a more radical level, that of opening the mind and directing the imagination." Second, the sacrifice engages the audience in a deeper feeling of community. In part of our being is a sense that we are members one of another, and the sacrificial rite or its tragic simulacrum enlivens this sense within us. Third, the personal agony that the rituals of actual human sacrifice are often designed to conceal—drums or cymbals, for example, drowning out the victim's cries—"the drama is by virtue of its nature as a fiction free to enact, and by virtue of its language empowered to elucidate and deepen to an extent beyond comparison." The drama, in other words, can arouse our sense of human individuality, of the uniqueness which we and every man in part pay up to achieve and participate in the community.

❧ ❧ ❧

As a critic Northrop Frye has resemblances to E. E. Cummings as a poet. He starts easily, clearly, delighting us with our own powers of accommodation. Then, and before we know it, we are dashing through an intellectual stratosphere filled with flying objects, hanging on for dear life. Frye is one of the most mind-opening of anthropological or archetypal critics, yet he is often hard to understand. The reason is partly, of course, that he ranges very high, very deep. But the reason seems also to be that in Frye the power of analogy has developed extravagantly but is not balanced by a correspondingly developed power of generalization. His essays keep extending horizontally, as it were, but not vertically, the parallel perspectives proliferating but the controlling idea or subsuming generalizations all too often either faintly whispered or in fact unspoken. What follows, about Frye's criticism of Shakespeare in the four chapters of A *Natural Perspective: The Development of Shakespearean Comedy and Romance* (1965), attempts to right the balance by suppressing some of the analogy and by stressing what I take to be the governing concepts.

Chapter I. Shakespeare's comedies, says Frye, and yet more, his romances, steer away from the illusionist realism Jonson practiced and praised. Shakespeare "does not ask his audience to accept an illusion: he asks them to listen to the story." And though

> we are assured that the Elizabethan audience would think
> very differently about the behavior of Isabella in Measure for
> Measure from anyone today who was expecting a problem
> play . . . it seems clear that no audience of Shakespeare,
> whether Elizabethan or modern, is allowed to think at all.

Shakespeare's comedies and romances are, in fact, less mirrorings of life than self-contained conventions that stylize their characters and "may force them to do quite unreasonable things." Further, Shakespeare seems at pains to render his manifold improbabilities yet more improbable, as when he doubles the absurdity of Claudio's succumbing to Don John's calumnies with the rigamarole of Margaret at the window, of Don Pedro's sympathetic imbecility, Beatrice's silence, Leonato's instant paranoia, and all the rest. "However we explain the difficulties, they seem to be there with the specific function of drawing us away from the analogy to familiar experience into a strange but consistent and self-contained world." Anachronisms work to this same effect— and the operatic features of the plays. Instead of the phenomenal world about us, "the late romances, *Pericles* in particular, . . . give us a drama beyond drama, a kind of ultimate confrontation of a human community with an artistic realization of itself."

Chapter II. Shakespeare's plays are objective: Shakespeare "refrains from trying to impose any sort of personal attitude on us, and shows no interest in anything except his play." "He seems to start out with an almost empathic relation to his audience: their assumptions about patriotism and sovereignty, their clichés about Frenchmen and Jews, their notions of what constitutes a joke, seem to be acceptable to him as dramatic postulates." Hamlet may speak of caviar to the general, but Shakespeare's motto seems to have been, "We'll strive to please you every day." He has no opinions, no values except dramatic structure. We know not his attitude toward Falstaff, nor his own private attitudes toward "legitimacy, divine right, order and degree, the chain of being, Christian eschatology, and the like . . . Shakespeare's plays reflect the anxieties of his time: they do not show that he shared those anxieties." Clearly, for Frye, the goal of biographical criticism is unattainable, its methods naïve. Shakespeare, as so many have said before, is impartial, but not because he is disengaged: "Shakespeare's impartiality is a totally involved and committed impartiality: it expresses itself in bringing everything equally to life."

Shakespeare's comedies are objective or impartial—popular. They are, as well, conventional, which is to say, they exhibit a certain kind of structure that "works through to its own logical end, whether we or the cast or the author feels happy about it or not. The logical end is festive, but anyone's attitude to the festivity may be that of Orlando or of Jaques." Shakespeare's problem plays, so-called, are to Frye's mind comedies wherein the working out of the structure conflicts with the moods we associate with comedy. But structure is more basic than mood and it is the structure that matters. " 'All's well that ends well' is a statement about the structure of comedy."

Shakespeare's comedies are primitive, archaic, deriving from "the region of origins and beginnings." "Shakespeare draws away from everything that is local or specialized in the drama of his day, and works toward uncovering a primeval dramatic structure that practically anything in the shape of a human audience can respond to." According to Frye, drama appears when the myth which accompanies and explains a ritual comes to enclose and contain it. "This changes the agents of the ritual into the actors of the myth. The myth sets up a powerful pull away from the magic: the ritual acts are now performed for the sake of representing the myth rather than primarily for affecting the order of nature." But drama recovers the magic it renounces not by acting directly on the nonhuman world but by assimilating it imaginatively to the human world.

Now "conventions are descended from myths" and "the literary convention enables the poet to recapture something of the pure and primitive identity of myth." Thus it is in Shakespeare's "problem" plays.

The "problem" of All's Well is not any Shavian social problem of how a woman gets her man, but the mythical problem of how Helena, like her ancestress Psyche, is going to solve her three impossible tasks: first of healing the sick king, then of presenting Bertram with a son of his own getting, and with his own ring, the talisman of recognition that . . . awakens his mind to reality.

Similarly, the problem in Measure for Measure is how Isabella's chastity, always a magical force in literature, is going to rescue both the violated Julietta and the jilted Mariana as a result of being exposed to the solicitations of Angelo.

Of Frye's extended analysis of *Cymbeline* as "the apotheosis of the problem comedies," combining "the *Much Ado* theme of the slandered heroine, the *All's Well* theme of the expulsion of the hero's false friend, the *Measure for Measure* theme of the confusion and clarifying of government, and many others," I regret I have not space to speak except to draw attention to his final point. In *Cymbeline* the force "which brings a festive conclusion out of all the mistakes of the characters, is explicitly associated with the working of a divine providence." *Cymbeline* adds "to the dramatic action . . . the primitive mythical dimension which is only implicit in the problem comedies."

Chapter III. Frye discovers at the core of most Renaissance comedy, including Shakespeare's,

the formula transmitted by the New Comedy pattern of Plautus and Terence. The normal action is the effort of a young man to get possession of a young woman who is kept from him by various social barriers: her low birth, his minority or shortage of funds, parental opposition, the prior claims of a rival. These are eventually circumvented, and the comedy ends at a point when a new society is crystallized, usually by the marriage or betrothal of hero and heroine. The birth of the new society is symbolized by a closing festive scene featuring a wedding, a banquet, or a dance. This conclusion is normally accompanied by some change of heart on the part of those who have obstructed the comic resolution.

The structure "normally begins with an anticomic society," with some "harsh or irrational law" as that of "killing Syracusans in *A Comedy of Errors*" or "disposing of rebellious daughters in *A Midsummer Night's Dream.*" Or "the anticomic theme may be expressed by mood"—as in Antonio's sadness at the beginning of *The Merchant of Venice,* the mourning habiliments of the characters at the beginning of *All's Well,* the melancholy of Orsino and Olivia at the start of *Twelfth Night.* The attempt to overcome the anticomic and irrational society of the play's beginning ushers in the structure's second phase, a "period of confusion and sexual license" (as the first period was a period of order and sexual restraint)—"the phase of temporarily lost identity." This theme finds expression in the confused identities of the moonlit lovers in *A Midsummer Night's Dream,* the convention of disguise, especially of sexual disguise, in Julia and Viola, in the substitution of Mariana for Isabella or Diana for Helena, etc. The final phase of the structure comes with the discovery of identity, which may have several forms. The individual may come "to know himself in a way he did not before." Katharina in *The Taming of the Shrew* is a case in point, or the courtiers in *Love's Labour's Lost,* or Benedick and Beatrice, Angelo, or Parolles. The discovery of identity may, again, take the form of marriage, for "the center of the comic drive toward identity is an erotic drive." In comic drama and romance, *contra* the Petrarchan convention of unfulfilled sexual identity,

> the action makes for marriage and the eventual possession of the mistress, and Shakespeare is expressing the contrast with courtly love poetry in its most concentrated form by developing an action in which a disappearing and returning heroine revolves cyclically around a male lover, and is usually the efficient cause of the conclusion.

Love triumphs over friendship and over lust. Finally, the discovery may be of social identity, of a new society. Whereas in Roman comedy, or Jonsonian, the new society tends to be one of youth, triumphant over their elders, in Shakespearean comedy, the new society reconciles the generations, "bringing the happy young couples into continuity with the society of their elders." *All's Well* illustrates the point clearly, as do the romances, all of them, and such historic comedies as *Henry IV* and *Henry V*.

At the end of the structure, when the new society has come into festive being, Shakespeare tends to treat the defeated forces as "states of mind rather than individuals." Shylock is an exception, and perhaps Malvolio, but in general the characters within the play, and the audience, without, are reconciled and participate in the new order. But there is always in us one part that remains observant instead of participant, and Shakespeare builds in his comedies (though not in his romances) characters who also remain observant, not participant—they acting, as it were, for that portion of ourselves which remains outside the play, as spectator. Frye finds two kinds of characters fulfilling this function: the fool or clown (Lavache, Touchstone, Feste) and what Frye elects to call the *idiotes* (i.e., the private person, idiosyncratic, resistant to the social or communal), who is "not a character type . . . but a structural device that may use a variety of characters." Usually the *idiotes* is "the focus of the anticomic mood, and so may be the technical villain, like Don John, or the butt, like Malvolio and Falstaff, or simply opposed by temperament to festivity, like Jaques." Touchstone is the clown, Jaques the *idiotes* of *As You Like It*, Lavache the clown and Parolles the *idiotes* of *All's Well*, Gobbo the clown and Shylock the *idiotes* of *The Merchant of Venice*, Dogberry the Clown and Don John the *idiotes* of *Much Ado*. Through these figures "we get fitful glimpses of a hidden world which they guard or symbolize," a world which, whether good, evil, ridiculous,

is never a wholly simple world, and [which] exerts on the main action a force which is either counterdramatic or anti-dramatic. Some of the most haunting speeches in Shakespeare

are connected with these shifts of perspective provided by alienated characters. What often happens is that something external to us is suddenly internalized, so that we are forced to participate in what we have been conditioned to think of as removed from us and our sympathies. Shylock's "Hath not a Jew" speech comes to mind.

Clown and *idiotes*, when the play comes toward its end, "place" the action and the new society for us.

In Shakespeare's romances, however, there is no detached spectator role at the end. This phenomenon jibes with another. Though "the normal action of a comedy moves from irrational law to festivity, which symbolizes a movement from one form of reality to another," the action of such a play as *The Winter's Tale*, is "from appearance to reality, from mirage to substance." This substance, however,

> has none of the customary qualities of reality. It is the world symbolized by nature's power of renewal; it is the world we want; it is the world we hope our gods would want for us if they were worth worshiping. But it is "monstrous to our human reason," according to Paulina, and its truth "is so like an old tale that the verity of it is in strong suspicion." Such things happen in stories, not in life, and the world The Winter's Tale leaves us with is neither an object of knowledge nor of belief.

Chapter IV. If I read Frye aright, the first two of his four chapters go to establishing the "conventionality" of Shakespeare's comedies, the second two to determining the nature of their extraordinary endings. I have come, now, to the fourth and final chapter, which makes its point repeatedly, each new formulation slightly enlarging the significance and simultaneously edging it the more sharply. To do it one kind of justice, I propose to enumerate these formulations.

(1) The comic drive is toward the discovery of an identity which emerges when the irrational society of the beginning "is dissolved and a new society crystallizes around the marriage of the central characters." This happy emergence is not perfunctory, as Johnson thought, but the consequence of a convention built into comedy's structure.

(2) "The mythical backbone of all literature is the cycle of nature." One half of this cycle presents the movement from spring to winter, from birth to death—a movement natural and rational, the pattern underlying tragedy and history plays. The other half of the cycle presents the movement from winter to spring, from death to rebirth, a movement natural yet to common sense irrational: "We can see that death is the inevitable result of birth, but new life is not the inevitable result of death." This movement provides comedy with its conventional structure and reveals that the power we associate with wish fulfillment is "a power as deeply rooted in nature and reality as its opponent." Further, "it is a power that we see, as the comedy proceeds, taking over and informing the predictable world."

(3) At the end of the romantic comedies there is a residual, irrational element.

> The drive toward a comic conclusion is so powerful that it breaks all the chains of probability in the plot, of habit in the characters, even of expectation in the audience; and what emerges in the end is not a logical consequence of the preceding action, as in tragedy, but something more like a metamorphosis.

(4) From tragedy we can infer axioms about fate and character; from comedy, about providence. In Shakespearean comedy, the characters act as though they were agents of providence.

(5) The irrational law at the beginning of comedy is "the comic equivalent of a social contract, something we must enter into if the final society is to take shape." This law centers on the

birth-death movement in nature. At the end this law "has been internalized, transformed into an inner source of coherence," as the new society has contained and absorbed the old.

(6) "In a typically festive conclusion, all previous conflicts are forgiven" but not quite forgotten. If they were forgotten, the experience would be pointless. But Hermia and Helena remember something, if faintly. And Bottom. And Hal. "We often have to think of the main action of a comedy as 'the mistakes of a night,' as taking place in a dream or nightmare world that the final scene suddenly removes us from and thereby makes illusory."

(7) The conclusion of comedy restores the "antecedent sense of the desirable; but it does not simply reproduce it, because we do not know what it was before we began to fashion it against the action" of the play. The purpose of the action is to define and clarify the new society, which is the old society "reformed and metamorphosed." (The sentimental gives us what was in our mind *before* the play began. Shakespeare's comedies give us, not childhood but innocence, a vision of what we have never seen, hence, a new vision.)

(8) The action of a Shakespearean comedy is dialectical as well as cyclical, then: "the renewing power of the final action lifts us into a higher world, and separates that world from the world of the comic action itself."

(9) The structure of Shakespearean comedy parallels that of the central myth of Christianity: "man loses a peaceable kingdom, staggers through the long nightmare of tyranny and injustice which is human history, and eventually regains his original vision." The regaining occurs not because of man's merit but because of God's grace, a distinction that "recurs all through Shakespearean comedy, where 'grace' is a centrally important thematic word."

(10) For Shakespeare and his contemporaries

the ordinary cycle of nature . . . is the middle of three modes of reality. It is the ordinary physical world that . . . man entered with his fall. Above it is the nature that God

> intended man to live in, the home symbolized by the biblical
> Garden of Eden and the Classical legend of the Golden Age,
> a world of perpetual fertility where it was spring and autumn
> at once. To this world, or to the inward equivalent of it, man
> strives to return through the instruments of law, religion,
> morality, and . . . education and the arts.

Music outwardly and female chastity inwardly symbolize the harmony of soul of regenerate man. Below our middle mode of reality "is the abyss of disorder which Shakespeare often summons up by the word 'nothing,' and symbolizes, most frequently, by the tempest. It is also the world of devouring time." Its subjective equivalents "are madness, illusion, or death itself." The three modes of reality relate to the structure of comedy thus: "As the comic action proceeds, the middle world of ordinary experience disappears into the world above it, and separates itself from the world below it." "The separation between redemption and destruction . . . constitutes the dialectic of romantic comedy."

(11) Comic action appears to present a turning around, but "the real turning around . . . is the reversal of the poet's presentation into the spectator's perception, and this reversal is completed when the comic action defines the world of its conclusion, and separates itself from the world of confusion and chaos below it."

(12) In certain of Shakespeare's plays, *The Two Gentlemen of Verona, As You Like It,* and *A Midsummer Night's Dream,* "the action moves from a world of parental tyranny and irrational law into a forest"—a green world which, with its miraculously potent dreams, magic, and chastity, symbolizes the golden world. In the romances this green world appears as a "natural" society which is in conflict with a courtly or sophisticated one. It is associated with a healer or preserver and is "the world in which the heroine—Thaisa, Fidele, Hermione—dies and comes back to life." Ultimately this natural society enters into the sophisticated society, informs it, and redeems it.

Space prohibits reviewing Frye's applications of these formulations to *The Tempest* (and I would hope that the reader might do that for himself), but we might hear his peroration:

> It is the wedding masque in which the dialectic of Shakespearean romance is most fully and completely stated. What the wedding masque presents is the meeting of earth and heaven under the rainbow, the symbol of Noah's new-washed world, after the tempest and flood had receded, and when it was promised that springtime and harvest would not cease. There is in fact a definite recall of the biblical scene:
>
> Spring come to you at the farthest
> In the very end of harvest.
>
> But these lines say more: they say that out of the cycle of time in ordinary nature we have reached a paradise . . . where there is a ver perpetuum, where spring and autumn exist together. It is not a timeless world, but it is a world in which time has a quite different relation to experience from ordinary time . . . In the world of the masque time has become the rhythm of existence, the recovery by man of the energy of nature. In the nonexistent world below, time is the universal devourer that has finally nothing to swallow but itself. Prospero's great speech at the end of the masque tells us that everything we perceive disappears in this time. That is, the world of the spectator is ultimately abolished. What is presented to us must be possessed by us, as Prospero tells us in the Epilogue. We are told that the characters, as usual, will adjourn to hear more about themselves, but we need not follow them, for it is our own identity that we are interested in now. If anything is to make sense of this play, no less than of Peter Quince's play, it must be, as Hippolyta says, our imagination and not theirs. When Prospero's work is done, and there is nothing left to see, the vision of the brave new

*world becomes the world itself, and the dance of vanishing
spirits a revel that has no end.*

In a sense Frye is an anthropologically sophisticated E. E.
Stoll. He gets away from character and comes to rest in convention, in structure as it derives from primitive ritual and myth. His
criticism clearly counters or complements that of the Coleridge-
Bradley tradition of psychological analysis. And it rebukes other
approaches as well. Frye rebuffs Johnson's complaint that Shakespeare's endings are amorally perfunctory. He answers Rymer and
Eliot by observing that their criticism neglects or takes literally
Shakespeare's conventions.[5] He negates the historical criticism
that explains the problems in Shakespeare's "problem" plays by
appealing either to Elizabethan sociology or Shakespearean realism. He silences (momentarily) the critics who derive biographical
inferences from objective and conventional matter within the
plays.

One important measure of Frye's value is clearly its contribution by negation to criticism's evolving dialogue about Shakespeare. Another measure, and greater, is his definition and ration-
alization of the Shakespearean comic and romantic structure—his
clear discrimination of the three main parts to the action, of the
clown and *idiotes* roles of alienation, of the dialectic that makes of
the plays' endings metamorphoses and miracles. Frye brilliantly
defines the structure and denominates the power by which it
charms us, haunts us, engages us, and ultimately liberates us. And
Frye does one thing further, which this treatment has too little
acknowledged. He explores the romances in depth, enabling us to
discover in each exfoliating patterns of symbolic resonance.

This is the positive view. The negative, ably argued by
Reuben Brower, protests that Frye's criticism is both circular and
reductive.[6] The argument "begins by establishing the ritual cycle
in drama through analogies between plays and actual ritual and
. . . ends by concluding that the meaning of the plays is to be

found in this generalized ritual cycle." Eventually, says Brower, "the critic and his readers must . . . conclude that all plays are one universal Play, that there are no individual meanings, but only the Meaning." The analogies are indeed there, and in the individual play, as in the human embryo, the pattern of origin and evolution may be found, but then, when the excitement of the discovery dwindles, where are we? As Brower puts it, "once the critic has pointed out the analogy, he may feel a little like Frost's Witch of Coös—'When I have done it, what have I done?' " Perhaps the answer is that the critic has quickened us to a life and power we had not so fully sensed before.

Arthur Sewell / 1903-

Relations to other critics, to Knight. Instances of wisdom.
The play as a working out of vision. Character as product
and agent of vision. Vision in comedy and history static, in
tragedy dynamic. The tragic hero's uncovenanted experi-
ence. "Tragedy and the 'Kingdom of Ends.'" Reservations
and final assessment.

The major critics resist easy classification. We may say that
Bradley is a moralist who treats characters as live, plays as history,
yet it is Bradley who wrote the great chapter on *"Construction* in
Shakespeare's Tragedies," and Bradley who opened up discussion
of the bestial imagery in *Lear,* the nightmare imagery of *Macbeth.*
Wilson Knight combines a formal concern for patterns of imagery
and themes in the embracing unity of a play's esthetic world with
the insights of anthropology. Harbage, the annalist, historian, and
sociologist, regards Shakespeare's plays formally, as psycho-moral
manipulations, pleasantly exciting, then pleasurably reassuring,
their audience. Arthur Sewell participates in a comparable plural-
istic comprehensiveness in his book, *Character and Society in*
Shakespeare (1951).

To make the point by names instead of labels, Sewell relates
to Stoll and Spivack in his feeling for character as a convention of
the theater, a relationship established between actor and audience.
The characters of comedy and history, he insists, "have no private
lives; they live in public, before an audience. This is obviously true

about . . . Launcelot Gobbo, but it is also true of Iago and Falstaff." Falstaff's "life within the play—the only life he has—is a sustained vaudeville turn." Iago can "speak about himself in the third person, as though he should take the audience into his confidence and say: 'You and I know this Iago well enough, but they can't catch him, not this poor trash of Venice, this nigger and this silly girl. Iago is much too fly for them.'" Sewell relates to Harbage in asserting that "the consistency of the character, like its significance, is generated within *our* moral attitudes" (my italics). "Unless Shakespeare had set our minds busy . . . on various kinds of evaluation, his characters could never have engaged us." Sewell relates, too, to Spurgeon and Clemen in his concern for imagery. He explores the thematic images of *The Merchant of Venice* and *Macbeth* in a manner reminiscent of Spurgeon at her most deft; he considers the *provenance* and form and action of images in *Othello* somewhat as Clemen does the images in *Richard II* and *Hamlet*. "In Iago's world," he writes, "everything is catalogued from observation. No image seems to have passed through his being . . . He has . . . a very large number of images of beasts; but these images are no more than emblems of men's weaknesses and vices." Again, "Iago rarely reveals a present emotion. His images always *refer to* an emotion of old standing, never generate the emotion in the moment, from the center." "Iago's is a pragmatic world, and his imagery finds its authority in social usage. Othello's world is the poetical aggrandizement of himself, and as he addresses he creates it."

Though Sewell is kin to many, he is closest kin to Wilson Knight and might be thought, if only he wrote more largely upon Shakespeare, to inherit the mantle from Knight that Knight inherited from Bradley. He has none of Knight's anthropology nor does he find in Shakespeare's career the same spiritual curve that Knight finds there. But he shares the radical conviction that the unity of a Shakespearean play is a unity of vision, that it subsumes all parts of the play, rendering character something less than actual person and, by virtue of its participation in the whole, something more. Sewell summarizes his position in these words:

> I have spoken . . . of vision, discovering itself in character and in conflict between characters, as though vision itself was unfolded in the play, and as though this unfolding was achieved through the embodiment in characters of various addresses to life, all presided over by one supreme and comprehensive address, which was Shakespeare's.

The essay is short, a mere 145 pages. It contains forty-seven consecutively numbered sections, this arrangement indicating the close, consecutive reasoning by which the argument develops. These sections are gathered up into six chapters which set forth the esthetic of vision I have briefly described, then develop implications of this esthetic, starting with the comedies and histories (briefly), through the great tragedies (expansively), and concluding with the Roman plays and the romances (briefly again). The style is classic to Knight's romantic—compressed, restrained, balanced. By virtue of its author's vision, and a vocabulary ever so slightly recondite, it quietly reverberates with wisdom —as the following passages may indicate. They are arranged in the order in which they appear in the book.

Of Shakespeare "darting himself forth" into Falstaff, Sewell says, "at most he does not assume the man; he assumes the attitude." Characters like Falstaff, Iago, Richard III "from moment to moment . . . seem to generate a mimesis of their own personalities, and only in the mimesis is the personality really known."

> When a comic person, of the servant type, makes puns, chops logic, comes to syllogistic conclusions, uses language above his station, as Shakespeare's servants often do, we argue the character, as a sort of hypostatization, from that play upon our social attitudes which is involved in the application of

certain verbal forms to matter unsuited to them. The disrespectful attitude to language is a disrespectful attitude to social order.

Sewell speaks of the "distillation of personality into style" that we recognize in Mercutio and the Bastard. Even in his private moments, Sewell says, Henry V is presented as a "public, a political character"—"as though a play about Mr. Winston Churchill should show him laying bricks, giving the V sign to a crowd of women workers, and talking to the survivors of a torpedoed destroyer. Every moment is, in its own way, an image of man in political society." Falstaff's speech on honor "is the spoken indignation of the individual in revolt against those irksome moral obligations which political order must impose. But, laugh as we may, we do not shuffle those obligations off, and we laugh because we cannot shuffle them off." "Hamlet is not a challenge to our psychological ingenuity; it is a challenge to the faith we seek to live by." "Is not Cordelia's conduct—even though, morally, she could do no other—the kind of conduct for which she must go down on her knees and ask forgiveness?" Wrily he remarks that "Angelo's marriage is not very different from Lucio's." "What do we do with Lear when we psychoanalyze his madness? We reduce him to the shabby validity of our generalizations." The fear in Macbeth "is precisely the same fear which prevented Hamlet from killing the king. It is the Either/Or of our human being." Of Coriolanus and Antony: "pre-eminence in bed or on the battlefield command a social admiration, even while they make us a little uncomfortable." "Is not Ajax the base-bred brother of Coriolanus? He 'professes not answering; speaking is for beggars; he wears his tongue in his arms.'" "Neither the nature of evil nor the nature of goodness is known the better or the more deeply for our reading of Timon." "Leontes is an acting part, rather than a character." "In the Romances all the characters are, in a sense, minor characters."

We return now to elaborate Sewell's critical position. To begin with, there is the playwright's address to the world, his comprehensive vision. The play is the dialectic by which he works out this vision, embodies it, communicates it. By "a prismatic breaking-up" of his vision, he creates his characters—or begins their creation, for actor and audience and communal moral attitudes have a share in them too. The characters are interacting terms of the play's dialectic, conflicting addresses to the world subsidiary to the presiding address of the poet. They have "two different but related activities," action and speech. The one— Macbeth, say, giving himself to darkness—eventuates in plot. The other—Macbeth coming "to terms with his dark universe in words, as he shapes for himself a poetic identity in language, in poetry," eventuates in style. The style is not the language an actual person would use; it is the personality rendered into mimetic verse, and the chief element in style is imagery. "Imagery creates the world as the character apprehends it . . . or rather, as the author imagines, in one activity, the character and the world as that character perceives it."

At this point we can recognize the Platonic harmonies of Sewell's thinking. Imagination creates the embracing, unifying vision which, in turn, creates the characters, themselves subsidiary visions, partial echoes of the central one, and these in turn, exist in and create their worlds by images, the products of imagination, visions yet more fractional than they. Worlds within worlds, visions within visions. Hence Sewell's probing into the imagery of *The Merchant of Venice* where the idea of order in an opulent commercial society finds expression in a host of images from almost everyone in the play and focuses on contractual relations and external law until, "in the last act the idea of order receives a subtle restatement, and becomes the theme of exquisite poetry. External law now gives place in Lorenzo's fancy to a harmony found in immortal souls." Hence the exploration of Angelo's imagery, which "scarcely ever reveals the darker recesses of his being" and betrays the fact that in him "Shakespeare has introduced a situation, a case, and a character, intractable to the working out of the comprehensive vision of the play." Hence the pitting of Othello's imagery against Iago's, the tracing of motifs in *Macbeth*, the touching on the imagery of clothes in *Lear*. Hence, most importantly, the idea that "the relation between character and vision in the tragedies can best be discovered in the nature of the imagery." To this we come shortly.

Character, as Sewell conceives it, is a fragment—or better, element—of the presiding vision, but

> in Shakespeare's mature plays even a minor character will enrich, diversify, and individually quicken the comprehensive view. Of that view he is the product, but in that view he is also an agent. The minor character is not merely a deduction from the theme of the play, related by a kind of dramatic geometry to the whole pattern. In him, as in a single brush-stroke in a picture, a moment of vision, a new angle of attitude, transforms to however small an extent, and lights up, the whole matter.

Barnardine in *Measure for Measure*, who refuses to be hanged because, drunk, he is not "fitted for it," is a case in point, or the clown who brings Cleopatra "the odd worm." But what does it mean to say that the character is both product and agent of vision? Product of Shakespeare's vision and agent to make that vision of ours? But this is banal and reduces Shakespeare to a dramaturgic Edgar Allan Poe, writing with a calculating eye to predetermined effects. The vision in both instances is Shakespeare's—the character both follows from that vision and alters it.

> Drama does not merely give scope to unacted desires; it acts and judges them; and the judgment is in the act of vision. Just as Coleridge could believe that the variety of Nature is, as it were, the other side of Mind, Mind getting to know itself, so we may suppose that the variety of characters in Shakespeare's plays is the other side of Shakespeare's vision, vision getting to know itself.

Rather than Poe, Shakespeare resembles Frost, who goes out on a curve of feeling as he writes, beginning in delight and ending in wisdom.

In the comedies and histories, Sewell finds, the vision is essentially static. It "is generated and deepened, but not transformed," by the characters, "and as we read the play we undergo an illuminating but not a changing experience." "In the comedies and the histories," that is to say, "there is never any real doubt about the world-picture into which the characters must be fitted." The Comic Muse, the ideal of political order, governs, regulates, brings things finally to the end that Shakespeare and we expected. "Our attitudes are never at a loss, and when Henry V comes into his kingdom we know that at last we are where we had hoped to be." In the tragedies it is different: "the hero undergoes an experience which puts all our previous attitude into question and which exacts from us, as from him, a transformation of vision which can accommodate and appropriate the new and uncovenanted experience." The reason is that the tragic hero is a citizen of and addresses himself to the metaphysical as well as to the secular world, this citizenship a matter not of label, as that Portia is a Christian or Pandulph a cardinal, but, ultimately, of language, of imagery. "Hamlet speaks in images which come from man's solitary experiences as well as from his experiences of social and political society." "Othello's mind . . . never expresses itself in secular terms. The invisible universe is all about him; the sun, the moon, and the oceans are the hiding-places of spiritual energies." Macbeth's "imagination draws on assurances and presences which do not come to him from temporal experience, and his discovery of this world of darkness has the authority of a revelation."

The tragic hero, addressing the metaphysical universe, has an uncovenanted experience that demands from him (and his creator, and us) a transformation of vision. The transformation derives from images, "dark materials" "from the unconditioned places of our being"—"Had Iago said 'Goats and monkeys!' it would have been no more than the language of the barracks; but for Othello

to say it is to return to the jungle and smell its beastliness."
Sewell distinguishes between images "derived either from experience settled and ordered in society or from experience unconditioned and private from our solitudes. Imagery may affirm a
public world or suggest and create a private world." Context will
often determine whether an image is of the first class or the
second, "but a preponderance of the second will demand from us
a continual and dynamic settlement after unsettlement, the
fashioning of a new order within disorder." Sewell sums his
argument thus:

> In the tragedies, then, we see the hero returned to dark
> and chaotic sources of being, and these sources, not only in a
> poetical figure, seem to manifest themselves in Nature, in the
> metaphysical universe, as well as in the soul of man. The
> generation of images, the fusion in language of imaginative
> energies into living personality, is a concrete representation, a
> mimesis, of a human soul in the very process of striving for
> identity, for ordered vision, in the prolonged encounter be-
> tween Chaos and Reason, seeking to fashion Chaos into Order.

This presents accurately, I believe, Sewell's central critical
doctrine and hints at its applications. Let us glance at a few of
these. The uncovenanted experience of the tragedies finds "an
elementary form . . . in the discomfitures that attend Shylock,
Malvolio, and perhaps Falstaff"—but the transformation has not
occurred in them or in us, so that our final response is troubled
and narrow, "little more than that less significant pity which we
give to unlucky people in real life." Again, the uncovenanted
experience of Brutus, Hamlet, and Cordelia derives from "our
common predicament," "that action is imperative for man, but
that all action whatsoever involves man in evil." And yet again, the
uncovenanted experience, involving always a conflict between the
temporal and the metaphysical, appears in three different modes in
Shakespeare. In *Othello*, the secular society of Venice, in which

Desdemona participates no less than Iago, is set beside but separate from the single human soul, Othello. In *Macbeth* the single human soul leaves society and plunges into darkness, seeking but never finding its "identity in the dark recesses of its own being." *King Lear* works toward a vision of the hero's identity "wholly involved with the life of society," the "kind of identity which comes to men when they are members of each other."

I shall not summarize the chapter, "Tragedy and the 'Kingdom of Ends,'" to which the last remarks above constitute an introduction—it would be somewhat like paraphrasing a lyric poem. The chapter is the apex to which the entire argument has wound. At its end, in the final paragraph, Sewell, like the heroes whose transformations he celebrates, finds a new address—thus,

> Only through grace, perhaps, if at all, can man find blessedness; and Shakespearean tragedy is tragedy simply because in it Fallen Man seeks to find rehabilitation in "infiniteness"—but without grace. The tragedy is in the failure, and perhaps the failure is general to the case of Man. The tragic character . . . will not resign himself to confinement in the secular world; but he has no certitude of status in a world more absolute. We cannot judge the tragic character in terms of our temporal moralities; neither can we schematize those mysteries of redemption which might at last exempt him from such judgments. He believes that he belongs to this world and he believes that he does not. He would jump the life to come—and yet he dare not. He comes to know that "the readiness is all," but that same ripeness, which releases him from the importunities of this world, discovers for him no other. Shakespearean tragedy is the product of the change in men's minds—the Renaissance change—by which men came to feel themselves separate from God; by which, indeed, the idea of God receded from men's habitual certitudes and became no more and often less than an intellectual construction, a merely credible hypothesis, a Being remote and not

certainly just or beneficent, perhaps the Enemy. In a world where anarchism was of recent development and men had not yet resigned themselves to a disabling opportunism man's perennial hunger for metaphysical being prompted Shakespeare to create supreme drama out of the question, How shall man find the intersection between that which is in time and that which is out of time? Or, to put the matter simply, and I do not think too simply, What shall we do to be saved?

Sewell's gift is to illuminate the tragic, the character suffering at the borders of the metaphysical universe an experience that forces upon him a moral metamorphosis. Certainly he deals little with the comedies and, in the histories, it is obviously Falstaff who (or should we say "that"?) engages him. No matter. What he says about the comedies jibes with what he says about the tragedies, and that, though general, dealing more with embracing contours than individual scene or line, derives from an esthetic which is richly consistent and abundantly applicable. To be sure the esthetic loses for us the psychological profundities of Bradley and Coleridge, Freud and the book's particular scapegoat, J. I. M. Stewart.[1] The gain is character in tune with Stollian and post-Stollian awarenesses, character as construct of actor and audience, working out of theatrical convention and shared moral attitudes, but character richer than Stoll or Harbage permits. This richness is several. In part, it is the richness of moral significance for us: to apprehend character as address to the world engaged with other addresses is to experience drama as meaning rather than entertainment. The deepening and illumination of the comic character, the transformation of the tragic character, are ours. In part it is the richness of moral significance for Shakespeare. No mere entertainer, no story teller with characters bigger than their plots, Shakespeare becomes again what he was for Knight, for Coleridge, a man addressing through his plays his universe, engaging in the dialectic which each must undergo, seeking his and our "salvation." Sewell gives us in a single, dynamic curve the moral esthetics of Shakespeare, his characters, ourselves.

When he comes to individual cases, I find myself in occasional disagreement. It is questionable, in such comedies as *Twelfth Night* and *Much Ado* with their deaths and resurrections, their hints of miracle and grace, that the regulating principle is the Comic Muse or Social Order. A fair case may be made, and by Coghill has been made, that divine beneficence in fact rules here in the Christian tradition.[2] Again, I cannot see Desdemona as significantly sharing with Iago a secular universe while Othello belongs uniquely to a metaphysical one. Many must feel that Desdemona and Othello share it against the secular world and that Othello, finally, sells out to the secular enemy. More deeply, I question the definition of the moral dilemma, that man must act but that action involves him in evil. If Shakespeare meant this, of Brutus, of Hamlet, of Cordelia, surely we might expect to find him saying it. He does not. Moreover, the statement is moot because its central term rests undefined. Is "evil" the displeasure of the gods, the turning from divine light, the tainting of the prejudiced soul, the producing of pain? Are the ethics here of intent or effect? Is the evil the result of action any more than of inaction? And is evil, in fact, evil or simply embarrassment? I quibble, perhaps, but to force the issue.

Disagreements do matter, but they do not come lightly, nor is Sewell's essential esthetic jeopardized. This and the book that contain it are remarkable and in the great tradition. As M. C. Bradbrook writes, "Here is esthetics and 'practical criticism' blended in a manner which is not often met with . . . In its rare combination of lucidity and depth this is a memorable work, one to be taken slowly, and to be 'chewed and digested.' "[3]

Notes

CHAPTER I

1. This chapter derives its illustrative quotations from the sources listed below. Where there are references to different works by the same author, these appear in the order they appear in the chapter. Works marked with * may be found in an immensely useful volume, *Shakespeare Criticism: A Selection*, ed., D. Nichol Smith (1916).

Joseph Addison, **Spectator*, No. 592 (September 10, 1714); No. 61 (May 10, 1711).

Francis Bacon, *The Advancement of Learning* (1605), Book II, Section IV.2.

Margaret Cavendish, *CCXI Sociable Letters* (1664), *Letter CXXIII.

John Dennis, *An Essay on the Genius and Writings of Shakespear* (1712), Letter I.

John Dryden, **An Essay of Dramatic Poesy* (1668); Preface to *Troilus and Cressida*, "Containing the Grounds of Criticism in Tragedy" (1679); *Prologue to *The Tempest* (1667, pub. 1670); Preface to *All for Love* (1678).

John Heminge and Henry Condell, *"To the Great Variety of Readers," Preface to *Mr. William Shakespeare's Comedies, Histories, and Tragedies* (1623).

Samuel Johnson, *Preface, *The Plays of William Shakespeare* (1765).

Ben Jonson, *"To the Memory of My Beloved, the Author Mr. William Shakespeare: and What He Hath Left Us," prefixed to the First Folio (1623); *"De Shakespeare nostrati," Timber: or, Discoveries* (1641); Prologue to *Everyman in His Humour* (1601).

Francis Meres, *Palladis Tamia: Wit's Treasury* (1598).

John Milton, *"An Epitaph on the Admirable Dramatic Poet, W. Shakespeare," prefixed to the Second Folio (1632); "L'Allegro" (1632?), *The Poems of Mr. John Milton* (1645).

Alexander Pope, *Preface to *The Works of Shakespear* (1725).

Nicholas Rowe, *"Some Account of the Life of Mr. William Shakespear," Preface to *The Works of Mr. William Shakespear* (1709).

Thomas Rymer, *A Short View of Tragedy* (1693), Chap. VII.

Sir Philip Sidney, *An Apology for Poetry* (1583?, pub. 1595).

Voltaire, Preface to *Brutus*, "Discours sur la Tragédie" (1731); Preface to *Sémiramis*, "Dissertation sur la Tragédie Ancienne et Moderne" (1748).

CHAPTER II

1. Robert W. Babcock, *The Genesis of Shakespeare Idolatry 1766–1799: A Study in English Criticism of the Late Eighteenth Century* (1931).

2. T. J. B. Spencer, "The Tyranny of Shakespeare," Annual Shakespeare Lecture of the British Academy, 1959, *The Proceedings of the British Academy*, XLV (1959), 171.

3. I must not give Johnson undue credit. His contribution is that he saw and endorsed at an important juncture of critical history what others had seen and argued for, if less successfully, before him. In Dryden's *Essay of Dramatic Poesy* (1668), for example, Neander argues that the soul of man is surely less heavy than his senses, which pass from the unpleasant to the pleasant in a twinkling, that contraries placed near each other set each other off, that continued gravity wearies the spirit, which needs relief, that "mirth, mixed with tragedy, has the same effect upon us which our music has betwixt the acts; which we find a relief to us from the best plots and language on the stage, if the discourses have been long."

4. As with his defense of tragicomedy, Johnson's attack on the unities of time and place is important less for its originality than for its authority and cogency. In Chap. 23 of his *Elements of Criticism*

(1762), Henry Home, Lord Kames, had argued that the reflective spectator is conscious that Garrick is not Lear, the playhouse not Dover Cliffs, and the noise not thunder and lightning: "And indeed it is abundantly ridiculous, that a critic, who is willing to hold candlelight for sunshine, and some painted canvasses for a palace or a prison, should be so scrupulous about admitting any latitude of place or of time in the fable, beyond what is necessary in the representation."

5. D. Nichol Smith, *Shakespeare in the Eighteenth Century* (1928), p. 80.

6. *Rambler*, No. 18 (August 12, 1758).

7. *Rambler*, No. 32 (November 25, 1758).

CHAPTER III

1. G. G. Gervinus, *Shakespeare Commentaries* (1849–1850), trans., F. E. Bunnett (1862), Vol. I, Introduction.

2. G. E. Lessing, *Hamburg Dramaturgy*, No. 11 (June 5, 1767), in *Selected Prose Works of G. E. Lessing*, trans., Helen Zimmern (c. 1890).

3. *Ibid.*, No. 15 (June 19, 1767).

4. *Ibid.*

5. *Ibid.*, No. 73 (January 12, 1768).

6. *Ibid.*, No. 81 (February 9, 1768).

7. *Ibid.*, No. 96 (April 1, 1768).

8. W. von Schlegel, *Course of Lectures on Dramatic Art and Literature*, trans., John Black (1815), rev., A. J. W. Morrison (1846).

9. *Hamburg Dramaturgy*, No. 70 (January 1, 1768).

10. Joseph Warton, *The Adventurer*, No. 122 (January 5, 1754); reprinted in *Shakespeare Criticism: A Survey*, ed., D. Nichol Smith (1916).

11. George Santayana, Introduction to *Hamlet*, *The University Press Shakespeare*, Renaissance Edition, XXX (1908); L. C. Knights, *An Approach to Hamlet* (1960).

12. E. M. W. Tillyard, *Shakespeare's History Plays* (1946); Lily Bess Campbell, *Shakespeare's "Histories": Mirrors of Elizabethan Policy* (1947).

13. Maynard Mack, "The World of *Hamlet*," *The Yale Review*, XLI (1952), 502–523; Harry Levin, *The Question of Hamlet* (1959).

CHAPTER IV

1. Robert W. Babcock, *The Genesis of Shakespeare Idolatry* (1931), pp. 125–126.
2. Asked his opinion of Morgann's *Essay*, Johnson remarked, "Why, Sir, we shall have the man come forth again; and as he has proved Falstaff to be no coward, he may prove Iago to be a very good character." James Boswell, *The Life of Samuel Johnson* (1791), for the year 1783, aet. 74.
3. The collection of this material has been accomplished in Samuel Taylor Coleridge, *Shakespearean Criticism*, ed., Thomas Middleton Raysor, 2 vols. (1930; 2d ed., 1960). From this a good selection has been made in *Coleridge's Writings on Shakespeare*, ed., Terence Hawkes (1959), and from this, with only slight exceptions, I have drawn the Coleridgean criticism quoted in this chapter.
4. T. M. Raysor, *op. cit.*, 2d ed. (1960), I, xxvi.
5. Anna Augusta Helmholtz, *The Indebtedness of Samuel Taylor Coleridge to August Wilhelm von Schlegel*, Bulletin of the University of Wisconsin, No. 163 (1907), 356.
6. Alfred Harbage, "Introduction," *Coleridge's Writings on Shakespeare*, ed., Terence Hawkes (1959), p. 25.
7. Coleridge, *Biographia Literaria* (1817), Chap. XIII.
8. John Middleton Murry, *Shakespeare* (1936), p. 295. The passages quoted later in this paragraph are from p. 296.
9. Addison, *Spectator*, No. 279 (January 19, 1712).
10. For Friedrich Schlegel's position, I am indebted to M. H. Abrams, *The Mirror and the Lamp: Romantic Theory and the Critical Tradition* (1953), p. 240, and through Abrams, to A. E. Lussky, *Tieck's Romantic Irony* (1932), p. 69.

CHAPTER V

1. Goethe, *Wilhelm Meister's Apprenticeship*, Bk. IV, Chap. 13, trans., Thomas Carlyle (1824). Goethe's main Shakespearean criticism appears in *Wilhelm Meister*; in *Shakespeare ad Infinitum* (*Schäkespear und kein Ende!*, 1815; *Goethe's Literary Essays*, arranged by J. E. Spingarn, trans., Randolph S. Bourne, 1921); and in Johann Peter

Eckermann, *Conversations of Goethe with Eckermann and Soret*
(1835, 1847; trans., John Oxenford, 1850; reprinted 1909). Unless
otherwise indicated, the material quoted from Goethe is from *Shakespeare ad Infinitum.*

2. Eckermann, p. 50.

3. *Ibid.*, p. 310.

4. *Wilhelm Meister*, Bk. III, Chap. 11.

5. *Ibid.*, Bk. IV, Chap. 16.

6. *Ibid.*, Bk. V, Chap. 6.

7. *Ibid.*, Bk. IV, Chap. 3.

8. *Ibid.*, Bk. V, Chap. 5.

9. Eckermann, p. 114.

10. *Ibid.*, p. 216.

11. *Ibid.*, p. 249.

12. *Ibid.*, p. 250.

13. The quotations in this paragraph are from *Wilhelm Meister*,
Bk. V, Chap. 7.

14. The quotations in this paragraph are from *Wilhelm Meister*,
Bk. V, Chap. 4.

15. Arnold's best known Shakespearean criticism is his fine sonnet of tribute that begins, "Others abide our question. Thou art free"
("Shakespeare," 1849), but he sounds the note of unblinking judi-
ciousness in his Preface to *Poems by Matthew Arnold, A New Edition*
(1853), where he speaks of Shakespeare's falling below the Ancients
in "clearness of arrangement, rigor of development, [and] simplicity of
style"; and later he complains of *Hamlet* that "it will never . . . be a
piece to be seen with pure satisfaction by those who will not deceive
themselves." "Hamlet Once More," *Pall Mall Gazette* (December 6,
1884), *Letters of an Old Playgoer* (1919), Chap. V.

16. Lamb's principal Shakespearean criticism appears in "On the
Tragedies of Shakspeare, Considered with Reference to Their Fitness
for Stage Representation," *The Reflector*, No. 4 (1811, reprinted in
Shakespeare Criticism: A Survey, ed., D. Nichol Smith, 1916)—my
concern in this chapter; in notes scattered through *Specimens of English Dramatic Poets Who Lived About the Time of Shakspeare* (1808,
subsequently collected under the title, *Characters of Dramatic Writers
Contemporary with Shakspeare*, 1808); and finally if indirectly, and
perhaps ultimately more influential than the others, in the *Tales from
Shakspeare* (1807) he wrote with Mary Ann Lamb.

17. Cf. Hazlitt's review, "Miss O'Neill's Juliet," *The Champion*
(October 16, 1814): Mrs. Siddons' "manner of rubbing her hands in

the night scene in *Macbeth*, and of dismissing the guests at the banquet, were among her finest things." *Hazlitt on Theatre*, ed., William Archer and Robert Lowe (1957—a reprinting of *Dramatic Essays*, Vol. II, 1895).

18. Francis Jeffrey, *The Edinburgh Review* (August, 1817), reprinted in *Shakespeare Criticism: A Survey*, ed., D. Nichol Smith (1916).

19. Unless otherwise indicated, quotations are from Hazlitt's *Characters of Shakespear's Plays* (1817).

20. Hazlitt, *Lectures on the English Poets* (1818).

21. Thomas Gray, Letter to Richard West, April, 1742; first published in William Mason, *Memoirs of Gray* (1775); reprinted in *Shakespeare Criticism: A Survey*, ed., D. Nichol Smith (1916).

22. Nevill Coghill, "The Basis of Shakespearian Comedy," *Essays and Studies of the English Association*, New Series, III (1950), 1–28.

23. In his Preface to *Man and Superman* (1903), Shaw blithely calls *Coriolanus* "the greatest of Shakespeare's comedies." For Lewis's remarks, see pp. 233–234 in this book.

24. The reviews quoted in this and the following paragraph originally appeared in *The Champion*, *The Examiner*, *The Morning Chronicle*, and *The London Magazine* in the years 1814–1820. They are conveniently collected in *Hazlitt on Theatre*, ed., Archer and Lowe (1957).

CHAPTER VI

1. *Shakespeare Commentaries* is the English title of G. G. Gervinus, *Shakespeare* (1849–1850), trans., F. E. Bunnett from the 2d German ed. (1862).

2. Walter Pater, "Shakespeare's English Kings," *Scribner's Magazine* (April, 1889); *Appreciations* (1889).

3. Harold C. Goddard, *The Meaning of Shakespeare* (1951), Chap. XIII, Sec. iii.

4. Augustus Ralli, *A History of Shakespearian Criticism* (1932), I, 353.

5. Hermann Ulrici, *Shakespeare's Dramatic Art* (1839).

6. Donald Stauffer, *Shakespeare's World of Images: The Development of His Moral Ideas* (1949). Hubler and Harbage are discussed hereafter, in Chaps. XV and XVI.

7. Ralph Waldo Emerson, "Shakspeare: or, The Poet," *Representative Men* (1850).

8. The comment on Shakespeare's gentleness appears in a letter to Evert A. Duyckinck, February 24, 1849, *The Letters of Herman Melville*, ed., Merrel R. Davis and William H. Gilman (1960); the quotation is from Melville's famous review, "Hawthorne and His Mosses," *The Literary World* (August 17, 1850).

9. Sidney Lanier, "Chaucer and Shakspere" (1880), *Music and Poetry* (1898).

10. George Puttenham, "Of Language," *The Arte of English Poesie* (1589), reprinted in *Elizabethan Critical Essays*, ed., G. Gregory Smith (1904), Vol. II.

11. This notion peculiarly afflicts the nineteenth-century critics of Hamlet, and even Bradley focuses on the Prince of Denmark without much regard to other questions. Gervinus had said "that the true point of unity in [Shakespeare's] works ever leads to the hidden grounds, from which their actions spring." But Gervinus himself customarily seeks the source of unity less in character than in idea.

12. George Santayana, Introduction to *Hamlet, The University Press Shakespeare*, Renaissance Edition, XXX (1908); L. C. Knights, *An Approach to Hamlet* (1960).

CHAPTER VII

1. F. G. Fleay recognized four periods (I. rhyming, II. comedy and history, III. tragedy, IV. Roman and final) in "On Metrical Tests as Applied to Dramatic Poetry. Part I. Shakspere," *The New Shakspere Society's Transactions* (1874), 1–16. F. G. Furnivall follows Fleay in his Introduction to the 1874 edition of Gervinus's *Shakespeare Commentaries*, trans., F. E. Bunnett. Furnivall, moreover, develops a biographical reading of the four periods which provides Dowden with a model, however primitive, for his own enterprise. According to Furnivall, the young and happy Shakespeare (period I) deepened in his knowledge of the world (period II), then suffered some sort of spiritual setback and wrote bitterly on such matters as betrayal (period III), but recovered faith and sanity, finally, in the restorative environs of Stratford (period IV).

2. Thomas De Quincey, "On the Knocking at the Gate in 'Macbeth,'" *The London Magazine* (October, 1823); reprinted in *Shakespeare Criticism: A Survey*, ed., D. Nichol Smith (1916).

3. Geoffrey L. Bickersteth, "The Golden World of 'King Lear,'" Annual Shakespeare Lecture of the British Academy, 1946, *The Proceedings of the British Academy*, XXXII (1946), 147–171; Jan Kott, "King Lear or Endgame," *Shakespeare Our Contemporary*, trans., Boleslaw Taborski (1964). Knight is discussed hereafter, in Chap. XII.

4. Samuel Smiles, *Self-Help: with Illustrations of Character and Conduct* (1859); T. J. B. Spencer, "The Tyranny of Shakespeare," Annual Shakespeare Lecture of the British Academy, 1959, *The Proceedings of the British Academy*, XLV (1959), 169.

5. H. A. Taine, "Shakespeare," *Histoire de la Littérature Anglaise* (1863), Bk. II, Chap. 4.

6. Sidney Lanier, "Chaucer and Shakspere" (1880), *Music and Poetry* (1898); Lytton Strachey, *Shakespeare's Final Period* (1906), *Books and Characters* (1922); D. A. Traversi, *Approach to Shakespeare* (1938). Harris, Jones, and Lewis are discussed hereafter, in Chap. XI; Murry and Spurgeon, in Chap. XIII.

7. Kenneth Muir, "Changing Interpretations of Shakespeare," *The Age of Shakespeare*, Vol. II of *A Guide to English Literature*, ed., Boris Ford (1955), p. 291. Of Swinburne's many works on Shakespeare, I have focused on the principal: *A Study of Shakespeare* (1880).

8. Pater wrote three essays on Shakespeare: "Measure for Measure," *Fortnightly Review* (November, 1874); "Love's Labour's Lost," *Macmillan's Magazine* (December, 1885); and "Shakespeare's English Kings," *Scribner's Magazine* (April, 1889). All three essays are included in *Appreciations* (1889).

CHAPTER VIII

1. Middleton Murry, *Pencillings* (1923), p. 95, quoted in *Shaw on Shakespeare*, ed., Edwin Wilson (1961). This volume ably brings together the Shakespearean criticism Shaw scattered through his letters and reviews (for the *Saturday Review*, 1895–1898), his prefaces, plays, and speeches; with one or two slight exceptions I have drawn from it the Shavian material quoted in this chapter.

2. From *Tolstoy on Shakespeare*, trans., V. Tchertkoff (1907), reprinted in *Shakespeare in Europe*, ed., Oswald LeWinter (1963). LeWinter's comments, quoted here, appear on p. 223.

3. Orwell has a different image. Tolstoy's reaction to Shakespeare, he says, "is that of an irritable old man who is being pestered by a

noisy child. 'Why do you keep jumping up and down like that? Why can't you sit still like I do?' In a way the old man is in the right, but the trouble is that the child has a feeling in its limbs which the old man has lost." George Orwell, "Lear, Tolstoy, and the Fool" (1945), *Shooting an Elephant and Other Essays* (1950), pp. 41–42.

4. Bradley, *Shakespearean Tragedy* (1904), Lecture VII, attacks *Lear* at this very point: "That which makes the peculiar greatness of *King Lear*,—the immense scope of the work; the mass and variety of intense experience which it contains; the interpenetration of sublime imagination, piercing pathos, and humor almost as moving as the pathos; the vastness of the convulsion both of nature and of human passion; the vagueness of the scene where the action .takes place, and of the movements of the figures which cross this scene; the strange atmosphere, cold and dark, which strikes on us as we enter this scene, enfolding these figures and magnifying their dim outlines like a winter mist; the half-realized suggestions of vast universal powers working in the world of individual fates and passions,—all this interferes with dramatic clearness even when the play is read, and in the theater not only refuses to reveal itself fully through the senses but seems to be almost in contradiction with their reports."

5. Lily Bess Campbell, *Shakespeare's "Histories": Mirrors of Elizabethan Policy* (1947). Tillyard, Harbage, and Spencer are discussed hereafter, in Chap. XV.

6. Francis Fergusson, "*Hamlet, Prince of Denmark:* The Analogy of Action," *The Idea of a Theater* (1949). Frye and Barber are discussed hereafter, in Chap. XVII.

CHAPTER IX

1. Bradley has other, important Shakespearean criticism in *Oxford Lectures on Poetry* (1909), which contains essays on "Hegel's Theory of Tragedy" (pretty much Bradley's own theory), "The Rejection of Falstaff," "Shakespeare's Antony and Cleopatra," "Shakespeare the Man," and "Shakespeare's Theatre and Audience"; but I have focused on *Shakespearean Tragedy* alone.

2. Charles F. Johnson, *Shakespeare and His Critics* (1909), p. 321.

3. *Ibid.*

4. Augustus Ralli, A History of Shakespearean Criticism (1932), II, 200.

5. Maynard Mack, "The World of Hamlet," The Yale Review, XLI (1952), 502–523. Knight is discussed hereafter, in Chap. XII.

6. The titles respectively of Mary Cowden Clarke's three volume work (1850–1852) and of L. C. Knights' essay (1933).

7. Kenneth Muir, "Changing Interpretations of Shakespeare," The Age of Shakespeare, Vol. II of A Guide to English Literature, ed., Boris Ford (1955), p. 291.

8. Ibid., p. 292.

CHAPTER X

1. Robert Bridges, "On the Influence of the Audience," The Works of William Shakespeare, Stratford Town Edition, X (1907).

2. Morgann, of course, had recognized this contrast long before: see in this book, p. 54.

3. Stoll's Shakespearean criticism begins early and continues late: "Anachronism in Shakespeare Criticism," Modern Philology, VII (1907), 557–575; "The Objectivity of the Ghosts in Shakespeare," Publications of the Modern Language Association, XXII, New Series, XV (1907), 201–233; "Shylock," Journal of English and Germanic Philology, X (1911), 236–279; "Criminals in Shakespeare and in Science," Modern Philology, X (1912–1913), 55–80; Othello: An Historical and Comparative Study (1915); Hamlet: An Historical and Comparative Study (1919); Shakespeare Studies, Historical and Comparative in Method (1927, 2d ed., 1942); "Cleopatra," Modern Language Review, XXIII (1928), 145–163; Poets and Playwrights (1930), Art and Artifice in Shakespeare (1933); Shakespeare's Young Lovers (1935); Shakespeare and Other Masters (1940). I have focused exclusively on Shakespeare Studies, rev. ed., corrected (1960), because it reviews and sums Stoll's principal contributions.

4. "The danger of studying [Shakespeare] alone," says T. S. Eliot in his Introduction to Wilson Knight's The Wheel of Fire (1930), "is the danger of working into the essence of Shakespeare what is just convention and the dodges of an overworked and underpaid writer; the danger of studying him with his contemporaries is the danger of reducing a unique vision to a mode."

5. Gabriel Harvey in a MS note to Speght's *Chaucer* (1598), in E. K. Chambers, *William Shakespeare: A Study of Facts and Problems* (1930), II, 197.

6. *His Infinite Variety: Major Shakespearean Criticism Since Johnson*, ed., Paul N. Siegel (1964), p. 130.

7. Levin L. Schücking, *Character Problems in Shakespeare's Plays* (1917), trans., W. H. Peters (1922).

CHAPTER XI

1. Frank Harris, *The Man Shakespeare and His Tragic Life-Story* (1909). Ernest Jones, *Hamlet and Oedipus* (1949), p. 132.

2. J. O. Halliwell, "The Last Days of Shakespeare," *The Saint James's Magazine*, I (1861), 285.

3. Walter Raleigh, *Shakespeare*, English Men of Letters (1907), Chap. I.

4. Jones, *Hamlet and Oedipus* (1949). This book constitutes the last of a series of revisions Jones gave to his original essay, "The Oedipus-Complex as an Explanation of Hamlet's Mystery: A Study in Motive," *The American Journal of Psychology*, XXI (1910), 72–113.

5. Otto Rank, "Das 'Schauspiel' in 'Hamlet,' " *Imago*, IV (1915–1916), 41–51.

6. Francis Fergusson, "*Hamlet, Prince of Denmark*: The Analogy of Action," *The Idea of a Theater* (1949), p. 111.

7. Wyndham Lewis, *The Lion and the Fox: The Rôle of the Hero in the Plays of Shakespeare* (1927).

8. Contrast Taine, who quotes Hamlet's description, in the closet scene, of his father—

A station like the herald Mercury
New-lighted on a heaven-kissing hill—

and comments, "This charming vision, in the midst of a bloody invective, proves that there lurks a painter underneath the poet. Involuntarily and out of season, he tears off the tragic mask which covered his face; and the reader discovers, behind the contracted features of this terrible mask, a graceful and inspired smile of which he had not dreamed." H. A. Taine, *A History of English Literature* (1861), trans., H. Van Laun (1871), I, 308.

CHAPTER XII

1. Knight's Shakespearean criticism begins with *Myth and Miracle* (1929), and proceeds through *The Wheel of Fire* (1930), *The Imperial Theme* (1931), *The Shakespearian Tempest* (1932), *Principles of Shakespearian Production* (1936), *The Crown of Life* (1947), *The Mutual Flame* (1955), and *The Sovereign Flower* (1958). Except for a few references to *Myth and Miracle*, I have focused exclusively on *The Wheel of Fire*, the work that brought Knight explosively and fully formed upon the Shakespearean scene.

2. *His Infinite Variety: Major Shakespearean Criticism Since Johnson*, ed., Paul N. Siegel (1964), p. 287.

3. Lytton Strachey, *Shakespeare's Final Period* (1906), *Books and Characters* (1922).

4. L. C. Knights, *An Approach to Hamlet* (1960).

5. I am thinking particularly here of Traversi's early volume, *Approach to Shakespeare* (1938), and of Mack's early essay, "The World of *Hamlet*," *The Yale Review*, XLI (1952), 502–523. Murry is discussed hereafter, in Chap. XIII.

CHAPTER XIII

1. Caroline F. E. Spurgeon, "The Revelation of the Man," Part I of *Shakespeare's Imagery and What It Tells Us* (1935).

2. D. A. Traversi, *Approach to Shakespeare* (1938). The other critics mentioned here are discussed in this or the preceding chapters.

3. John Middleton Murry, *Shakespeare* (1936).

4. John Aubrey, *Brief Lives*, quoted by E. K. Chambers, who dates the passage dealing with Shakespeare 1681: *William Shakespeare: A Study of Facts and Problems* (1930), II, 252–254. Nicholas Rowe, "Some Account of the Life of Mr. William Shakespear," Preface to *The Works of Mr. William Shakespear* (1709), in *Shakespeare Criticism: A Survey*, ed., D. Nichol Smith (1916).

5. William Wordsworth, "Scorn Not the Sonnet" (1827), lines 2–3: "with this key Shakespeare unlocked his heart."

6. Edward A. Armstrong, *Shakespeare's Imagination* (1946), rev. ed. (1963).

CHAPTER XIV

1. M. C. Bradbrook, "Fifty Years of the Criticism of Shakespeare's Style: A Retrospect," *Shakespeare Survey*, VII (1954), 9. Spurgeon develops her concept of undersong, which is our concern here, in "The Function of the Imagery as Background and Undertone in Shakespeare's Art," Part II of *Shakespeare's Imagery and What It Tells Us* (1935).

2. L. C. Knights, *How Many Children Had Lady Macbeth?* (1933), *Explorations* (1946).

3. C. S. Lewis, "Hamlet: The Prince or the Poem?" Annual Shakespeare Lecture of the British Academy, 1942, *The Proceedings of the British Academy*, XXVIII (1942), 139–154.

4. Maynard Mack, "The World of *Hamlet*," *The Yale Review*, XLI (1952), 502–523; Robert B. Heilman, *The Great Stage: Image and Structure in King Lear* (1948), and *Magic in the Web: Action and Language in Othello* (1956).

5. Cleanth Brooks, *The Well Wrought Urn* (1947), Chap. 2.

6. This is the English title of the 2d ed. (1951) of Clemen's *Shakespeares Bilder. Ihre Entwicklung und Ihre Funktionen im dramatischen Werk* (1936). My quotations are from the 2d ed., but I have avoided, I believe, including material that was not in the first.

7. Lamb, note to the selection from *The Two Noble Kinsmen* in *Specimens of the English Dramatic Poets* (1808). Clemen seems more conscious of coherence than Lamb, and Lamb more than Taine. "Shakespeare flies," says Taine, "we creep. Hence comes a style made up of concepts, bold images shattered in an instant by others still bolder, barely indicated ideas completed by others far removed, no visible connection, but a visible incoherence; at every step we halt, the track failing; and there, far above us, lo, stands the poet . . ." *A History of English Literature* (1861), trans., H. Van Laun (1871), I, 309.

CHAPTER XV

1. Samuel Johnson, "Dryden," *Lives of the Poets* (1779–1781).

2. S. C. Chew in his review of Spencer's *Shakespeare and the Nature of Man*, *Books* (January 10, 1943).

3. Jenkins, "Shakespeare's History Plays," *Shakespeare Survey*, VI (1953), 1–14.

4. Spencer quotes from A. O. Lovejoy, *The Great Chain of Being* (1936), pp. 101–102.

5. My concern here is with Harbage's *Shakespeare and the Rival Traditions* (1952); in Chap. XVI, I examine his *As They Liked It* (1947); but his contributions to Shakespeare study extend far beyond these. To mention only the most salient, *Annals of the English Drama, 970–1700* (1940), *Shakespeare's Audience* (1941), and *Theatre for Shakespeare* (1955).

6. G. B. Harrison's review of Harbage's *Shakespeare and the Rival Traditions*, *The Saturday Review*, XXXVI (October 10, 1953).

7. T. S. Eliot, "Hamlet and His Problems" (1919) and "Shakespeare and the Stoicism of Seneca" (1927), *Selected Essays, 1917–1932* (1932).

CHAPTER XVI

1. These prefaces, published in different years from 1927 on, have been gathered in Harley Granville-Barker, *Prefaces to Shakespeare*, 2 vols. (1946–1947).

CHAPTER XVII

1. Francis Fergusson, "*Hamlet, Prince of Denmark*: The Analogy of Action," *The Idea of a Theater* (1949), p. 117. Frye is discussed in the final part of the present chapter.

2. Frank Kermode, review of Northrop Frye, *A Natural Perspective*, in *The New York Review of Books* (April 22, 1965).

3. Philip Edwards, "The Year's Contributions to Shakespearian Studies, 1. Critical Studies," *Shakespeare Survey*, XVI (1963), 155.

4. Frank Kermode, review of John Holloway, *The Story of the Night*, in *New Statesman*, LXII (December 29, 1961).

5. "I have never," says T. S. Eliot, "seen a cogent refutation of Thomas Rymer's objections to *Othello*." "Hamlet and His Problems" (1919), *Selected Essays, 1917–1932* (1932), p. 121. For Rymer's objections, see above, p. 5.

6. Reuben Brower, review of Northrop Frye, *A Natural Perspective*, in *Partisan Review*, XXXIII (1966), 132–136.

CHAPTER XVIII

1. J. I. M. Stewart, *Character and Motive in Shakespeare* (1949).
2. Nevill Coghill, "The Basis of Shakespearian Comedy," *Essays and Studies of the English Association*, New Series, III (1950), 1–28.
3. M. C. Bradbrook, "The Year's Contributions to Shakespearian Study, 1. Critical Studies," *Shakespeare Survey*, VI (1953), 150.

Index

Addison, Joseph, 4, 8, 11, 14–15, 17, 73, 75

All's Well That Ends Well, 27, 28, 47, 123, 142, 152, 166, 170, 171, 309, 311, 318, 338, 373, 374, 375

Antony and Cleopatra, 9, 11, 18, 31, 32, 48, 57, 85, 122, 124, 126, 144, 148, 171, 172, 176, 188, 198, 200, 217, 218, 221, 230, 233, 235, 250, 260, 261, 269, 271, 273, 307, 310, 311, 313, 314, 318, 319, 321, 324, 325, 327–334, 342, 362, 363, 367, 368, 369, 386, 388

Aristotle, 9, 37, 39, 88, 121, 242

Armstrong, Edward A., 259, 270–280, 287, 294, 327

Arnold, Matthew, 93

As You Like It, 50, 101, 165, 166, 167, 169, 221, 222, 266, 309, 310, 312, 338, 355, 356, 371, 375, 379

Aubrey, John, 262

Babcock, Robert W., 25

Bacon, Francis, 11, 145, 214, 253

Barber, C. L., 184, 344, 354–361

Barry, Spranger, 113

Beaumont, Francis, 306

Bible, 299, 363, 364, 365, 366

Bickersteth, Geoffrey L., 144

Booth, Junius Brutus, 113

Bowdler, Thomas, 74

Bradbrook, M. C., 281, 393

Bradley, A. C., xxii, 51, 117–118, 157, 182, 184, 186–204, 206, 209, 224, 243–244, 247–248, 270, 285, 297, 349, 351, 353, 361, 381, 383, 384, 392, 401, 403

Bridges, Robert, 85, 205–209, 210, 213, 268, 335, 336, 342

Brooks, Cleanth, 288–290

Brower, Reuben, 381–382

Bunnett, F. E., 116

Campbell, Lily Bess, 49, 184

Campbell, Mrs. Patrick, 167, 175

Carlyle, Thomas, 25

Cavendish, Margaret, 9
Chapman, George, 253, 306
Chaucer, Geoffrey, 104, 105, 106
Clarke, Mary Cowden, 58, 202
Clemen, Wolfgang, 268, 290–295, 384
Coghill, Nevill, 106, 107, 393
Coke, Edward, 210
Coleridge, Samuel Taylor, xx, xxi, xxii, 19, 25, 63–79, 89, 90, 93, 106, 110, 111, 122, 133, 149, 157, 164, 186, 187, 189, 199, 201, 202, 206, 223, 239, 268, 277, 279, 283, 285, 290, 312, 327, 349, 381, 388, 392
Collier, John Payne, 63
Comedy of Errors, The, 156, 310, 374
Condell, Henry, 8, 278, 327
Copernicus, Nicolaus, 303
Coriolanus, 29, 57, 85, 89, 102, 105, 112, 123, 124, 153, 196, 198, 200, 208, 216, 233–234, 236, 273, 284, 311, 324, 362, 369, 386, 400
Corneille, Pierre, 37, 39
Cymbeline, 44, 47, 96, 97, 105, 110, 111, 123, 124, 125, 166, 172, 174, 250, 266, 324, 373, 379

Daly, Augustin, 165
Dante, 121, 131, 192
Dekker, Thomas, 253, 306
Dennis, John, 10, 29
DeQuincey, Thomas, 144
Donne, John, 214, 303
Dowden, Edward, 77, 116, 117, 130, 139–151, 152, 153, 154, 155, 157, 167, 168, 169, 171, 186, 223, 224, 239, 248, 290
Dryden, John, 4, 6–7, 8, 9, 11, 73, 121, 196, 297, 396

Eckermann, Johann Peter, 81, 84
Edwards, Philip, 361
Eliot, T. S., 26, 65, 315, 385, 404, 408
Elizabeth I, 213, 223
Emerson, Ralph Waldo, xxiii, 25, 130

Essex, Robert Devereux, 2nd Earl of, 223, 227

Fergusson, Francis, 184, 228, 355
Fitton, Mary, 221, 224
Fleay, F. G., 401
Fletcher, John, 8, 306
Frye, Northrop, 184, 344, 355, 361, 370–382
Furnivall, F. J., 116, 401

Garrick, David, 94, 113, 166
Gervinus, Georg Gottfried, 35, 116–130, 149, 150, 161, 162, 163, 182–183, 184, 228, 230, 313, 361, 401
Goddard, Harold C., 120
Goethe, Johann Wolfgang von, 69, 80–93, 122, 131, 133, 138, 164, 183, 217, 257
Granville-Barker, Harley, xxii, 322–335
Gray, Thomas, 103
Greene, Robert, 262
Griffith, Mrs. Elizabeth, 53

Hall, Edward, 303
Halliwell-Phillips, J. O., 220
Hamlet, xix, xx, xxi, 5–6, 8, 10, 13, 28, 29, 33, 36, 45, 46, 48, 50, 51, 52, 63, 66–67, 70–74, 78, 80, 81–83, 89–93, 94, 95, 96, 97, 99, 101, 103, 114–115, 117, 118–119, 121, 122, 123, 124, 126, 127, 128, 130, 135–138, 142, 144, 146, 147, 148, 150, 152–153, 167, 168, 170, 172, 173, 181, 182, 187, 191, 192, 193, 196, 197, 198–199, 200, 201, 202, 203, 206, 209, 211, 213–214, 215, 216, 217, 218, 221, 222, 223, 224–228, 231, 233, 234, 238, 239–240, 242, 243, 249–250, 255, 258, 266–268, 270–271, 273, 279, 284, 285, 287, 304, 308, 310, 313, 314, 315, 319, 320, 321, 324, 336, 337, 338, 340, 342, 355, 362, 367, 368, 384, 386, 389, 390, 393, 401
Harbage, Alfred, 65, 126, 184, 209,

304–314, 318, 322, 335–344, 351, 383, 384, 392
Harris, Frank, 77, 147, 177, 219–223, 224, 227, 236, 257, 259, 270, 279
Harrison, G. B., 305
Harvey, Gabriel, 214
Hawthorne, Nathaniel, xxiii
Hazlitt, William, 100–115, 157, 167, 186, 187, 200, 243, 323, 324
Hegel, George William F., 184
Heilman, Robert B., 287
Helmholtz, Anna Augusta, 64
Heminge, John, 8, 278, 327
Henry IV–I, 8, 9, 33, 46, 48, 52, 53–54, 58–62, 76, 77, 102, 105, 111, 118, 124, 126, 143, 150, 152, 181, 182, 202, 209, 211, 212, 213, 214, 216, 232, 236, 263, 292, 306, 308, 309, 310, 321, 336, 337, 338, 361, 371, 375, 378, 384, 385, 386, 390, 392, 398
Henry IV–II, 60–61, 77, 102, 105, 121, 124, 143, 147, 261, 263–264, 304, 308, 309, 310, 316–318, 319
Henry V, 6, 9, 45–46, 77, 112, 123, 124, 152, 162, 165, 173, 209, 216, 265, 273, 308, 309, 375, 386, 389
Henry VI, 6, 105, 148, 155, 273, 292
Holloway, John, 361–370
Hooker, Richard, 145, 214
Horace, 10, 39, 121
Hubler, Edward L., 126, 314–322
Huxley, Aldous, 317

Ibsen, Henrik, 166, 169, 170, 171
Irving, Henry, 165, 167, 210

Jeffrey, Francis, 100–101
Jenkins, Harold, 297
Johnson, Samuel, xx, xxi, 2–3, 4–5, 8, 9, 14, 16–18, 19, 20–34, 35–36, 39, 41, 44, 45, 46, 47, 48, 50, 51, 52, 65, 67, 69, 70, 73, 74, 75, 84, 90, 93, 97, 105, 107, 121,

150, 164, 168, 184, 186, 199, 202, 220, 297, 315, 335, 336, 385, 398
Jones, Ernest, 77, 147, 219, 223–229, 236, 259
Jonson, Ben, xx, 4, 6, 8, 9, 13, 134, 160, 253, 305, 306, 307, 327, 370, 375, 377
Julius Caesar, 5, 9, 10, 76, 85, 89, 111, 142, 148, 165, 172, 175, 196, 198, 200, 216, 218, 222, 227, 233, 248, 266, 273, 283, 311, 324, 335–336, 338, 390, 393

Kames, Henry Home, Lord, 397
Kean, Richard, 113–115, 160
Keats, John, 261, 316
Kemble, John Philip, 113
Kermode, Frank, 361, 362
King John, 24–25, 33, 123, 172, 176, 222, 263, 264–265, 266, 270, 282, 283, 284, 285, 336, 338, 386
King Lear, 10, 13, 28, 33–34, 46, 48, 49, 51, 52, 68–69, 99–100, 105, 111, 115, 117, 134, 140, 144, 147, 148, 149, 150, 153, 171, 172, 174, 178–181, 182, 190–191, 192, 194, 195, 196, 197, 198, 199, 200–201, 203–204, 216, 218, 221, 222, 234, 235, 236, 239, 241, 249, 268, 270, 271, 273, 284, 287, 304–305, 308, 309, 310, 313, 314, 315, 319, 320, 321, 324, 325, 338, 340, 342, 362, 363–367, 368, 369, 383, 386, 390, 391, 393, 403
Kittredge, George Lyman, 336
Knight, G. Wilson, xx, 130, 144, 201, 238–251, 259, 290, 294, 297, 383, 384, 392
Knights, L. C., 48, 202, 239, 287
Kott, Jan, xix, 144

Lamb, Charles, 89, 91, 93–100, 115, 157, 186, 294
Lanier, Sidney, xxiii, 130, 147
Lessing, Gotthold Ephraim, 35–37, 39, 43, 178

Levin, Harry, 50
LeWinter, Oswald, 177
Lewis, C. S., 287
Lewis, Windham, 112, 147, 229–237, 257, 261, 269, 270
Locke, John, 252
Lorraine, Robert, 167
Lovejoy, A. O., 408
Love's Labour's Lost, 25, 78, 127, 128–129, 149, 156, 157, 158, 159, 161, 162, 171, 221, 222, 266, 291–292, 309, 312, 324, 356–361, 374
Lowell, James Russell, xxiii, 117, 118, 130–138, 150, 184, 201

Macbeth, 10, 13, 16, 18, 48–49, 51, 70, 74, 84–85, 89, 90, 94, 95, 98, 102, 104, 113, 115, 119, 121, 123, 144, 148, 149, 150, 171, 172, 173, 174, 175, 188, 189, 192, 194–195, 196, 198, 199, 200, 201, 207, 210, 211–212, 213, 217, 218, 221, 241, 242, 243–248, 250, 261, 273, 284, 285, 286–287, 288–290, 308, 309, 310, 339, 340, 342, 362, 363, 369, 383, 384, 386, 387, 388, 389, 391
Machiavelli, 45, 231, 232, 303
Mack, Maynard, 50, 202, 248, 287
McManaway, James, xxiii
Marlowe, Christopher, 155, 156, 210, 213, 253, 306
Marston, John, 305, 306, 313
Measure for Measure, 24, 27, 28, 47, 76, 105, 118, 124, 125, 142, 154, 158–161, 162, 163, 168, 170, 172, 199, 201, 206, 207, 240, 249, 255, 282, 310, 311, 319, 321, 336, 338, 370, 373, 374, 386, 387, 388
Melville, Herman, xxiii, 130
Merchant of Venice, The, xix, 24, 25, 46, 50, 52, 73, 101, 124–125, 129, 208, 209–210, 212, 213, 216, 221, 223, 260, 266, 282, 285, 308, 309, 310, 312, 324, 325, 336, 355, 356, 374, 375, 376, 384, 387, 390
Meres, Francis, 4

Merry Wives of Windsor, The, 9, 12, 312
Middleton, Thomas, 306, 307
Midsummer Night's Dream, A, 20, 45, 46, 101, 115, 130, 143, 156, 217, 266, 285, 308, 311, 356, 361, 374, 379, 380
Milton, John, xxii, 4, 8, 52, 73, 103, 134, 285
Montagu, Mrs. Elizabeth, 53
Montaigne, Michel de, 131, 303
Morgann, Maurice, 52–62, 70, 73, 77, 82, 83, 93, 98, 202, 205, 209, 212, 398, 404
Moulton, Richard G., 325
Much Ado About Nothing, 9, 25, 46–47, 76, 78, 120, 129, 152, 165, 166, 169, 171, 172, 176, 207, 208, 216, 221, 266, 285, 308, 344, 345, 355, 371, 373, 374, 375, 393
Muir, Kenneth, 152, 202
Murry, Middleton J., 69–70, 77, 147, 164, 248, 259, 261–270, 285

Orwell, George, 402–403
Othello, 5, 10, 18, 33, 37, 47, 52, 70, 74, 76, 96, 98, 101, 105, 111. 114, 117, 118, 121, 123, 125, 126, 127, 147, 150, 153, 165, 170, 176, 181, 182, 187, 189, 191, 192, 194, 195, 196, 197, 198, 199, 200, 201, 203, 208, 210, 211, 213, 216, 217, 221, 222, 231–232, 233, 235, 236, 241, 249, 250, 266, 284, 287, 308, 309, 310, 320, 321, 324, 340, 342, 344, 345–353, 362, 368, 369, 384, 385, 388, 389, 390, 393, 398

Partridge, Eric, 257
Pater, Walter, 117, 157–163, 189, 201, 229, 361
Pericles of Athens, 12, 105, 154, 308, 310, 371, 379
Poe, Edgar Allan, xxiii
Pope, Alexander, 4, 7, 9, 15–16, 17, 44, 45, 66, 73, 111
Priestley, Joseph, 14

Prynne, William, 210
Puttenham, George, 132

Quiller-Couch, Arthur, 325

Racine, Jean Baptiste, 37
Raleigh, Walter, 223
Ralli, Augustus, 65, 120, 121
Rank, Otto, 227
Rape of Lucrece, The, 214
Raysor, Thomas Middleton, 64, 65
Richard II, 48, 70, 78, 107–109,
    111, 118, 122, 123, 124, 143,
    155–156, 160, 161, 162, 172,
    176, 260, 262, 263, 265–266,
    284, 293–294, 308, 311, 314,
    342, 384
Richard III, 45, 47, 94, 102, 113–
    114, 123, 126, 147–148, 166,
    167, 175, 176, 198, 208, 211,
    217, 262, 263, 273, 293, 337,
    344, 345, 352, 385
Richardson, William, 53
Robertson, Forbes, 167
Robinson, Henry Crabb, 63
Romeo and Juliet, xxii, 15–16, 18,
    33, 37, 42–43, 64, 66, 69, 73, 76,
    77, 78, 93, 96, 101, 113, 114,
    117, 119, 120, 124, 126, 127,
    146, 148, 150, 155, 161, 167,
    171, 176, 188, 196, 216–217,
    222, 223, 258, 275, 276–277,
    284, 285, 308, 310, 311, 312,
    313, 319, 324, 338, 340, 386
Rowe, Nicholas, 9, 102, 262
Rubens, Peter Paul, 84
Rymer, Thomas, 5, 10, 22, 23, 205,
    385, 408

Saintsbury, George, 65
Santayana, George, 48, 65
Schlegel, Augustus Wilhelm von,
    xix, xxii, 37–51, 57, 64, 65, 66,
    67, 69, 70, 74, 75, 78, 80, 85,
    87, 88, 93, 105, 122, 131, 133,
    199, 201, 239, 285
Schlegel, Friedrich von, 78
Schücking, Levin L., 182, 215–219,
    230
Sewell, Arthur, 344, 383–393

Shakespeare, William
Nature
    Genius, xx, 4, 5, 8, 24, 37, 52,
        55–56, 65–67, 76–77, 81,
        84, 90, 102, 103, 104–105,
        133, 134, 199, 261, 262,
        266, 277–278, 279, 294,
        326–327, 387; *see* Art: pro-
        ficiencies: Organicism; and
        Characterization
    Fancy, 22, 67, 90, 102; *see*
        Characters: Fairies, witches,
        ghosts
    Mimetic power, xxi, 4–5, 8–9,
        20–22, 75, 81–82, 89–90,
        177, 262–263; *see* Charac-
        terization
    Knowledge of the mind, 55,
        68, 78; *see* Characterization
    Rhetorical power, 5, 6, 8–9,
        34, 57, 74, 84–85, 90–91,
        102, 171, 182, 205–208,
        216–217, 277–278, 335–
        342, 384; *see* Characteriza-
        tion
Art: deficiencies
    General, 5–7, 9, 65, 91, 164–
        165, 180–181, 198–199,
        206, 399
    Theatrical indecorum (tumults,
        bad manners), 5–7, 13–14,
        50, 135–136, 181, 206
    Stylistic indecorum (failure
        to blot, bombast, puns), 4–
        7, 14–18, 24, 30–31, 73–
        74, 133, 160, 180–181, 199,
        206, 277, 291–292, 315,
        385–386
    Indecency, xxi, 7, 23, 74–75,
        168–169, 206, 311–312
    Poetic injustice, 6, 10–11, 27–
        28, 37, 74, 75, 162–163
    Anachronisms, 23, 44–45, 85,
        135–136, 371
    Deviation from character types,
        xx, 13, 29
    Plot negligence, 6, 23, 24, 92–
        93, 165, 180, 199, 377
    Tragicomedy, xx, 12–13, 15, 29–
        30, 39–40, 52, 67, 84, 396
    Disunity (and unity) of ac-

Shakespeare, William, Art (*Cont.*)
tion, time, and place, 5, 6,
11–12, 13, 29, 30–32, 40–
41, 52, 57–58, 69, 84, 92–
93, 134, 183, 295, 396–397;
see Perspectives: Esthetic;
Esthetics of delusion, recitation, illusion

Art: proficiencies
Possession of art, judgment,
xx, xxi, 9, 37, 43, 51, 52, 56,
57, 65–67, 110, 133, 268
Artistic development, 139–144,
153–157, 262–264, 266–
267, 268, 290–295
Dramatic structure, 45–47,
194–198, 325–326, 328,
329–330, 349–350, 371,
372, 373–381; *see* Nature:
Rhetorical power; Art: proficiencies: Unity of interest,
Organicism
Unity of interest, impression,
idea, world, 40–43, 50, 51,
64, 81, 85, 105, 109–111,
122, 126–130, 131, 149,
151, 160–162, 200–202,
240–241, 242–243, 277,
284, 384–385, 387, 401; *see*
Art: proficiencies: Dramatic
structure and Organicism;
Meanings
Organicism, 44, 45, 51, 64, 65–
70, 75–76, 110, 149, 151,
201–202, 242, 244–248,
283–284, 293, 295; *see* Art:
proficiencies: Dramatic structure and Unity of interest

Style
Language, 23, 90, 103, 131–
133, 134, 154, 161, 232,
235, 358–359
Verse, 103, 109, 154–157, 166,
174–176, 230–231, 234,
262, 328, 332–333, 334
Imagery, 9, 67–68, 103, 133–
134, 175–176, 190–191,
201, 241, 243, 248, 253–
261, 263–264, 268–269,
270–295, 301, 302, 304–
305, 364, 384, 387–388,

389–390
Wit, 17–18, 67, 359
Humor, 142–144
And the Theater, 90–92, 93–100,
103–104, 113–115, 165–
166, 167, 172, 210–213,
215–218, 262, 263–264,
323–335, 357, 403
Characterization, 29, 54–57, 76–
77, 84–85, 102–103, 133–
134, 173, 205–209, 210–
212, 214–218, 250, 262,
268, 279, 336, 351, 357,
385, 387, 388

Characters
As actual or "real," 56, 58–62,
83, 104–105, 198, 202, 297,
344, 351; *see* Perspectives:
Biographical
As dramatic or unreal, 58, 62,
103, 166, 181, 205–218,
242–243, 245–248, 337,
344–349, 352, 383–385, 387,
388
Heroines, 105–106, 142, 230
Villains, 98, 209, 211, 216,
344
Choral characters, 57, 120, 338
Fairies, witches, ghosts, 36, 90,
99; *see* Nature: Fancy

Plays
Comedies, 4, 7, 22–23, 105,
106–107, 122, 127, 140,
147, 354–361, 370–381, 389
Histories, xix, 7, 31, 37, 49–
50, 108, 109, 111–113, 127,
140, 143, 147, 159, 160,
265–266, 284–285, 340–
341, 342, 389
Tragedies, 4, 7, 9, 10, 22, 23–
24, 86, 88–89, 101, 105,
121–122, 127, 140, 147,
172–173, 187–189, 192–
198, 208, 229–237, 242, 295,
303, 340, 389–390; the
tragic hero, 173, 174, 188–
189, 193–195, 208, 229–
237, 294, 362, 367–370,
389–392
Romances, 141, 354–361, 386

Shakespeare, William (*Cont.*)
And His Age, 3–4, 5, 7, 9, 13, 15, 22, 69–70, 91–92, 103, 131–132, 133, 169, 177, 183, 206, 209–210, 213, 214, 215–217, 229–236, 263–265, 268, 270, 298–305, 306–314, 319, 321–322, 363–364, 371, 391–392
Meanings, Moral and Amoral, Philosophical, Visionary, Religious, 5, 23, 26–29, 30, 38–39, 46, 47, 48–49, 74–75, 85, 105, 106, 112, 120, 121–126, 150–151, 161–163, 164–165, 170–174, 177, 182–184, 193–195, 206–208, 231–237, 240, 244–247, 249–250, 256, 265–268, 276, 285, 294, 298–305, 307–312, 314–315, 316–322, 335, 338–342, 350–351, 355–361, 362–366, 370–381, 385, 386–393; *see* Art: deficiencies: Poetic injustice; Art: proficiencies: Unity of interest
Perspectives
Neo-classical, 3–36, 37–39, 41–42, 64–66, 93, 215
Romantic, 37–40, 41–43, 64–66, 87–89, 93, 133, 134
Biographical, 22, 77–78, 82, 117, 130, 139–147, 153, 167–171, 219–237, 239, 248, 253–268, 270–280, 314–315, 317–322, 371, 401, 405
Historical, *see* And His Age
Esthetic, 159–160; Esthetics of delusion, recitation, illusion, 30–32, 41, 79, 96–99, 205
Impressionist, 192
Expressionist, *see* Characterization and Perspectives: Biographical
Psychoanalytic, 223–228, 278–279, 386
"Interpretative," 241–243, 244–248, 251, 287

Anthropological or Archetypal, 229–237, 249, 251, 269, 354–363, 367–382
History of Shakespearean Criticism, xxiii, 25–26, 178, 183–184
Shaw, George Bernard, 25, 93, 112, 157, 164–177, 183, 184, 185, 223, 313, 341, 400
Siddons, Mrs., 95, 113, 119
Sidney, Philip, 11–12, 13, 27, 39, 50, 121
Siegel, Paul N., 215, 238
Smiles, Samuel, 145, 167, 168
Smith, D. Nichol, 32–33, 65
Sonnets, 146, 314–322
Sophocles, 38, 39, 88
Spencer, T. J. B., 25–26, 145
Spencer, Theodore, 184, 296–305, 322
Spenser, Edmund, 214
Spivack, Bernard, 344–353, 383
Spurgeon, Caroline, 147, 252–261, 270, 279, 281–290, 293, 294, 297, 384
Stauffer, Donald, 126
Stewart, J. I. M., 392
Stoll, E. E., 182, 184, 209–215, 218, 336, 349, 351, 352, 353, 381, 383, 392
Strachey, Lytton, 147, 239
Swift, Jonathan, 14
Swinburne, Algernon Charles, 164, 165, 168, 175, 262, 290, 349

Taine, Henri A., 145, 405, 407
Taming of the Shrew, The, 102, 163, 169–170, 171, 273, 308, 312, 374
Tempest, The, 22, 67, 75, 94, 123, 135, 172, 174, 216, 217, 239, 248, 250, 266, 268, 280, 285, 304, 307, 308, 310, 312, 321, 380–381
Terry, Ellen, 167
Tillyard, E. M. W., 49, 184, 296–305, 322
Timon of Athens, 46, 102, 122, 124, 144, 208, 210, 222, 233, 234, 235, 236, 238–239, 249,

Timon of Athens (*Cont.*)
  250, 255, 313, 338, 339, 340,
  362, 368, 369, 386
Titus Andronicus, 211, 216, 291,
  308, 339, 344, 345
Tolstoy, Leo, 25, 117, 177–185,
  209, 270, 313
Traversi, Derek A., 147, 248, 259
Tree, Beerbohm, 165
Troilus and Cressida, 6, 11, 70,
  105, 142, 153, 170, 171, 188,
  221, 222, 233, 234, 238, 240,
  242, 243, 249, 250, 284, 285,
  305, 310, 311, 312, 314, 318,
  319, 321, 338, 342
Twelfth Night, 46, 105, 120, 169,
  222, 233, 266, 282, 307, 308,
  309, 310, 312, 313, 319, 355,
  356, 374, 375, 390, 393

Two Gentlemen of Verona, 24, 25,
  142, 149, 156, 206, 262, 292,
  307, 312, 338, 374, 379
Tyrwhitt, Thomas, 53

Ulrici, Hermann, 122

Venus and Adonis, 74, 155, 318
Voltaire, 5–6, 14, 29, 35, 36–37,
  52, 178, 205

Warton, Joseph, 46
Whately, Thomas, 53
Whiter, Walter, 252, 253
Winter's Tale, The, 50, 144, 261–
  262, 272, 273, 310, 312, 318,
  335, 376, 379, 386
Wordsworth, William, 262

NORTON CRITICAL EDITIONS

AUSTEN *Emma* edited by Stephen M. Parrish
AUSTEN *Pride and Prejudice* edited by Donald J. Gray
BRONTË, CHARLOTTE *Jane Eyre* edited by Richard J. Dunn
BRONTË, EMILY *Wuthering Heights*, Revised edited by William M. Sale, Jr.
CARROLL *Alice in Wonderland* edited by Donald J. Gray
CLEMENS *Adventures of Huckleberry Finn* edited by Sculley Bradley, Richmond Croom Beatty, and E. Hudson Long
CONRAD *Heart of Darkness*, Revised edited by Robert Kimbrough
CONRAD *Lord Jim* edited by Thomas Moser
CRANE *The Red Badge of Courage* edited by Sculley Bradley, Richmond Croom Beatty, and E. Hudson Long
Darwin edited by Philip Appleman
DEFOE *Moll Flanders* edited by Edward Kelly
DICKENS *Hard Times* edited by George Ford and Sylvère Monod
John Donne's Poetry selected and edited by A. L. Clements
DOSTOEVSKY *Crime and Punishment* (the Coulson translation) edited by George Gibian
DREISER *Sister Carrie* edited by Donald Pizer
FIELDING *Tom Jones* edited by Sheridan Baker
FLAUBERT *Madame Bovary* edited with a substantially new translation by Paul de Man
HARDY *The Return of the Native* edited by James Gindin
HARDY *Tess of the D'Urbervilles* edited by Scott Elledge
HAWTHORNE *The House of the Seven Gables* edited by Seymour L. Gross
HAWTHORNE *The Scarlet Letter* edited by Sculley Bradley, Richmond Croom Beatty, and E. Hudson Long
HOMER *The Odyssey* translated and edited by Albert Cook
IBSEN *The Wild Duck* translated and edited by Dounia B. Christiani
JAMES *The Ambassadors* edited by S. P. Rosenbaum
JAMES *The Turn of the Screw* edited by Robert Kimbrough
MELVILLE *The Confidence-Man* edited by Hershel Parker
MELVILLE *Moby-Dick* edited by Harrison Hayford and Hershel Parker
NEWMAN *Apologia Pro Vita Sua* edited by David J. DeLaura
The Writings of St. Paul edited by Wayne A. Meeks
SHAKESPEARE *Hamlet* edited by Cyrus Hoy
SHAKESPEARE *Henry IV, Part I*, Revised edited by James L. Sanderson
Bernard Shaw's Plays edited by Warren Sylvester Smith
SOPHOCLES *Oedipus Tyrannus* translated and edited by Luci Berkowitz and Theodore F. Brunner
Edmund Spenser's Poetry selected and edited by Hugh Maclean
STENDHAL *Red and Black* translated and edited by Robert M. Adams
SWIFT *Gulliver's Travels*, Revised edited by Robert A. Greenberg
The Writings of Jonathan Swift edited by Robert A. Greenberg and William B. Piper
TENNYSON *In Memoriam* edited by Robert Ross
Tennyson's Poetry selected and edited by Robert W. Hill, Jr.
THOREAU *Walden and Civil Disobedience* edited by Owen Thomas
TOLSTOY *Anna Karenina* (the Maude translation) edited by George Gibian
TOLSTOY *War and Peace* (the Maude translation) edited by George Gibian
TURGENEV *Fathers and Sons* edited with a substantially new translation by Ralph E. Matlaw
VOLTAIRE *Candide* translated and edited by Robert M. Adams
WHITMAN *Leaves of Grass* edited by Sculley Bradley and Harold W. Blodgett
A Norton Critical Edition of Modern Drama edited by Anthony Caputi
Restoration and Eighteenth-Century Comedy edited by Scott McMillin

LITERATURE IN THE NORTON LIBRARY

Ammons, A. R. *Tape for the Turn of the Year* N659

Austen, Jane *Persuasion* Introduction by David Daiches N163

Behn, Aphra *Oroonoko; or, The Royal Slave* Introduction by Lore Metzger N702

Brace, Gerald Warner *The Garretson Chronicle* N272

Browne, Sir Thomas *The Complete Prose of Sir Thomas Browne* (Norman J. Endicott, ED.) N619

Browning, Robert *The Ring and the Book* Introduction by Wylie Sypher N433

Burgess, Anthony *A Clockwork Orange* Afterword by Stanley Edgar Hyman N224

Burney, Fanny *Evelina* N294

Campion, Thomas *The Works of Thomas Campion* (Walter R. Davis, ED.) N439

Conrad, Joseph *The Arrow of Gold* N458

Conrad, Joseph *Chance* N456

Conrad, Joseph *The Rescue* N457

Creeth, Edmund, ED. *Tudor Plays: An Anthology of Early English Drama* N614

Darwin, Charles *The Autobiography of Charles Darwin* N487

Edgeworth, Maria *Castle Rackrent* N288

Eliot, George *Felix Holt the Radical* Introduction by George Levine N517

Fielding, Henry *Joseph Andrews* Introduction by Mary Ellen Chase N274

Fuller, Margaret *Woman in the Nineteenth Century* Introduction by Bernard Rosenthal N615

Gaskell, Mrs. Elizabeth *Mary Barton* Introduction by Myron F. Brightfield N245

Gissing, George *The Odd Women* N610

Gogol, Nicolai V. *Dead Souls* Introduction by George Gibian N600

Gogol, Nicolai V. *"The Overcoat" and Other Tales of Good and Evil* N304

Gosse, Edmund *Father and Son* N195

Gregory, Horace, TR. AND ED. *The Poems of Catullus* N654

Hamilton, Edith, TR. AND ED. *Three Greek Plays* N203

Harrier, Richard C., ED. *Jacobean Drama: An Anthology* N559 (Vol. I) and N560 (Vol. II)

Hawthorne, Nathaniel *The Blithedale Romance* Introduction by Arlin Turner N164

Herrick, Robert *The Complete Poetry of Robert Herrick*
(J. Max Patrick, ED.) N435

Hogg, James *The Private Memoirs and Confessions of a Justified Sinner* Introduction by Robert M. Adams N515

Homer *The Iliad* A Shortened Version translated and edited by I. A. Richards N101

James, Henry *The Awkward Age* N285

James, Henry *"In the Cage" and Other Tales* N286

Jonson, Ben *The Complete Poetry of Ben Jonson* (William B. Hunter, Jr., ED.) N436

Kavanagh, Patrick *Collected Poems* N694

Lawrence, T. E. *The Mint* N196

Lederer, William J. and Eugene Burdick *The Ugly American* N305

Lucian *Selected Satires of Lucian* (Lionel Casson, TR. AND ED.) N443

Lynn, Kenneth S., ED. *The Comic Tradition in America: An Anthology of American Humor* N447

Mackenzie, Henry *The Man of Feeling* Introduction by Kenneth C. Slagle N214

Martz, Louis L., ED. *English Seventeenth-Century Verse* (Vol. I) N675

Meredith, George *Diana of the Crossways* Introduction by Lois Josephs Fowler N700

Meserole, Harrison T., ED. *Seventeenth-Century American Poetry* N620

Mish, Charles C., ED. *Short Fiction of the Seventeenth Century* N437

O'Flaherty, Liam *"The Wounded Cormorant" and Other Stories* Introduction by Vivian Mercier N704

Peacock, Thomas Love *Nightmare Abbey* N283

Plautus *"Amphitryon" and Two Other Plays* (Lionel Casson, TR. AND ED.) N601

Plautus *"The Menaechmus Twins" and Two Other Plays* (Lionel Casson, TR. AND ED.) N602

Reeve, F. D., TR. AND ED. *Nineteenth Century Russian Plays* N683

Reeve, F. D., TR. AND ED. *Twentieth Century Russian Plays* N697

Richardson, Samuel *Pamela* Introduction by William M. Sale, Jr. N166

Riding, Laura *Selected Poems: In Five Sets* N701

Rilke, Rainer Maria *Duino Elegies* N155

Rilke, Rainer Maria *The Lay of the Love and Death of Cornet Christopher Rilke* N159

Rilke, Rainer Maria *Letters of Rainer Maria Rilke, 1892-1910* N476

Rilke, Rainer Maria *Letters of Rainer Maria Rilke, 1910-1926* N477

Rilke, Rainer Maria *Letters to a Young Poet* N158

Rilke, Rainer Maria *The Notebooks of Malte Laurids Brigge* N267

Rilke, Rainer Maria *Sonnets to Orpheus* N157

Rilke, Rainer Maria *Stories of God* N154

Rilke, Rainer Maria *Translations from the Poetry* by M. D. Herter Norton N156

Rilke, Rainer Maria *Wartime Letters of Rainer Maria Rilke* N160

Rizal, José *The Lost Eden* *(Noli Me Tangere)* (Leon Ma. Guerrero, TR.) N222

Rizal, José *The Subversive* *(El Filibusterismo)* (Leon Ma. Guerrero, TR.) N449

Rose, Martial, ED. *The Wakefield Mystery Plays* N483

Ruskin, John *The Literary Criticism of John Ruskin* (Harold Bloom, ED.) N604

Seneca *The Stoic Philosophy of Seneca* Essays and Letters (Moses Hadas, TR. AND ED.) N459

Shaw, George Bernard *An Unsocial Socialist* Introductions by R. F. Dietrich and Barbara Bellow Watson N660

Solzhenitsyn, Aleksandr *"We Never Make Mistakes"* Translated by Paul Blackstock N598

Stansky, Peter and William Abrahams *Journey to the Frontier: Two Roads to the Spanish Civil War* N509

Stendhal *The Private Diaries of Stendhal* N175

Tolstoy, Leo *Resurrection* The Maude Translation, with an introduction by George Gibian N325

Trollope, Anthony *The Last Chronicle of Barset* Introduction by Gerald Warner Brace N291

Turgenev, Ivan *"First Love" and Other Tales* N444

Vaughan, Henry *The Complete Poetry of Henry Vaughan* (French Fogle, ED.) N438

Whitman, Walt *Leaves of Grass* The Comprehensive Reader's Edition (Harold W. Blodgett and Sculley Bradley, EDS.) N430

Wollstonecraft, Mary *A Vindication of the Rights of Woman* Introduction by Charles W. Hagelman, Jr. N373

Wycherley, William *The Complete Plays of William Wycherley* (Gerald Weales, ED.) N440

Zukofsky, Louis *All: The Collected Short Poems* N621